HOCKEY!

HOCKEY!

The Story of the World's Fastest Sport

NEW EXPANDED EDITION

by Richard Beddoes
Stan Fischler
Ira Gitler

Macmillan Publishing Co., Inc.
NEW YORK
Collier Macmillan Publishers
LONDON

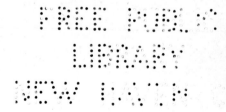

Macmillan Publishing Co., Inc.
866 Third Avenue, New York, N.Y. 10022
Collier-Macmillan Canada Ltd.

Library of Congress Catalog Card Number: 72-176062

Third Edition 1973

Second Printing 1974

Printed in the United States of America

To the many personalities who helped begin our love affair with hockey, and those who have kept it glowing ever since: the players, pro and amateur; the officials; the writers; and the fans.

Lefty Adelson, Marv Albert, Ty Anderson, Syl Apps, Alger Arbour, Dom Baolto, Alex Barilko, Bill Barilko, Charlie Barton, Andy Bathgate, Jean Beliveau, Doug Bentley, Maxwell Herbert Lloyd Bentley, Bob Blume, Garth Boesch, Emile (Butch) Bouchard, Frank Boucher, Joe Breu, Carl Brewer, Jim Burchard, Bill Burley, Tommy Burlington, Norm Burns, Arley Carlson, Herb Carnegie, Ossie Carnegie, Red Carr, Eddie Cassola, Bill Chadwick, King Clancy, Leo Coar, Bill Coggins, Jim Coleman, Ab Collings, Jimmy Conacher, Bill Cook, Bun Cook, Manny Cotlow, Art Coulter, Ray Crew, Hank D'Amore, Vern De Geer, Joe Desson, Cecil Dillon, Gordie Drillon, Red Dutton, Bobby Edel, Win Elliot, Lloyd (Bingo) Ernst, Jack (Tex) Evans, Bill Ezinicki, Larry Feltham, John Ferguson, Johnny Flynn, Louie Fontinato, Don (Duck) Forman, Whitey Fountain, Arnie Fox, Irving Fox, Emile (Cat) Francis, Danny Gallivan, Paul Gardella, Joe Giaimo, Rod Gilbert, Hank Goldup, Gladys Goodding, Jim Goodie, Jackie Gordon, Herb Goren, Phil Goyette, George Gravel, Aldo Guidolin, John Halligan, Jerry Heffernan, Ott Heller, Camille Henry, Jimmy Hernon, Foster Hewitt, Dutch Hiller, Mickey Hopp, Gordie Howe, Harry Howell, Whitey Huddleston, Bob Johnson, Charlie Joyce, Bill Juzda, Alex (Killer) Kaleta, Bingo Kampman, Mauno Kauppi, Forbes Kennedy, Ted Kennedy, Herbert Khaury, Bert Korwin, Bobby Kuhn, Eddie Kullman, Al Laney, Edgar Laprade, Claude Larochelle, Bert Lee, Tony Leswick, Bill Libby, Tommy Lockhart, Vic Lofvendahl, Ken McAuley, Bucko McDonald, Hub Macey, Dick McGrath, Manny McIntyre, Murdo McKay, Fleming Mackell, Redvers MacKenzie, Bob MacLean, Stan McLellan, Frank Mahovlich, Robert Markel, Howie Meeker, Fred Meier, Pop Melis, Freddie Metcalfe, Nick Mickoski, Bill Moe, Leo Monte, Pete Morin, Ethel Mullany, Muzz Murray, Joe Nichols, Buddy O'Connor, Baz O'Meara, Don Perry, Nick Pidsodny, Bones Raleigh, Chuck Rayner, Allie Regan, Kenny Reardon, Arthur Reichert, Leo Reise Jr., Henri Richard,

Maurice Richard, Whitey Rimstad, Moe Roberts, John Rode, Al Rollins, Stan Saplin, Bob Schanz, Richie Scheiblich, Larry Schildkret, Sweeney Schriner, Dick Selby, Dick Sieminski, Mickey Slowick, Mr. and Mrs. Cooper Smeaton, Lenny Speck, Joe Spendley, Winston Standup, Wally Stanowski, Gene Stuart, Red Tilson, Dr. David Tracey, Paul (Boxcar) Waldner, Dick Williams, Ward Wilson, Gump Worsley, Larry Zeidel, Dick Aslin, Ron Ward, Edgar "Chirp" Brenchley, Hy Buller, Gerry Cosby, Len Dobbin, Rollie Duranceau, Lidio Fogolin, Armand "Bep" Guidolin, Sam B. Gunst, Andy Hebenton, Wally Hergesheimer, Ivan Irwin, Eben Ludlow, Pentti Lund, Waikko "Joe" Lund, Bill Mosienko, Dean Prentice, Harry "Hard Rock" Torgerson, Frank Traverso, Steve "Turk" Turek, Dick Dillman, Tim Ryan, Dan Baliotti, Frank Brown, Vinnie Claps, Pete Connors, Mike Cosby, Bill Daley, Steve Devaney, John Dillon, Dale Eccles, Mike Finnen, Jimmy Franks, Danny Greenhall, Harold Hursley, Mitch Jennings, Sally Lark, Sal Marchiano, Nick Milos, Mo Mulligan, Leo Ornest, Guy Roche, Bob Stampleman, Pete Tavis, Phil Vitale, Lynn Welshman, Matty Yorke.

Contents

THE PRESENT

PART FOUR
THE GAME

PART FIVE
CONTROVERSIES

ACKNOWLEDGMENTS

The Trail of the Stanley Cup by Charles L. Coleman, published by the National Hockey League, for details on the death of Owen McCourt, the Dawson City Challenge and Joe Malone's scoring.

Ronald Andrews, NHL Publicity Director and Statistician, for information contained in the statistical sections.

Andy O'Brien and *Weekend Magazine* for Newsy Lalonde's all-time all-meanie team.

The Encyclopedia of Sports, by Frank G. Menke, for documentation on the origin of ice hockey.

John Halligan, Larry Zeidel, Fred Katz, Jack Zanger, Paul and Richard Friedman, Charlie Barton, Del MacKenzie, Wayne Cooper, Joe Kadlec, Joe Gordon, Jon Washington.

Introduction

Hockey on ice is among the most modern of sports, probably originating in Canada less than 100 years ago. There is some evidence that it was played, in crude fashion, in Halifax, Nova Scotia —a ball batted up and down a frozen surface.

All honorable data suggest that students at McGill University, in Montreal, took the crude elements of hockey and formed them into a definite game, with standard rules of play. The first game was played in Montreal, on March 3, 1875, at the Victoria Skating Rink.

Since then it has become Canada's national game, described by poet Al Purdy as "a Canadian specific." Hockey achieved that status, wrote Canadian author Scott Young, "because it is the combination of blood, sweat and beauty."

The sport is constantly changing, still evolving as a pastime of skill and violence. It was played with seven players on each side until 45 years ago. Then the number was reduced to six. Teams used to be staffed with seven or eight men, but rosters expanded to the present 18. Substitution every 60 or 90 seconds provides fresh troops for more speed.

Fifteen years ago the curved stick and the goalkeeper's mask were innovations; expansion is what happened to the waistlines of fat hockey players after that last helping of French fries.

Now the curved stick slaps the puck up to speeds of 120 miles an hour, and it is a rare goalie who does not protect his features with a mask. Hockey has expanded professionally from coast to coast on this continent, and is played from Alaska to Mexico. It is a major winter sport in many European countries—in Russia, Sweden, Czechoslovakia, Great Britain, Germany, Switzerland, Italy, Poland and Bulgaria. Japan and Australia have been represented in Olympic hockey tournaments.

Most of the players who perform in the two major professional hockey leagues are Canadian. Since Canada is still grappling with its fierce frontiers, the Canadian personality in hockey represents many qualities required of the pioneer: vigor and humor, strength and perseverance, survival of the fittest.

John Kieran said it for everybody who cares about the game when he sang on the sports pages of the *New York Times*: "Oh, for pep and speed and action,/There's only one attraction,/That's hockey—give me hockey any time!"

PART ONE
The Old Six

Boston Bruins

BOSTON HOCKEY for 30 seasons, from 1924 to 1953 inclusive, was the cunning concoction of Arthur Howey Ross, the stubborn bear of the Bruins who managed their early conquests of the Stanley Cup, in 1928–29, 1938–39 and 1940–41.

Ross died in 1964, the victim of crippling arthritis and blurred eyesight and the remorseless rigors of 78. He groped through the last years, puzzled and fretful, and this made it too easy to forget what he had been.

What Ross had been was a persistent and inventive mind, an abrasive personality to match Tommy Gorman and Conn Smythe and Jack Adams in skirmishes that began when the Bruins played their first game on December 1, 1924. Before that, as an aggressive defenseman, he had been a shrewd, agile rebel.

His searching genius as a manager produced the puck and nets used almost universally in hockey today. Prior to his design, the nets were a primitive twine, so tight that pucks often bounced off the rear of the net and back into play. He sponsored a bulky, pliable mesh which made practically certain that any puck shot in, stayed in. He advocated, and had approved, a puck with a bevelled edge. He developed the first fiber guard on the back of skate boots to protect the vulnerable Achilles tendon.

Ross also was the first operator to pull his goalkeeper in a Stanley Cup playoff. The tactic, considered amazing at the time, did not work when Ross attempted it on March 26, 1931. He lifted goalie Cecil (Tiny) Thompson for a sixth attacker in the last minute, but

Montreal's Canadiens preserved their 1–0 lead. Canadiens won the series three games to two, and subsequently beat Chicago by the same margin for the Stanley Cup.

Ross developed a respect for money when he was a rookie bank clerk from the Ontario whistle stop of Naughton. Cobalt, he always contended, made him the highest paid player in hockey history— $1,000 for two games against despised rivals from the enemy mining town of Haileybury.

He was a hardy philosopher even then, 60 years ago, who believed in winning if he had to gouge eyeballs to do it. He did it to Haileybury in a rowdy doubleheader, to the unspeakable delight of Cobalt supporters.

"Jubilant fans pressed the thousand bucks on me," he recalled, years later, when he was inducted into the Hall of Fame. "They also gave me a sack of silver nuggets which had, by God, a good, game quality."

Money was the root of what owners considered Ross's rebellious evil in the early months of World War I when he was "barred for life" by the slightly comic National Hockey Association.

The league included Ottawa Senators, Montreal Canadiens, Quebec Bulldogs, Torontos, Toronto Shamrocks and Montreal Wanderers, who controlled Ross's playing rights. He quarreled with Samuel Lichtenhein, the monumental tightwad who owned the team and wanted to restrict salaries to $600 a man for a 20-game season.

Ross, taking no particular trouble to mask his moves, began signing players for higher guarantees if they would help him form a new league.

Lichtenhein blocked the revolt by directing T. Emmett Quinn, the obedient NHA president, to convene an urgent association meeting. "Ross is trying to undermine us," Lichtenhein insisted. "The bastard has got to go."

Elmer Ferguson, a venerable hockey historian still writing sports for the *Montreal Star*, was the unpaid secretary of the tribunal. "There were only two teams represented," Ferguson remembers. "Canadiens and Wanderers. President Quinn had the proxies for the other teams, and when he said 'aye' to Lichtenhein's motion to banish Ross, Art was gone. Then we all went for a drink."

The ban stuck for exactly three weeks, from November 28, 1914 to December 18, when Ross was signed by the Ottawa Senators. His expulsion was ignored, even by Lichtenhein, and he helped Ottawa win the league championship. The team won by dismissing the Wanderers in a home-and-home totals-goals series, winning the first 4–0 and holding on to lose the second 1–0.

"Wanderers were pretty sure they could overcome the four-goal deficit in the second game," Elmer Ferguson recalls. "But they reckoned without the canny Ross. He devised a new form of defense for the second game, which saw Ottawa line up with four men out in front of the goalkeeper. Wanderers could only pierce such a defense for one goal."

Thus, the genesis of the defensive gesture called kitty-bar-the-door.

Ross played until 1918 when he was 32, turned to refereeing, then scented fresh money in the satchel of Charles Francis Adams of Boston. Adams was a chore boy in a grocery store in Newport, Vermont, who grew up to own a chain of groceterias; part of the bread, reported to be $15,000, purchased a National Hockey League franchise for Boston.

The Bruins won six games out of 30 in their first season, represented by an inferior crew that finished last. The best players were Jimmy Herberts and Carson Cooper, two outstanding amateurs from Ontario.

Two years later, when Frank and Lester Patrick peddled their depressed Western Canada League, Adams obtained the players who anchored Boston's first Stanley Cup team. He got a bargain fit for a grocery clerk, as it were: Duke Keats, Perc Galbraith, Harry Oliver, Harry Meeking, and the inimitable Eddie Shore—all for $50,000.

Adams was noted for many things, not including reckless spending, but he appreciated courage as that abused word fits hockey. One night Shore, the baleful defenseman, received brutal attention from the Big Three-S Line of the Montreal Maroons.

The three—Nels Stewart, Babe Siebert and Hooley Smith—had a collective butcher's touch. They broke his nose, slashed his face, detached him from his teeth. Shore defiantly kept playing, scarcely able to see out of one black eye. Afterward, in the Boston dressing room, he was greeted by Adams. "Here," Adams said, thrusting a $500-check at his bruised warrior. "Use this as a poultice for your face."

Ross and Adams made perfunctory gestures to Boston patriots by signing George Owen, an all-around Harvard athlete, to play defense. But Owen was gone by the spring of 1929 when the Bruins won their first Stanley Cup. Shore was the combative cog of that team, as he would continue to be until Boston won a second Cup 10 years later.

Cecil (Tiny) Thompson had arrived to play goal by 1929, a position he handled with such vigilance that he would win the Vezina Trophy four times in the decade before he was replaced by Frank Brimsek of Eveleth, Minnesota.

The defensive flamboyance of Shore and Thompson was complemented by the Dynamite Trio, the first of two distinctive attacking units formed by Ross. The second, in the late thirties, was the Kraut Line of Milt Schmidt, Woody Dumart and Bob Bauer.

The Dynamiters had Ralph (Cooney) Weiland at center between Norman (Dutch) Gainor on left wing and Aubrey (Dit) Clapper on the right. Weiland, 64, coached Boston's last Cup conquest, in 1940–41, and has presided over Harvard's hockey team since 1951.

Clapper, rangy and amiable, had a steady genius that lasted from 1927 to 1947, a record for nonstop playing in the NHL until 1965. Since then Red Kelly and Allan Stanley and Bill Gadsby have survived 20 years of big league play. Clapper's permanence in a demanding game was the one feat admired by Gordon Howe of Detroit four years ago. "There's one thing I want to do," said Howe, who has done it all. "That's last 20 years, like Clapper."

Now Howe is beginning his twenty-fourth season and the end of his playing span is still off there, beyond the hockey horizon. "No telling how long Howe will last," Clapper says, squinting against the smoke of his cigarette in his plumbing shop in Peterborough, Ontario. "Gordie's so strong, he could last 25 years—or more."

Dutch Gainor, the third Dynamiter, died several years ago in a mental institution at Oliver, Alberta, victim of a boozy, capricious youth. He is regarded as the first to deceive opposing players with a quick double shift—faking one way, faking the other, then veering in the first direction after giving the opponent tangled feet.

The Bruins won their first Cup with dominating ease, winners of five consecutive games against Canadiens and Rangers. Weiland, a slick, black-haired sophomore, scored both goals as Thompson twice shut out Canadiens 1–0. They finished first five times in the American Division in the nine seasons between 1929–30 and 1937–38; they were first three more times immediately after the divisions amalgamated in 1938–39. The four years between 1937 and 1941 produced two Stanley Cups and the palmiest era in Bruins' history.

They set the longest undefeated record in the NHL: 15 wins and 8 ties between December 22, 1940, and February 25, 1941.

The playoffs of 1939, won by the Bruins in series against the Rangers and Leafs, belonged to Mel (Sudden-Death) Hill. "Who's Hill?" fans were demanding as they contemplated the Boston demolition crew of Brimsek, Shore, the Krauts, Clapper, Flash Hollett and the gifted Bill Cowley. The answer was that Hill was a chunky 175-pound athlete from Glenboro, Manitoba, who specialized, for a brief 12 days, in beating the Rangers in overtime.

Boston won the best-of-seven semifinal four games to three; Hill secured three of the wins with overtime goals. Boston won the first three games, Rangers won the next three and, after the regulation 60 minutes of the seventh, they were tied 1–1. Hill untied it with a goal after 48 minutes of overtime. Coach Lester Patrick of the losing Rangers had reason to be rueful. "I turned Hill down because he was too small . . . I didn't think he could stand the strain of a full season and the tough playoffs." Hill didn't provide any heroics in the Cup final against Toronto, but none was needed. The Bruins dismissed the Leafs in five games.

The Krauts dominated Boston's last Cup triumph in 1941. They twice got behind Toronto before winning a seven-game semifinal which went the limit, then whipped Detroit four in a row for the major prize. Milt Schmidt, in his last season before leading Bauer and Dumart in three years of war, scored three goals and assisted on four others in a personal rampage against Detroit.

In the 28 seasons since then the Bruins qualified a scant four times for the Cup final. Each time—in 1945–46, 1952–53, 1956–57 and 1957–58—they were beaten by the Canadiens. In each series the intensely competitive Schmidt was a worn link with the Bruins' bearish past; finished as a Stanley Cup player after 1953, he was installed as coach before the 1956–57 final. Among the latter-day Bruin stars were Fern Flaman, Bronco Horvath, Vic Stasiuk and Johnny Bucyk.

In more recent Cup appearances, the Bruins caught the overpowering Canadiens in the middle of the five consecutive championships. The first game of the 1957 series was typical: Canadiens won 5–1, Rocket Richard providing the margin with one of his churlishly inspired four-goal performances.

"It was," Boston goalie Don Simmons admitted, "humiliating."

Simmons used a word that fit the Bruins between 1959–60 and

1966–67, eight deplorable seasons when they finished fifth twice and sixth six times. There has always been some wolf in Boston hockey, but in those years the wolves were coyotes scavenging near the cellar.

In 1967–68, rebuilt around the precocious Bobby Orr, they came in third in the East Division of the expanded NHL. They were knocked out of the playoffs in four successive games, by the Canadiens.

In 1969, in the most exciting playoff in a decade, the Canadiens beat the Bruins in six tense games in the Eastern final.

"Always," muttered manager Milt Schmidt, "it's the Canadiens."

But Boston's boisterous partisans fervently believe that their bashing Bruins are heirs apparent to the Montreal mantle. Their vigorous renaissance coincided with the expansion of the NHL from six teams to 12.

The records indicate how the Bruins have been inflated in a time of flattening out everywhere else, except in Montreal. In 1968–69 Boston smashed many records and still finished behind Montreal in the East, three points out of first place.

They scored 303 goals, 39 more than the old mark established in one season by Chicago; Phil Esposito, a tall, mischievous center, obtained 126 points, 29 more than anyone accumulated before; they were the most penalized team in hockey history, 1,297 minutes compared to the 1,121 in penance served by Detroit Red Wings in 1964–65.

The collective sin of the Bruins was saluted by a derisive banner hung in the grimy Boston Garden, "PLAY DIRTY AND WIN!"

They weren't all roughhouse, as Dink Carroll commented in the *Montreal Gazette*: "The 1969 Bruins set many scoring records, paced by the Esposito–Ken Hodge–Ron Murphy line. But their firepower isn't all concentrated in one line. Two other trios—Fred Stanfield–John Bucyk–John McKenzie and Turk Sanderson–Ed Westfall–Glen Sather—can also put the puck in the net.

"The Bruins were better defensively, if only because Gerry Cheevers is much sharper in the nets. There is also Ted Green, along with Bobby Orr, Dallas Smith and Don Awrey, on a solid defense."

Besides expansion, one other circumstance altered the Boston case. They were the beneficiaries of a one-sided swap in the summer of 1967—Esposito, Hodge and Stanfield received in a trade with Chicago for defenseman Gilles Marotte, center Pit Martin and Jack

Norris, a minor-league goalkeeper. With a friend like Milt Schmidt found in Chicago manager Thomas Ivan, he can put up with a lot of enemies.

Harry Sinden, an intense 37-year-old coach who never played a game in the NHL, was given control of the club in 1966–67 after guiding a Boston affiliate, Oklahoma City Blazers, to the championship of the Central Pro League. He has a taste for turbulence.

The Bruins slathered Toronto Maple Leafs four consecutive times in the 1969 semifinals, twice by monstrous margins. They won the first two games at home, 10–0 and 7–0. Esposito tied a Stanley Cup record with six points, four goals and two assists, in the first rout.

The Boston future was at least as optimistic as Montreal's. Each team protected only 14 players and two goaltenders in the 1969 draft, under a complicated draft system, but several Bruins were exempt from the draft.

Orr, for example, had completed three years in the NHL, but was exempt because he was still eligible for junior hockey the previous winter; officially he was designated as "a first-year pro."

Five other Boston prospects—Rick Smith, Tom Webster, Steve Atkinson, Jim Harrison and Garnet Bailey—were also exempt as first-year professionals. Glen Sather was the only regular lost in the draft, gone to Pittsburgh Penguins.

The Bruins seemingly replaced the Montreal Canadiens as hockey's contemporary dynasty in May 1970 when they captured the Stanley Cup. To accomplish the feat Boston first eliminated New York in six games. Then the Black Hawks and Blues went down in four straight games each.

The general who directed the Bruins to the 1970 championship was Sinden, who disgusted with the frugal financial policies of the front office—he was being paid only $18,000 a season—suddenly accepted a $40,000 a year managerial job with Stirling-Homex, one of the largest manufacturers of prefabricated homes on the continent.

Sinden was replaced by Tom Johnson, the Bruins' assistant general manager, who had no experience as a coach either in the NHL or amateur hockey. The Bruins finished first in the East Division under Johnson as Esposito set new records with 76 goals and 152 points, and Orr broke all existing scoring marks for defensemen with 37 goals and 102 assists for 139 points. (The 102 assists surpassed all forwards as well.) Ken Hodge set a point record for right wings with 105 and Johnny Bucyk one for left wings with 116.

Each had over 60 assists which were also record breakers. The
Bruins passed their old 303 goal high by 96. Twenty-five were
short-handed, another record. About the only thing they didn't
break was their penalty minute mark. (The Vancouver Canucks
raised [or lowered] this standard to 1,371, which stood until the
1972–73 Philadelphia Flyers came along.)

Many people questioned the validity of the incredible scoring
statistics and attributed them to the inflationary effect of expansion,
but there was no doubt of Boston's potency. That is, until their old
nemesis, the Montreal Canadiens, turned them into paper champs
in the spring of 1971.

When the Bruins finished first again in 1971–72 and went on to
win the Cup for the second time in three years, dynasty talk was
revived. Then the old guard started slipping away. Ted Green,
considered expendable, wound up with the New England Whalers
of the WHA; scrappy John McKenzie jumped to Philadelphia of
the "other league"—as the NHL preferred to call it—and flakey,
flamboyant Derek Sanderson went with him; Ed Westfall was
drafted by the Islanders; and, most disastrous of all, goalie Gerry
Cheevers set up housekeeping in front of the Cleveland Crusaders'
nets.

Before 1972–73 was over, Sinden was back and Schmidt was
moving toward the exit which, at the end of the campaign, would
be his gateway to the new Washington, D.C., franchise; Johnson
was ousted in favor of Armand "Bep" Guidolin, coach of the Bruins'
AHL farm team, the Boston Braves; Sanderson was cut loose by the
Blazers and was welcomed back to Beantown; and Jacques Plante
became a straw thrown by Toronto and grasped at by the Bruins.

For a while Plante held fast in the Boston goal; Bobby Orr's
gimpy knee seemed trouble-free; and Guidolin's tough practices
gave the rollicking Bears some needed discipline. They passed the
Rangers to finish second but in the first round of the playoffs, Orr
was neutralized, Plante was demoralized by long bombs and Phil
Esposito's knee was fragmentized by a Ron Harris bodycheck. The
Rangers won in five and the dynasty became more fling than Ming.

Chicago Black Hawks

WRITERS HESITATE to let the facts fracture a good story, but debunking charming legends is the sacred duty of researchers bound to place the National Hockey League in its most accurate perspective.

One of the hardiest yarns in hockey is the Curse of the Muldoon, all about the sorcery and witchcraft a soremouthed loser is said to have invoked to prevent Chicago Black Hawks from ever finishing first in the NHL.

The Hawks finally won their first pennant in 41 years in 1966–67, and there was defiant rejoicing at the final rejection of the Curse. The authors, ever gimlet-eyed, wish to knock off that whimsy. There never was any Curse of the Muldoon, except in the nimble imagination of James X. Coleman, the great kidder among Canadian sports columnists.

More than 20 years ago, Coleman was sitting at his desk in the *Toronto Globe and Mail*. He was burdened with the task of composing a column for the early editions.

He sat staring vacantly at the blank copy paper in his typewriter while the clock's hands moved inexorably toward deadline. The fate he had feared for years had overtaken him at last. The dread day had arrived when he had nothing to write—no lances to splinter, no gags, no quips, no fragment of an idea freshly minted or slightly used.

Coleman sat groping, squirming, straining, and his palms grew moist with nervousness. He ripped the paper from his typewriter, rolled in new sheets and glowered at them. Time marched, but nothing else.

It was 26 minutes to the first edition. His desperate thoughts landed on the Black Hawks, who had exhibited their customary hilarious act of teetering on the brink of first place, then toppled with unseemly haste into second, or lower. Inspiration filled Coleman's agitated mental vat.

"I got it!" he hollered at Ralph Adams, who was presiding over the sports copy desk.

"I hope you've got a column," Adams muttered. "The boys in the composing room are asking whether you think we're putting out a weekly or what."

"I got it!" Coleman repeated. "I'll write that the reason the Hawks never finish first is that Pete Muldoon put a curse on 'em!"

Adams was properly skeptical. "It's an addlebrained notion that nobody will believe," he said. "But it might stand up for one edition, if you get a lucky bounce."

When it is 26 minutes to deadline, the last frayed thread is about to break and plunge the sword of Damocles in a hack's back. In tight, the sportswriter throws nothing back. Coleman typed feverishly:

> The Hawks are victims of a hex Pete Muldoon put on them many years ago, after he was fired as coach. He had a stormy session with Major Frederic McLaughlin, the strange eccentric who owned the Hawks when they were admitted to the NHL in 1926.
>
> Muldoon coached the Hawks to a third-place finish in their first year, but McLaughlin was not impressed. "This team was good enough to be first," he said.
>
> Muldoon was amazed at McLaughlin's criticism, but not to the point of shutting up. "You're crazy!" he fumed.
>
> McLaughlin was outraged by such heresy. "You're fired!" he roared.
>
> Muldoon flared back in a black Irish snit. "Fire me, Major, and you'll never finish first! I'll put a curse on this team that will hoodoo it till the end of time!"
>
> And so, kiddies, that's why the Hawks always fail to grab the flag in the NHL. They cannot beat the Curse of the Muldoon . . .

The fiction caught on, perhaps to the amazement of Jim Coleman. The Curse of the Muldoon became an entertaining chapter in the folk literature of hockey, often paraded as fact by romantic writers on the beat. Coleman teased it along with an annual reprinting of the story of Muldoon's black magic.

The authors hate to be meddlesome belittlers, but the facts are a trifle less fanciful. There was a Pete Muldoon and he did coach the Hawks in 1926–27, but reliable informants say he never cussed, let alone cursed, in his whole antiseptic life. There was a Major McLaughlin, a millionaire coffee baron and husband of a movie actress named Irene Castle, and he was eccentric. He had the ludicrous notion in 1938, for example, that natives of the United States with such unlikely names as Ike Klingbeil and Fido Purpur could play in the NHL.

Muldoon died a few years ago in Seattle, apparently without knowledge of Coleman's curse. McLaughlin died without witnessing the Hawks finish first. But in 1967 the Hawks did it for the first and only time, and, in the interests of accuracy, the Muldoon Myth can be mercilessly shot down.

Major McLaughlin was coaxed into hockey in 1926 by Lester Patrick, when the Old Silver Fox was peddling the Pacific Coast Hockey League to Eastern enthusiasts. McLaughlin did not know a hole in the ground from the usual comparison about hockey, but he obligingly gave Patrick $200,000 for the Portland Rosebuds. The Portland package included Dick Irvin, Mickey Mackay, George Hay, Rabbit McVeigh, Percy Traub and Bob Trapp.

McLaughlin was a prominent American polo player in his blue-blooded youth and, in maturity as a hockey owner, refused to become unhorsed. He was always riding to battle with his coaches, hiring and firing them on frantic whim.

The Hawks finished third in the American Division in their first season, behind Rangers and Boston, but McLaughlin detached the robes of authority from Coach Muldoon. He replaced Muldoon, to start the 1927–28 season, with Barney Stanley, who had played in the West at Vancouver, Calgary, Regina and Edmonton.

The Hawks, under Stanley's administration, were wretched. They won seven games out of 44 in 1927–28 and Stanley professed to be perplexed. One afternoon, disgusted, he walked into McLaughlin's office in the cavernous Chicago Stadium. "For the life of me," Stanley said, "I don't know what's the matter with this team."

The Major hardly raised his aristocratic eyes from the paper he was reading. "If you really want to find out quick what's wrong," he snapped, "take a look in the first mirror you come to!"

From that thorny point, McLaughlin went through coaches faster than Bobby Hull can whap a slapshot. Or, to be accurate, much faster. Chicago coaches met each other getting on and off trains; McLaughlin did everything except install a revolving door in the Stadium to hasten their departure.

Edward Fitkin, who now flacks publicity for Los Angeles Kings, once observed: "For a coffee king, McLaughlin sure had caffeine nerves."

The Major at least had an uncontrollable itch in his trigger finger. He shot down 13 coaches in his first 10 years in the NHL, hiring three and firing two of them in 1932–33. He successively employed Godfrey Matheson, Emil Iverson and Tommy Gorman that season, dismissing the first two with ample provocation. Matheson, a Winnipeg opportunist and comic, was a hilarious choice. When goalkeeper Charlie Gardiner was injured and unable to practice, Matheson used a dressmaker's dummy in his place.

Frank Patrick, working for Boston in the early thirties, once asked a Chicago forward, Johnny Gottselig, "Who would you say was the worst coach you ever had in Chicago?"

"I don't know," Gottselig said. "I'd say it was a photofinish between a half a dozen of them."

Tommy Gorman, a knowing hustler from Ottawa, coached the Hawks to a semblance of respectability in 1933–34, when they won the first of two Stanley Cups under Major McLaughlin's bizarre ownership. The Hawks ended the regular schedule in second place behind Detroit in the American Division, then eliminated the Montreal Canadiens and Montreal Maroons in successive playoff series to reach the Cup final. They subdued the Red Wings three games to one, principally because of goalie Gardiner's heroics.

Gardiner was a cocky Hibernian, born in Edinburgh, Scotland, and raised in Winnipeg, Manitoba. He had suffered from notorious nonsupport with the Hawks since 1927, the only reputable Chicago representative through two seasons when the team won only 14 and tied 11 of 88 games. Gardiner was the league's all-star goalkeeper in 1930–31, 1931–32 and again in 1933–34, Chicago's first championship year and his last. In eight Stanley Cup games, Gardiner lost one, tied one, and achieved two shutouts for a stingily spectacular goals-against average of 1.5.

Although the Hawks had suffered regularly at the hands of Red Wings in Detroit for years, when they opened for a final series in the Olympia on April 3, 1934, they hiked eyebrows up into hairlines by winning 2–1. They repeated two nights later, 4–1. The series switched to Chicago and, before 17,700 fans, Detroit's Herbie Lewis, Larry Aurie and Ebbie Goodfellow temporarily restored Gardiner to the mortals. They beat him, 5–2. The fourth game required 30 minutes and five seconds of overtime before Mush March scored the Cup-winning goal for Chicago, on a pass from Doc Romnes. Detroit's Goodfellow was serving a penalty when March's shot turned the Hawk partisans wild.

The next day, high on jubilation, Gardiner was gleefully wheeled through the Chicago Loop by Roger Jenkins, a teammate. Jenkins was paying off a bet: he had bet Gardiner he couldn't stop the Wings.

Two months later, on June 13, Gardiner was wheeled into an operating room in a Winnipeg hospital. It was too late to save his life, at 30, from a brain hemorrhage.

Bill Tobin, the squat, gray man who managed the Hawks for 30 years, would say, "Hockey was Gardiner's life." Tobin, the manager, was known as Mysterious Mister T, the great little what-is-it of the Hawks. He was an agile broken-field runner who outlasted a generation of managerial contemporaries; coaches were constantly purged but he always survived the perils of running a habitually brutal team.

Baz O'Meara wrote in the Montreal *Star* after Tobin died in 1963: "Tobin was the warp and woof of hockey." But while he woofed, the Hawks warped. They had the most lamentable record in NHL history until Tommy Ivan replaced Tobin as manager 13 years ago.

Tobin's survival depended on his tolerance for the addled notions of his superiors. In 1938 he went along, very straight faced, with an odd order from Major McLaughlin. "Ice me a team of all American players," McLaughlin demanded. Tobin obliged, instead of counseling against making the Hawks a bigger joke than they were. Chicago's All-American roster included Mike Karakas from Aurora, Minnesota, Bun LaPrarie from Sault Ste. Marie, Michigan, Milt Brink, Al Soumi and Butch Schaeffer from Eveleth, Minnesota, and Ike Klingbeil from Hancock, Michigan. They won one game in six— they whipped New York Rangers—before sanity prevailed and McLaughlin abandoned his America First scheme.

In the 11 seasons between 1946–47 and 1956–57, the Hawks were a lame wing that drooped in last place nine times. Tobin blandly blamed the conditions on the refusal of other clubs to deal with Chicago. "Unmitigated nonsense!" Conn Smythe of Toronto said in

1954. "The Hawks have had a chance to buy players from us, but Tobin is so cheap that he wouldn't pay 10 cents to see the Statue of Liberty take a swan dive into New York Harbor." Tobin probably was all the things they said about him at his funeral—affable, genial, inoffensive. Smythe's critique suggested that as a hockey executive, however, he was a splendid gin rummy player.

The Hawks won their second Cup in 1938 in outrageous circumstances cut to fit their flaky proprietor. They were a remote third in the American Division, winners of a mere 14 games, 30 points behind the first-place Boston Bruins.

Alex Levinsky, a Toronto furniture dealer, played defense for Chicago then, and he remembers: "We were so bad that I thought we'd be eliminated in our first playoff series by the Canadiens. So I packed all my clothes in my car and sent my wife home to Toronto." Levinsky laughed as old athletes do when the glow of old upsets are on them: "But we kept winning and I was still living out of the car a month later."

The Hawks beat the Canadiens two games to one, after losing the first of a three-game series. They subdued New York Americans, after losing the first of another three-game series. That qualified them, stumbling and hiccuping, to play Toronto in the best-of-five final. They were 10-to-1 longshots against a Maple Leaf squad which banished the powerful Bruins in three successive games.

The Hawks were coached by Bill Stewart, an irascible egomaniac whom McLaughlin recruited from the ranks of referees and umpires. Stewart refereed in the NHL for nine seasons and began umpiring in the National League in 1933. He was a native of Fitchburg, Massachusetts, the only native American to coach a team in the NHL.

Paul Thompson was an ornament among the Chicago zircons in 1938, allied with Earl Seibert, Johnny Gottselig, Lou Trudell, Doc Romnes, Levinsky, Carl Voss and Mike Karakas. But historians most remember a very substitute goalkeeper named Alfred Moore.

The Hawks reeled into the final without goaler Karakas, whose big toe had been broken in the series against New York Americans. Bill Stewart sought to replace him with Dave Kerr, a superb player with New York Rangers, but Conn Smythe said the hell with that.

Kerr did dress with the Hawks shortly before the first game in Toronto, but Smythe vetoed him as a substitute. Stewart blew one of his celebrated fuses. He seized the butcher knife which the players used to cut tape for their sticks and ran to the door.

"Where's that sonofabitch Smythe? I'll murder him!" Stewart was tackled before he could make the door, knocked down by Levinsky, a former Leaf. Stewart would argue later, and until he died four years ago, that he had been assaulted by ruffians in blue Toronto jerseys.

The Hawks, loudly agitated, then reluctantly accepted Alf Moore as a substitute goalie. He was a modest minor leaguer who had spent the season in Pittsburgh and returned home to Toronto.

Legend, the sort of nonsense that surrounds the Hawks, suggests that Stewart obtained Moore from a Toronto beer hall, where Alfred was wetting an enormous thirst. "Who, me?" Moore is supposed to have said, puzzled and gently burping back beer fumes when Stewart beckoned.

"Yes, you," Stewart muttered. "Unfortunately."

The Chicago players shared Stewart's disgust as Moore dragged on cumbersome equipment. Lou Trudell looked up from tying his skates and grumbled, "Why did it have to be you?"

"Beg pardon?" Moore said, allegedly full of hops. "I believe I will stone them."

The Leafs conned Moore for an early goal, but, head clearing and aided by a strong defense, he blunted every other Toronto thrust. He thwarted the Leafs by a 3–1 majority, to the vast delight of beer drinkers.

Turk Broda was the Toronto goalie that spring, still professing to be stunned by his rival's performance. "We threw everything at old Alf but the building," Broda insists.

Moore, delighted, had a rebuttal for jeering fans in the building. After the game ended, he thumbed his nose at the Toronto bench.

Moore, gray and sober 31 years later, gives lie to the barroom myth. "I'd been asked to attend the game by the Hawks, so they must have known they were in trouble for a goalkeeper." The Leafs, through the recalcitrant Smythe, prompted NHL President Frank Calder to rule Moore ineligible for the remainder of the series. "I wasn't unhappy about that," Moore says. "I guess I was happy. I'd had my moment."

Coach Stewart, forced to seek another reserve goalie for the second game, found someone named Paul Goodman. He was found— and no one ever denied it—2½ hours before the game in a movie theater. Goodman was not so good, beaten 5–1 as Toronto tied the series. Three days later, when the series switched to Chicago, Mike Karakas's broken toe was repaired sufficiently for him to play goal.

The third game was tied 1–1 when Doc Romnes untied it for Chicago at 15:55 of the third period. The Leafs protested that the shot hit a goalpost but the referee, a gimlet-eyed fellow named Clarence Campbell, ruled the puck went in the net. A Chicago mob of 18,946, gratified at the 2–1 triumph, cheered the man who would become NHL president in 1946.

The fourth game was a 4–1 romp for the Hawks, an easy conquest on goals by Cully Dahlstrom, Carl Voss, Jack Shill and Mush March. Karakas, the wounded goalie, was carried off by his jubilant team-mates. Bill Stewart skidded across the ice, hollering in the codfish accents of New England, the lights reflecting off his bald head.

Paul Thompson, an all-star left wing that year and now a cattle rancher in Kamloops, British Columbia, has an explanation for the outcome of the chaotic series. "There are some fanciful stories about Moore and Stewart," Thompson says, "but we really won the Cup by roughing up Red Horner."

Horner was the herd sire of the Toronto defense, a bullish competitor of immense wrath. In the first game he cross-checked Doc Romnes and fractured his nose in six places. In the third and fourth games, in Chicago, the Hawks retaliated. "We cut Horner down," Thompson said, "Chicago gangland style."

Bill Stewart, the victorious coach, discovered that glory was indeed fleeting when a man worked for Major McLaughlin. The next season, when the Hawks sank to their customary subterranean level, Stewart was fired. Thompson replaced him and held the job, with indifferent success, until 1944.

Thompson's administration was distinguished by the recruiting of the Bentley brothers, Doug and Max, from the Canadian prairies. They were ponies in a game where it is wiser to bet on horses, but each made it to the individual winner's enclosure: Doug won the scoring championship with 73 points in 1943, Max won it twice, back to back in 1946 and 1947, with respective totals of 61 and 72 points.

But between 1943–44, when they lost the Stanley Cup in four straight games to the Canadiens, and 1960–61, when they beat Detroit in six, the Hawks did not qualify for the Cup final. It was a long time between champagne cocktails and there were years in the late forties and the early fifties when it seemed the Chicago franchise would fold. The club's financial turmoil settled when the junior Jim Norris saved the operation in 1952.

Norris's influence in the NHL—because of his family's interest in

Detroit, Chicago and New York—was enormous. He bought players and extracted favors from his NHL partners, particularly from Conn Smythe of Toronto and Frank Selke of Montreal, who received help from Norris in their horse-racing ventures. "Norris saved the game in Chicago," Smythe insisted at Big Jim's funeral in 1966. He saved it by pouring $2,000,000 into the Black Hawks, to resurrect them from the verge of extinction in 1953 to the Stanley Cup in 1961. They were drawing fewer than 4,000 fans a game before Norris funneled funds and enthusiasm into the franchise.

The Chicago fans, boisterous at the best of times, were loud and derisive in the worst of times. They used to wait for Norris to leave Chicago Stadium so they could pelt him with abuse. He customarily holed up, after grievous defeats, in the dressing room. Tommy Ivan, the thoughtful, dapper general manager, sat with him. "Think the fans have gone now?" Norris would say after a half hour of mourning. If Ivan said yes, they took the long walk up the street to their cars.

Norris was given, in convivial moments, to extravagant gestures. In 1962, in a Toronto hotel room where the bartender was working overtime, he offered $1,000,000 for Frank Mahovlich, the former Maple Leaf left wing. The deal aborted after the principal Toronto owners—John Bassett, Harold Ballard and Stafford Smythe—could not agree to give up their superstar. That the offer was made at all illustrates the casual side of a very rich man's son, one who was once revered as the chief tentacle of Octopus, Inc., the monopolistic International Boxing Club.

Big Jim was indifferent to his huge inheritance. "I hope you don't think I built up the family fortune," he told one interviewer. "I'm doing my best to dissipate it." This careless attitude may have caused his problems with the IBC, grimy circumstances that eventually prompted the United States Supreme Court to abolish the IBC as a cartel in restraint of trade.

"Getting into boxing was the worst thing that ever happened to me," Norris testified before a Senate subcommittee. That was in 1960, after he admitted catering to Frankie Carbo, a mysterious underworld figure who owned pieces of 50 to 100 important fighters, among them two middleweight champions and a lightweight champion. "Carbo was the expediter," Norris admitted. "He convinced several big-name fighters to perform on the IBC's televised shows."

Whatever his conduct of boxing, Norris was a factor for good in the NHL. He had strong, abiding ties with hockey since childhood.

"Racing is pure luck," he once said. "In boxing, the outcome has nothing to do with the promoter. But hockey—it's a team sport where psychology and desire are half the game."

It is a team sport, but the Hawks' success during Norris's jurisdiction depended on several key players. They won the Cup in 1961 because Bobby Hull, Stan Mikita, Pierre Pilote and goalie Glenn Hall were arriving into stirring primes. Hull, Mikita and Pilote had graduated from the St. Catharines (Ontario) Teepees, a thriving junior farm operated for the Hawks by Rudy Pilous. His reward, in 1957, was to succeed Ivan as coach, the twenty-fourth in 30 years.

Pilous lasted until 1963, removed from authority after repeated failures to finish first. The Hawks missed by one point in 1962–63, beaten out of the pennant by Toronto. Several players expressed disenchantment with Pilous, particularly Eric Nesterenko, a taciturn right wing. "Pilous," Nesterenko grumbled, on the record, "couldn't coach a girl's softball team."

Such insurrection cost Pilous his job, which Norris and Ivan gave to Billy Reay, who had successfully coached Chicago's pro farm in Buffalo. "D'you have any advice for me?" Reay asked Pilous when they met at a Montreal race track in the summer of 1963.

"Yes," Pilous said. "Be goddamn sure you finish first."

Reay finally managed it, in 1966–67. Major McLaughlin was dead by then, as were Bill Tobin and Jim Norris; and the Hawks were owned by Arthur Wirtz, who had been a partner in the IBC. The Curse of the Muldoon was at last kicked off a wharf into Lake Michigan.

A year later the Hawks began to sag, mainly because Ivan traded Phil Esposito, Ken Hodge and Fred Stanfield to Boston for Gilles Marotte, Pit Martin and a minor-league goalie named Jack Norris. The three ex-Hawks, all young forwards, were responsible for the big Boston surge last winter. The rangy Esposito set an NHL record for points in a single season, 126.

Now, when hockey men watch Ivan pass by, they marvel, "There goes the guy who made a monster out of Boston."

But despite the Bruins' rise, the Black Hawks weren't dead for long. They miraculously finished first in the East Division in 1970 and then were transferred to the West Division in 1970–71 and finished on top once more. They wiped out Philadelphia in four straight games of the opening round of the 1971 playoffs; took the Rangers in an exhausting seven-game, semifinal set; and succumbed to the Canadiens in the seventh game of the final series.

In 1971–72 and 1972–73 Chicago continued to dominate the West Division although the victory margin over second place Philadelphia was only eight points in the latter season. This coincided with the migration of Bobby Hull to the Winnipeg Jets of the World Hockey Association in the summer of 1972. With Hull, however, they were eliminated in four straight games by the Rangers in the 1972 play-offs. Without him in 1973 the Hawks went through St. Louis in five and calmly strangled the Rangers in the same number, even though they lost the first game at home. They uncovered a fine rookie defenseman in Phil Russell; Pit Martin continued to prove that they had at least gotten one player in the Phil Esposito deal; Tony Esposito flopped and stumbled and kept the puck out; and Dennis Hull, out of his big brother's shadow, skated brilliantly.

Then came the Canadiens and, although the Hawks fought with great heart including a back-to-the-wall, 8–7 triumph in the highest scoring game of modern Cup history, they bowed to the Flying Frenchmen in six games. With the score tied, 4–4, in the last period of the final encounter they could have used the kind of *big* goal that the Golden Jet supplied them with for so many years.

Detroit Red Wings

JACK ADAMS was five weeks short of 73 when he slumped over his desk in Detroit on May 2, 1968, dead of a heart attack. It was appropriate that in the end John James Adams was doing best what he cared about most. He was absorbed in hockey, in charge of the Central Professional League, still caught up in the game that transported him from Fort William, Ontario, to the Hall of Fame on the shore of Lake Ontario, in Toronto. The distance isn't far in miles, but few qualify for the trip.

Adams was among the advance men who blazed the NHL to a big-league level—combative, bold, frank, cussed, big-headed and amiable, one with Art Ross and Lester Patrick and Tommy Gorman, with Dick Irvin and Leo Dandurand and Frank Selke and Conn Smythe. Only Selke and Smythe are left from those puck pioneers.

All of the little universe of hockey in the twentieth century was contained in Adams's mind and interwoven with his life. It wasn't simply that Jack "knew them all," as they say of certain men of vintage. Adams influenced them all; he reacted on them, and they on him. He discovered stars, or invented them. He rose above issues or ignored them, or turned them inside out. He thought loyalty was a two-way street for management and players alike, which is why he helped stifle the first players association in 1957.

But what completed the picture for Jack's intimates was an irreverence that kept himself in perspective. "Let me tell you about the old Vancouver Millionaires," he would say. "A bad hockey team, and I was one of its bad players." He may have been giving himself all the worst of his athletic assessment. In three seasons in Vancouver, 1920 through 1922, he led the Pacific Coast Hockey Association once in penalties and once in goals.

After 1927 Adams guided the Detroit franchise through 35 seasons, to 12 first-place finishes and seven Stanley Cups. In one tyrannical span—from 1949 to 1955—the Red Wings finished first seven successive times, an athletic success unsurpassed by even baseball's New York Yankees in their dominant years. Adams would bristle like a new broom when the inevitable comparisons were made between the Wings and the Yankees. "We are not the Yankees of hockey," he would insist. "The Yankees are the Red Wings of baseball."

Detroit was admitted to the NHL in 1926 when a syndicate purchased the Victoria Cougars for $100,000. The club's president was Charles Hughes, a prominent member of the Detroit Athletic Club. For their money, the partners obtained players like Frank Fredrickson, Frank Foyston, Clem Laughlin, Art Duncan, Jack Walker, Slim Halderson and Frank Sheppard. Of that motley squad, Fredrickson, Foyston and Walker have been admitted to the Hall of Fame.

Duncan inspired the Cougars to a last-place finish in the American Division of the NHL, winners of 10 games in 44. The team played across the Detroit River in Windsor, Ontario, because construction of the Olympia in Detroit was not finished. By the spring of 1927 the Cougars were frantic for fresh money and new managerial talent. They had blown $84,000 at the gate; they were targets for scorn at home and contumely on the road.

Meanwhile, Adams, retired as a player at 32, had helped Dave Gill manage Ottawa Senators to a Stanley Cup triumph over Boston Bruins. Frank Calder, the mild, stocky NHL president, approached him with a proposition. "I think Detroit might be looking for a firebrand like you," he said. "I'll phone Charles Hughes and set up an appointment."

Adams would reveal, long after: "When I walked in to see Hughes, I had a psychological advantage. I was no cap-in-hand applicant for employment. He had finished last and lost a ton of money, and I'd been involved in winning the Stanley Cup. I told him he needed me more than I needed him—and he agreed."

The Detroit franchise hit the skids before the bottom fell out of the world's economy in the crash of 1929. The Cougars were lucky, Adams recalled, if they attracted 80,000 fans a year, not all of them paid. "One night in 1930," Adams said, "we played an exhibition game for some charity run by Frank Murphy, the Detroit mayor. It was a cash collection, pay what you could. Just before the game started we heard there was a guy driving up and down Woodward Avenue outside the Olympia. He had five bags of potatoes and wanted in. We took his spuds and gave him standing room."

The club's name was changed from Cougars to Falcons after a newspaper competition to pick a new tag, but the team remained depressed. They traveled on day coaches and browsed on cheese sandwiches wrapped in wax paper. Frank Sheppard, one of the nondescript forwards, told Adams he had figured a way to retire in luxury. "I'll open a string of hot-dog stands where the train stops," Sheppard said, drooling at the prospect. "The crummy meals you guys eat, I'll be rich."

"We were this depressed," Adams once said. "If Howie Morenz, the great Montreal star, had been available for $1.98, we couldn't have afforded him."

The Falcons had one respectable season in their first eight— 1933–34, the year they finished first in the American Division, beat Toronto in a semifinal playoff to qualify for the Cup final, then lost in four games to Chicago's Black Hawks. The Falcons retreated to the cosy womb of last place the next season, and, in the spring of 1935, Adams was in Montreal watching the Maroons beat Toronto for the Cup. He got in conversation with Frank Patrick, his old boss in Vancouver who was then presiding over the Boston Bruins.

"If I had Cooney Weiland," Patrick said, mentioning Detroit's nifty center, "Boston would be in this final."

"If I had Marty Barry," Adams retorted, in reference to Boston's big, dour center, "Detroit would win the Stanley Cup."

The deal was made; "Big stuff," Adams recalled, "between two freewheeling paupers."

It is fashionable for hockey operators to say of a swap that "it was a trade that helped both teams." It is not always true, but the Weiland-for-Barry barter indeed assisted both Boston and Detroit. Weiland became the pivot between Dutch Gainor and Dit Clapper on Boston's Dynamite Trio. Barry was inserted between Larry Aurie and Herbie Lewis to form the set of forwards chiefly responsible for Detroit's first Stanley Cup triumph, in 1935–36.

Adams was unaware of prosperity around the corner, however, until he arrived at his office in the Olympia one April morning in 1935. The rink was in receivership and there were rumors the Falcons would collapse.

The girl on the switchboard had a big smile on her, for no reason Adams could fathom.

"There's a call for you from Chicago," she told Jack. "The new owner wants to talk to you."

"New owner? Of this club? Who?"

"Mr. James Norris," the switchboard operator said. "The large grain millionaire."

"Adams?" a gruff voice said, when Jack got connected to Norris. "I'll be in Detroit this afternoon. Meet me with the bankers when I take over that lousy club." James D. Norris, Sr., always spoke in such autocratic fashion, in a firm, crisp tone of voice which suggested that if you cared to argue, you would do him a favor by arguing with someone else. Adams, habitually argumentative, did not quarrel with his new boss.

"I remember that afternoon Norris took over," Adams said, after the old wheat baron died in 1952. "He was bald and he had heavy black eyebrows and a round face. His nose was broad and flat, like somebody had hit it."

Norris was a 56-year-old czar of commerce when he purchased the Falcons, but he had always had an interest in hockey that began when he was a boy in Montreal. Norris had played for a team inspirationally called the Montreal Winged Wheelers as a young man and, in the middle of the depression, defied the NHL by operating an outlaw league for two years in Chicago. As a millionaire, he built a rink on his estate at Lake Forest, Ill., where every chauffeur Norris hired had to be able to skate so he could play hockey with the kids.

"We'll call this team the Wings," Norris informed Adams on the first day they met. "In fact, we'll call it Red Wings. Our emblem will be a winged wheel, which ought to sit good with Henry Ford and the Detroit car people." He fixed Adams with a sharp gaze. "And I'll give you a year on your job—on probation."

Adams never signed a contract with Norris and came, in relaxed moments, to call him Pops. "Pops was the bankroll and the boss and after he took over, Detroit hockey never looked back."

The dynasty was begun quickly in the 1935–36 season. Adams coaxed Norris into buying Syd Howe from St. Louis Flyers for $35,000, a lavish price at the time, and encouraged spending about $17,000 to acquire Hec Kilrea from Toronto. The Wings won the American Division and whipped Toronto three games to one for Detroit's first conquest of the Stanley Cup.

They repeated in 1936–37, the first team to finish first and win the Cup in two consecutive seasons. They achieved the prize in spite of crippling injuries, reduced to nine players in beating New York Rangers for the Cup. A journeyman goalie recruited from New York Americans, Earl Robertson, was a prominent replacement for the injured Normie Smith.

Adams believed the Wings of Aurie, Barry and Lewis, of Syd Howe, Ebbie Goodfellow, Johnny Sorrell, Hec Kilrea, Bucko McDonald and Mud Bruneteau were good enough to last. "I stood pat," Adams admitted after they finished last in 1937–38, "and I should have been dealing. After this flop, I'll never hesitate to bust up championship clubs."

The Wings did not qualify for the Cup final again until 1942, and then Adams sustained what he called "the bitterest blow" of his career. They won the first three games of a best-of-seven final and were leading the fourth game with 15 minutes to play, when the Leafs rebounded to win four straight games. It was the greatest comeback or worst collapse, depending on your sentiments, in Stanley Cup history.

In the fourth game, Adams always insisted, the Wings were victims of incredibly inefficient refereeing by the official, Mel Harwood. The Wings lost the pivotal fourth game, 4–3, yielding two goals in the last 15 minutes. Afterward, the embattled Harwood was surrounded by three riled Detroit players—Grosso, Eddie Wares and Sid Abel. Adams skidded across the ice to join them.

"Jack was only going to protect the referee," said young Jim Norris, then a vice-president of the Wings. Norris's tongue was tucked firmly in his clean-shaven cheek.

Adams was charged with hitting the referee, although he protested, not quietly: "I didn't get within 10 feet of that guy!"

Calder, the NHL president, repudiated Adams's protest by suspending him for the balance of the series. Grosso and Wares were fined $100 each for abusing the referee. Thus clipped, the Wings subsided in the last three games, beaten four games to three in Toronto's rousing reversal.

"To me," Adams would say, much later, "the 1942 series was controlled by the Toronto papers and Conn Smythe. They influenced Calder into favoring the Leafs."

Adams kept needling Calder the next time the governors convened, in the summer of 1942. "You're through persecuting me!" he hollered at the man who had suggested, 17 years before, that he apply for a job in Detroit. "I'm through being your goddamn patsy!" Adams always believed that his protest insured that Detroit subsequently received even breaks from referees. Calder, whom the public believed could be intimidated by domineering governors like Smythe and Adams, died before completion of the 1942–43 season. He did not live to witness the Wings, led by Abel and Carl Liscombe, subdue Boston Bruins in four successive games in the Cup final.

Toronto and Montreal, with stronger farm systems and fewer players in World War II, dominated the NHL in the late forties. The Wings weren't back to win the Cup until 1949–50 when, in a rigorous seven-game final, they beat Rangers four games to three.

"That series," Adams praised, "gave my kind of player a chance to shine. I mean guys like Sid Abel, with the hard glow of dedication." Abel had been a left winger before the war, but when he came back Adams shifted him to center ice. "Sid had bad legs but lots of heart, so I put him in a position where he wouldn't have to do all the driving skating along the wing."

Detroit came down to the last game of the 1950 final tied three games each with the aroused Rangers. Abel was playing between Ted Lindsay and Gerry Couture, missing Gordie Howe who had been critically injured in a semifinal against Toronto.

"Abel was clearly played out," Adams said. "But late in the game, when he was knocked down, he still managed to score the tying goal on his knees. That kept us alive, and Pete Babando came off the bench to score the winning goal in the twenty-eighth minute of overtime."

Abel subsequently coached Chicago Black Hawks in 1952–53 and 1953–54, then returned to the Wings as coach in the last years of Adams' administration. When Adams was relieved of command in 1963, Abel succeeded him. Adams did not like it much.

Tommy Ivan, whose surname was pruned from Ivanoff, was the Detroit coach in the 1949–50 championship. He is a neat, agile man, five inches over five feet, who came up through the Red Wing system in the same fashion as a player is groomed. Ivan's playing career ended as a young amateur in Brantford, Ontario, when a puck smashed his face. He stayed in the town as the coach of a kids team, then joined the Detroit organization as coach of their juniors in the Ontario towns of Guelph and Galt. Ivan served in the Canadian army in World War II, then graduated to Detroit's pro farm at Omaha, Nebraska. He was boosted to the Indianapolis Capitals in the American League in 1946–47 and tapped to replace Adams, by Adams himself, as bench boss of the Wings in 1947–48.

"Adams," Ivan says, "is the best thing that ever happened to me." He continued to feel that way even after leaving the Wings in 1954 to become general manager of the Black Hawks, in one of the whole-sale manipulations of personnel by the Norris family between Detroit and Chicago.

The Red Wings under Ivan were the young Wings of Terry Sawchuk, Red Kelly, Ted Lindsay, Alex Delvecchio and the great Howe. They practiced early in the mornings, on Ivan's cunning theory that "If you get them up early enough, they'll get to bed early enough."

The Detroit farms were producing big-league players by the platoon 20 years ago, and castoffs for Chicago by the brigade. In the four-year period between 1950 and 1954, the Hawks siphoned 19 players plus Ivan from the Wings.

Detroit prospects were surrounded at tender ages. For example, scout Bob Kinnear spotted goalie Terry Sawchuk in East Kildonan, Manitoba, when Sawchuk was 14. The late Fred Pinckney stumbled upon Howe in a Saskatoon schoolyard when Howe was a gangly 13. Carson Cooper recruited the graceful Kelly and combative Lindsay from St. Michael's College in Toronto, a few blocks from the rink of the Maple Leafs. "The boys were so young when they came to the Wings," Adams used to say, "that when I came home from a trip they would rush up to me yelling, 'Daddy! Daddy! What did you bring me?' "

The Wings always finished first in the early fifties and in 1951–52, in a stunning display, they won the Stanley Cup in the minimum number of eight games. Goalie Sawchuk—supported by a defense of Kelly, Leo Reise and Bob Goldham—yielded five goals in eight trouncings of Toronto and Montreal. Four of his conquests were shutouts, responsible for the picayune average of 0.62 goals per game against him. No goalkeeper has ever frustrated playoff opponents in such stingy fashion.

Adams loudly contended that Howe was the greatest all-round player he ever saw. "I'm a strong admirer of Rocket Richard," a reference to Montreal's flaming competitor, "but for pure versatility, high purpose and team contribution, My Guy is the greatest." Adams cited Howe's unselfishness in the 1951–52 season as characteristic. "He was going for 50 goals to tie Rocket's record, so I told Ivan to use him a lot in our last few games. But Gordie kept passing the puck to Abel. Finally Tommy asked him what he was up to."

Howe drawled in his slow, laconic way, "Oh, Ol' Boot has a bonus for getting 20 goals, y'know," using Abel's nickname, Bootnose. "If he's in front of the net, I'm gonna give him the puck."

They both missed their marks. Abel got 17 goals and Howe was stopped at 47. He would get 49 the next season but, for all his uncommon power and talent, Howe never reached 50.

Howe is the one Wing that Adams guaranteed a job in Detroit as long as he could lace up skates. Adams made similar promises to others of his "boys," notably Ted Lindsay and Red Kelly, but they departed after celebrated rifts with their cantankerous mentor.

Lindsay, scarred and rebellious, was shuffled to Chicago in 1957 after he attempted to organize the first NHL players association. Adams considered Lindsay's union activity a disloyal act against the we're-all-chums-together attitude management preferred. "When Lindsay came to us from Toronto he was a fine boy," Adams protested. "He and Howe and Abel made a great forward line. But as he got older, it became a question of whether he was going to run the team or I was. So," with a dismissing wave of the hand, "I shipped him to Chicago." Lindsay played three years for the Hawks and did not return to Detroit until after Adams was dismissed in 1963. Then, 39 and returning for a last Red Wing hurrah, Lindsay came back to play one more year for Sid Abel. He scored 14 goals in Detroit's rush to first place in 1964–65.

Kelly was in his thirteenth season with the Wings when Adams let him go in 1960. He appeared to be slumping as a defenseman and Adams tried to trade him to New York for Bill Gadsby. Kelly refused to join the Rangers. Adams, convinced Kelly was through, then swapped him to Toronto for Marc Reaume, a journeyman defenseman. The Kelly swap did nothing to elevate Adams' seventh sense of managerial genius. In Toronto, working for Coach Punch Imlach, Kelly switched from defense to center ice and helped the Leafs win four Stanley Cups. He also served two terms in the Canadian parliament as the Liberal member for the Toronto constituency of York West.

Adams was jolted emotionally when Pops Norris died in 1952, but he slipped into a smooth arrangement with Marguerite Ann Norris, 26-year-old daughter of the old grain merchant. Just before the old gentleman's death, some skeptics were asking questions about Norris's NHL monopoly. "The NHL," Jim Coleman scoffed in the Toronto *Globe and Mail,* "stands for Norris House League."

On the surface, at least, Norris did seem to be seizing controls of other teams besides the Wings. He owned chunks of Chicago Stadium, where the Black Hawks played, and Madison Square Garden, home of the Rangers. Prior to the death of the senior Jim Norris, however, the family attempted to clarify the muddled situation. Young Jim, then president of the International Boxing Club, gave up his financial interest in the Red Wings. He joined his younger brother, Bruce, and Arthur Wirtz in purchasing the Chicago Stadium and the Black Hawks. The elder Norris in turn surrendered his holdings in the Stadium and bought young Jim's interest in the Wings. No direct link between Norris and other NHL teams was ever proved, but the player deals between Detroit and Chicago had the look of a family compact. Jack Adams insisted that the interest of Pops Norris in hockey was purely altruistic. "Why, I saw Pops once give $40,000 to the New York Rangers, no questions asked, just to help keep them from folding."

Detroit won the Cup for the last time in 1954–55, just before Montreal Canadiens set off on a despotic span of five in a row. Bruce Norris, a tall, fair-haired man, had returned to run the Wings and he decided, after the Wings sagged to fifth in 1961–62, on rearranging the front office.

Adams, in Norris's view, had to go. There was a groping for sugar to coat the firing, lame excuses that Adams ought to have a little more time to himself, a little more leisure to spend with his wife, Helen. Jack brushed aside all speculation when asked about his departure. "I was," he said bluntly, "kicked out."

The Wings' athletic fortunes did improve immediately after Adams long association with them ended. Under Abel, they qualified for the Cup final in 1962–63 and 1963–64, losing each time to Toronto. They were in the final again in 1965–66, beaten in six games by Montreal.

Adams spent the last three years of his life presiding over the Central Pros, back in hockey but never quite getting over his firing by the Wings. Three years ago, in New York, he received the Lester Patrick Trophy as the man who had done the most for hockey in the United States. Howe, his Guy was there, and Howe had the grace to acknowledge Adams's paternal attitude. He turned toward Jack in a banquet room at Toot Shor's and said, "Close to my father, up very close, it's you."

Adams got up to speak at the end, caught up in the melancholy thought of ongoing time. "May God take all of you in His arms," he said, "but not too soon."

Under Abel the Red Wings floundered in recent years. They finished sixth in 1967–68 and fifth in 1968–69.

A brief revival occurred in 1969–70 when the Detroit sextet finished third in the NHL's East Division. Bolstered by defenseman Carl Brewer and high-scoring Frank Mahovlich, the Red Wings appeared to be a playoff threat until they were shellacked by Chicago in four straight games in April 1970. Then a succession of setbacks crippled the team.

Brewer walked out on the team in mid-summer soon after Ned Harkness, the former Cornell University coach, was named the Red Wings mentor. Harkness immediately made his presence felt with a series of edicts which annoyed several veterans. By the start of the season the Detroiters were riddled with dissension with Harkness at the center of the controversy.

Eventually, Harkness was removed as coach but, surprisingly, installed as general manager. His bench replacement was ex-Red Wing defenseman Doug Barkley. As manager, Harkness cleaned house, trading Mahovlich to Montreal, Peter Stemkowski and Bruce MacGregor to New York, while negotiating several other deals. By the end of the 1970–71 campaign in which they missed the playoffs, the Red Wings boasted of a young and seemingly eager team and Harkness appeared to have wiped most of the troublemakers out of his lineup. Through it all, Gordie Howe remained and vowed to play through the 1971–72 season. A chronic case of arthritis, however, dimmed his chances; and when the Wings lined up for the first faceoff in the fall of 1971, "number 9" was missing from the line-up, retired to a vice-presidential post in the organization.

Without him, The Wings rose from seventh to fifth, four points behind Toronto the last Eastern playoff qualifier. Barkley, after a weak start, was replaced by former Red Wing forward, iron man Johnny Wilson, who rallied the team to the near miss.

In 1972–73 the Wings again missed but only by two points, this time to Buffalo. Even though they had gone over the .500 mark and earned 10 more points in the standings over 1971–72, it was still as good as a mile. Wilson was then dismissed in favor of Port Huron's tempestuous, towel-tossing Ted Garvin, who had been named to the International League's first all star team as coach.

Garvin's nucleus consists of 52-goal scorer Mickey Redmond,

40-goal man Marcel Dionne, promising speedster Henry Boucha and a Ken Dryden-type goaltender up from the Virginia Red Wings, American Hockey League rookie-of-the-year Doug Grant.

Montreal Canadiens

MONTREAL CANADIENS had won the Stanley Cup on the late afternoon of May 11, 1968, for the fifteenth time. Inside their cluttered dressing quarters, in the old Montreal Forum, victory champagne was being poured from long, green bottles down long, dry throats. Then Hector (Toe) Blake, the thick-set, perspiring coach, 55 years old, made a simple announcement: "I think this is it. I think I'm quitting. This was the longest season, and one of the hardest, with my fightingest team."

It occurred to Blake that he was abandoning the best back-of-the-bench job in hockey. "I'd like to coach Canadiens for a hundred years, but," heavily, wearily, "the tension is too terrific. On the days of some games, this year, I was almost not human."

Blake did retire to the prosperous tranquility of his Montreal tavern, retained by Canadiens in the relaxed capacity as assistant to Sam Pollock, the club's cunning general manager. Pollock was succeeded by the squat Claude Ruel, who was 29 when he accepted the job, the youngest coach in the National League.

Casual fans would think Blake's unparalleled success might ease his stubborn, gnawing urge to win. No man, on the sod or under it, matched his distinguished stewardship in the NHL: nine first-place finishes in 13 years, eight Stanley Cup triumphs, five in succession in an all-conquering span between 1955 and 1960.

But today, winning today, was the spur that continually raked Blake's psyche. His dressing-room oratory was loud, sometimes pro-

33

fane, often with whipcracks in it. "Get mad!" he would advise his
subordinates, unquietly, when they were losing. "You're better than
they are! Look up! Up!"

If a player looks high enough in the Montreal boudoir, he can
see eight Canadiens of medieval generations staring back at him.
Georges Vezina is in the gallery, and Howie Morenz, Joe Malone
and Aurel Joliat, Sylvio Mantha, Herb Gardiner, Newsy Lalonde
and Rocket Richard. Every one of them is in the Hall of Fame.

Underneath the unsmiling portraits, in red block letters, is an
inspirational line written in combat during World War I by the
Canadian poet, John McCrae: "To you from failing hands we throw
the torch, Be yours to hold it high . . ." Dick Duff, an irreverent
Montreal left wing, once said, "Nobody grabbed McCrae's message
quite like Blake. He always let us know that if we didn't catch the
torch, he'd light it under us."

In the early years of Blake's command, in the seasons immediately after he replaced the late Dick Irvin in 1955, the Canadiens
required no inspirational literature. They formed a swift, dominant
crowd that reeled off five consecutive Cup conquests, the Canadiens of Rocket Richard and Bernard Geoffrion and Bert Olmstead,
of Doug Harvey and Tom Johnson and Jacques Plante and Tom
Johnson and Dickie Moore and the big, young Jean Beliveau.

It was customary for Blake's detractors to sneer, "Even a sports
writer could win coaching that mob. All you gotta do is open and
shut the gate." That mob reckoned that any best-of-seven-game
series was a four-game set. If it took them any longer to win, it was
a mistake. If they didn't win at all, it was a scandal.

Athletic dynasties end when the legs collapse, or the farms stop
producing; but Blake, rebuilding with unknowns supplied first by
Frank Selke, then by Sam Pollock, won the Cup three times in his
last four years. When he retired, only three players—Henri Richard,
Claude Provost and the big, eldering Beliveau—remained from
his first Montreal team in 1955–56.

In his last season, Blake was forced to integrate five rookies into
the line-up when his veterans were injured. He guided them, cussing
and goading, from last place at Christmas to the Stanley Cup by
Mother's Day. Before he quit, he had erased all the raps against him
as a pushbutton coach.

Observers were inclined to forget, as they marveled at Blake's
abrasive crotchets and coaching genius, that he was called the Old

Lamplighter when he was the left-wing confederate of Rocket Richard and Elmer Lach. He lit a red lamp 260 times behind enemy goalkeepers.

Blake's playing career was distinguished, more or less, by courtly conduct. In one season, 1945–46, he won the Lady Byng Trophy as the athlete best combining exemplary manners with impressive play. In later years, as Canadiens' curator, Blake took special pains to prove that his winning the Byng was an extreme form reversal. He was in constant rebellion against what he considered the oppressive heel of authority.

Eight years ago, as one notorious example, he became agitated by the decisions of referee Dalton McArthur of Maple, Ontario. He skidded across the ice in Chicago after losing a playoff game and directed a right-hand wallop at McArthur's startled expression. Enchanted witnesses claim it was the best blow thrown in the Chicago Stadium since Tony Zale was punching the face off Rocky Graziano 20 years ago in their wild middleweight quarrels. Vice was its own reward in the McArthur case. Blake was fined $2,000 by NHL president Clarence Campbell for his intemperance, the largest single rebuke ever assessed in hockey history.

The penalty did not noticeably deter Blake, however, from unloosing his temper whenever he felt abused. Two fans accused him and the scarred Claude Provost of assault after a noisy night of bloodletting in the Los Angeles Sports Arena on November 19, 1967. They were fitted for an impressive lawsuit of $655,000. Bernard Weisman, of Northridge, California, testified that he was booing Blake and the Canadiens, and that he moved close to the Montreal bench to administer close-range needling. Somehow, he said, he came away with a gash on his scalp requiring 23 stitches to shut after being struck by a stick wielded by Provost or Blake. Weisman demanded, as balm, $405,000. A Los Angeles woman, the second plaintiff, claimed she suffered a concussion after being hit by a stick in the same incident. She suggested, by writ, that $250,000 would be adequate to repair the damage. Blake and Provost were acquitted of malicious assault in July, 1968.

Blake's departure from the Canadiens did not mean the team would be bereft of his spiritual encouragement. There was talk, during extensive renovations to the Forum in the summer of 1968, of hanging his portrait in the dressing room with Richard and the rest. It would be a blunt reminder about that business with the torch.

The Canadiens were organized on December 10, 1909, eight years before the conception of the NHL, and have always been the personification of Gallic flamboyance, of French elan and speed. But in the last 20 years the team has been a harmonious amalgam of French- and English-speaking players, split between the Richards, Provost, Beliveau, Rousseau, Bouchard, Plante and Cournoyer, for instance, and the Harveys, Reardon, Moore, Duff, Lach, Olmstead, Harris, Backstrom, Worsley and Blake. They are a muscular microcosm of Canada's bicultural and bilingual community, representative of 4,000,000 French-Canadians and those among the 17,000,000 other Canadians who are not fans of the Toronto Maple Leafs.

The English-speaking Canadiens kid their French-speaking playmates as "Pepzees" or "Gorfs." Pepzee is a quaint term peculiar to the Montreal patois ever since a soft-drink strike depleted supplies of Coca-Cola. "We 'ave no Coke," the Montreal storekeepers would apologize, "but we 'ave Pepzee."

"Gorf" of course is "frog" spelled backwards, and the English-speaking Canadiens like the uncomplicated goaler Lorne (Gump) Worsley make of that what they will. Lumpy Gump, who is built like a badly packed army dufflebag, was the punchline for a joke told by the jovial Provost during the team's visit to Expo 67 two years ago. Provost conducted a question-and-answer session for his companions, based on the vigilant security precautions taken to protect Charles DeGaulle. The reedy old mossback who generally managed France had offended many Canadians by calling for Quebec's secession from the rest of the country.

"Who guard the President of the United States?" Provost asked. And answered himself, "The Secret Service."

"Who guard the Prime Minister of Canada?" Provost demanded.

"The Royal Canadian Mounted Police," he replied.

Then, in his thickest Pepzee accent, "Now, *mes frères*, who guard De Gaulle?"

"Gump Worzlee!" he shouted.

The Flying Frenchmen, which became the Canadiens' flashy sobriquet, were not started by French sportsmen. They were inspired one December night in 1909 by a Scottish baker and a pugnacious Irish contractor. The Eastern Canada Hockey Association was the only pro league in existence, and it was sagging.

James Strachan, whose family was big in the baking industry, managed the Montreal Wanderers. One winter night in 1909 he was in earnest conversation with Ambrose O'Brien of Renfrew, Ontario, heir to railroad riches surrounded by his father. "There's 70 per cent of Montreal's population that's French," Strachan told O'Brien. "A club of French-Canadian players would be a successful attraction in this town."

O'Brien momentarily deflected the notion. He instead sought admission for his home team, the Renfrew Millionaires, into the Eastern Canada league. He was refused and, typically bull-headed, formed his own league.

O'Brien had his own team, the Millionaires. He founded the Montreal Canadiens and backed them with $5,000 to guarantee the players' salaries. He coaxed James Strachan to transfer the Montreal Wanderers to the new league, and financed two more teams, Cobalt and Haileybury, from Ontario's thriving nickel belt. He called the league the National Hockey Association, which became the immediate predecessor of the NHL. O'Brien's audacity destroyed the floundering Eastern League, which collapsed when Ottawa Senators and Montreal Shamrocks withdrew to join him.

Canadiens played their first game on January 5, 1910, against Cobalt, in a cramped sardine can called the Jubilee Rink. They attracted 3,000 noisy partisans to watch seven-man hockey played in two 30-minute periods.

Their first captain and manager, Jean Baptiste (Jack) Laviolette, was perfectly cast for a French-Canadian clientele. He was swift, and his uncommonly long black mane streamed behind him as he burst down the ice to provide shots on goal for Edouard (Newsy) Lalonde and Didier (Pit) Lepine. Joe Cattarinich, who would later join Leo Dandurand as co-owner of the club, played goal. Cattarinich yielded six goals to Cobalt, but his teammates responded with seven.

Canadiens won only one other game in the 12 played during their first season, but O'Brien made a 50 per cent profit. He sold the team to a Montreal wrestler who called himself George Kennedy. He called himself Kennedy because his father, whose surname was Kendall, refused to have a wrestler in the family.

Kennedy played the good-guy role outside the ring, as Newsy Lalonde would remember years after. "Kennedy led us to our first Stanley Cup in 1916," Lalonde recalled last summer, when he was 82, "without once raising his voice or swearing."

Three years later, in the spring of 1919, the Canadiens played in the only Stanley Cup final ever canceled. They were on the Pacific Coast, combating the Seattle Metropolitans, when the area was caught in the massive epidemic of influenza that followed World War I.

Several of the Canadiens were felled by flu, including Bad Joe Hall, a smooth vigorous center who had been born in England. Lalonde roomed with Hall and urged the Englishman to stay in bed. Hall refused, persisting in wearing his Canadiens' sweater until he died of pneumonia on April 6, 1919. Hall's death prompted officials to cancel the championship with the series locked at two wins each and a tie.

Hall was 38 when he died, a 15-year veteran who was called Bad Joe because of his implacable, muscles-first approach. Lalonde, often called the meanest man in hockey history, testifies: "Hall was the meanest."

Kennedy died in 1921, never fully recovered from the flu, and Canadiens were sold to Louis Letourneau, Joe Cattarinich and Leo Dandurand, then operating a race track in Cleveland. Their agent, Canadien coach Cecil Hart, bought a bargain for $11,000. Dandurand peddled the team in 1935, in the tatters of the Depression, to the Canadian Arena Company for $165,000. The company, backed by the respected Senator Donat Raymond, retained the team for 22 years before selling to the Molson brewing family for more than $1,000,000.

The successive Montreal managements have catered to the hero-hungry French-Canadian minority, occasionally to the point of harmless deceit. One year the operators attempted to pass off one Claude Hennessy Burke, an Irishman from New Brunswick, as Claude Bourque. But such capers were seldom necessary, for there was a steady flow of bona fide Frenchmen—Aurel Joliat, Albert (Battleship) Leduc, George Boucher, Billy Boucher, Sylvio Mantha, Wildor Larochelle, Johnny Gagnon and Armand Mondou.

Their early hero, however, bore a lively Gallic-sounding label but, ironically, Howie Morenz was from German-Swiss stock. A cartoon in a Montreal newspaper put Morenz in gaudy perspective, *"Morenz est synonyme de la vitesse."* The quintessence, in sluggish English, of excitement.

The goaler of the early time, from 1911 until 1926, was the tall sober Georges Vezina, who kept his cool so carefully that he was endorsed as the Chicoutimi Cucumber. Goalkeepers still compete for the trophy awarded in tribute to him. He collapsed in action (ah, there, Joe Hall) and died, on March 27, 1926, a victim of tuberculosis.

Canadiens sank through the thirties, no special power after Morenz died in 1937—until Rocket Richard arrived in the early forties. They took the Stanley Cup in 1943–44 and 1945–46, under the late Dick Irvin's jurisdiction, but Canadiens' commanding dominance began two years later. They have won the Cup 12 times since Frank Selke was given the robes of authority on July 25, 1946.

Selke was a small electrician from Kitchener, Ontario, who apprenticed in hockey's front-office affairs under disputatious Conn Smythe in Toronto. He quit the Maple Leafs after Smythe returned, quarrelsome and prickly, from World War II.

Selke didn't resemble an empire maker, short, trim, looking like a business agent for the embalmer's union; but few empire makers have looked the part. His first look at Montreal's empire, Stanley Cup champions and all, did not inspire optimism. "I told Senator Raymond that no other team could match his top six players—Bill Durnan in goal, Ken Reardon and Butch Bouchard on defense, and the Punch Line of Blake, Richard and Elmer Lach. But there were no reserves, no farm system."

Senator Raymond requested Selke's solution, and got it. "We must build a chain of farms in every Canadian province, like Toronto has. It will take money." Senator Raymond gave Selke carte blanche. Money was invested in young players and new teams across the country. One winter Selke spent $300,000 to keep Montreal's farm affiliates solvent. Another year, anxious to turn Jean Beliveau professional, he bought the entire Quebec Senior Amateur League.

Selke was retired by the Molsons in 1964, a reward he didn't necessarily appreciate. He was replaced by the shrewd, agile Sam Pollock, whom he had groomed and who kept Canadiens on top through the coaching era of Blake.

Nor was there any sign of decline in the first year of Claude Ruel's stewardship. The Canadiens subdued, in succession, New York Rangers, Boston Bruins and St. Louis Blues in the all-conquering sweep to their fifteenth Stanley Cup.

However, dissension set in during the 1969–70 campaign, during which the Canadiens finished out of the playoffs on the final night of the season. Ruel remained the coach at the beginning of the 1970–71 season but soon was replaced by his assistant, Al MacNeil. Suddenly, the Montrealers rallied and finished a respectable third in the East Division. They were regarded as heavy underdogs against Boston in the opening playoff round but whipped the Bruins in seven games; bested the North Stars in six; and went on to win the

Stanley Cup from Chicago in another thrilling, seven-game struggle with rookie goaltender Ken Dryden playing all 20 games after only six regular season games as his NHL experience.

MacNeil, although a winner, had ruffled the feathers of Henri Richard during the final series. The captain publicly denounced his coach when he failed to get a full turn, but scored the winning goal of the series. After the season MacNeil returned to the Nova Scotia Voyageurs and St. Louis mentor Scotty Bowman, Anglo but bilingual, came back to his old organization to replace him.

Under Bowman the Canadiens were third again but were pushed out in the quarterfinal of the playoffs by the Rangers. A year later they had again ascended to the top of the East Division and, in disposing of Buffalo, Philadelphia and Chicago, drank champagne from the Stanley Cup for the eighteenth time since World War I.

Richard, apparently not ready to retire at 37, skated like a junior; passed Red Kelly as the player to have participated in the most playoff games; and had his name inscribed on the Cup for the eleventh time, another record. Even with Richard's retirement there is still Yvan Cournoyer, Jacques Lemaire, Guy Lafleur, Frank and Peter Mahovlich, Jacques Laperriere, Serge Savard, and Guy Lapointe. Formidable!

With the Boston "dynasty" shattered it seemed likely that the Canadiens, with an abundance of talent centered on the parent club, bolstered by the Voyageur farm team and heavily endowed by the clever manipulations of Pollock in stockpiling junior draft choices, should be in the throne room for some time to come.

New York Rangers

THE NEW YORK RANGERS unquestionably never would have been born were it not for the immediate success of their predecessors in Manhattan, the New York Americans. The fact has been overlooked by many contemporaries, but it was the Americans who introduced big-league hockey to New York. That the national game of Canada would make a hit in Gotham seemed axiomatic to those associated with hockey. Amateur teams had been playing it for years in rinks around the metropolitan area since the turn of the twentieth century. To succeed on a big-time level, hockey needed a push, and that push—which eventually developed into a shove—was provided by a Canadian-born hockey writer, William "Bill" MacBeth.

A warm, persuasive type, MacBeth was on good terms with practically everybody. One of his acquaintances was William "Big Bill" Dwyer, a bootlegger who had parlayed his liquor investment into a multimillion-dollar operation. Meanwhile, George Lewis "Tex" Rickard, who was born in Kansas City and raised in Texas, who had made a small fortune promoting fights, came to New York, where he immediately became a promotional genius. When, in 1924, the New York Life Insurance Company announced it was foreclosing the mortgage on the old Madison Square Garden and would, in its place, erect a 40-story office building, Rickard decided he would promote a new Garden.

With the assistance of a syndicate of businessmen—Rickard called them "my 600 millionaires"—he organized the new Madison Square

Garden Corporation. Construction began on January 9, 1925, and from that day on Rickard began wondering just what events he'd need to attract people to the huge new arena. He realized that boxing, his favorite sport, would not be enough, and he sought advice from colleagues about promoting other attractions. One such adviser was Col. John S. Hammond, former military attaché in Argentina whom he had met during his cattle ventures.

Just to be sure about hockey's possibilities, Colonel Hammond visited the old Mount Royal Arena in Montreal for a look at top-grade hockey. That was all he needed. Convinced that hockey would be a winner in New York he returned to the United States and tried to persuade Rickard that he should obtain a National Hockey League franchise. But Rickard, a Midwesterner ignorant of the "Canadian Game," was unimpressed with Colonel Hammond's reports. This naturally perturbed Colonel Hammond, who realized that the NHL had two franchises available for the buying.

One of them was the Hamilton (Ontario) Tigers. While Rickard fiddled, Big Bill Dwyer, on MacBeth's advice, moved in and purchased the Tigers for $75,000. Knowing that Rickard was cool to hockey, Dwyer wasn't concerned when the Garden charged him a steep rental fee for the new team, which he dubbed the Americans. Bill was nonplussed because he had money and a "guarantee" from the Garden that his Americans would be the only hockey team in town. Dwyer might have guessed that the Garden would renege on its promise immediately after his Americans played their opening game in New York on December 15, 1925, against the Montreal Canadiens.

Pomp and circumstance dominated the evening. The Governor-General's band of Canada, the West Point band and the cream of society attended the event that won the hearts of the spectators. Two goals by Billy Boucher helped Montreal to a 3–1 victory over the Americans, but the fans were more intrigued by the speedy game, the collisions and the general excitement. It was obvious that NHL hockey was to stay in New York.

This bothered Rickard. Although he was renting the Garden to the Americans, he suddenly decided he also would like to have a second New York club playing out his arena, one that would be wholly owned by the Garden. Colonel Hammond already had suspected Rickard would be wooed by hockey's popularity and had gone about the business of laying the groundwork for a new team. The colonel had heard about a bright young Canadian named Conn

Smythe, who was successfully managing teams in Toronto. He invited Smythe to come to New York and organize the Rangers.

Smythe, like Dwyer, found the Garden brass less than appealing, and a month after he was hired, he quit, returned to Canada and became the power behind the Toronto Maple Leafs. Smythe was replaced by Lester Patrick who, along with his brother, Frank, had established a reputation as a hockey promoter and innovator in Western Canada after an immensely successful career as a player. The new team, which already had been tagged Tex's Rangers, was to be managed and coached by Patrick. Lester, who was called the Silver Fox, because of his obtrusive white mane, forged an awesome hockey machine led by Frank Boucher, a former member of the Royal Canadian Mounted Police, and Bill and Bun Cook.

Dwyer, quite naturally, was furious when he learned of Rickard's plans for a second hockey team in New York. Big Bill wasn't concerned about the new competition but he was annoyed that the Garden reneged on its promise. Dwyer's wrath was the first act of hostility for what was to prove to be an extraordinarily keen rivalry between the Rangers and Americans, one that matched in intensity the bitterness between the city's New York Giants and Brooklyn Dodgers in baseball. From the financial viewpoint there was no competition. Since the Garden owned the Rangers, Colonel Hammond's boys got in rent-free whereas the Americans' rent bill grew steeper and steeper.

Garden officials have preferred to overlook the history of the Rangers' intrusion on the Americans' existence. Both teams attracted great crowds in their early years and left little doubt that New Yorkers would support two hockey teams. But the Garden in its greediness made it more and more difficult for the Americans to exist and the club went out of business in 1942 but not until it played an important part in the success of the Rangers and hockey in Manhattan and even changed its name to Brooklyn Americans for a year. The Rangers benefitted indirectly because of the Americans' image of rambunctiousness. Dwyer's club had an air of illegitimacy while the Rangers seemed to carry themselves with dignity and their president, Colonel Hammond, liked to boast about it. The Americans, obviously, couldn't make such claims.

There was the time the Americans were training at New Haven, Connecticut, in 1928. Their quarters were in the Garde Hotel, a hostel that the Americans' manager, Thomas Patrick (Tommy) Gorman, nearly saw destroyed before his eyes. "One night," Gorman later recalled, "Lionel Conacher was playing cards in a room with Billy Burch and others. All of a sudden Red Green threw an apple core and hit Conacher in the eye. Lionel leaped from his chair and chased Red down a hall. Green slammed a door behind him at the end of the hall only to have big Conacher draw back and make a shoulder lunge at the closed door. Conny missed the door but he crashed into the wall so hard that some of the back section of the building actually collapsed—with Conacher and Green beneath it. It cost the hockey club $500."

The Garden management let no opportunity pass to harass the Americans. Once, during the 1928–29 season, Colonel Hammond summoned Gorman to his office to complain about the Americans' deportment. He berated Gorman and insisted that at that very moment his players were cavorting in a big party at a flat on Fifty-first Street around the corner from Madison Square Garden. Gorman dashed from the office, got the assistance of two detectives and found the party. When they burst into the party they discovered not one of the Americans but nearly a dozen Rangers—celebrating the birthday of their defenseman, Ching Johnson.

There was little Colonel Hammond could do about his Rangers' conduct. They were so impressive on ice, almost from their very start at the Garden, that reprimands hardly ever were ordered.

Unlike the Americans, the Rangers won their first game at the Garden, on November 17, 1926, against the Montreal Maroons. New York won the game, 1–0, on Bill Cook's goal at 18:37 of the second period. Seabury Lawrence, who covered the game for the *New York Times*, observed: "On their first appearance the Rangers made a distinctly favorable impression. Bunny and Bill Cook, playing the wings, and Boucher at center, distinguished themselves by particularly skillful stick work and clever skating."

Boucher, who in time would become coach and then manager of the Rangers, selected the 1927–28 version of the team—then, only two years old—as one of the two finest Ranger teams. "The 1927–28 squad," said Boucher, "won New York's first Stanley Cup. It had two very strong lines, a remarkably effective defense and good goalkeeping."

To win the Stanley Cup, the Rangers eliminated Pittsburgh and Boston in the semifinals to advance against the Montreal Maroons in the finals. "It was tremendously difficult for a Ranger team in those days," Boucher observed. "We couldn't play the finals on our home ice in New York because the arena was booked with another attraction; we had to play every game at the Montreal Forum."

The Maroons were bolstered by such stars as Nels Stewart, Babe Siebert, and Hooley Smith. They defeated the Rangers, 2–0, in the opening game. When New York's goalie Lorne Chabot was injured in the second game, the Rangers asked Montreal manager Eddie Gerard for permission to borrow either Alex Connell, a competent goalie for Ottawa, or minor leaguer Hughie McCormick. Both goalies were in the stands and would have been adequate replacements for the injured Chabot but Gerard refused to permit such substitution. The Rangers were perplexed. They had no substitute goaltender and no forward or defenseman who felt competent enough to wear the pads. Finally, Lester Patrick, the 45-year-old manager who had never played goal in his life, volunteered.

Inspired by their Silver Fox, the Rangers contained the Maroons until early in the third period when Bill Cook scored to put New York ahead, 1–0. Montreal at last beat Patrick at 14:20 of the third period forcing the game into overtime when Frank Boucher scored to win the game for the Rangers. But Montreal defeated New York, 2–0, in the third game and needed but one win for the Cup. Again, Boucher was the hero scoring the only goal of the game, forcing a fifth and final contest on Montreal ice. Naturally, the Maroons were favored. They had won the Cup two seasons earlier and a goal in the fifth game loaned suspicion that they would win it again, especially when the Rangers were penalized early in the match.

By this time Lester Patrick had replaced the injured Lorne Chabot with an obscure goalie named Joe Miller, who achieved little distinction in the NHL. To many, the mere mention of his name was a joke and not necessarily because of the joke book. "He'd been named Red Light Miller," Boucher remembered, "because he had played for the New York Americans. They had a losing team then so, naturally, Joe was a losing goalkeeper. Frankly, I never thought he was bad and, as things turned out, he was just magnificent in the last game."

Shorthanded because of a penalty, the Rangers nevertheless controlled the puck, thanks to Boucher's expert stickhandling. The one-time Mounted Policeman even managed to launch an attack and was being guarded by Mervyn (Red) Dutton. "I knew his weakness," Boucher said. "If you pushed the puck through his legs, instead of watching you he'd look down at the puck. I tried the

trick and, sure enough, he looked down. By the time he looked up
I was around him. I picked up the puck, skated in on Clint Benedict, Montreal's goalie, and flipped it into the right hand corner."

The Rangers still weren't out of danger. They were penalized
again and once more Boucher was dispatched to the front. This time
he controlled the puck at center ice. "I played it off the boards," he
said, "hoping to pick up my own rebound and keep it in our possession." But he shot it too far ahead; so far, in fact, that Montreal
defenseman Dunc Munro raced for the puck that was sitting almost
midway between the two opponents.

"I was watching him," said Boucher. "He skated for it. Then, I
could almost hear him think, 'By God, I can't get there in time.'
He seemed to stop in one motion and then he changed his mind
and went for the puck. By this time I was there. I just swooped
over to one side, let him go by and then I had the whole ice to
myself." Boucher placed the puck in exactly the same spot as he
had earlier in the game. The final score was 2–1. The Rangers had
won their first Stanley Cup.

The Rangers didn't win the Stanley Cup again until 1932–33
although they had powerful teams. In 1932 Conn Smythe's Maple
Leafs routed New York, 6–4, 6–2, 6–4, marking the first time that
a team had won a Stanley Cup final in three straight games. The
Leafs trailed only once in the entire series, in the second game when
Bun Cook and Doug Brennan gave the Rangers a 2–0 lead after one
minute of the second period. Toronto then scored six consecutive
goals to humiliate Patrick's team.

A year later the Rangers were the toast of hockey. Once again
the Cook Brothers and Boucher reaffirmed their superiority. The
players whom Smythe originally had signed when he was asked to
organize the Rangers dominated play as the New Yorkers won the
best of five series in four games. Bill Cook scored the decisive goal
in the fourth and final game to give the Rangers a 1–0 victory. Two
Toronto players, Alex Levinsky and Bill Thoms, were in the penalty
box when the 35-year-old Cook scored. In addition to the Cook
Brothers and Boucher, another ace for the Rangers was Cecil Dillon
who scored eight goals and two assists. Three of the goals were
scored against Toronto. Although Dillon never received the press
that some of his more illustrious colleagues did, he was regarded by
Patrick as the greatest he had ever seen.

A canny boss, Patrick realized that some of the cornerstones of
the early Ranger teams were crumbling and had to be replaced. He

organized a farm system and during the mid and late thirties, fresh players began graduating from teams in Philadelphia, New York (Crescents) and various points in Canada. The Cooks eventually gave way to the likes of Bryan Hextall, Phil Watson, Alex Shibicky and two sons of Patrick, Lynn and Murray (Muzz).

The Americans were having less success. They never won the Stanley Cup and began to suffer at the gate. Their rent kept rising and Big Bill Dwyer soon was arrested and sent to the penitentiary for bootlegging. When he was released he had little of his original fortune and was in no position to back the Americans anymore. It was then that Red Dutton, who had plenty of NHL experience as a player, stepped in to save the Americans and prevent the Garden from applying the boot. Dutton desperately tried to keep the Americans afloat. He was the team's manager and chief cheerleader and became its number one character. Once, the Americans were playing in Detroit and Charlie (Rabbit) McVeigh was the linesman. Dutton and McVeigh had been old pals since childhood. They had fought together in World War I and played together in the early days of the Americans. It was Red who recalled that McVeigh was deaf but nonetheless recommended him as an NHL linesman although he knew Rabbit also was getting a pension from the Canadian government for his war disability.

In this game Dutton manifested no sympathy for McVeigh. Too many of the linesman's calls were going against the Americans. Dutton ranted and raved and tried to get McVeigh's attention whenever play stopped near the Americans' bench but McVeigh ignored him. When the game ended, Dutton rushed over to McVeigh and startled his old pal with a big "hello." Dutton inquired about his health and told McVeigh he had a friend in the government who could get him a pension increase. McVeigh was touched by the apparent sensitivity under fire.

"Aw, Red," he said, "that would be great. But what would you tell the Pension Board about my case?"

Suddenly, Dutton's voice rose several decibel counts. "I'll tell them," shouted Dutton, "you're blind, you little squirt."

Had the Americans been able to stay competitive with the Rangers in the late thirties they might have had a chance to survive but the Rangers had developed a new dynasty with their young players and, in 1939–40, were the most feared club in hockey. Boucher had retired to become coach and Patrick was the manager. Despite his fears that his sons would embarrass him, Patrick was gratified that both Lynn and Muzz had developed into competent players, Lynn as a forward and Muzz as a defenseman. With the likeable Boucher behind the bench, the youngsters exhibited excitement and class.

"I'd encourage suggestions," said Boucher. "The boys would come up with them and then we'd practice the new ideas. One of them was the box defense whereby the four players killing a penalty arrange themselves in a box formation in front of a goaltender. A more sensational one was an offensive penalty-killing combination. Instead of playing a tight defensive game, the Rangers were thirsty for goals, even when they were shorthanded due to a penalty.

"When we were a man short," Boucher explained, "we'd send out three forwards and one defenseman and we'd forecheck in their own end. This team was so good it would score more goals over a season than it would have goals scored upon it during the penalty-killing."

On November 23, 1939, the Rangers played a 1–1 tie with the Canadiens. From that point on they won 14 games and tied five for a 19-game unbeaten streak, a club record. Boucher believed it easily could have been extended to 25; but it didn't because the Rangers were too smart for their own good. "We were playing in Chicago in the twentieth game of the streak," said Boucher, "and we were playing rings around them. It was the kind of game we should have won hands down but, for some strange reason, we couldn't score a goal and were down, 1–0, going into the third period."

During the intermission Boucher convened his men and came up with another revolutionary idea. If the Rangers hadn't tied the score —they were convinced Chicago wouldn't score another goal—by the final minutes New York would pull goalkeeper Davey Kerr, but not in the usual way. Normally, a team would wait for a whistle and a face-off before replacing the goaltender with a sixth skater. This, of course, enables the opposition to prepare for the extra man. "We decided," added Boucher, "that it would be better to put in the goalie without making it obvious—to do it on the fly. And that was the plan."

Chances are the strategy would have worked except that Boucher neglected to inform Lester Patrick of the plan. Normally this wouldn't have mattered since Lester didn't occupy the bench. But this night in Chicago he rejoined the players on the bench. Lester was distrustful of the Chicago timekeeper, so when the clock turned to within minutes of the end he got off the bench and sat next to the timekeeper who was located between the Black Hawks' and Rangers' benches.

"By this time," said Boucher, "we had the puck in their end. The signal was given for Kerr to come off the ice and the extra forward to go on. And that's exactly what happened. Except that Lester only noticed the extra forward and didn't realize that Kerr had been removed."

Believing that Boucher had made the mistake of allowing too many men on the ice, the frantic Lester beseeched Boucher to remove the sixth skater before the referee saw him. "Paul Thompson, the Black Hawk coach, heard him," said Boucher. "And when he saw six men in his zone he started screaming. We were about to put the puck in the net when the referee blew his whistle to give us a penalty. Then he turned around and saw Kerr out of the nets and realized there shouldn't have been a penalty at all. But it was too late. Some adroit strategy backfired, and Chicago won the game, 1–0."

Boucher's mighty Rangers won their next five games in a row for an overall record of 24 victories or ties in 25 games. They defeated Boston, four games to two in the Stanley Cup semifinal round and faced Toronto in the finals. Three of the games—including the final two—went into sudden-death overtime and in each of the contests the Rangers scored the winner. With the series tied 2–2, the last three games were scheduled for Maple Leaf Gardens' ice because Madison Square Garden was unavailable. The Rangers won the fifth game, 2–1, at 11:43 of the first overtime and won the sixth game at 2:07 of the first overtime and the Stanley Cup. The Rangers were paced by Phil Watson, Bryan Hextall, Dutch Hiller, the Patrick Brothers, Alex Shibicky and the Colville Brothers, Mac and Neil. Only two players on the Cup-winning team—Dave Kerr and Art Coulter—had not come up through the Ranger farm system. It appeared that the Ranger dynasty might last another decade. But World War II put an end to that. Muzz Patrick was the first to enlist and, in time, the Rangers were to lose more good players to the armed forces than any other team.

The war years were disastrous to hockey in New York. The Americans, confronted by high rentals on the one hand and the loss of top players to the armed forces on the other, capitulated in 1942. The Rangers continued but they hardly were a representative hockey club. They finished sixth for four straight seasons and set all kinds of records for ineptitude. They went 25 games without winning

between January 23, 1944 and November 11, 1944 (21 losses and
four ties) and on January 23, 1944 were defeated, 15–0, by the
Detroit Red Wings. They were so bad that even Boucher came out
of retirement to play a few games for them and was better than
many of his regulars.

If there was any solace for the Rangers in the war years it was in
Boucher's sense of humor and the laughs supplied by many of the
characters who peopled the Garden from 1942 through 1950 when
the Rangers again reached the Stanley Cup finals. One of the comic
characters was Phil Watson, who, despite his name, was part-French-
Canadian and whose English was often twisted and well-salted with
French expressions. Watson was a turbulent center who played
superbly with Hextall and Lynn Patrick. He was the architect of
many a key goal and played the game with great intensity. Often,
his temper would get the best of him and he'd become involved in
assorted brawls, most of which he lost. But it never prevented
Watson from trying again.

Once, he clashed with Bingo Kampman, a Toronto defenseman
of monumental strength. Kampman lifted Watson off the ice, twirled
him around his head and then deposited the Ranger over the boards
into a box seat. Another time he was having trouble with Bucko
McDonald, then an aging Maple Leaf. After a lengthy debate,
Watson finally came up with what he thought was the perfect
squelch, except that he misplaced his words. "Bucko," Watson
shouted, "you're nothing but a been-has!"

In the postwar years the Rangers were involved in another stunt,
one that might have shaken the world of psychology, had it worked.
The Blueshirts were in a losing trough at the time and needed help.
Someone mentioned that a certain Dr. Tracy had successfully im-
planted athletes with a positive psyche.

The psychologist accepted the invitation to try his powers of per-
suasion on the skaters. The burly doctor entered the dressing room
prior to a game with Boston. He was particularly attentive to Tony
Leswick and appeared to have mesmerized Tony while Pentti Lund,
Alex Kaleta and Buddy O'Connor looked on with a mixture of amusement and amazement.

Amazement was the reaction of the Garden fans as the Rangers
held Boston to a 3–3 tie going into the final minutes of play. But
the Bruins' Bill Quackenbush broke the spell with a long shot that
crazily hopped past goalie Chuck Rayner and the Rangers lost, 4–3.

That ended it for Dr. Tracy, but he didn't stop trying. He tried persuading the Rangers that he realized his mistakes. "You've got to let me at the goolie," Dr. Tracy insisted. "He's not relaxed."

The Rangers have had players of every conceivable ethnic extraction, but how many recall the only Chinese player to wear the Blue? That would be Larry "King" Kwong, who graduated from the Rovers to the Rangers in the 1947–48 season.

Kwong was a speedy skater, but lacked size and scoring ability and eventually was relegated to the minors. But not after Gotham headline writers had a field day with his name. The most overused banner was: "There's Nothing Kwong with the Rangers That a Few Goals Won't Cure."

Slowly, the Rangers began to lift themselves to a plateau of respectability if not stardom. During the 1947–48 season they reached the Stanley Cup semifinal round but were quickly eliminated by the Detroit Red Wings. They made another bid for the Cup in the 1949–50 season. By this time Boucher had become manager of the team and Lynn Patrick the coach.

It was a good club, hardly great, but possessed a number of talents. Chuck (Prince Charlie) Rayner, who was with the last New York Americans team, was the Ranger goalie. There were stalwart forwards including Pentti Lund, Tony Leswick and Edgar Laprade and hefty defensemen such as Gus Kyle, Pat Egan, Jack Lancien and Allan Stanley.

The club grabbed the attention of the league when it upset Montreal's Canadiens—armed with Maurice Richard, Bill Durnan and Butch Bouchard—in the semifinal round, four games to one. When the Rangers defeated the Canadiens, 3–0, in the final game on Montreal ice, people began considering the New Yorkers a genuine darkhorse contender for the Stanley Cup. Coach Patrick was less diffident. He unabashedly declared:

"If the boys can keep the sharp edge, we're a cinch to take the Stanley Cup."

As much as they admired him, newsmen took Lynn and his prediction lightly. And for good reason. Ringling Brothers Barnum and Bailey Circus already had camped in Madison Square Garden, compelling the Rangers to play all their "home" games on the road. That their opponents would be the awesome Detroit Red Wings offered even less comfort to the local strategists.

Right off the bat, the Rangers were nearly wiped off the ice. The Red Wings romped to a 4–1 win at Detroit's Olympia in the opening game. Patrick was furious. He blamed the loss on overconfidence and made known that he had promoted his Lilliputian goalie from New Haven to the Ranger roster in case he was needed—that Emile Francis, who today needs no introduction.

The second and third games were held on neutral ice or, if you will, Ranger "home" ice—Maple Leaf Gardens in Toronto. All tickets were sold 45 minutes after they went on sale, which says it all for Toronto as a hockey town. After the two games in Toronto, all other games would be played in Detroit.

Maple Leaf Gardens was not expected to be any special balm for the Blueshirts, but Red Wing coach Tommy Ivan sensed trouble. "It'll be tough for us," he said before the second game of the series. "I'm still scared of them. The series will go more than four games."

Ivan didn't realize how prophetic he was.

The Rangers whomped the Red Wings in the second game, 3–1, on Laprade's two goals and another by defenseman Pat Egan and now the finals were tied at one game apiece. What's more, the supposedly phlegmatic Toronto fans adopted the Rangers as their own and rooted for New York as passionately as they would have for the Leafs. But they had little to cheer about in the third game, played at the Gardens. Detroit blanked the Rangers, 4–0, and returned to Olympia expecting an early trip to Florida to celebrate their playoff win. The Wings had good cause for optimism; they led the series, two games to one and all the remaining games would be on Detroit ice.

"We'll win the next two games and wind this series up in a hurry," the Wings promised.

The promise began crumbling at the last second of the second period, with the Wings ahead, 2–0. Buddy O'Connor scored at 19:59 of the middle period making it 2–1 Detroit and although Detroit scored early in the third, the Rangers were carrying a hot hand. Laprade made it 3–2 at 8:09 and Kyle tied the game at 16:26, setting the stage for sudden-death overtime. Here's how Joe Nichols described the early overtime action in the *New York Times*:

"The Rangers tried to keep up their heavy rushes, but the Wings took over and thrice sent their star pointmaker, Ted Lindsay, in on Rayner. Two of his drives were easy enough, but the third seemed to have him beaten and only a miraculous save kept the disk out of the cage."

Then, the Rangers counterattacked.

Ed Slowinski robbed Detroit's Joe Carveth of the puck behind the Red Wing net. He skimmed a pass to Don "Bones" Raleigh 20 feet in front of the cage. The beanpole center was checked by defenseman Jack Stewart and started to fall as the puck reached him. But he took a desperate backhand swipe at it and fell on his stomach, his eyes riveted on the net.

Somehow, the puck skidded to goalie Harry Lumley's right. The big netminder flashed out his right skate but the rubber barely eluded the goalie's blade, hit the goal post and went into the net at 8:34 of the sudden death, tying the series, 2–2. "No one in the place expected Raleigh to touch the puck, much less score," observed Bill Lauder, Jr. in the *Herald Tribune*.

When it was over, Patrick admitted that Raleigh had no business being on the ice at the time; "He was so tired," said Lynn, "I wanted to keep him off but Nick Mickoski had just been hurt, so I had no choice. I needed bodies and I got a goal."

With the series tied at two goals apiece, the spectre of injuries clouded the Ranger camp as the Blues prepared for game five. Mickoski had suffered a dislocated shoulder and Jackie Gordon was lost for the rest of the series with torn knee ligaments. And, of course, there was the problem of playing another game at unfriendly Olympia.

No matter. Game five was on and the Rangers went out and took a 1–0 lead on Dunc Fisher's goal at 7:44 of the second period, then saw the lead evaporate with less than two minutes remaining in the game when Lindsay sunk his own rebound. The Rangers treated Lindsay's goal as an idle annoyance to be brushed aside as one would a fly on one's knee. And if anyone else was to secure the game, who else but Bones Raleigh, on a pass from, who else but Ed Slowinski. Which is what happened.

The speed, let alone the duplication of the goal, arrested the imagination of the 12,610 spectators. The play evolved with only a minute-and-a-half gone in the overtime, Slowinski captured the puck behind the net, fed Raleigh who unleashed a 10-foot shot that found an opening between Lumley's pads.

"Eddie did all the work," Raleigh insisted. "It was the best pass I've ever had." So New York led, three games to two, and needed one win in the next two games to win the Cup.

The sixth and what Ranger followers believed would be the last game of the series was held at Olympia on Saturday, April 22. To many observers it should have been the finale and those who saw the game or heard Bert Lee describe it on the radio still have difficulty believing the Rangers ultimately lost. But, they did and here's how the tragedy developed:

Before the Red Wings could find their groove, the Rangers had contrived a 2–0 lead in the first period on goals by Stanley and Fisher. Lindsay reduced the lead by one in the period's final minute but Lund scored at 3:18 of the second to make it 4–2 New York. Again the Red Wings retaliated, tying the score late in the second, and, again the Rangers went ahead in the third on Leswick's goal at 1:54.

The fact was, there was too much Lindsay for the Rangers. The combative left wing stickhandled through three Rangers to tie the score at 4:13. Sid Abel scored the winner at 10:34 after snaring his own rebound in front of Rayner.

And now it was time for the climactic seventh and final game, April 23, at Olympia. For two periods it appeared the Rangers had the Stanley Cup in the bag. Goals by Stanley and Leswick gave them a 2–0 lead after the first period. Detroit tied it in the second at 2–2 but O'Connor put New York ahead again at 11:42 of the middle period.

That was the Rangers' last moment to exult in a lead. Jim McFadden soon was to beat Stanley to the puck and shoot an "impossible" angled shot past Rayner to tie the score. There was nothing left but excruciating overtime; the first goal deciding the game and the Cup winner.

"You could see it coming," said Patrick. "Once the overtime started I figured we were through. The boys just had nothing left."

Well, not quite nothing. They traded blow-for-blow, shot-for-shot with the Red Wings at the hostile Olympia for 20 minutes of the first sudden death and very nearly won the Cup. A shot by Mickoski had Lumley beaten but the puck hit the goal post and went the wrong way.

Now it was the second overtime and the Rangers were still there. But they were tiring fast and you could see the end coming. "The Wings had carried the play to the fading Blueshirts," wrote Lew Walter in the *Detroit Times*, "and had missed goals by hairline margins."

Detroit's George Gee was one who barely missed scoring the winner. He was put in the clear by Pete Babando. Rayner moved slowly out of his cage, 10, 12, 15 feet. Gee shot, Rayner sprawled and smothered the puck. Referee Bill Chadwick, now the color announcer for Ranger home games, whistled a face-off in deep Ranger zone, to the left of the net.

Patrick sent out Buddy O'Connor, Alex Kaleta, Nick Mickoski, Pat Egan and Allan Stanley. Detroit's unit consisted of Gee, Babando, Doc Couture, Leo Reise and Marcel Pronovost. Gee was to take the face-off against O'Connor.

The Red Wing paused and skated back to Babando. "Move over behind me," Gee said. "You're too far to the left." They proved to be prophetic words.

"I moved over," Babando said later. "I still wasn't far enough because Gee beat O'Connor to the draw and whipped the puck back to my right. I had to reach for it to catch it on my backhand."

More than eight minutes had ticked away in the second sudden death when Gee won the draw. Rayner was at the near corner of the net as the puck moved toward Babando. The Ranger goalie's view was obscured by Stanley, his defenseman.

"When the puck hit my stick," Babando recalled, "I just let fly through the scramble. I wasn't sure the shot was on the net."

It was.

The puck followed a straight line, two feet off the ice. It flitted past Gee, past Stanley and past Couture toward a three-foot opening at the right corner. Rayner knew the shot was coming but he couldn't find the puck because of the confusion of bodies in front of him. "I never saw it coming," said Rayner. At the last second he fell to the ice kicking out his left pad in a spreadeagle split. But he felt nothing hit his pads.

Intuitively, his head turned behind to the left—toward the net. The puck was there in the corner, along with the Rangers' shattered dreams.

When the cheering had subsided and the Rangers had wiped away their tears, Red Wing captain Sid Abel walked into the New York dressing room and gave the Blueshirts the finest testimonial they could have received short of winning the cup. Abel pumped Rayner's hand, looked around the room and said to the other New Yorkers: "Don't you guys know when to quit?"

The Rangers suffered another depression in the early fifties but, this time, manager Boucher had planted the seeds of what was to be another successful farm system. The chief source of talent would be the Guelph (Ontario) Biltmores of the Ontario Hockey Association Junior A Division. Exceptional youngsters such as Andy Bathgate, Harry Howell, Dean Prentice, Aldo Guidolin, Lou Fontinato and Ron Murphy were being groomed in Guelph for delivery to the NHL. But the crisis in New York worsened and Boucher was compelled to promote the youngsters before they were ripe for the NHL. Impatient, the Garden brass finally coerced Boucher into stepping down as manager. He was replaced in the spring of 1955 by Muzz Patrick and Phil Watson was hired as coach.

Capitalizing on the youngsters developed by Boucher's farm system, Watson guided the Rangers to the playoffs in 1955–56, 1956–57, and 1957–58. There was every likelihood that he would do it again in 1958–59 but the team suddenly folded in the last two weeks of the season and was beaten out by the Maple Leafs. Watson eventually was fired and the Rangers sank into the trough again until the 1961–62 season when Doug Harvey, the former star of the Montreal Canadiens' defense, signed as player coach and directed the club to the playoffs where Toronto eliminated the Rangers in a six-game semifinal.

Another playoff famine developed and the fortunes of the Rangers appeared dismal under Patrick's managership until he was relieved of the position in the fall of 1964 and replaced by Emile Francis. The dynamic Francis immediately began rebuilding.

The Francis regime produced a hockey team that emphasized balance more than stars and combined robust play with classical passing maneuvers. Husky skaters such as Reg Fleming, Vic Hadfield and Orland Kurtenbach lent the muscle so conspicuously lacking in other Ranger teams while the line of Phil Goyette, Don Marshall and Bob Nevin displayed the brand of passing and scoring that was reminiscent of the Cook Brothers and Boucher.

When goalie Jacques Plante temporarily retired, Francis obtained Ed Giacomin from the Providence Reds of the American League. Untried in the NHL, Giacomin alternately starred and then erred grievously in his rookie season. But Francis stuck by his goalie. The decision would ultimately make or break the manager. Giacomin again was erratic in his sophomore year and then, suddenly, recovered to win the first All-Star Team nomination. The Rangers finished in the playoffs for the first time in four years and Francis clinched his job.

He also managed to lure Bernie (Boom Boom) Geoffrion out of retirement after Geoffrion had coached the Quebec Aces of the American League for two years. Onetime NHL scoring champion, Geoffrion infused the Rangers with a dressing room spirit they had lacked and bolstered the power play. Despite a worsening ulcer condition, Geoffrion helped the team to its second playoff berth in two years in 1967–68 and then succumbed to a serious stomach operation. Upon his recovery he was offered the coaching job by Francis and took over bench duties at the start of the 1968–69 season until illness forced him to quit in 1969.

Geoffrion had inherited a solid defense featuring Harry Howell, Arnie Brown, Jim Neilson and Rod Seiling—all developed by Francis—and solid forwards such as Rod Gilbert, Jean Ratelle, Dave Balon and Ron Stewart. He also was aware that the Rangers had been unable to win the Stanley Cup since 1940 and have not finished first since 1942. The familiar cry of "Wait 'til next year" had become a bore with Ranger fans and its alteration became Geoffrion's major target. But when Geoffrion departed, Francis guided the club to third place, and the Rangers were wiped out of the 1969 playoffs in four games by Montreal.

New York finished fourth in an 11th hour grab of a playoff berth in April 1970 but lasted only through the first playoff round in which the Bruins eliminated the Rangers in six games.

Determined to catch Boston in 1970–71, Francis executed several changes in the Rangers lineup. He dealt defenseman Arnie Brown as well as rookies Don Luce, Jim Krulicki and Mike Robitaille to Detroit. In return he obtained defenseman Dale Rolfe and forwards Bruce MacGregor and Peter Stemkowski. Rookie center Syl Apps Jr. was sent to Pittsburgh for utility forward Glen Sather.

Although New York finished second in the East, far behind Boston, the Rangers rallied to eliminate Toronto in the first round of the 1971 playoffs and then played valiantly before losing to Chicago in the seventh game of the semifinal. Stemkowski was a hero, winning two games with sudden death goals, one in a third overtime.

The frustrations of failing to finish first or win the Stanley Cup continued to plague Francis' flock. The only team in the league to make the playoffs for seven consecutive years through the spring of 1973, the Rangers entered the Cup finals in 1972 for the first time in 22 years by beating Montreal and whipping Chicago but bowed in six games to Boston. The following year they rid themselves of their Bruin tormentors in the first round only to be shocked out in five games by the Black Hawks in the semifinals.

Rangers developed a new star in rookie Steve Vickers, who combined with the Bulldogs, Walter Tkaczuk and Billy Fairbairn, to form their most solid line. The highly-rated GAG Line (goal-a-game), which accounted for 139 goals in 1971–72, dropped to 94 in 1972–73 and in the playoffs only Rod Gilbert acquitted himself in an above-average manner. Jean Ratelle continued his poor life-time playoff performance and Vic Hadfield, after a bumpy season, marred by his defection from Team Canada and a series of crippling injuries, failed to ignite any sparks.

Emile Francis, who brought the once-lowly Rangers to respect-ability and serious contention, still found the Holy Grail of hockey beyond his grasp. Before the 1973–74 season he relinquished his dual role of general manager-coach and turned over the bench reins to former Ranger center Larry Popein who had been coaching in the New York organization at Providence. This move did not seem likely to bring the Cup to Manhattan, a place it had not rested since before World War II.

Toronto Maple Leafs

THE TORONTO MAPLE LEAFS, as we know them today, have roots extending back to 1917 when a club known as the Toronto Arenas was admitted to the National Hockey League. Eddie Livingstone, a Toronto lawyer, ran the Torontos and somehow managed to antagonize his colleagues in Ottawa and Montreal, the other hotbeds of the young NHL just after World War I. In 1919 the Toronto Arenas were replaced by the Toronto St. Patricks (St. Pats), managed by Charles Querrie, a former lacrosse star who had become a sportswriter.

While Querrie was running the St. Pats, a young, dynamic man named Conn Smythe was becoming more and more vocal in Toronto hockey circles. Smythe had a heroic air because of his exploits in World War I. He had gone overseas with the Fortieth Battery, transferred to the Air Force; been shot down while on reconnaissance duty; been made a prisoner of war; been placed in solitary confinement by the Germans after he had tried to escape; and, after the armistice, he returned to Toronto to coach the University of Toronto Junior Hockey Team (alias Varsity). In time Smythe's teams grabbed headlines. He became coach of the Senior Team at the University (Varsity Grads) and won the Allan Cup, emblematic of senior hockey supremacy in Canada, in 1926. The following year the Grads went on to the Olympics. Smythe didn't make that trip. He had been contracted by Colonel John Hammond, president of the newly organized New York Rangers, to obtain hockey players for the Manhattan franchise. Smythe, who had set the NHL as his target, relished the assignment until he suffered a severe personality collision with Colonel Hammond and was dismissed.

The Ranger president had heard that Babe Dye was a superb player and requested that Smythe obtain him. The colonel became furious when he learned that Smythe was at a football game and missed a chance to buy Dye for the Rangers. In a typical counter-attack, Smythe insisted he didn't want Dye at any price. He explained that he was organizing a young team and Dye was an older player. Colonel Hammond didn't buy the logic and dismissed Smythe after presenting him with a check for $7,500. This was $2,500 less than the original price he had signed for but Smythe didn't care.

Smythe bore no grudge against Tex Rickard, president of Madison Square Garden. After Smythe's dismissal, Rickard approached his former employee and asked whether he thought the Rangers could hold the powerful Montreal Maroons to a respectable score in the first game the Rangers would play at the Garden. "If you keep your eyes open," countered Smythe, "you'll see the Rangers win. This is a pretty good hockey club, Mister."

When the Rangers did win Rickard was so impressed he sought out Smythe, hoping he'd return to the Garden fold. "I wouldn't work for Madison Square Garden for any price," said Smythe, betraying what was to develop into one of the sharpest antagonisms in the NHL.

Always the sportsman, Rickard, upon hearing how Smythe had been shortchanged $2,500, ordered that the money be given to the young Torontonian. Smythe bet the found money on a football game between the University of Toronto and McGill University, won, and then bet on the Rangers in a game against the Toronto St. Pats, won again, and then was ready to make his big bid in the NHL.

Later, with a group of ex-World War I veterans, Smythe and the syndicate bought the Toronto St. Pats from Charlie Querrie for $165,000. At first it looked like a buy. But after the first season's receipts totaled only $113,000, some of the supporters began to wonder. Smythe was undaunted. He remained convinced that there was a bonanza in professional hockey and believed the bonanza lay in the building of an ultramodern arena. Since Smythe had changed the name of the St. Pats to the Maple Leafs it was only natural that the new structure be called Maple Leaf Gardens. However, it wouldn't have been at all illogical to have named it

Smythe Gardens, for the inspired promoter spurred the project forward during one of the most despairing periods in the nation's history. Maple Leaf Gardens was in the planning-financing stages at the moment when the stock market crashed in 1929. To keep the construction moving, workmen accepted part of their pay in stock. When money ran out, one of Smythe's chums, J. P. Bickell, always managed to produce a few hundred thousand more.

Part of Smythe's genius was his ability to surround himself with men of equal energy and foresight. One such man was Frank Selke, who suggested, when Smythe's St. Pats were losing: "Just fire the old men you have playing on your team now. Replace them with these young bucks I have with me on the [Toronto] Marlboros. Do that and you'll never look back."

Selke was right, but it would take more than inexperienced young players. What Smythe needed was a superstar to draw the fans to Maple Leaf Gardens and, without skimping on money, he went out and got him. As luck would have it—and Smythe had a surplus of luck—Frank (King) Clancy, a wiry defensive star, was put up for trade by the Ottawa Senators. Smythe offered the Senators $35,000 plus two hockey players whose value he estimated at $15,000. In those days the price was considered exorbitant, even for a player of Clancy's ability; but the flamboyant defenseman was soon to prove that Smythe was wise in spending heavily for him. "It undoubtedly is fair to say," wrote Milt Dunnell, sports editor of the *Toronto Daily Star*, "that one person more than any other, was responsible for lifting the mortgage: King Clancy. Getting the King was one of the smartest moves Smythe ever made." With Clancy as the nucleus, Smythe built a powerful club that won the Stanley Cup for the Maple Leafs in 1931–32. His goaltender was Lorne Chabot, never the best but always more than adequate. In addition to Clancy, his defense was anchored by Clarence (Hap) Day, the team captain who had given up a career as a pharmacist to play for the Leafs. In addition there was Alex Levinsky, Harold (Baldy) Cotton, Irvin (Ace) Bailey, Andy Blair, Frank Finnegan and Red Horner, all able pros.

A strong trio in the club was the Kid Line of Joe Primeau at center, Charlie Conacher at right wing and Harvey (Busher) Jackson at left. "This threesome was truly a sight to behold," wrote Selke in his biography *Behind The Cheering*. "When coach Dick Irvin sent the trio onto the ice the fans teetered on the edges of their seats and an electric tension seemed to permeate the entire auditorium. There have been other great forward lines in hockey but none could match the frenzy that greeted Toronto's Kid Line in the mid-thirties."

As hockey teams go, the Leafs of the early thirties certainly could pass for an ice version of the St. Louis Cardinals Gashouse Gang along with the Americans of New York. Pranks were the order of just about any day and, usually, Clancy was the butt of them. One day, Charlie Conacher and Hap Day decided to readjust Clancy's alarm clock by setting it ahead a few hours. They then ordered the room clerk in the Boston hotel at which they camped to phone Clancy and tell him he was late for the game. When Clancy got the message and stared at the readjusted clock, he speedily dressed, dashed down the hotel stairs and out the door where he hailed a cab. He demanded that the cabbie get him to Boston Garden extra fast because he was late for the start of the hockey game. When the driver told him it was more than two hours before game time, Clancy ordered the cab around and returned to the hotel where Day and Conacher were sitting in the lobby unable to contain their laughter.

Although Clancy was the court jester of the Leafs he also was a leader of sorts simply because he refused to admit defeat. One night the Leafs were involved in a major brawl with the Montreal Maroons. Clancy mistakenly selected Harold Starr, an enormous Maroon defenseman, as his opponent. Starr wiped the ice with Clancy, sat on the Toronto player and thoroughly routed him until Clancy bellowed "Let me up! Let me up!" Starr complied but, in so doing, added, "Well, I licked you good, eh, Clancy?"

While the witnessing players convulsed themselves with laughter, Clancy replied at the top of his lungs: "Starr, you never saw the day you could lay a hand on me!"

In some ways Harold (Baldy) Cotton was as amusing a character as Clancy. He hurled his body around the ice without fear of collision and, as a result, often found himself at odds with the law of gravity. One writer commented: "Cotton's goal-scoring stance was often on one or even both ears."

Smythe was just as ebullient as his players. One summer when hockey news was practically nowhere to be read, Leo Dandurand, a part owner of the Montreal Canadiens, phoned Smythe just to pass the time of day. As a conversation piece, Dandurand wondered what Smythe thought about the possibility of a trade. "I'll give you my goaltender, George Hainsworth for yours, Lorne Chabot," said

Dandurand. "A change of scenery might be good for both of them."

Of course Dandurand was sure Smythe wouldn't bite. After all, Chabot had played excellent hockey for him. But before Dandurand could grasp what was happening, Smythe replied: "It's a deal" and hung up. When the Montreal official recovered, he phoned Smythe and the two worked out a mutually satisfactory release date for announcing the deal.

Smythe's record wasn't perfect. He often was outwitted by Major Frederic McLaughlin, the socialite owner of the Chicago Black Hawks. McLaughlin had a ploy that often duped Smythe. He would call the Leafs' boss and suggest that one or two of the Black Hawk stars were becoming jaded in Chicago. Perhaps Smythe was interested in them. His appetite sharp for a deal, Smythe would take the first available train to Chicago to talk trade with McLaughlin. However, by the time he arrived, Smythe discovered that the Major had cooled considerably on the subject of a deal and would suggest negotiating for some second- or third-line skater that didn't really appeal to Smythe. But he had made that long trip. "First thing you knew," Smythe admitted, "you'd buy some guy who wasn't worth a nickel. It was either that or return to Toronto empty-handed."

The Leafs' Stanley Cup triumph in 1931–32 was the tip-off that Smythe had developed a dynasty. In the following season the Leafs finished first in the Canadian division of the NHL and Harvey Jackson led the division in scoring. The Leafs then engaged the Boston Bruins, who finished first in the American division, in the first round of the Stanley Cup playoffs. The best of five series was tied, 2–2, when the final—and most spectacular game—was held at Maple Leaf Gardens on April 2, 1933.

For three periods the teams struggled without a score, forcing the game into sudden-death overtime. There was no score in the first sudden-death and none in the second. As the energy-sapping contest labored on into the third and fourth sudden death Art Ross of the Bruins and Smythe asked NHL President Frank Calder for permission to halt the game at the end of 100 minutes so that the clubs could resume fresh the next night. "Nothing doing," Calder replied, "the game must be finished tonight."

The Bruins came up with an alternate suggestion; they'd toss a coin and the winner would move on to the next round. Smythe and the Leafs agreed. They moved out to center ice and prepared to begin the ritual, but the 14,539 spectators were appalled by the idea and urged the Leafs to continue the game. The Toronto club agreed to continue although Calder had suggested that each team remove its goaltender to make scoring easier but the players refused this idea and the gruelling contest resumed.

Shortly after the four-minute mark of the sixth overtime—each overtime period lasted 20 minutes—Andy Blair of the Leafs captured the puck from Eddie Shore, the Bruins' all-star defenseman. Blair passed the puck ahead to tiny Ken Doraty who raced into Boston territory and scored the winning goal at 164:46 (4:46 of the sixth overtime) for a 1–0 victory. The game ended at 2 A.M. on April 3 and was the longest game played in the NHL up until that time.

The heroic Doraty soon was traded to Cleveland as Smythe began paring the Leaf roster to make way for new blood. Detroit bought Hec Kilrea, Hal Cotton went to the New York Americans with Hap Day and Chicago bought Andy Blair. By 1936 King Clancy had retired and the Conacher–Primeau–Jackson era was rapidly coming to an end. Smythe assiduously replaced them but with not quite the same success as he enjoyed in the early thirties, though he did manage to obtain some interesting characters.

One of them was Bingo Kampman, a huge defenseman who had played for the Sudbury team that won the Allan Cup. Kampman was perhaps the strongest man ever to play in the NHL and often would perform tricks to display his power. A favorite was—after, naturally, placing some small bets—to lift a full-scale table by biting into its sides with his teeth and then, by sheer force, lifting it off the ground.

Another colorful type was Walter (Turk) Broda, a goaltender Smythe discovered by accident. The Leaf boss had visited Windsor, Ontario, to scout Earl Robertson, a goaltender then playing for the Windsor Bulldogs. Although Smythe was impressed with Robertson he was even more entranced by the youth who was playing opposite him for the Detroit Olympics. After the game, Smythe asked Jim Norris, president of the Detroit Red Wings, what he wanted for the goaltender. Norris, certain that Smythe was referring to Robertson, asked for $8,000. When Smythe told him he wanted Broda he asked for the same price. It was a steal, judging by the fact that Broda played 15 years for the Leafs and became known as the best clutch goalie in the NHL.

Smythe was equally as fortunate one afternoon when he and his wife were watching a football game between McMaster University and a Toronto intermediate club. Smythe's attention was arrested by a large McMaster halfback who appeared to be manipulating the game with an assortment of runs, catches and kicks. After the game Smythe inquired whether the player knew how to play hockey. He was told that Sylvanus Apps was, indeed, an accomplished hockey player, not to mention the best pole vaulter in Canada.

Apps, however, was not persuaded that he should pursue a hockey career with the pros. He wanted to compete in the 1936 Olympics and also considered other careers when the Olympics were over. But he agreed to meet with Smythe when the games ended. Once Apps returned he couldn't refuse Smythe's offer. He signed with the Maple Leafs and became one of Canada's most respected hockey players. He won the Calder Trophy as rookie of the year in his first season and, in time, became captain and leader of the Leafs during their golden era of the late forties.

Many observers contend that the Toronto hockey renaissance began in 1941 when Clarence (Hap) Day, the former Leaf defenseman, was named coach of the club. The choice was not surprising. Day had joined the Leafs in 1926 and, except for three years, remained one of the most loyal and effective Toronto players until he was traded to the Americans in 1937–38. "Anything good about a man can be said about Day," Smythe commented.

With Day running the team, the Leafs finished second, only three points behind the Rangers, and promptly knocked off New York in six games of the Stanley Cup opening round. They wound up meeting the Detroit Red Wings in the finals and appeared a good bet to defeat the Red Wings who had finished fourth, 15 points behind Toronto. But the Detroit club was guided by manager Jack Adams who had a habit of lifting his club to extraordinary heights against the Leafs. "We may not have the greatest hockey club in the world," Adams said on the eve of the first game, "but we're loaded with fighting heart. And if there's anything that wins championships it's just that."

Detroit then proceeded to win the first three games of the best of seven championship round and thoroughly startled the Leafs, not to mention the hockey world. From all appearances the Leafs were finished and the fact that coach Day decided to bench high-scoring Gordie Drillon and defenseman Bucko McDonald merely confirmed the critics' suspicions. In their place Day inserted an unheard of utility player, Don Metz, and vowed to use more of his brother, Nick Metz. However, the strategy appeared futile. The Wings took a 2–0 lead early in the second period. Still, the Leafs persisted. They tied the score 2–2, fell behind 3–2 in the third period, tied it again on Sylvanus Apps' goal and won it on a score by Nick Metz. The defeat angered the Detroiters to such an extent that Don Grosso and Eddie Wares of the Red Wings became embroiled in an argument with referee Mel Harwood and were fined $50 and $25, respectively. At this point Jack Adams raced across the ice and began tossing punches at Harwood. NHL President Frank Calder required a police escort from the Olympia Stadium and later announced the indefinite suspension of Adams and prohibited him from taking any further part in the bench management of the Red Wings. Ebbie Goodfellow handled the Wings in the remaining games of the series.

The Leafs mauled Detroit, 9–3, in the fifth game, then topped the Wings, 3–0, in the sixth game back at Olympia. Never before had an NHL team lost the first three games of a Stanley Cup final and rebounded to win the next four. But on April 18, 1942, the Toronto club defeated the Red Wings, 3–1, at Maple Leaf Gardens, and Hap Day was enroute to many more NHL records.

Curiously, in the 1944–45 season, the Leafs again encountered the Red Wings in the Stanley Cup final and this time Toronto won the first three games and lost the next three to Detroit. But the Red Wings couldn't duplicate the feat of 1942 and dropped the final game, 2–1, and the series. Although Day had now won two Stanley Cups in only four years of coaching the accomplishments were merely a prelude for things to come.

Smythe, who again led a Canadian expedition to France, returned to Toronto after World War II and became deeply involved in running the team again. He was dismayed over the 1945–46 team, which ran fifth, and insisted that the new Toronto club would be built around a few veterans and liberally sprinkled with youth. No doubt, the club provided more action than Smythe had bargained for. The team finished second to Montreal and then defeated the Red Wings and Canadiens to win the Cup they weren't supposed to win for another two years. It was the beginning of one of the greatest hockey machines the NHL had ever known.

"I should have figured it out years ago," Smythe said. "Youth is the answer in this game. Only the kids have the drive, the fire and ambition. Put the kids in with a few old pappy guys who still like to win and the combination is unbeatable."

The pappy guys were portly goalie Turk Broda, whom Smythe was to describe as "the best playoff player in all hockey"; Syl Apps, a majestically tall center, described by writer Vince Lunny as "a Rembrandt on the ice, a Nijinsky at the goal mouth"; Nick and Don Metz, the supreme utility players, who killed penalties with extraordinary efficiency and took regular turns on the forward line; and Wally Stanowski, who skated like Sonja Henie and hit like Gus Lesnevich.

But without the kids there wouldn't have been any mustard and without the mustard the Leafs would have been a bland, second-rate outfit. Nobody symbolized the kids more than "Bashing" Bill Barilko, who had the face of a Beatle, the body of a bronco and the brashness of a gate crasher. Smythe imported Barilko from the Hollywood Wolves, a minor league team, and Barilko exploded on the NHL scene, in the midst of the 1946–47 season, although he was practically barren of hockey rudiments. His skating was so poor he would run several yards on the points of his blades to catapult himself into motion. His sense of strategy was crude, but he developed his "snake hips" bodycheck so well opponents stayed away from his side of the ice if they could help it, and he loved to win. And so did his mates. But more than that, they loved to fight.

The Leaf line-up was something out of a Golden Gloves program. There was (Wild) Bill Ezinicki, who once had four teeth knocked out in a homestretch game; he was suffering from pain and nervous shock, yet returned to score the winning goal against Boston. And the impudent Gold Dust Twins, defensemen Jim Thomson and Gus Mortson. Not to mention such rollicking types as Howie Meeker, Joe Klukay, Vic Lynn, Ted (Teeder) Kennedy and Garth Boesch, the only mustachioed player in hockey.

They punched, clutched, grabbed and thoroughly infuriated their foes. They so enraged Montreal coach Dick Irvin after a win at the Forum that Irvin kicked a live Santa Claus out of the Canadiens' dressing room.

They were inventive. Boesch and Barilko created the tandem Maginot Line knee-drop. A split second before an enemy would shoot the puck they'd drop to their knees, blocking the shot—a technique that later was copied by other defensemen around the league. Nick Metz and Klukay devised the modern penalty-killing style of vigilant forechecking.

And, in time, they were to have a superstar, although they lacked him at first. In fact, the Leafs were so bereft of supermen it was something of a local joke in Toronto because they failed to place a single player on the league All-Star Team even though they had won the Stanley Cup in 1947. "We may not have the all-stars," countered their coach Hap Day, "but we have the champions."

Instead of treating them with respect, many opponents regarded Smythe's Leafs as if they were the Dead End Kids. "They are the worst team in the league for holding, tripping and interfering," snapped Ranger coach Frank Boucher. But Smythe couldn't have cared less. If the Leafs indulged in jungle warfare it was only because they were reflecting the behavior of their master who had shown bravery in two world wars. Major Smythe won the Military Cross in 1916 and then transferred to the Royal Flying Corps where, as a reconnaissance pilot, he was "mentioned in dispatches." The Germans captured him after he crashed behind the lines in 1917, and he spent 14 months in a prison camp.

He was supposed to be too old to fight in World War II, but he organized an antiaircraft battery and shipped out to England. One night, during a unit softball game in the south of England, the Little Major was playing third base. With two out and runner on second, Smythe moved back of third to catch a pop fly. Just as he reached for the ball the runner from second crashed into him and Smythe fell to the ground. His ribs were broken and twice he fell unconscious. But he wasn't going to be stopped. "Any guy who peeps about this can expect a court-martial," he said.

They took him to a civilian doctor who patched Smythe's side where there were four broken ribs. And four days later he led his men into France.

Less than a month later a German reconnaissance plane dropped flares over the battery's headquarters. One of them fell into a tarpaulin covering an ammunition truck. Realizing that the ammunition might erupt within seconds, Smythe directed removal of the flare.

But before the soldiers could move, the truck exploded, killing two men. A chunk of shrapnel hit Smythe, grazed his spine and missed paralyzing him permanently by a fraction of an inch. Lying amid the dirt and metal, Smythe refused to quit: "I'm all right," he shouted at his troops, "get those fires out!"

This was the spirit Smythe transmitted to his Maple Leafs and they reflected it like soldiers. To some it came naturally. Howie Meeker, the speedy crew-cut right wing on the new Kid Line, had been wounded overseas when a grenade blew up in his face. He was told by doctors he'd never play hockey again. Meeker was unimpressed. In 1947 he won the Calder Trophy as NHL's rookie of the year. Vic Lynn, also of the Kid Line, was not a super scorer but he was big and rough and hit hard. Ted Kennedy, the third member, couldn't skate a lick but whenever you looked up he had the puck. As a unit, their gears meshed perfectly.

Losing in Smythe's book was sinful, but losing AND getting pushed around was utter heresy. In the spring of 1947 the Red Wings pulverized the Leafs, 9–1, in the opening round of the Stanley Cup semifinals. This annoyed Smythe. But the fact that Detroit's fearsome Black Jack Stewart had clobbered his young defenseman, Jim Thomson, with a left hook and wasn't slugged back infuriated him.

"Nobody," warned Smythe, "pops anybody in this club without getting popped back. I'm not interested in hockey players who don't play to win. You can take penalties, but you gotta play to win." In the next four games, Thomson laid the beef on Stewart and the Leafs swept all four games and the series.

There was a bromide that Smythe would fire any player who won the Lady Byng Trophy for gentlemanly conduct but that wasn't entirely true. His captain, Syl Apps, was a chronic contender for the Byng and Smythe would proudly introduce Apps to audiences as "Syl Apps, our captain, who does not smoke or drink." Coincidentally, Smythe himself never smoked nor drank.

With Apps at the helm, the Leafs upset Montreal in six games to win the Cup in April 1947, but Smythe, enthused as he was, still was slightly dubious about his budding powerhouse. When the 1947–48 season opened the Leafs were a good team the way the Los Angeles Dodgers were a good team and won the pennant in 1966. But the Dodgers had Sandy Koufax and the Leafs didn't. The Koufax that Smythe wanted—and knew he needed for first place— was a superstar playing for the Chicago Black Hawks. His name was Max Bentley, a wiry center who skated like a scared jack rabbit and shot like a bazooka and who had led the league in scoring the previous two seasons.

With the swift, smooth Apps and the tenacious, tough Kennedy in his line-up, Smythe had two of the best centers in the league but that wasn't enough; not for the superteam he wanted to create. "Strength down center is the key to a great team," he said. And when the Leafs fumbled their way through the opening month of the season he knew he needed Bentley, so Smythe opened negotiations with Chicago President Bill Tobin.

Tobin had to deal. Even with aces such as Max and Doug Bentley, the Hawks were floundering around last place with no

signs of improvement. Tobin offered Smythe $15,000 each for Gus
Bodnar, Elwyn Morris, and Bob Goldham. Smythe was furious. "I
repeatedly told Tobin that we're after players, not money." But
Smythe had the answer. He came up with a package of five first-rate
players—Gus Bodnar, Bud Poile, Gaye Stewart, Bob Goldham, and
Ernie Dickens—and offered them to Tobin for Bentley and an un-
known rookie, Cy Thomas. It was an astonishing proposal because
Bodnar, Poile and Stewart comprised the Flying Fort line and
Goldham and Dickens were a defense combination. So, all that
Tobin lacked for a complete team was a goaltender.

Smythe, of course, was taking a gamble of enormous proportions.
Max Bentley, for all his talent, was hypersensitive and hypochon-
driacal. The split with brother Doug might ruin him mentally and
artistically. And who could tell when his numerous imaginary aches
and pains would return to plague him and the Leafs.

But Smythe had become obsessed with visions of Max in the
royal blue and white Leaf uniform. He made the offer and on
November 3, 1947, Tobin accepted to complete what then was
described as "the greatest mass trade in professional hockey history." Smythe had parted with four extremely popular players in
Bodnar, Poile, Stewart, and Goldham and now he had a lot of
explaining to do.

"Our purpose in making the deal," he told stunned Leaf fans,
"relates to the center ice position. If anything were to happen to
Syl Apps we would be desperate. I feel it's quite a gamble but it's
worth it." Bentley was valued at $75,000 on the hockey market and
Thomas, $15,000. The Chicago package was priced at $95,000.

Although the deal had been rumored for several days, the Bentleys were stunned by the announcement. Their 74-year-old father,
William Bentley, said it was a mistake. "If I were they," said Papa
Bentley from his farm in Deslisle, Saskatchewan, "I wouldn't have
done it."

Max was heartbroken. "Having to play without my older brother,"
Max said, "made me feel like I lost my right arm." And, for a while,
it seemed that way. As a Leaf, Max went 10 straight games without a
goal until he found himself. Then he started scoring and never
stopped.

Unlike his new teammates, Max was a fragile pacifist who needed
police protection. Fortunately, the Leafs had handsome Bill Ezinicki
around and that was enough to distract anybody from Max. Ezinicki
was not much bigger than Bentley but he had sinewy arms and a

body that bulged from daily weight-lifting. He had a passion for free-skating that was outdone only by his passion for bodychecking. "I love to bodycheck," he'd say. "I don't care if they bodycheck me. In fact, I love that, too."

He also had a passion for tape. He'd stick reams of tape around his stick, his knees and his shoulder guards. And he had a passion for drinking water. He was, in fact, a very passionate hockey player and tough.

He'd collide with opponents—usually bigger opponents—from every direction. Sometimes, he'd wait for an opponent to speed in his direction, then he'd bend forward, extend his hips and the foe would fly over him and to the ice. Then, there was the "Ezzie orbit" which ex-Montreal Canadien defenseman Glen Harmon recalled:

"He'd circle his own defense and catch an opposing puck carrier circling from the far side of the defense. We were playing against him once and Ken Reardon came down in a mad rush. He was off-balance, circling, head down, one knee bent and frantically concentrating on retaining possession of the puck when Ezzie caught him with what we called 'the Ezinicki iron shoulder pad'—a regular shoulder pad reinforced with tape.

"Ezzie's shoulder caught Kenny squarely on the jaw. Kenny went down with a crash, rolled over, lurched unsteadily on his knees, then to his skates. His legs were so wobbly he looked like he was giving one of those comic drunk routines. His eyes were actually crossed."

The Canadiens had a theory that if they could neutralize Ezinicki they could beat the Leafs. Jim Coleman, columnist for the Southam newspaper chain in Canada, described one such expedition: "Ezinicki performed in a robust manner and took a whack at everyone without bothering to examine their license plates. Les Canadiens were looking for him, too, but scored only one point when Glen Harmon cross-checked Ezzie on the chops and escaped without a penalty." Other Canadiens went after Ezzie and took penalties. "Those penalties cost Canadiens two goals," added Coleman, "and Leafs won, 3–1."

A week later the Canadiens tried again. "Canadiens continued to spend a lot of time in a futile attempt to soften up Ezinicki," wrote Jim Vipond in the *Toronto Globe and Mail*. "The Toronto winger took them all on singly, two at a time and on one occasion was mixed up in a melee with four of the enemy. He hit Maurice Richard so hard once that the Rocket crashed into the door to the Leafs' bench, knocking it off the hinges."

Ezinicki was adored in Toronto and vilified wherever else he played. In Detroit, the Red Wings charged him with deliberately injuring goalie Harry Lumley. In Boston, *Globe* writer Herb Ralby said, "Toronto has the leading candidate for the most hated opponent in Ezinicki."

On November 8, Ezinicki crumpled Ranger center Edgar Laprade to the ice with a bodycheck. Laprade suffered a concussion and Ranger coach Frank Boucher protested to NHL President Clarence Campbell with a scathing telegram:

LAPRADE IN HOSPITAL WITH CONCUSSION FROM CHARGE BY EZINICKI AFTER WHISTLE ON AN OFFSIDE PLAY. REFEREE GEORGE GRAVEL CLAIMS HE DID NOT SEE OFFENSE. HOW MUCH LONGER IS EZINICKI GOING TO GET AWAY WITH ELBOWING, HIGH-STICKING AND DELIBERATE INJURIES TO OPPONENTS? BELIEVE CURB MUST BE PUT ON THIS PLAYER IMMEDIATELY.

Smythe swiftly counterattacked and urged Campbell to fine Boucher $1,000 for "acting in a manner prejudicial to the league." Smythe's trump card was a movie of the action. He offered to have a special screening for Boucher and six New York writers who were visiting Toronto. Boucher refused, and Smythe chortled: "They don't want to see a legal bodycheck. It might give their players a bad habit."

Eleven days after the incident Campbell completed his investigation and exonerated Ezinicki. "Reports of the officials," said Campbell, "show that the check by Ezinicki was perfectly legal and not a charge. The injury to Laprade was not caused by Ezinicki's stick but by Laprade striking the ice as he fell."

Soon after Campbell's decision Smythe was named president of Maple Leaf Gardens and Ezinicki was toasted by some of his most fearsome opponents. "He's a tough little guy," said Montreal's Ken Reardon, "but he's definitely not dirty. He can check and pester you and sometimes hurt you, and he can make you mad, but he's not dirty. Because he's short he can hurt. Those low bodychecks of his enable him to throw his shoulder into your stomach."

Ezzie's linemates were Boy Scouts by comparison. Leaf wing Harry Watson was a passive type who never seemed to get out of second gear and into high. Captain Syl Apps was positively angelic, but always played in high gear.

"Apps is the cleanest player I've known," said his coach, Hap Day. "I used to figure I came pretty close to being that myself. I didn't drink and I didn't smoke but I used to do my share of swearing. That's where Apps has me beaten. He doesn't smoke; in fact, he never started. He never bends an elbow except to twist his stick over an opponent's wrist. The strongest language he ever uses is 'By hum' and 'Jiminy Christmas'."

One night Boston defenseman Flash Hollett extracted two of Apps' teeth by shoving the thick wooden shaft of his stick in Syl's mouth. The Leaf captain muttered, "By hum, this has gone far enough," and then leveled Hollett with a flurry of punches.

Apps shocked the hockey world late in the 1947–48 season with an announcement that he'd retire after the playoffs. This was unheard of. The captain was only 33, physically fit, one of the NHL's leading scorers, the most popular player in Canada, and apparently capable of reaching the 200-goal plateau early the next season. "Sure I'd like to finish with 200 goals," Apps said in explaining his decision, "but I've got my family to think of and I can't go on playing forever, so I've made up my mind to retire."

Stunned as they were, the Leafs had too many jokers around to remain melancholy for very long. Whenever there was need for a gaff —or, whenever there was no need for one—goalie Turk Broda had one handy. The corpulent netminder, who looked more like a haberdashery salesman, was alternately laughed with and laughed at.

Once, after shutting out the Red Wings, Turk was rushed by his happy teammates. But Broda ignored them. He was busy scooping up a bunch of cigars a fan had tossed in his direction. When one of the Leafs tried to shake his hand, Turk insulted his pal. The player had accidentally skated over one of Turk's cigars.

"I wish they'd stop complimenting me," Turk complained. "It makes me nervous. Every time I read those nice things about me I get a nasty hunch that Smythe's getting ready to sell me to Chicago. I don't carry enough life insurance to play for Chicago. I'll just have to go out and play a bad game so that the boys will pan me and Smythe will be forced to keep me around for a couple of years."

Then there was droll Nick Metz who, like Apps, was to announce his retirement at the end of the season. Metz often played wing on the Max Bentley line although Nick insisted he never knew whether it was Max or brother Doug or one of the other numerous Bentleys skating with him.

"I used to play baseball against the Bentleys," Metz liked to tell the boys in the dressing room. "There were five of them and you couldn't tell 'em apart. Max, who was the best, would get a hit, reach first and then there'd be a huddle of the five Bentleys. When the conference broke up there would be a Bentley on first all right, but it always seemed to be Max who was batting again. Trouble was, we never could prove it."

The Leafs' trainer was Tim Daly, a short, fat, churlish ex-fighter who delivered lines in fractured Brooklynese. His banter was enough to keep an injured man in the line-up rather than on the dressing room table, and his vocabulary was just this side of incomprehensible. Once, when the Leafs were failing to bodycheck, he observed, "There's too much sediment on this team." Another time, a rookie asked Tim how his arm had become seared. Daly replied, "A hot pipe leans against me."

If Tim's phrase-warping turned off some Leafs, it never bothered Ezinicki who was a regular visitor to Daly's quarters. Ezzie owned an insurance policy with a $100 premium that guaranteed $5 for every stitch required to close an injury received in a hockey game. Ezzie regarded the patchwork the way a housewife would trading stamps. "It's just like double indemnity," he'd say.

Lurking almost unnoticed behind this merry menagerie was Clarence (Happy) Day, the Leaf coach and former Toronto defenseman who had established his niche in 1942, his rookie coaching year. After the third loss to Detroit, Day calmly told his men: "Forget the idea that you have to take four games in a row." Two weeks later the Leafs had done what had never been done before—or since; they rebounded, won four straight games, and the Cup.

If the acid in the Leafs' winning formula was supplied by Smythe, the glue belonged to Day. As a defenseman he never was reluctant to drape himself over an opponent and his defensemen did likewise. "When Day was playing defense," ex-Leaf Babe Pratt explained, "it cost the opposition triple money for sweaters. He used to rip them right off the players' backs with his clutch."

The Leafs displayed the same respect for Day that they observed with Smythe. Toronto's practices were severe but never to the point of creating dissension. One afternoon Boston defenseman Pat Egan stopped in Maple Leaf Gardens as the Leafs completed the last minutes of a torturous practice. "That's why they're goin' to win everything," said Egan. "Day could tell those kids to go into the wall head first and they'd do it."

One of those kids was Howie Meeker, a fighter from the Ezinicki mold. Meeker, who later was to become a member of Canada's Parliament, was fast and tough and had a congenital desire to fight with Gordie Howe of Detroit and Tony Leswick of the Rangers. Al Nickleson of the *Toronto Daily Star* described a bout with Leswick: "The two started shoving and the action ended when Meeker picked Leswick up in a crotch hold, threw him to the ice with a body slam and, with Meeker atop, Leswick's head hit the ice, leaving him a groggy fellow."

Meeker added: "I had my fist back ready to give it to him but then I saw the glazed look in his eyes and I changed my mind."

Toronto's metamorphosis occurred in December after Max Bentley rediscovered his scoring touch. The Kid Line had reached its peak. The Apps line was never better balanced. While Ezinicki exploded everywhere, Apps and Watson collaborated for goal after goal; and every once in a while Ezzie would get one, too. Max, the dipsy-doodler, took a regular turn at center with Nick Metz and Klukay and worked the point on the power play. Later in the season young Sid Smith made his debut with Bentley. Despite claims by experts that other teams had better power plays, the Leaf onslaught was as awesome as any the NHL ever has known, and the balance wheel was Bentley. He'd play the right point. On the face-off the Leafs would outmuscle their opponents for the puck, then pass it to Maxie. Instead of trying the noisy and erratic slapshot so overused today, Bentley would cradle the puck on his stick and thread his way through the opposition with a series of peripatetic feints until he was within wrist-shooting distance of the goal. Then, he'd blur a quickie to the net. "Max," said Detroit's respected manager Jack Adams, "comes close to being the greatest player in the game."

Bentley's secret weapon was his quick wrists. "I got 'em," he explained, "from milking cows as a kid. There were eight cows on my father's farm in Saskatchewan and every day since I can remember, when I'm on that farm I milk the cows. Two hours in the morning and two hours at night."

Max's father, William, confirmed the ingredients of the secret weapon. "There's nothing like milkin' cows to build steel in your wrists," said old William Bentley. "My boy has milked enough cows to stretch from here to the Rocky Mountains, standin' tail to tail; and he's scored enough goals to make me the proudest man in Canada." Then, a pause: "Just forget the part about the Rocky Mountains. The cows would really only reach about 2,000 miles."

By late February, Max's line had scored 45 goals, the Apps line,

41. There was a pattern to the Leafs' scoring. They'd fall behind in the first and second periods, then surge to victory in the third. But, despite their balance and power, they were closely pursued by the Red Wings, themselves a potent outfit. The Wings had a superb young goaltender in Harry Lumley, a solid defense backed by Jack Stewart, Bill Quackenbush and Red Kelly, and the scoring of the production line—Sid Abel, Gordie Howe, and Ted Lindsay.

On March 10, with only five games remaining in the regular schedule, the Wings moved ahead of Toronto by a point. Then the Leafs rebounded and, as the final weekend approached, Toronto held a one-point lead over Detroit. The teams were to meet in a home-and-home series starting Saturday night in Toronto. If the Leafs won the opener they'd have the championship.

But more than first place was on the line. Goalies Turk Broda and the Wings' Harry Lumley were battling for the Vezina Trophy. Each had 138 goals scored against him. And captain Syl Apps, who insisted he would not return next season, needed three goals to reach the 200 mark.

Both goalies were riddled with a case of the nerves on Saturday but Lumley was the worse of the two. Twice the Wings took the lead and twice Lumley flubbed and Toronto tied the score. A goal by Apps—his 198th—put the Leafs ahead to stay in the second period and they scored again in the third to win, 5–3.

"Now," said defenseman Gus Mortson, "we're playin' the second game for Turk. He's been great for us all season . . . we'd just better win."

Next game Broda excelled. "I guess I was too nervous," said Lumley. Nervous or not, he never had a chance. Less than two minutes after the opening face-off at Detroit's Olympia, Harry Watson put the Leafs ahead. Now it was Apps' turn. He needed two goals for 200. He finally scored at 3:21 of the second period for number 199. Three minutes later, Watson cracked the Detroit defense and had Lumley at his mercy. A split second before he was to shoot, he spotted Apps moving in on his right. He slid the puck to his captain who blasted it into the webbing at 7:11 of the second. Early in the third period, Apps climaxed the evening with his 201st career goal and a hat trick. The Leafs won, 5–2, and Broda captured his second Vezina Trophy. "Now," said Ezinicki, "we've got to keep the Stanley Cup."

Toronto's opening-round opponents for the Stanley Cup, the third-place Boston Bruins, were big, tough and fast. "They'll beat the Leafs and win the Cup," predicted Ranger coach Frank Boucher, who had accurately declared at the beginning of the season that Montreal would be upset by New York and would finish fifth.

Boston was led by Frankie "Mr. Zero" Brimsek in goal, Milt Schmidt and Woody Dumart up front and a capable defense of Jack Crawford, Murray Henderson, Pat Egan, Fern Flaman and Clare Martin. In the first game at Maple Leaf Gardens, they punished the Leafs for two periods and built up a substantial 4–2 lead with only eight minutes remaining in the game. This time it appeared that the Little Major's troops would be routed, except that eight minutes was a long time for the Leafs. At 12:02 Apps took a long pass from Wally Stanowski, skated around Egan and blasted a hard shot at Brimsek that slipped through his pads. One minute and 23 seconds later the puck came to Jim Thomson at the point. The tall Leaf defenseman had not scored a goal all season. This time Thomson's shot sailed over Howie Meeker's shoulder and past Brimsek before the goalie ever saw it.

The game went into sudden death overtime and at 17:02 Nick Metz passed to Max Bentley whose shot was blocked by Brimsek. But the goalie allowed the puck to drop in front of him just as Metz swooped by. "Shucks," drawled farmer Nick afterward, "it was a set-up. All I had to do was bang it in." Which he did and that was that for the Bruins.

In the second game played at Toronto, Ted Kennedy scored four goals and Max Bentley one as the Leafs romped, 5–3, moving the series to Boston for the third and fourth games. And, once again, the Leafs had too much power. Artistically, they easily dispatched the Bruins with two goals in the first period, one in the second and two in the third. Fistically, they left matters to Harry Watson, the tall husky left wing.

Watson, the passive type with all the ability to be a high scorer and all the strength to be heavyweight champion, long had been criticized for his lack of zip and failure to annihilate smaller, pesty opponents who antagonized him. This time he was bothered by big defenseman Murray Henderson who was to be mashed in one of the most one-sided, bloody bouts hockey has known.

"The usually mild-mannered Toronto winger went berserk," observed Jim Vipond in the *Toronto Globe and Mail.* "He shed his gloves and peppered the Boston defenseman [Murray Henderson] with a series of hard, short jabs to the face. Watson landed at least eight blows and Henderson was forced to retire to the Boston dressing room with a flattened nose."

Dr. Horace MacIntyre, the Leafs' physician who had treated players for more than 20 years, said he had never seen a nose so badly smashed.

Boston fans were furious over the double manhandling their team was getting. A group behind the Leaf bench began harassing the visitors early in the first period and continued their baiting throughout the game. When referee George Gravel asked the police to remove the offending spectators, Bruin president Weston Adams interceded and the fans remained and screamed even louder.

"One fan threatened to hit me," coach Hap Day recalled, "and I told him I'd be waiting at the end of the game. I turned around as soon as the game ended and the two of us tangled. I slipped to the floor and lost my fedora."

Most of the Leafs had departed for the dressing room before the riot had erupted, but defenseman Wally Stanowski lingered by the Toronto bench anticipating trouble. Stanowski went after the fans and the several others who joined in pummeling Day. Ted Kennedy and Garth Boesch, who had walked part way to the dressing room, doubled back and the melee spread to the ice. One fan bashed Boesch to the ice from behind. The Toronto defenseman was dazed and had to be taken back to the hotel and put to bed. The attacker ducked into the crowd and ran away into the promenade.

By then, police, linesman George Hayes and Bill Smith, a member of Smythe's World War II battery, had waded into the angry mob and held them off until Day and the players could get to the dressing room. When Weston Adams attempted to seek out Conn Smythe in the Leaf quarters he was promptly ejected by Smythe. "It's a disgrace, a positive disgrace," snapped Smythe. "The police did nothing. If they had put that fan out in the first period all the trouble would have been prevented."

The Boston press unanimously denounced the fans' conduct. "THUGS ATTACK TORONTO STARS," screamed the headline on the front page of the Boston Herald. "Most unsporting demonstration in Boston's hockey history," commented hockey writer Henry McKenna.

More than double the usual number of police were stationed at Boston Garden for the fourth game on April Fools' Day and the Bruins won, 3–2. But it was merely a dying gasp. Kennedy's goal at 5:52 of the third period buried the Bruins, 3–2, in the fifth game and now the Leafs were ready for the hated Red Wings who had eliminated the Rangers in six games.

"We get paid to play the other teams," carped Detroit captain Sid Abel before the opener. "The Leafs? We'd play them for nothing."

Bookies listed Toronto as 2–1 favorites to win the Cup and the experts were saying the final round represented the Leafs' test of omnipotence. "It takes a really good team to win the Cup or the league championship," said Tommy Munns, sports editor of the *Toronto Globe and Mail*, "but only a really great team can win the Cup one season and retain it the next."

Hap Day's dilemma in the opening game was finding a replacement for defenseman Gus Mortson who had suffered a double fracture of the left leg in the second period. But the Leafs were so steeped in competent reserves it was no problem at all. He moved veteran Wally Stanowski into the opening and Stanowski set up the fifth Toronto goal in the 5–3 win.

Max Bentley's electric shot inspired the Leaf attack in the second game. He scored twice and linemates Harry Watson and Bill Ezinicki scored one apiece as the Leafs curbed Detroit, 4–2.

So decisive were the wins, the Detroit camp strained for an explanation. Finally, Jack Adams scooped up some hoary bromides and accused the Leafs of holding and interference. He said defenseman Bill Barilko had never made a legal check in his life. "I'm not alibiing for the way we played or because we lost," moaned Adams. "I'm not alibiing for the future. I'm not asking anybody for anything except a square deal."

All Adams got when the series switched to Detroit for the third game there was more of the withering Leaf power, and battering defense fronted by that super money player, Turk Broda. The fat man stopped Detroit and the game remained scoreless until the last minute of the second period when Ezinicki skittered out of the Toronto zone with Harry Watson at his side. An hour later, Smythe was to describe them as "the two best wingers in the game at the moment."

Once inside the Detroit blue line Ezzie dropped the puck and skated ahead, blocking goalie Harry Lumley's vision. Watson trapped the puck and fired a hot backhander behind Lumley. Burly Vic Lynn scored the second and final goal late in the third period snapping home a pass from Ted Kennedy.

Paul Chandler, hockey writer for the *Detroit News*, summed up the situation, "It is the Red Wings' misfortune that Toronto is a great team with an uncanny ability to rise to almost every important occasion."

The final occasion was the fourth game of the series and the Leafs, as usual, rose.

Few teams have ever been so thoroughly demolished in their home ice in the final game of the Stanley Cup finals as the Red Wings that April 14, 1948. The onslaught started at 2:51 of the first period when Ted Kennedy sunk Max Bentley's rebound past Lumley, and it ended at 14:37 of the third period when rookie Les Costello took a Bentley pass and scored Toronto's seventh goal.

In between there were scores by Garth Boesch, two by Harry Watson, another by Kennedy and one by Syl Apps. The final score was 7–2, but the Red Wings goals were mere tokens. "There was never any doubt about it from start to finish," Jack Adams glumly admitted. Coach Tommy Ivan, dazed by the endless attacking waves of Leafs, could never devise an adequate defense: "We just couldn't do anything about it," he said.

Although it was Toronto's fourth Cup win in seven years the Little Major's troops couldn't contain their exuberance. Once they trundled into the dressing room Broda was stretched on the knees of Bentley and Klukay and doused with a bottle of Coke by Meeker. Smythe shed a coat and hat and settled on a trunk and beamed: "This is the greatest team I ever had. They never failed me and for the first time in my life I didn't have to give them a pep talk in the final series."

Laughing in the corner with pure childish joy was the man who lifted the Leafs to the plateau of complete supremacy. Max Bentley, who at the age of 16 had been rejected by the Montreal Canadiens and told by a doctor he couldn't play hockey again because of a bad heart, led the Leafs in scoring during the regular season and finished second to Ted Kennedy in the playoffs.

"He's an even better player than I thought," said Smythe. "He gave us the third center we needed to give us the Murderer's Row of hockey—three 25-goal centermen."

The next day they stepped off the Detroit train in mid-afternoon to be hailed by tens of thousands of Torontonians. With the Queen's Own Rifles band leading the parade, the Little Major and his troops rolled under a torrent of ticker tape in open cars from Union Station to the City Hall, where an additional 10,000 fans cheered Captain Apps when he was introduced to the throng.

It was the last time Apps would be seen as a Maple Leaf. He

stuck to his retirement decision as did Nick Metz although team-mates tried to persuade them to change their minds. "If Syl would only come back for one more season," said Bentley, "we could be a cinch to repeat next year."

Young Ted Kennedy was named captain but without Apps and Metz the Leafs finished fourth the next season and appeared doomed against the Bruins in the Stanley Cup semifinals. Instead, they routed Boston in five games setting up a rematch with Detroit in the finals. The Wings had stampeded into first by a comfortable margin, 18 points ahead of the Leafs. But once the Wings faced Toronto again, they disintegrated. The Leafs romped to an unprecedented third straight Cup in four consecutive games.

A year later Detroit finally got revenge. They put the Leafs out in the seventh game of a sudden death semifinal round and it looked like the Toronto machine had permanently broken down. But it wasn't true. Bill Barilko scored the winning goal against Montreal in a sudden death overtime of the fifth game of the 1951 finals and the Leafs regained the Cup. A few months later Barilko was flying over the thick forests of Northern Ontario when the engine of his single-engined plane failed. The aircraft plunged to the ground, carrying the Leaf defenseman to his death. And with him went the great Toronto dynasty.

More than a decade went by before the Leafs were to win another Cup. After a series of mediocre efforts both on the ice and in the front office, the Toronto management signed George (Punch) Imlach as general manager and coach. An abrasive type with a very positive attitude, Imlach rebuilt the Leaf club with some extraordinary moves. He obtained Red Kelly from Detroit after Kelly had been considered jaded as a defenseman and immediately converted him to center. He liked Johnny Bower, an ancient goaltender who had been rejected by the Rangers, signed him and made him a regular. Meanwhile, the Leaf farm system was producing such impressive youngsters as Carl Brewer, Bobby Baun, Bob Pulford, Frank Mahovlich and Dave Keon.

Stimulated by Imlach, the Leafs duplicated the Hap Day feat of three straight Stanley Cups between 1962 and 1964 and appeared headed for even greater things because of the profusion of youth in the line-up. But Imlach's hard-nosed style began grating some of his more sensitive younger players. First, Brewer quit, then others complained. When the NHL expanded to 12 teams in 1967, Imlach unloaded Baun and Douglas but still overtones of mutiny were heard. When the Leafs finished a poor fifth—and out of the play-offs —for the first time in a decade in the 1967–68 season there were rumblings that even more cuts would be made, possibly even Imlach himself.

But his triumphs still fresh in the minds of his bosses, Imlach hung on and continued to direct the club through the 1968–69 season. However, his influence was waning and the era of the triumphant Leafs once again had come to an end.

Imlach was fired on April 4, 1969, after a long feud with club president Stafford Smythe, son of the Maple Leafs founder. Smythe hired minor league coach John McLellan as the new club mentor and Jim Gregory as the manager.

The new regime enjoyed little success during the rebuilding year of 1969–70 but in 1970–71 several young players such as Jim Dorey, Mike Pelyk, Brian Spencer and Rick Ley enabled Toronto to reach a playoff berth.

The Leafs also obtained veteran goalie Jacques Plante from St. Louis and young goalie Bernie Parent from Philadelphia, giving them an excellent goalkeeping combination.

Despite their relative youth, the Leafs played competently in the 1971 playoffs, forcing the New York Rangers to a sixth game before bowing out in sudden-death overtime. Thanks to the insightful and calm coaching of McLellan and the maturation of the rookies, the Leafs appeared destined for better things in years to come. One of the results of the 1970–71 season as concerned the Leafs was the adoption of the new "third-man" rule. Not that they were the only offenders, but their bench-clearing battle with the Rangers in the playoffs was the third time Toronto was involved in this kind of mass brawling. The league decided that fines were no deterrent to a practice it found abhorrent. (Some governors, in fact, like Stafford Smythe and William Jennings were balky in paying and even succeeded in getting their assessments lowered.) So it was decided and instituted before the 1971–72 season that any man who leaves the bench while a fight is in progress gets a game misconduct and a minor penalty against his team. The third-man rule states that any player who is on the ice and intervenes between two other fighters, even as an alleged peacemaker, gets an automatic game misconduct. These rules have proved far more effective than a trip to the wallet in curbing mass brawls.

Meanwhile the Leafs had other headaches. In 1971–72 they were again fourth but only by a few points and the Bruins eliminated them in five games. Any bright hope for the future went behind a big cloud labeled WHA that summer. The Leafs were one NHL team hardest hit by defections to the new league. They lost their top goaler Parent to Philadelphia Blazers; defensemen Rick Ley and Brad Selwood to New England; and tough center-ice man Jim Harrison also jumped to the Alberta Oilers. Plante could not shoulder enough of a load and near the end of the season, when Toronto saw they were doomed to a dismal sixth place finish, they dealt him to Boston.

Paul Henderson, hero of the Team Canada-Russia series, was hampered by injuries and scored only 18 goals while playing only 40 games. Bobby Baun's injured neck forced him into retirement after five games. Bright spots among the younger players were forwards Darryl Sittler and Rick Kehoe.

After the season McClellan went the way of all coaching flesh.

PART TWO
The Expansion

New Growth

BEFORE THE SEASON of 1942–43 the Brooklyn Americans, as the record book tells it, "retired from League" and the National Hockey League settled into the six-team circuit that was to be its format for the next 25 seasons. Over that span, especially in the 1960's, the word "tight" was often used to describe the governing body of the world's most exclusive skating club. Writer Jack Olsen, in an article, "Private Game: No Admittance" (*Sports Illustrated*, April 12, 1965), pictured the NHL as "A tight little island of close-fisted, inbred standpatters with a stranglehold on a grand professional game." His view was not particularly singular. Until February 8, 1966, when Clarence Campbell formally announced the addition of six new teams, the idea of expansion was generally as welcome among NHL leaders as a forward in the goal crease.

The earliest wave of expansion might be said to have started in 1924 when the Boston Bruins became the first team from the United States to join the league. In the same year, the Maroons presented Montreal another club to vie with the Canadiens. The following year, Hamilton Tigers franchise, which had replaced Quebec Bulldogs in 1920, was sold to New York, becoming the Americans, and the Pittsburgh Pirates were admitted. By the beginning of the 1926–27 season the ranks had swelled to an all-time high of 10 teams. In addition to Bruins, Maroons, Canadiens, Americans and Pirates, there were the Toronto Maple Leafs, Ottawa Senators and three new entries: New York Rangers, Chicago Black Hawks and Detroit Cougars. The League was divided into two five-team divisions,

Canadian and American; the New York Americans lined up with the four north-of-the-border clubs. From that time until 1967, anything resembling expansion was really only migration.

The Pittsburgh franchise became the Philadelphia Quakers in 1930; in 1931 Philadelphia folded. Ottawa, which had suspended operations for the 1931–32 season, returned in 1932–33, became the St. Louis Eagles in 1934 and molted into oblivion in 1935. Three seasons later the Maroons disbanded, beating the Americans to the ash heap by four years.

After World War II, hockey, like all professional sports, began to reclaim its stars and solid regulars. The one-sided games of the wartime years subsided into more normal scores as the retreads and teen-agers returned to the minors. Not only was the caliber of play up but so were the attendance figures. In the postwar boom there was much ready money and sports shared amply in the entertainment dollar. The last place Black Hawks of 1946–47 drew a crowd of 20,000 to Chicago Stadium as far along in the season as late February, and the Rangers, who had suffered much humiliation in the war years, again had a respectable team to attract consistently good crowds.

In May 1952 Jim Hendy, general manager of the Cleveland Barons, thought that his club was on the verge of leaving the American Hockey League to become the National Hockey League's seventh member. It had taken six months of beaverish activity to reach this point. A Cleveland sports columnist wrote: "Our city has been awarded a franchise in the NHL. This is the most pleasurable news of the year." He was a trifle premature.

Despite all indications that the Barons were "in," two months later they were turned down. "What do they want?" wailed Hendy, and the NHL answered with the following stipulations: $425,000 to cover the franchise, league reserve fund and working capital and 60 per cent of the stock to be owned by Cleveland residents. Hendy fulfilled these requests. His backers were solid and he seemed to have the support of the member teams. He built up a farm system along major league lines. President Clarence Campbell came out in favor of the Barons acceptance as a boon to hockey interest in the United States.

With seemingly only the formalities to be dispensed the NHL shot a "no" from a curved stick. Included in the money raised to fulfill Cleveland's requirements were substantial advances against TV and radio earnings and concessions, extending over two seasons.

In the eyes of the NHL governors this was not "working capital." Application denied.

It was probably a combination of reasons that made the NHL ultracautious. From the past there were the spectres of all those failed franchises of the 1930s. In the present were new financial problems. Although there was no depression, the postwar prosperity was over and people were not going out to see losers. The NHL had two of these, Chicago and New York. Between 1949–50 and 1956–57 the Black Hawks finished last seven out of eight times. From 1950–51 through 1954–55 the Rangers were fifth four times and in the cellar once. In that period there was nothing so enervating as a midweek struggle between the two weak sisters. At one such contest, a 1–1 tie that neither team seemed eager to break, the Ranger management decided not to open the balcony in deference to the size of the crowd. One literally could hear a puck drop. With fences such as these to mend, it was little wonder that the league sought new lands reticently. Instead, they strengthened from within.

The Black Hawks, with deliberate help from the stronger clubs, moved to fifth in 1957–58 and were not out of the playoffs again until 1969. Once their farm system began to produce the likes of Bobby Hull and Stan Mikita they became more self-sufficient. The Rangers, after a pocket renaissance from 1955–56 through 1957–58, fell back to the role of perennial also-ran until 1966–67, with the exception of 1961–62. They were joined by Boston, which did not participate in one Stanley Cup game from the spring of 1960 up to the spring of 1968. However, there was one important difference between the doormats of the fifties and the sad sacks of the sixties— the home town rooters were filling the arenas to watch the latter play. More specifically, they were coming to watch hockey. Television, described by Clarence Campbell in 1951 as "the greatest menace of the entertainment world," had helped magnify the great appeal of the ice sport in already established areas and spread its magnetic aura to unlikely corners, even where it had been only a dirty word. (In Nashville "hockey," prior to the arrival of the Dixie Flyers of the Eastern League, was a local joke. It took the natives a while before they could view the sign "Hockey Tonight" outside the arena without having a fit of thigh-slapping hysterics.)

What began as local televising of certain home games—or parts of games—by each team in the early fifties, eventually reached the network stage. In 1956–57 Columbia Broadcasting System inaugurated a Saturday afternoon series from Boston, Chicago, Detroit and

New York. Meanwhile, the Canadian Broadcasting Company's "Hockey Night in Canada" added TV to go along with the weekly Saturday night radio broadcasts. None of these telecasts hurt attendance but, in fact, boosted it in certain areas. The Rangers finished last in 1965–66 but their practice of televising their Saturday night road contests made so many new fans for hockey that a pasteboard to one of their games at Madison Square Garden had become, through several losing seasons, one of New York's "hot tickets."

In the sixties, hockey not only spread to the South, but towns like Ft. Wayne, Indiana, in the International Hockey League were attracting bigger crowds to their games than "major league" cities in other winter professional sports like basketball. Before the 1961–62 season, San Francisco and Los Angeles joined the Western Hockey League. The success of these franchises in large population centers already represented by major league teams in baseball and football, became a constant spur to NHL expansion as the sixties unfolded. The American Football League set up shop alongside the National Football League in 1960. Faced with the possibility of a third league, the National and American Leagues of baseball each added two teams for the 1962 season. That spring, columnist Jim Murray of the *Los Angeles Times* wrote: "The National Hockey League makes a mockery of its title by restricting its franchises to six teams, waging a kind of private little tournament of 70 games just to eliminate two teams.

"Other big money sports are expanding," he continued, "but hockey likes it there in the back of the cave. Any businessman will tell you that in a dynamic economy you either grow or perish. Baseball had to be dragged kicking and screaming out of its rut. Football groped its way on the end of a short rope. Hockey just can't sit there in the dark forever, braiding buggy whips."

At the same time, Harold Ballard, one of the owners of the Toronto Maple Leafs, said: "If the right kind of people come to us with $5,000,000 and the right kind of plans, we'll listen. We'd be crazy not to." Although mitigated by some of the requirements, this was one of the rare positive statements on expansion to come from the NHL hierarchy at that time. Clarence Campbell's position for the league was couched in more conservative terms. "The league . . . is not actively promoting or encouraging expansion of the number of its members at this time," he stated drily. "But it is prepared to consider each individual application on its own merits."

By 1964 rumblings from the West Coast were edging toward the seismic. Coley Hall, a Director of Vancouver, but then the owner of the San Francisco Seals, said, "The time has come for the NHL to realize that Los Angeles and San Francisco can't wait; our hockey fans are just as major-league-conscious as fans of baseball and football and feel they should be up there. An angry feeling is developing."

One of the more testy, anonymous quotes from the Pacific territory to reach print at that time was, "If the NHL won't expand to us, why don't we go outlaw, raid them groggy and find out if their control over hundreds of young players through B and C forms will stand up in law?"

The next flurry of expansion excitement also came in 1964 from the Pacific Northwest. At the Western Hockey League's annual meeting in Seattle, Stafford Smythe, former president of the Toronto Maple Leafs, revealed that his club was willing to erect an $8,000,-000 coliseum, seating 20,000, in downtown Vancouver in time for the opening of the 1966–67 season. Smythe envisioned Vancouver as a member of a new six-team division. His accomplice, Ballard, saw the new entry as part of the old circuit along with Los Angeles, San Francisco and St. Louis. Ballard made it clear that the Leafs' interest in Vancouver would be confined to building and operating the arena, with the franchise to be independently owned. What eventually became the main stumbling block was the contingency that the city donate the property for the arena site.

At first the City Council appeared to have agreed to this offer but almost immediately the motion was described as "a noncommittal resolution." Mayor William Rathie of Vancouver advocated a green light on the proposal. Although he won an election, the land grant was voted down by the taxpayers of Vancouver.

When the original proposition had come from the Maple Leafs, Clarence Campbell called it "kite flying" and added his presidential weight by stating: "I know that as of this minute they are not speaking for anybody official in the National Hockey League." However, he did say of Smythe and Ballard: "I agree with them that expansion is inevitable. With a show as good as ours, economics may someday either induce or force expansion."

The arguments against expansion were many. Travel expense was one. A major league baseball team stays three or four days in one city when on the road; a hockey team plays one-night stands. Lack of talent was another. When baseball moved to Los Angeles and San Francisco it gave those cities established teams, but when it expanded it presented new teams that were hardly competitive.

Campbell cited the "formation of a clown club" without directly naming the New York Mets. "We don't want any clown teams in the National Hockey League," he concluded. It was common thinking—and this prevailed until proved wrong during the actual playing of the 1967–68 season—that there were simply not enough good players available to make up two more NHL teams, let alone a new six-team division.

At the conclusion of the 1963–64 season it was reported that the NHL had played to 94.5 of its total seating capacity; this in a year when the fifth-place Rangers finished 17 points from the last play-off spot, and the Bruins trailed the New Yorkers by another six points. ("I'm for expansion," wrote one waggish columnist, "on the condition that it first include New York and Boston.") The stand-patters could say, "What can we gain by expanding and adding to our expenses?" and the answer would have been, "Nothing," if not for one factor—television. Aware of the lucrative deals garnered by baseball and football, the most forward-thinking of the NHL governors realized that in order to snare the TV dollar, major league hockey would have to extend its nets over the length of the United States.

On March 11, 1965, at a special meeting of club owners in New York's Plaza Hotel the NHL announced that it was expanding with the formation of a second six-team division, and would begin evaluating applications from responsible groups. The official acceptance in February 1966 found Los Angeles, San Francisco, St. Louis, Pittsburgh, Philadelphia and Minneapolis-St. Paul as the representatives of the new division. St. Louis was a surprise since they had not filed a formal application. Buffalo and Baltimore had been rejected. So had Vancouver and this rankled many Canadians. After all, here were six additions to the NHL and not one city was located in the country that was the cradle of hockey.

It is generally conceded that the younger governors like Canadiens' David Molson and Rangers' Bill Jennings were the prime movers in the expansion. For the daring jump to be successful, it was realized that the arrangement for stocking the new teams had to be equitable. When the Board of Governors thought they had a fair plan devised, the general managers balked. President Campbell explained the delay with: "I never met a generous general manager."

The approved plan called for each existing team to protect one goalie and 11 other players. When they lost one, they could fill with another. This would go on until each new team had a roster of 20 players. The old teams would lose their number 12, 14, 16, 17 and 18 men to the expansion clubs. When the established teams' general managers heard this they moaned. The new members seemed satisfied. Only Campbell was reported to be not completely pleased. However he felt that an extended back-up plan that called for *all* teams to be able to protect two goalies and only 14 others for the 1968 and 1969 drafts would help in the equalization. "The new teams won't have trouble picking out which 14 to protect," he said, "but the older teams . . . they're going to have problems.

"I visualize definite improvement in the new teams by 1968–69 because of the back-up plan," Campbell added, "By 1970, they should have a glorious field day and I hope they do."

On June 6, 1967, the expansion draft was held in Montreal and the new teams received an opportunity to see what they were going to get for their initiation fee of $2,000,000. When the cigar smoke had cleared, there were those observers who felt the neophytes had been taken when they wound up paying $100,000 each for bodies that ordinarily, under the regular draft price, cost only $30,000. Of course, for $2,000,000 one not only received 20 players but also an area in which to skate—provided one had the rink.

Even the players, pleased by the doubled job opportunities, had differing opinions. Forward Billy Hicke, drafted by Oakland (then California) Seals said of the new owners: "They didn't get a fair shake. The league was charitable with goaltenders, but that was all. Of the 20 players each team drafted, only six or seven are of NHL caliber."

Later, toward the tail end of the season, Philadelphia Flyer defenseman Ed Van Impe waxed positive about the new division. "Expansion was a good thing for hockey. These teams are good teams. There were a lot of good hockey players who never had a chance until this year. It's hard to imagine until this year, there were only 120 spots open for major-league hockey players. Now it's 240. Expansion hasn't hurt. These guys are proving they belonged."

One thing expansion did was create more holdouts. Players who knew that they were vital to the new teams—especially the all-important goalies—drove hard bargains. The older players realized that this was their last chance to cash in.

At the conclusion of the season, even the league's most ardent critics had to concede that the NHL version of expansion had been the most successful of any professional sport. The new teams, with the exception of Oakland, were all contenders for the four playoff spots. While Philadelphia finished first with 73 points, Pittsburgh was fifth, two points out of fourth, with 67 points. The six new clubs won 40, tied 18 and lost 86 in competition with the established division, a figure even a clairvoyant would have rejected in October.

The West Division playoffs were so closely played that all three series went the full seven games and one-third of these games were decided in sudden death overtime. When the St. Louis Blues bowed to the mighty Montreal Canadiens in four one-goal victories—two of them in overtime—the creators of expansion could sit back and admire an artistic triumph.

How did the new teams reach this level so quickly? Top caliber goal-tending, certainly; lots of extra effort, for sure; complacency on the part of the old teams, partially: prevailing over all, the feeling that the major league bench warmers, the locked-in minor leaguers and the fringe faction were all better than they had been rated. And, of course, the theory of different combinations was given a thorough testing. You know—A may not play well with B and C, but put him with D (digger in the corners) and S (speedy up and down his wing) and you will see a different hockey player. The individual stars are always important but hockey is a team game, and an inventive coach can make a whole out of a lot of seemingly disparate parts.

For all the huzzahs over expansion's initial bloom, there were some who warned that there might be a sliding back when the juniors that the East Division clubs were able to protect would come to maturity and jet the old teams a few strides ahead again. Others warned of the consequences of trading away future choices in the universal draft of 20-year-olds. (Minnesota, for one, was heavily indebted to Montreal in this area.) The open draft of juniors began in 1967, but the size of established teams' sponsored lists didn't begin to really shrink until after 1968 as the phasing out process neared its conclusion. Before the 1968 draft only 33 untouchables were left. 4,500 were available and the figure was greater in 1969. Anyone turning 20 is eligible and the days of signing a fledgling at 14 are over. Scouting has become more important than ever.

In the fall of 1970 Vancouver and Buffalo made their respective debuts in the NHL following a realignment of divisions. Chicago was moved to the West Division while the two new entries joined the East section.

Atlanta and the New York Islanders, a Nassau County entry, made their appearances in 1972–73, the former in the West and the latter in the East. Accepted, and slated to begin play in 1974–75, are franchises representing Kansas City and Washington, D.C.

In 1973 a European league was in the formative stage with an eye toward eventual competition on some sort of international basis. Today the NHL, tomorrow the world—or the World Hockey Association.

In August 1973 the NHL announced that when Washington and Kansas City enter the league for the 1974–75 season the realignment of teams and divisions will look like this:

Division I: Atlanta, New York Islanders, New York Rangers, Philadelphia

Division II: Detroit, Los Angeles, Montreal, Pittsburgh, Washington

Division III: Chicago, Kansas City, Minnesota, St. Louis, Vancouver

Division IV: Boston, Buffalo, California, Toronto

When two new teams are accepted for the 1976–77 season, one will join Division I and the other will be placed in Division IV.

At the end of the season twelve teams will make the playoffs, three from each division. Divisional leaders will draw a bye in the first round, and the other eight teams will play each other determined by the number of points earned during the regular season: highest against lowest, second highest against second lowest, etc. These series will be best two out of three. In the quarter-finals the pattern will revert to the usual four out of seven but opponents will still be determined by seasonal point totals. This will carry through to the finals where the points will decide which finalist receives the advantage of the extra home game.

Los Angeles Kings

THEY LAUGHED when the Los Angeles Kings skated out to start their first season in the NHL. Twenty of 24 experts picked them to finish last in the West Division. After all they reasoned, Terry Sawchuk was the only player to have spent the entire previous season with a major league club, and even those who had NHL experience in the past were fringe players. Besides, Sawchuk was 37 and at the tail end of a great career. What they hadn't reckoned with, in addition to the intangible qualities of the unproven players, were the administrative abilities of Jack Kent Cooke and the two Irishmen he hired to help him, Lawrence Emmett (Larry) Regan and Leonard Patrick (Red) Kelly.

Cooke, who had become a multimillionaire through his radio, publishing and baseball interests in his native Canada, was a surprise winner in the Los Angeles franchise sweepstakes over four other bidders, including a group headed by Dan Reeves, owner of the Los Angeles Blades of the Western League. When the city gave him a hard time about using the Sports Arena, where the Blades and Cooke's own Lakers of the National Basketball Association had played, he threatened to build his own edifice, and did.

His choice of general manager, Larry Regan, did not set any imaginations on fire, coming as it did after a draft in which most observers felt the Kings came up short. Regan, a clever center with Bruins and Maple Leafs, who won the Calder Trophy in 1956–57 at the ripe old age of 26, had served as player coach of Pittsburgh's American League club in 1961–62 and spent three years as manager-

96

coach of the Innsbruck, Austria, team before returning to North America and one season as a player with the Baltimore Clippers in 1965–66. Then he was hired by Cooke as head scout for the new organization and began traveling around the United States and Canada, evaluating hockey players in preparation for the big draft. "He works as hard as I do," said Cooke of Regan. This was high praise, coming from someone described by California columnist Bud Tucker as "the kind of man who wants to die in his own arms."

The draft itself became the scene of the first interdivisional joust. The combatants were Cooke and Maple Leaf owner Stafford Smythe. Cooke, the shy, unassuming, self-effacing Los Angeles Bonaparte, was a morning glory, Smythe testified, at Malvern Collegiate in Toronto. Cooke, in rebuttal, deflected such praise as exactly the gratuitous stuff he expected to hear from "the little field marshal." Cooke was peeved at Smythe and the Leafs for reneging on an alleged agreement to leave Red Kelly unprotected until the eighteenth round when the Kings would then draft him as nonplaying coach. Before the eighteenth round came close, Kelly was back on Toronto's protected list. "It was either a double-cross or a monumental mistake," cried Cooke.

Both Cooke and Kelly complained to Clarence Campbell, Red claiming that he had agreed to play one more year for Leafs the previous season with the understanding that they would give him his freedom to accept a job in the new division. The argument was finally settled when the Kings traded their seventeenth round pick, defenseman Ken Block for Kelly. Ironically, their eighteenth round choice, Bill (Cowboy) Flett, who turned out to be one of the bright surprises of the season, was drafted from the Leafs.

Kelly, an all-star defenseman with Detroit in the first part of his career, and a three-time 20-goal man and Stanley Cup star as a center with Toronto in the last portion, is mild-mannered and soft-spoken with a quiet sense of humor. His strongest curseword is "hang" but he can be tough when he has to be. This and his great patience helped him win the respect of the players. In his first season as a coach, the tobacco farmer from Simcoe, Ontario, and former Liberal member of Canadian Parliament from Toronto's York West, proved to be as resourceful as he was in his playing days.

Before their home rink opened the Kings played six home games in the Long Beach Arena and eleven games in the Los Angeles Sports Arena. Nevertheless, they got off to a surprisingly good start. A skating club that could beat you by scoring in bursts, they knocked in four in one period at Chicago; four in 10 minutes in Detroit; and three in six minutes against Oakland. When they beat Toronto 4–1 on November 9, before close to 10,000 Los Angeles customers, Cooke, a former Ontario Hockey Association Junior A player who had laced on skates for the first time in 28 years to lead the Kings onto the ice when they opened their training camp in September, was beside himself with joy. To make it even sweeter, two of the King's goals were scored by speedy Ed Joyal, drafted from the Leafs.

As it became apparent that Los Angeles was nobody's pushover, Cooke offered: "You would have thought that these experts back east would have recognized the advantages in having depth of talent and would have picked my club and the Philadelphia club as the strongest." Jack-laden Jack was referring to the fact that he had shelled out many shekels to Eddie Shore for the franchise of the Springfield Indians of the AHL. (Philadelphia had purchased Quebec of the same league.) One of the players who came with the franchise was six-foot-two defenseman Bill White, who scored 11 goals, 27 assists and compiled 100 penalty minutes in playing all 74 games for the Kings. One of the top defensemen in the West Division, White is not a fast skater but a skillful one with an accurate, if not overpowering, shot.

During the season players were rushed up from Springfield to help Los Angeles out of dry periods like the one in which they managed only two wins and a tie in 13 games—12 of them against expansion opponents. Diminutive winger Howie Menard and defensemen Jim Murray and Brent Hughes were three who answered the call at different intervals. Heavy-hitting rearguard Dave Amadio spent time with the Massachusetts Kings as well as with the Los Angeles crownshirts.

Much of the Kings' success came from unheralded players like Ted Irvine and Bill Flett. Lowell MacDonald, who netted 21 goals, and Joyal, who shot in 23 on his way to 57 points and second place in West Division scoring, were unexpected stars but had played in the NHL before. Irvine, an 18-goal man, and Flett, who led the team with 26, came directly from the Central League.

Flett is called "Cowboy" because of his off-season activities as a calf roper in rodeos in and around Calgary. "It's a tough way to make a buck," he says. "You get bruised up more than in hockey." On the ice, Flett is the bruiser at six-foot-one, 195 pounds. In his first season he acquired 97 minutes in penalties but his strength was put to other uses as well. On March 10 in New York, the Rangers and

Kings were tied 3–3 in the last minute of play. Cowboy, who had gotten Kings' first goal of the game, blew down the right alley, powered his way past defenseman Jim Neilson, and handcuffed Ed Giacomin with a vicious high shot. Flett and the rebound wound up together to the left of the net and, while balanced on one leg, he sailed the puck in before the goalie could recover. There were 20 seconds left to play. The Rangers' season-long Sunday nonlosing streak had been broken, and the Kings had their tenth win over established teams, the best any expansion club achieved in 1967–68.

By the end of November, the Kings, early division leaders, were looking up at the Philadelphia Flyers. They spent the rest of the season that way, except for a brief time when they shared the top spot. Going into their final game they trailed Philly by two points. A win would not only have given them a tie in points but one more victory than the Flyers, who had a final game to play on the following night.

On the evening of March 30, the Kings had a 2–0 lead over the Oakland Seals—the last place team but a particularly tough nut for the Kings to crack—but were tied 2–2. Defenseman Bob Wall shot a third goal for the Kings but it was disallowed because the referee said Flett was in the crease when the puck went in. Cowboy Bill felt the goal should have counted because he was knocked into the crease by Seal defenseman Aut Erickson. "That call cost us a thousand bucks a man," said Kelly, but he will never know how Philadelphia might have played against Pittsburgh the following night if it was necessary for the Flyers to win.

During the regular season, 45 of the Kings' games found the tall, contact-lensed rookie Wayne Rutledge in goal. Terry Sawchuk, injured in training, and again later on in the campaign, played in only 36. Sawchuk's average was 3.07; Rutledge's 2.87. When the playoffs arrived, however, Sawchuk got the call from Red Kelly. Opening at home against the North Stars, terrible-tempered Terry won 2–1 on goals by Joyal and White, and then achieved his twelfth Stanley Cup shutout as MacDonald and Joyal, again, provided the goals. The reputedly loose Los Angeles defense permitted only 18 shots on goal.

Back in Minnesota for games three and four the North Stars rallied for 7–5, 3–2 wins. When the series returned to Los Angeles, Kelly inserted Rutledge and Wayne responded with 27 saves and a 3–2 victory, as Joyal scored his third goal of the playoffs and center Gordon Labossiere, who had only 13 during the pennant race, hit for two. Then, with a chance to wrap it up on the road, the Kings blew a 3–1 lead in the last period and lost it at 9:11 of overtime.

For the seventh and deciding game, Kelly went back to his one-time teammate, the veteran Sawchuk. Disaster struck early as Minnesota took a 3–1 lead by the end of the first period. After Joyal made it 3–2 at 6:12 of the second, the North Stars poured in five goals within eight minutes and finished on the long end of a 9–4 score. As the rout became apparent, Sawchuk was assaulted with refuse and abuse. It demonstrated that in one year, expansion fans had reached parity with the boors who inhabit some of the established division rinks. Before the following season, Sawchuk had departed for a third term in Detroit, traded for young forward Jimmy Peters, son of a man who had been Terry's teammate on the Red Wings in 1950–51.

As bitter as defeat can be in the final game of a series that goes the distance, the Kings had many reasons to exult after their infant season. Picked for last, they had come within an ice-shaving of first; they had a relatively young club; and leaders like Kelly, Regan and—Jack Kent Cooke.

In 1967 Clarence Campbell, talking of St. Louis owner Sid Salomon's power in Democratic Party politics, called him "the only guy in the NHL who can walk into the White House without an invitation." He may have reckoned without the feisty owner of the Kings. Cooke was born pushing and shoving, in the felicitous phrase of David Lilienthal, "as the sparks fly upward." Some observers of the NHL believe he could barge into the White House unannounced, or, in a pinch, buy it.

Cooke has established quantities of brass, but few things he touches have turned to it. He formerly owned the Toronto baseball club, an enterprise that made money under his flashy guidance. He was loud and large in Toronto broadcasting when he owned station CKEY and in Toronto publishing when he was the proprietor of *Liberty* and *Saturday Night*. He subsequently quit his Canadian heritage when he emigrated to Los Angeles to assume United States citizenship.

The NHL's loftiest intellects either knew Cooke before they granted him admission, or they knew about him. Neither condition necessarily led to liking. Certain of the governors manage to conceal their enthusiasm for him pretty well; his swift flair for flamboyance and success annoys other operators who need elbow room for their own conceit. But Cooke was admitted to NHL society because he has other attributes that appeal to the autocratic manner of the governors. He has sufficient power to vote yes or no without referring to a board of directors. He combines the overcharged imagination of a carnival huckster with a business sense sharp enough to beat Old Man Scrooge down to the nearest pfennig.

Cooke's pitch to the governors, during the inaugural expansion meetings, was typically florid. He promised to build an arena that would be his version of the ancient Roman Forum. His plans for the lavish playpen seemed to include shops, a convention center, a railroad station, a public library and recognition of the USA. The arena was built, in the Los Angeles suburb of Inglewood, and opened to noisy fanfare on December 30, 1967. (The Flyers beat the Kings 2–0 before a national TV audience and Cooke displayed his distaste for defeat in a postgame interview.) Cooke authorized a brochure on the building, constructed for $16,000,000 and seating 15,651 for hockey, to proclaim: "The Forum, already internationally known, is acclaimed as the finest arena built since the original Roman Coliseum." The lavish blurb seemed to be slicing the baloney a trifle thick, since the restroom and concession counters appeared inadequate whenever crowds exceeded 5,000. Line-ups were common, just as they must have been when Christians were tossed as tidbits to lions in the days of Rome's depraved nobility.

The day Cooke won his franchise in February 1966 in New York, his big smile was an arch of triumph wrapped around teeth. "I'm an American now," he shouted, "but I feel like I've just been elected King of England!"

The men he joined in the NHL were aware that, if they weren't wary, Cooke could elect them page boys. Staff Smythe managed to strike a philosophical stance: "Oh, you might get scuttled by Cooke, but there's always room for one more in the rat's nest."

There was a certain perversity in the reaction of the other NHL governors to Cooke. They admire Cooke's style of rattle and roll because, in several instances, it matches their own. He may have been dealt in for the cussedness of it. You have to dance with a man before you can step on his feet.

Despite Cooke's decibel count and flair for publicity his team lacked both glitter and oomph. The Kings lost their coach, Red Kelly, to the Pittsburgh Penguins. General manager Larry Regan then took over as coach but the Kings finished out of the playoffs both in 1970 and 1971 and Cooke was a much quieter man as the 1971–72 season began.

Regan continued as coach into that season but eventually was replaced by Fred Glover, deposed leader of the California Golden Seals. The result was a disastrous last-place finish in which their lowly 49 points was 11 less than the sixth-place Seals.

Changes were in order. The first was the retirement of hard-nosed center Bob Pulford from the ice to behind the bench. Using some leaves out of Washington Redskins' coach George Allen's book on conditioning and attitude, Pulford instilled some pride into the Kings. Terry Harper, acquired from Montreal, helped stiffen the defense along with Gilles Marotte. Goals against was cut by 60 from a team high of 305 in 1971–72 as another ex-Canadien, goal-keeper Rogatien Vachon, checked in with a 2.85 average for 53 games. Rookie forwards like Vic Venasky and Don Kozak showed promise and Bob Berry, Mike Corrigan, and Butch Goring scored lots of goals. Big blonde Juha Widing piled up the assists.

Despite an improvement of 24 points, the Kings finished sixth, this time in an eight-horse race. However, they were only three points behind fourth place St. Louis. The effervescent Cooke was slowed by a heart attack but his team's progress was illustrated by fan interest which picked up considerably for the first time since the Kings' bright beginning.

Minnesota North Stars

"SUDDEN DEATH" is a term most often heard in hockey at Stanley Cup playoff time when it is synonymous with the first goal scored in the overtime used to decide tie games. In their first taste of playoff hockey, the Minnesota North Stars were involved in five overtime games, winning two and losing three, but they suffered their biggest loss of the season in the early morning hours of January 15, 1968 when 29-year-old Bill Masterton died from a massive internal brain injury sustained in a game against Oakland two days before.

If Masterton's death was not exactly sudden, the injury that made it almost immediately inevitable happened with a swiftness cloaked in the routine. With four minutes gone in the game, Masterton moved toward the Oakland goal and slid a pass to his right wing, Wayne Connelly. As he did, he was checked by Seal forward Ron Harris, bounced off Seal defenseman Larry Cahan and went catapulting backward, striking his head on the ice with such impact that blood gushed from his ears and nose. Connelly, rushing to aid him, heard Masterton murmur, "Never again, never again."

At Fairview-Southdale Hospital in Minneapolis, where Masterton lay unconscious for 30 hours before dying, five doctors, including two neurosurgeons, were powerless to help him by operating, owing to the seriousness and nature of the injury. In the tragedy's aftermath some Minnesota players mentioned that Masterton had complained of dizziness after being checked heavily in a game against

Boston, two weeks earlier, but had not reported it to the management. There is credibility in the double injury theory. When North Star general manager-coach Wren Blair described the fatal play, he said: "He hit so hard that I'm sure he was unconscious before he fell. I've never seen anyone go down that way."

The violent body contact of hockey and the speed at which the game is played have often caused people to wonder why there aren't more fatalities.

On March 6, 1907, Owen (Bud) McCourt, the leading scorer for the eastern Ontario town of Cornwall, was killed in the old Federal Amateur Hockey League. The league, comprising Cornwall, Ottawa Vics, Montagnards and Morrisburg, was an ancestral association of the NHL.

Early in the second half of a game which Cornwall won, 11–3; McCourt began to brawl with Art Throop of Ottawa. Several players intervened, including Charles Masson of Ottawa.

McCourt was removed from the game with a severe cut on his head and, after falling unconscious, was taken to the hospital. He died the following morning.

A coroner's inquest, presided over by Dr. C. J. Hamilton of Cornwall, issued a solemn verdict:

"That Owen McCourt came to his death by a blow from a hockey stick in the hands of Charles Masson during the progress of a game of hockey played in the Victoria rink in the town of Cornwall March 6, 1907. And, that in the opinion of this jury, although there is no evidence of ill feeling previous to the assault, there was no justification by personal provocation for the blow at the hands of the said Charles Masson. After hearing the evidence, your jury recommends that legislation be enacted whereby players or spectators encouraging or engaging in rough or foul play may be severely punished."

Masson, the defendant, was subsequently arraigned on a charge of murder. He was represented before a Magistrate Danis by lawyers R. A. Pringle and J. A. Chisholm. James Dingwall, the county attorney acting for the Crown, strenuously objected when the charge was reduced to manslaughter.

The manslaughter charge was tried before Judge Magee and a jury in Cornwall on April 10, 1907. The witnesses included referee Emmett Quinn, Zian Runnions, Alfred Young, Jack Williams, John Ryan and William Bannerman.

Several witnesses swore that McCourt was struck by another Ottawa player before Masson's blow. Judge Magee, uncertain which stick assault had been fatal, acquitted Masson on April 12.

There is no record of Masson having played organized hockey again.

The NHL has had several near misses in its 52-year span, with Ace Bailey, Gordie Howe and several other less celebrated close calls, but until Masterton's death no one had ever been killed in a league game. Almost immediately there was a clamor that the wearing of protective helmets be made a league rule. Like all college players, Masterton had worn one when he played for the University of Denver but discarded it after he joined the professionals.

Bobby Hull, the Chicago supershooter, testified: "We should all be wearing them, except we're just too damn vain."

Hull's slick playmate, Stan Mikita, managed to contain his vanity. "I plan to wear one from now on," he promised. "I want to spend the summers cutting grass instead of pushing up daisies."

Mikita maintained his promise for the balance of the 1967–68 season. He encouraged his wings, Doug Mohns and Ken Wharram, to also wear helmets—a circumstance that prompted reporters to call them the Head Line.

Canadiens' Bobby Rousseau had abandoned his helmet in mid-season, before the unfortunate incident, but he didn't return to it. "I agree everybody should wear a helmet," said Rousseau. "But I gave up mine when I was playing badly and my play has improved since then. I don't know how to put it, but with the helmet on, I couldn't sense players coming from behind. Without it, I can sense they are there." Traded to Minnesota in 1970, he donned it again.

In the generations since Owen McCourt's death, players added shoulder pads, kidney pads, shin guards, ankle guards and instep shields to their equipment. The padded armor weighs about 25 pounds. But until Masterton's death, 61 years after McCourt's, few professionals wore protectors for their face and head. There was no agreement that helmets should be mandatory, even after the Masterton fatality.

Clarence Campbell spoke with presidential authority. "Masterton's accident was a normal hazard of our business. Serious situations like it have been rare in the NHL because of the inordinate skill of the players."

The NHL's dean of boys added: "There have always been some critics who demand helmets. The fact is that the very best ones money can buy are available to the teams, if the players want them. It's an optional thing. It was tried one time in 1933, after Ace Bailey's injury, but the experiment was a dismal failure. Some players just won't wear a helmet."

Ironically, if not for expansion, Masterton would probably be alive today. The formation of the new division, which doubled the employment opportunities in the NHL, was the incentive that brought back a man who had been out of professional hockey for four years. After finishing sixth in American Hockey League scoring race as a member of the Cleveland Barons in 1962–63, Masterton played only for the United States National team in the hours after his regular job in contract administration at Honeywell.

Although he scored only four goals and eight assists with the North Stars, Masterton was considered a big asset to the team by Wren Blair. "Because he had the habit of giving it everything he had for every second he was on the ice," said Blair, "Bill was the type of hockey player who didn't have to score a lot of goals to help a club." After the 1967–68 season the NHL Writers Association created a Bill Masterton Memorial Award to be given to the player who most fit the description "unsung hero." Claude Provost of Canadiens was the first recipient.

The tragedy hit the North Stars hard. Blair talked about it on the plane as he headed for the All-Star Game in Toronto. "It's a terrible thing, tragic. I haven't slept in three days. I got the final word early this morning, but I waited up until about seven o'clock before I woke the players to tell them. They took it pretty badly."

Minnesota proceeded to lose their next six games. They seemed to be in a state of shock. But they regrouped under the highly resourceful, volatile Blair to win six out of their next seven games and maintain second place at a time when it was possible for them to skid to fifth in a tightly packed race. From training camp on, Blair, renowned as the discoverer of Bobby Orr, manipulated and juggled his line-up with the skill of a master prestidigitator. The man who won Canada's Allan Cup with the Whitby Dunlops in 1956 and 1958, and the World Championship at Oslo with the same team in the latter year, later guided the Boston farm team at Kingston, Ontario, in the Eastern Professional League to regular season and playoff titles in 1962–63. He is eminently qualified to handle his dual role of general manager-coach. In fact, at the time he was running the Dunlops, he was directing the Clinton Comets of the Eastern League to a championship.

Blair demonstrated from the start that he would not tolerate any nonsense. When veterans Pete Goegan and Len Lunde didn't like their contracts, he fined them and let them stew. When Goegan did finally report he never did attain top shape, and after working as fifth defenseman and warming the bench, he ended in the minors where Lunde had long since departed. The North Stars, an offensive-minded team, had trouble with their backline. Elmer (Moose) Vasko, coaxed out of retirement, was slow to round into form, and Jean-Guy Talbot, failing to impress, was traded to Detroit for Bob McCord.

Forwards like Ted Taylor, Duke Harris and André Prononvost shuttled between the North Stars and the minors, and 19-goal-man Parker MacDonald spent time with the Memphis South Stars before rejoining the parent club. After Masterton's death, Blair obtained the services of slick playmaker Bronco Horvath on loan from Rochester for a brief spell. When the going got sticky, he didn't hesitate to call up from Memphis George Standing and Ted Mc-Caskill, two men who had been in the Eastern League the year before. What proved to be his best move was a midseason deal in which he obtained forwards Milan Marcetta and Jean-Paul Parise from Rochester in exchange for Taylor, Harris, Lunde, Murray Hall and Don Johns. Marcetta, in his first shot at the majors, capped the season with seven goals in the playoffs; Parise, a hard worker in the corners, who had been cut by the Oakland Seals in training camp, had 11 goals and 16 assists in 43 games.

Blair had not done too badly in the draft, either. Selectees such as Wayne Connelly, Ray Cullen, André Boudrias, Dave Balon and Mike McMahon all had productive seasons. Connelly, on the verge of stardom with Boston, came into his own at Minnesota, firing 35 goals to lead the West Division in that department. Cullen, drafted from Detroit, scored 28 as he and the French Flyer, Boudrias, each produced 53 points. McMahon, a wily puck handler who had failed to make it in New York as a raw rookie a few seasons before, led all defensemen of both divisions in scoring with 14 goals and 47 points. But, eventually, all but Cullen were sent to other clubs.

Criticized for plucking Cesare Maniago from New York, Blair's judgment was upheld by the fine play of the dinosaurian netminder, who compiled a 2.77 average in playing more games, 52, than any other goaler besides Ed Giacomin or Charlie Hodge. Three of his six shutouts were in the middle of a scoreless streak of 188 minutes and 37 seconds that stretched from 16:28 of the third period against

Pittsburgh on December 10 to 5:06 of the first period with Philadelphia on December 21. Enroute, Cesare froze out Los Angeles twice and Oakland once.

North Star governor Gordon Ritz, a former center ice man at Yale before moving into radio and television in Minneapolis, praised Blair for his acumen. "I'm not denying that some of our high draft choices didn't pan out," he admitted, "but I wish more people would give Wren credit for quickly recognizing this and doing something about it. In this regard I compare him to the shrewd merchant who sees that a certain brand of goods isn't selling, so he marks the goods down for a quick sale in order to at least get some of his investment out of it."

Ritz also nominated Blair's predraft agreement with Canadiens' general manager Sammy Pollock as NHL "deal of the year." By promising not to touch Claude Larose and pick Dave Balon instead, North Stars were able to purchase Boudrias and McMahon from Montreal. In the 1968 draft, Blair caught up to Larose. In order to bolster his defense corps (the Stars had given up 226 goals, the high in the West Division), he also picked up the Hillman brothers, Wayne from New York and Larry from Toronto, and Duane Rupp from Maple Leafs. He felt secure enough to trade his captain, Bob Woytowich, to Pittsburgh for a 1972 draft choice.

Blair did not have his owners buy a minor league team as Los Angeles and Philadelphia did because he considered it "financially unsound." Instead he acquired the rights to eight members of the Canadian National Amateur team and one United States team player. "With the extra players we now have," Blair claimed in October 1967, "players we bought or borrowed, I have stocked Memphis. I can finish fifth and make more money than Los Angeles can by finishing first."

Blair was able to make this claim because of the nature of the Minnesota franchise. The Metropolitan Sports Center, where the North Stars skate, was built for $6,000,000—approximately one-third of the cost of the Los Angeles Forum—in suburban Bloomington, adjacent to Metropolitan Stadium, home of the baseball Twins and football Vikings. From the first announcement that Minnesota would have an NHL team, enthusiasm ran high and season tickets sales soared. Minnesota has long been a hotbed of hockey in the United States. Most of the American players to reach the majors have been Minnesotans like Cully Dahlstrom, Doc Romnes, Sammy LoPresti, Mike Karakas, Frank Brimsek, and Tommy Williams.

In the days after World War I, in the old Central League, stars like Frank (Moose) Goheen, Ivan (Ching) Johnson, Taffy Abel, Tiny Thompson and Cooney Weiland thrilled northern fans. All made it to the majors except Goheen, who declined to leave Minnesota when drafted by the Bruins in 1925, but he is in the Hall of Fame along with Johnson, Thompson and the home-grown Brimsek.

Another Minnesota product to make his mark in the NHL was the colorful, hard-rock defenseman, Johnny Mariucci from Eveleth, who starred with the Chicago Black Hawks before and after World War II. From 1952 to 1966 he served as ice coach of the University of Minnesota where he had played on the unbeaten 1940 AAU hockey champions and, under Bernie Bierman, as an end on the Big Ten champion football teams of 1937 and 1938. As director of United States player development for the North Stars and, later, assistant to the general manager, Mariucci is a fine representative of Minnesota's hockey tradition.

The president of the North Stars, likeable, gentlemanly Walter Bush, is another Minnesota native who has been actively involved with hockey on many levels for a long time. A former Dartmouth player, lawyer Bush organized and later ran the United States Central League in the 1950s; then coached the Minneapolis club of that league from 1958 through 1962. He also managed the United States National team in 1959 and their Olympic team in 1964. Since 1959 Bush has been a director of the Amateur Hockey Association of the United States.

Although Minnesota sagged at the end of 1967–68 to finish fourth, they rallied in the playoffs. They eliminated Los Angeles in a tough, seven-game series, fighting back from 2–0 and 3–2 positions. Marcetta won game six with an overtime goal and then the Stars routed the Kings in Los Angeles, 9–4. In an even more gruelling set with St. Louis, the North Stars played only two home games due to the presence of an ice show at Sports Center. Nevertheless, they carried the Blues to seven games before bowing 2–1 in double overtime. The series had four overtime games in all, only one of which the North Stars won. However, in Bill Goldsworthy, they had the leading Stanley Cup scorer of goals (eight) and points (15). They also uncovered a 20-year-old rookie center, Walt McKechnie, who came up from the Phoenix Roadrunners to score three goals and two assists in nine games.

From the beginning of the season the fans turned out in great numbers—the North Stars led the West Division in average attend-

ance with 11,762 per game—but they were not too vocal until Blair
chided them. After reading his criticisms of their quiet rooting, they
littered the ice with programs and newspaper in protest of Bill
Friday's officiating during a 3–2 loss to Pittsburgh and were silent
nevermore.

Most of the North Stars enjoyed being in the cold climate. One
was André Boudrias, who had played in Houston for two years and
had found it strange to come out of a swimming pool and on to an
ice rink. When André Pronovost was called up from Memphis, he,
too, was happy. He said that the cold weather made him feel more
like playing, that his three sons would get more ice time in the vast
amateur hockey programs that operate in the Minneapolis-St. Paul
area, and that his wife liked the change. "The only fur she could
wear in Memphis," said Pronovost, "was her mink stole."

Players such as Boudrias came and went as the North Stars
attempted to gain an air of respectability which eluded them until
the 1970–71 season. Having failed previously to hire a truly sound
hockey coach, manager Wren Blair finally found his man in 1970
when he appointed Jack Gordon to the post.

A veteran of the American League managing and coaching wars,
Gordon had spent several years as aide to Rangers manager Emile
Francis. By hiring Gordon, Blair infused the North Stars with a
healthy helping of class. He also, via the trade route, obtained several new faces, including defenseman Ted Harris, who became the
team captain, Doug Mohns and Ted Hampson. These veterans
complimented such venerable types as goalies Gump Worsley and
Cesare Maniago as well as young talents such as Jude Drouin and
Danny Grant.

Although they finished fourth in the West Division, the North
Stars rose and smote the heavily favored St. Louis Blues in the opening round of the Stanley Cup playoffs and then encountered the
Montreal Canadiens. The North Stars lost in six games but gained
new esteem by their strong showing.

They followed this by their strongest showing since coming into
the league—86 points and a second-place finish—but their old
adversaries, the St. Louis Blues, eliminated them in sudden death
of the seventh game of the first Stanley Cup round.

In 1972–73 they garnered 85 points, only eight behind first-place
Chicago and the same number attained by the Philadelphia Flyers,
but finished third because they lost the season's series to the
Flyers. This pointed up another one of those little, irritating in-

equities in the NHL system. Each team won all its home games against the other during the regular season but there were three played in Philly and only two in Bloomington.

Minnesota managed to win one at the Spectrum during the play-off round but the Flyers won two in Minny as well as two at home for a 4–2 edge.

Before the regular campaign ended, an injured Gump Worsley retired for the umpteenth time. For once it seemed like it might stick but in May 1973 he announced that he would return to share the North Stars' nets with Cesare Maniago, who posted two shut-outs in the playoffs. This enabled them to trade young Gilles Gilbert to Boston for crack center Fred Stanfield. Up front, tough guy Dennis Hextall blossomed as the team's scoring leader with 82 points, followed by Jean-Paul Parise, Drouin, and Grant. The North Stars' biggest problem seemed to be the weighting of their youth-experience balance too heavily on the latter side of the scale.

California Golden Seals

IN THE *Hockey News* poll of writers held prior to the start of
the 1967–68 season, only three writers figured that the California
Seals—as they were then called—would finish out of the playoffs.
No one thought that they would finish last, and seven writers gave
them sufficient first-place votes to make them the consensus choice
to lead the expansion division in its first year of competition. What
was it that made everyone regard the Seals so highly? Why was it
that they were so wrong? In a season that found only six points
separating the first- and fifth-place teams, the Seals were 20 points
in the cellar.

The masters of hindsight trace the root of the Seals' problems
to the firing of general manager Rudy Pilous by Barend (Barry)
Van Gerbig, the then-28-year-old owner of the team. Jet setter Van
Gerbig, who owns pieces of Standard Oil of New Jersey and Union
Carbide, resembles a blond beachboy just in from the surf. He
played goal for the varsity team at Princeton and graduated to marry
the daughter of Douglas Fairbanks Jr. His godfather is Bing Crosby.

Writer Stewart Warner, in the *Toronto Star Weekly*, described
Van Gerbig as "something of an absentee owner—he missed Oakland's 6–0 victory over Los Angeles, which snapped their 11-game
winless streak, because he was helping organize the Crosby golf
tournament. But he kept sufficiently in touch with the team to
decide he didn't like Pilous's style."

When Bert Olmstead sat down at the Montreal draft meeting of
June 1967, he had been general manager-coach of the Seals for a

month. Without an astute general manager, armed with informed scouting reports, Olmstead was like a total paraplegic at a grab bag. What he got was a gaggle of over-30 hockeyists who would soon prove that they could play like over-40s bearing no resemblance to Gordie Howe. That the Seals had also drafted the young sons of old-time greats King Clancy, Babe Pratt and Bryan Hextall, would not help them either.

One of the main reasons for the optimistic preseason evaluation of the Bay Area team was their supposedly solid defense. In goal they had Charlie Hodge, who had starred with the Canadiens; on the blue line experienced hands like Bobby Baun and Kent Douglas of Toronto and Larry Cahan, a man with NHL experience who had been outstanding in the Western League for the past two seasons. Hodge held up well under heavy duress. He played in 58 contests— only Ed Giacomin appeared in more—and allowed only 2.86 goals per game. He might have done better with more help from his friends. In October, Olmstead said of Douglas: "Kent should be the best pointman on the power play and one of the best at getting the puck out of his zone in the league." Later he was traded to Detroit for forwards Ted Hampson and John Brenneman and defenseman Bert Marshall; he wound up the season with the unique distinction of playing 76 games in a 74-game schedule.

Hampson finished as the Seals leading scorer but he arrived too late and there were not enough of his ilk. Toronto veteran Billy Harris started well but soon became very unhappy. Another center, Wally Boyer, drafted from Chicago, didn't find himself until the last part of the season. The team's leading goal scorer, Billy Hicke, was troubled by an asthma condition that benched him for various stretches. He still managed to knock home 21 of the Seals league low of 153. Gerry Ehman potted 19.

In addition to their 11-game nonwinning skein, the Seals also put a string together that totalled 14, including 13 losses in succession. The flinty Olmstead was wearing a deep rut behind the Seals' bench with his bemused travels up and down, past the backs of his stalwarts. As a player with Montreal and Toronto, Dirty Bertie, as the hostile fans in other cities referred to him, was a fiercely serious competitor who equated losing with something infinitesimally close to dying. He had been known to fight with teammates if he felt they weren't pulling their weight, and reputedly once tussled with Maurice Richard himself in the Canadien dressing room when he pointed his finger at the Rocket for making the mistake that sent

Montreal down to defeat. In the fifties he particularly infuriated New York fans, who regarded him as an intimidator of smaller men who would hide, taunting, behind linesmen when Rangers' destroyer of Canadiens, Lou Fontinato, was nearby. They retold stories of Olmstead's alleged beating of a Pullman porter with incriminating glee and chimed in with a chorus of "I-told-you-soes" when he was forced to report late to the Maple Leafs before the 1958 season, because he was answering an assault charge in Vancouver, involving a gentleman of small size. Sneaky and mean, but a superb playmaker who excelled in the heavy going of the corners, Olmstead expected the same kind of dedication when he became a coach. At Vancouver in the Western League he had finished third and then guided his team to the playoff finals before being defeated by Seattle.

The play of the Seals rankled Olmstead. "They're just not trying," he said. "I've tried everything to get them to snap out of it. I've insulted and I've threatened. But they've just quit." In another enlightened moment he added: "If I was a player, I don't even know whether I'd want to be associated with this bunch. I'd be tossing a few of them out of that dressing room on their cans. They have no pride. A lot of them are getting a chance of a lifetime, and they're reacting like playing in the NHL is a prison sentence."

During a Christmas night brawl with the Bruins, Bert Murray Olmstead from Scepter, Saskatchewan, waved a wand in the form of a hockey stick as he chased a belligerent Bruin fan along the Boston Garden ice level and was fined by Clarence Campbell for his intent. Nothing he did roused his club and, in February, Bert escaped from his prison behind the bench and turned the line-changing and pacing over to his assistant general manager-coach, Gordie Fashoway. Several faces relaxed and, coincidentally, Billy Harris returned. Olmstead not only alienated his players. He locked the dressing room door to reporters and wouldn't reveal his home phone number. Former Western League star Eddie Dorohoy offered this characterization of Bertie: "If Olmstead did public relations for Santa Claus, there wouldn't be any Christmas."

Part of the Seals' attendance problems—and this could have been cured with a few wins—was concerned with which specific area they were to pledge allegiance. They had inherited the nickname of the old San Francisco entry in the Western League but were playing their games in the new Oakland-Alameda County Coliseum Arena. The Cow Palace in San Francisco where the old Seals cavorted had been rejected as a home because of poor sight lines. By November, the team that had been named the California Seals, in order to represent both San Francisco and Oakland, became the Oakland Seals. "It was the desire of the league that we try to identify with San Francisco," Van Gerbig explained. "This is a different situation from Minneapolis and St. Paul. The only way we could identify with both cities would be to play in the middle of the bridge. There should be no kidding ourselves. We're Oakland."

In the 1946 edition of James C. Hendy's *Official Hockey Guide*, issued prior to the start of the 1945–46 season, there is an interesting paragraph in the report on the old Pacific Coast Hockey League by its then president George J. Campbell. It read: "Added interest in the popular ice sport was injected into the game when it was disclosed that the Oakland entry, which formerly played all its games in San Francisco's Winterland, this year will be based in Oakland at the Ice Arena. Negotiations for the transfer began last year when Oak fans swarmed across the bay for Oak home games." In 1967 there were no swarms of San Franciscans crossing over the bridge nor were there hordes of nearby Oaklanders traveling to the County Arena. An exception was Charles Schulz, creator of *Peanuts*, who would drive 60 miles to see the Seals.

As early in the season as November there were rumors that Van Gerbig had threatened to move the Seals out of California if attendance didn't improve. By the time the Board of Governors convened for their March meeting in New York, there had been feelers to the Seals from Labatt Breweries of Canada Ltd., and two wealthy Canadians, Max Bell of Calgary and Frank McMahon of Vancouver. Labatt offered a loan of $680,000 (the amount that the league specified that the Seals had to come up with by May 15) in order to move the franchise to Vancouver. Other interested bidders were Mel Swig, former owner of the old San Francisco Seals of the Western League; Ralph Wilson, owner of the Buffalo Bills football team; and Charles Finley, owner of the Oakland A's baseball club.

At the meeting a move to Vancouver was vetoed by an 8–4 vote. The league could still become healthy, and they were in no mood to depart from a large population area so vital to any television plans. (The CBS TV contract specifically stipulated the inclusion of the Bay area.) In August the Seals were purchased by the owners of the Harlem Globetrotters, Potter Palmer and George Gillett of Chicago, and John O'Neil Jr. of Miami. (They were aided by the loan from Labatt.) The three also have financial interests in the

Atlanta Braves, the Miami Dolphins and the Atlanta Chiefs soccer team. Palmer and O'Neil had been partners, along with Van Gerbig, in the original Seal franchise. It was announced that Van Gerbig's future association with the team would be in an advisory capacity only. President Frank Selke Jr. became the general manager and a new man was hired to replace Bert Olmstead. He was Fred Glover.

Glover, a player-coach during the last six of his 16 seasons with the Cleveland Barons, was voted "most valuable player" seven times in the AHL and holds numerous scoring records in that league. Called "No Kid Glover," in deference to his toughness during his playing days, the new Seals' coach is another who actively detests losing but he is not in the brooding mold of Olmstead. Canadiens' tough guy John Ferguson, who played under Glover at Cleveland, salutes him when he says, "Glover influenced me a lot. He's the greatest competitor I've ever seen. I saw him get beaten in some fights and then go right back in and tangle with the same guy in the next game. I learned a lot from him. I'll always remember his advice 'never let anyone fight you off the puck.'" At Cleveland, Glover reputedly would fine any player $100 if he was caught talking to a member of the opposition.

Before the 1968–69 season, Glover was not the only new face in the Seals' dressing room. Only seven of the 20 originally drafted by the club remained. It was hoped that Bryan Watson and Carol Vadnais, drafted from Canadiens, and Gary Jarrett and Doug Roberts, acquired from Detroit for Bobby Baun, would help Glover move the Seals upward.

In front of the nets, Glover inherited, in addition to the diminutive Charlie Hodge, the six-foot-three Gary Smith. Smith, while promising, had, in his first season, an alarming tendency to stickhandle the puck across his blue line. Symbolic of the Seals NHL debut was one of his rushes. He had outskated two of his teammates.

Few NHL goalies ever were bombarded the way Smith was during the 1969–70 and 1970–71 seasons. Prior to the latter campaign, Charles Finley, owner of the Oakland Athletics, bought the NHL club and changed its name to California Golden Seals. He added colored skates, new jerseys and several other gimmicks but the Seals finished with the worst record of either division.

With the help of a big trade with the Bruins, engineered by general manager Garry Young, former Boston Director of Player Personnel, that sent Vadnais and winger Don O'Donoghue for forward Reg Leach and defensemen Bob Stewart and Rick Smith,

THE TEAMS

Art Ross, former manager and one of the key developers of the Boston Bruins, receives Hall of Fame plaque from NHL president Clarence Campbell on September 1, 1959. The league now commemorates Ross by naming a trophy, for scoring leadership, in his name. He also was inventor of the modern puck now in general use.

(Courtesy of Dick Beddoes)

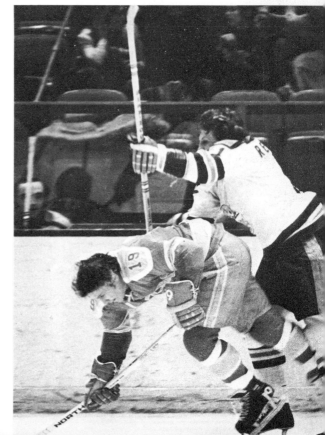

John McKenzie, player of the Vancouver Blazers (left) bounced by Craig Reichmuth of the New York Golden Blades
(Courtesy of Stan Fischler)

Two of Chicago's greatest scorers, Max Bentley (center) and Doug Bentley (right), are escorted by former Toronto player and coach Joe Primeau. The Bentley brothers played together with the Black Hawks in the early and mid-forties until Max was traded to Toronto in 1947.
(Courtesy of Dick Beddoes)

Bobby Hull (left), and Stan Mikita, one-two supershooters of Chicago Black Hawks, pictured in 1963-64 season. *(Courtesy of Dick Beddoes)*

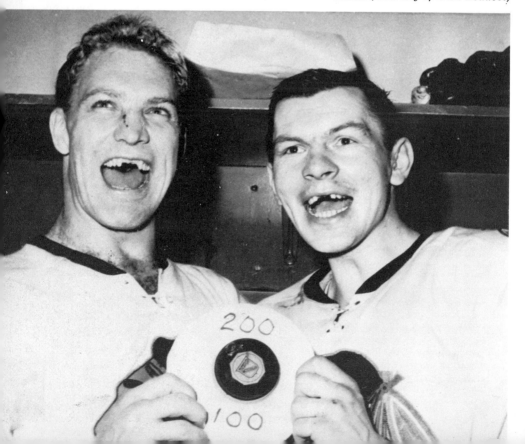

Hank Bassen, former goaltender with the Detroit Red Wings, makes an extraordinary save on Boston Bruin forward Wayne Connelly, while Detroit defenseman Howie Young looks on.
(Courtesy of Stan Fischler)

Jack Adams (right), former manager and coach of the Detroit Red Wings, receives testimonial tray from Red Dutton, former defenseman with the New York Americans who later became president of the NHL. *(Courtesy of Dick Beddoes)*

Hector (Toe) Blake with three players prominent in five consecutive Cup triumphs for Montreal between 1955 and 1960. The three, from left, are Jacques Plante, Rocket Richard and Bernard (Boom Boom) Geoffrion. Canadiens won eight Stanley Cups in 13 years under Blake's guidance. *(Courtesy of Dick Beddoes)*

Two outstanding goalies for Montreal Canadiens, Jacques Plante (left) and Bill Durnan. Plante pioneered the use of a mask. As Canadiens, both men won the Vezina Trophy six times as the best players at their position. Plante won it a seventh time in a spectacular comeback with St. Louis Blues in 1968-69. *(Courtesy of Dick Beddoes)*

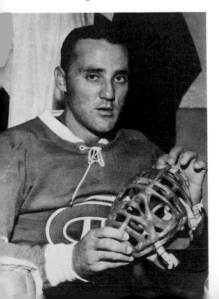
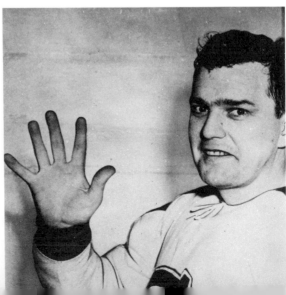

"Le Gros Bill," Jean Beliveau, captain and supercenter of the Montreal Canadiens, hems in rising New York Ranger star Walt Tkaczuk. Twice winner of the Hart Trophy, Beliveau scored the sudden-death goal in double overtime that eliminated the Boston Bruins from the 1969 Stanley Cup playoffs. He retired to the Canadiens' front office after Montreal's Cup win in 1971. (Courtesy of Dan Baliotti)

Davey Kerr, the first New York Ranger goalie in the club's history to win the Vezina Trophy, kicked too late on this shot by Paul Haynes of the Montreal Canadiens. The Rangers, however, won the game, 7–3, at New York in January 1939. (Courtesy of Stan Fischler)

All-time New York Ranger scoring leader Andy Bathgate rifles a shot into the lower corner past Montreal Canadiens' goalie Jacques Plante's outstretched glove. Canadien defenseman Dollard St. Laurent is at Bathgate's left. (Courtesy of Stan Fischler)

Goalie Ed Giacomin comes out of his crease to make a diving save. Defenseman Arnie Brown kneels at right. Giacomin was first team all-star in 1966–67 and second all-star for the next three seasons. In 1970–71 he again made first team and shared the Vezina Trophy with Gilles Villemure.
(Courtesy of Orazio Belfiore)

Fiery Phil Watson, former New York Ranger center, who as their coach steered them into the play-offs three consecutive seasons from 1955–56 through 1957–58.
(Courtesy of Stan Fischler)

Roy (Shrimp) Worters, one of the smallest—and finest—goaltenders in NHL history, sprawls to kick the puck away at Madison Square Garden during a game against the Boston Bruins. Notice that both a member of the Americans at the left and the Bruins on the right are wearing baseball caps—a common sight in the late twenties and early thirties. *(Courtesy of Stan Fischler)*

The Original Kid Line of hockey consisted of (left to right) Charlie Conacher, Harvey (Busher) Jackson and Joe Primeau, who guided the Toronto Maple Leaf attack in the early thirties. Primeau later became Leaf coach. *(Courtesy of Dick Beddoes)*

Four keys to the Toronto Maple Leaf kingdom: (left to right) Babe Pratt, Ted Kennedy, Conn Smythe and Max Bentley. Pratt starred for the Leafs in the early forties, while Kennedy and Bentley played for the Toronto 1947–48 club which won the Stanley Cup. Smythe was one of the founders of the Leafs and also was a manager and president of the team. *(Courtesy of Dick Beddoes)*

Walter (Turk) Broda, considered one of the finest goaltenders in NHL history and the goaltender on the Toronto Maple Leaf team that won three consecutive Stanley Cups in 1947, 1948 and 1949. Broda was renowned for his ability to play well in clutch games. *(Courtesy of Dick Beddoes)*

Here, Broda drops to one knee while making a save against New York Ranger left-wing Lynn Patrick during a game at Madison Square Garden in 1938. Patrick is being taken out of the play by Toronto defenseman Reg Hamilton.

(Courtesy of Stan Fischler)

George Armstrong, captain of the Toronto Maple Leafs during the sixties, carries the Stanley Cup through a crowd celebrating the Leafs' Stanley Cup victory in 1962. Running interference for Armstrong on the right is Harold Ballard, executive vice-president of the Leafs. *(Courtesy of Dick Beddoes)*

Rangy Ken Dryden came out of Cornell University to lead the Montreal Canadiens to the Stanley Cup in 1971 and capture the Conn Smythe Trophy as the outstanding performer in the playoffs. In 1971–72 he took down the Calder Trophy as best rookie and in 1972–73 won the Vezina Trophy as top goaltender before backstopping the Canadiens to another Cup triumph in the spring of 1973. (*Daniel S. Baliotti*)

New York Islanders' first-round, amateur draft choice in 1972, bonus baby Billy Harris started slowly in his and the Islanders' initial season but came on to lead the club in scoring with 28 goals and 50 points. His strong performance with a weak team marked him as one of the stars of the future.

(*Daniel S. Baliotti*)

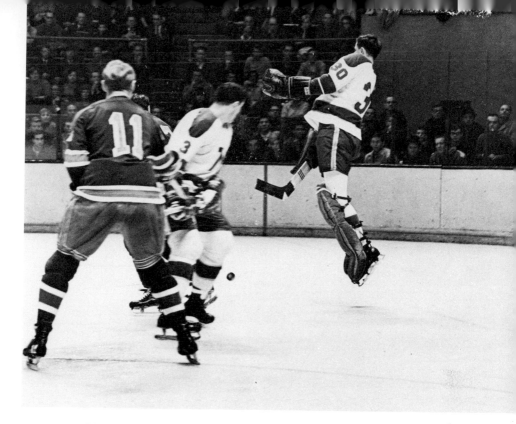

TWO WAYS OF MAKING A SAVE: HIGH AND LOW
HIGH

Minnesota North Star goaltender Cesare Maniago makes jump save against New York Rangers. Ranger forward (number 11) is Vic Hadfield. North Star defenseman (number 3) is Bob McCord. (*Courtesy of Orazio Belfiore*)

LOW

This time Maniago does a split as he gloves puck spectacularly. Minnesota defenseman (number 6) is Mike McMahon; New York wing is Bob Nevin (number 8).

(*Courtesy of Orazio Belfiore*)

The Oakland–Alameda County Coliseum Arena, familiarly known as the "Jewel Box," where the California Golden Seals play the majority of their home games.
(Courtesy of the California Golden Seals)

The Spectrum, Philadelphia's $12,000,000 sports and entertainment center, pictured while under construction. It opened in September 1967. Early in 1968 heavy winds tore holes in its roof, causing the Flyers to take to the road for an extensive period.
(Courtesy of the Philadelphia Flyers)

Philadelphia Flyers' Pat Hannigan is stopped by Pittsburgh Penguins' goalie Les Binkley during first game ever played at the Philadelphia arena, the Spectrum. *(Courtesy of the Philadelphia Flyers)*

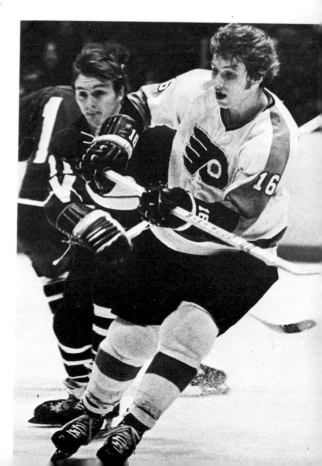

Bobby Clarke, young ice leader of the Philadelphia Flyers who finished second to Phil Esposito in the NHL scoring race with 37 goals and 67 assists. Despite a diabetic condition, Clarke shows amazing stamina, killing penalties and appearing on the power play, as well as taking his regular turn.

(Photo: Dan Baliotti)

Former Philadelphia defenseman Larry (the Rock) Zeidel, center of many an ice imbroglio. Zeidel sat out the 1968–69 season rather than report to the minor leagues. He then retired from hockey to take a job as a stockbroker and also worked as a color commentator for Flyer TV games in 1971–72. *(Courtesy of the Philadelphia Flyers)*

Ron Ward, one of the great success stories in the WHA's maiden season, just after registering his 100th point of the season on March 3, 1973 at Madison Square Garden against the Cleveland Crusaders. Bob Whidden is the goalie at left. Defenseman Wayne Muloin, at right, has tried unsuccessfully to fill in for the wandering Whidden. Before the 1973-74 campaign, Ward's New York Raiders became the Golden Blades and traded him to the Vancouver (formerly Philadelphia) Blazers for the man who topped him in the scoring race, 124 to 118, Andre Lacroix. *(Harvey Cohen)*

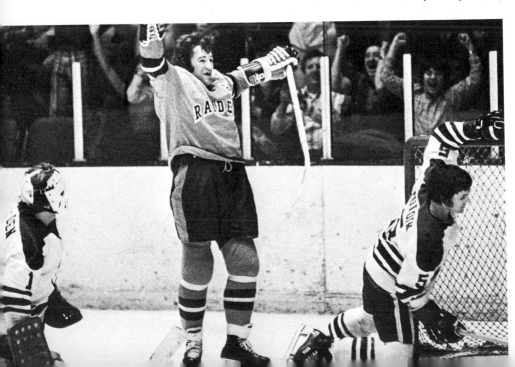

Center Andre Lacroix, who had three 20-goal seasons with the Philadelphia Flyers of the NHL, vegetated with the Chicago Black Hawks in 1971-72 and then jumped to the Philadelphia Blazers of the WHA where he commenced to lead the new league in scoring with 124 points. (*Courtesy of New York Golden Blades*)

Ted Green, captain of the New England Whalers, winners of the first Avco World Trophy, emblematic of the World Hockey Association championship. Green, cast off by the Boston Bruins, played very steadily in anchoring the Whalers' defense through divisional and playoff triumphs. (*Courtesy of New England Whalers*)

Pittsburgh's $22,000,000 Civic Arena, sometimes called the "Igloo" because of its shape. The team name of Penguins derives in part from this. Main business district of city is located a few blocks away. *(Courtesy of the Pittsburgh Penguins)*

the Seals improved. For a while it looked as if they might make the playoffs but they slumped and missed by seven points. Vic Stasiuk had replaced Glover early in the campaign but he was fired to let Young take over a dual role for 1972–73. Then the team was wrecked by wholesale jumping to the WHA. The Seals lost top defenseman Paul Shmyr and forwards Tom Webster, Gerry Pinder, Norm Ferguson, Bobby Sheehan, and Wayne Carleton and once more fell to last while winning a mere 11 games. Young, who Finley claimed had signed players to exorbitant contracts without his knowledge (if he had done more of this the Seals might have maintained their team), was let out and Glover, fresh from a release by the WHA Cleveland Crusaders, was rehired.

Amid rumors of more defections and the possibility of Finley selling the club, the Seals pointed toward 1973–74 by signing some of their top players like rookie sensation Hilliard Graves, Craig Patrick, Walt McKechnie, and Bob Stewart. A better showing figured to help sagging attendance but in the long run the solution seemed to center around a move back across the bridge to San Francisco.

Philadelphia Flyers

THE HISTORY of sports is dotted with examples of front running teams having the roof cave in on them, figuratively speaking, but the Flyers of Philadelphia may have been the first to have one literally blow away from them. To their everlasting credit they finished first in the West Division of the National Hockey League for 1967–68 although they did not play one game in Philadelphia during the month of March. For 31 days these nomads of the NHL were buffeted about like a rowboat in a typhoon, living out of suitcases, away from their families and the friendly faces of the Philly fans.

As they battled with Los Angeles for the top position the pressures were great. "It hasn't just been worrying about first place," explained Lou Angotti, then the Flyers scrappy captain, "but also worrying and wondering where our next few games would be played. If you don't think it affects a team, you're crazy. Why we'd get up some mornings feeling seedy. You wouldn't know what was going on. That's because you're on the move all the time. I know there are going to be ups and downs for as long as we're playing hockey. But when you take everything into consideration, anything that happens after this will have to rank second to the things that happened this year."

The trouble started in the latter part of February when a strong wind rent a hole in the top of the Spectrum, Philadelphia's new $12,000,000 arena which resembles a huge brick and glass sardine can. Then on March 1 it happened again. This time the damage was greater and Mayor Harold J. Tate ruled that the building was unsafe and should be closed. The Flyers played a "home" game in New York against Oakland and another in Toronto against Boston, before finally settling in Quebec City, site of their training camp and domain of their top farm team, the Quebec Aces, as their home away from home. After they had beaten Minnesota at the Quebec Coliseum, defenseman Joe Watson, who had scored the winning goal, said: "If we have to play away from Philly, this is the best place to play. The guys who played here in Quebec in past years give it that little extra because they know the fans who supported them in the past are out there cheering them on. This is important, having the support of the fans."

In New York, where the fans love an underdog, they had booed the Flyers and cheered the Seals. "We won't go back there," grumped general manager Bud Poile, "unless it's for the Stanley Cup finals." In Toronto, on the other hand, the fans supported them against the hated Bruins, but the magnanimous Maple Leaf management charged the Flyers 50 per cent of the gate as their rink rental.

Meanwhile the hole in the Spectrum's top became the most famous flaw in Philadelphia since the Liberty Bell. In the new Madison Square Garden a fan was complaining about the small number of seats from where one could actually see the entire rink. A second fan offered the fact that although the Spectrum contained 2,500 less seats than the Garden, one could see well from anywhere in the building. "Yeah," chimed in a third party, "you could even fly over in a heeliocopter and see da game troo da roof." The Spectrum had become a joke—but not to the Flyers—and in Philadelphia it had become a political puck. It took 19 days for the city government to reach a decision to begin repairs on the building. Finally, with two games remaining in the regular schedule, it was announced that the Spectrum would reopen in time for the Stanley Cup playoffs.

During the troubled time there was talk that the Flyers would be leaving for another location permanently, even though in their first season they had scored a solid hit with the fans. It was estimated that the Flyer organization lost approximately $400,000 when they were unable to play their last seven home games at the Spectrum. "We felt sure we'd play before sellout crowds," cried Poile.

The team that had shaved Los Angeles 73 to 72 for the Clarence Campbell Bowl came home from the regular season closer at Pittsburgh with a four-game losing streak. (The last loss, by a 5–1 margin, was due, in part, to a champagne party that began at 1:30 A.M. on the morning of the game, actuated by the news from Oakland that the Seals had tied the Kings, thereby making it impossible for them to catch the Flyers.) Though elated, they were a road-weary band.

On April 4, in the opening playoff game against St. Louis, the Flyers' first tilt in the Spectrum since February 29, they managed only 14 shots at Glenn Hall and were beaten 1–0. Then home cooking seemed to take effect and two days later, lanky, right winger Léon Rochefort, who had scored 21 goals during the season, climaxed a 41-shot barrage by beating Hall in the third period for a 4–3 win.

In St. Louis, the Flyers lost 3–2 in double overtime, despite 54 saves by Bernie Parent, and 5–2, to put their backs against the wall. Then they regrouped at their beloved Spectrum and thrashed the Blues 6–1, knocking Glenn Hall out of the box with three first-period goals. Rookie Rosaire Paiement, an Eastern Leaguer the previous season, who had been called up as an emergency replacement from Quebec, took four shots and scored three goals. A bloody, 20-minute brawl in this game was a reprise of a regular season imbroglio between these two teams.

Back in St. Louis, it was Philly's turn to apply the double overtime sudden death. Unassisted, left wing Don Blackburn, only a nine-goal man during the season, notched his third playoff goal midway in the second extra period to tie the series. The Flyers were coming home again and things were looking up. After all, hadn't they held a 7-to-1 edge—with 2 ties—against the Blues over the 74-game haul. To their disappointment, they found out that Stanley Cup play is something else again as St. Louis eliminated them, 3–1, before 14,646 of the Philly faithful in a hard-fought game. The Flyer president, Bill Putnam, had said that in order to recoup some of the losses from the March wanderings his team would have to reach the Cup finals. While they didn't do that, the Flyers did establish a foothold for major league hockey in Philadelphia that should last for some years to come. Observers had felt they would have to win in order to interest the fans. When they scored victories over Boston, New York, Montreal and Detroit in the first part of the season, they had the Brotherly Lovers hooked.

Putnam is a positive thinker. During the season he stated: "I never had any doubts that we'd have a very fine club. I knew right from the time we first put a team together at the draft meeting in

Montreal last June." Like the Los Angeles Kings, the Philadelphia organization purchased an American League team, the Quebec Aces, before the Flyers ever took to the ice. This gave them depth and experience—and an unexpected auxiliary home—that was a large factor in their success. Much credit should go to the men who set up the Flyers: president Putnam; general manager Norman (Bud) Poile and coach Keith Allen.

Putnam, tall, affable and quietly classy, was a vice-president with J. P. Morgan and Company in New York, when in 1965 he moved to Los Angeles to become executive vice-president of Jack Kent Cooke, Inc., where he played a large role in acquiring the Lakers basketball team for Cooke Enterprises. From January 1966 through the end of the 1969–70 season he guided the Flyer interests. His associates, in the beginning, included Jerry Wolman, president of the Philadelphia Eagles in the National Football League.

Wolman purchased the Eagles five years ago for $5,505,500, after building a fortune in the construction game. About the time of his involvement in hockey, he estimated his net worth at $38,000,000. "My father was a fruit dealer," Wolman explained. "He didn't have any money, so I started borrowing in 1947 and began building sub-divisions. I also went broke, before the postwar boom made me rich."

Wolman sustained financial woe in the middle of the first expansion season, and sold his share of the Philadelphia hockey franchise to Ed Snider, former Eagles vice-president. They had been business partners since 1955, when Wolman assisted Snider's rise from a record distributor to a wealthy sports promoter. Wolman's untidy departure left Snider with 60 per cent of the hockey franchise, Putnam with 25 and Joe Scott, a Philadelphia sportsman, with 15.

Both Poile and Allen had successful records in the Western League as coaches and general managers; Poile at Edmonton and San Francisco; Allen at Seattle. Poile, who scored 107 goals with five NHL teams during his career, was an all-star with the Black Hawks in 1948. Allen, who played only 28 games for the Red Wings, was an outstanding minor league defenseman, and is another in a long line who have proven that you don't have to be a NHL star to be a fine coach. Both men, in their mid-40's, had been around long enough to know the talent on the farms. They picked up two 22-year-old goalies from the Bruins, Doug Favell and Bernie Parent, who were good enough to share in the winning of the Vezina

Trophy race of the season's first half, and finish third overall with a combined average of 2.42. Each man registered four shutouts.

From Chicago, they snared defenseman Ed Van Impe, runner-up to Bobby Orr for the Calder Trophy in the previous season, defenseman John Miszuk, center Lou Angotti and wingman Pat Hannigan. Boston also yielded to them defenseman Joe Watson and forwards Gary Dornhoefer and Forbes Kennedy. From Montreal came Jean Gauthier, Leon Rochefort and Garry Peters; from Toronto, Brit Selby.

Forwards such as Don Blackburn, Bill Sutherland and Ed Hoekstra, who had never before received a chance to play in the NHL (Blackburn had been with Boston for six games in 1962–63), were allowed to display their talents in the big time thanks to expansion.

From Quebec there were the familiar NHL names like Claude LaForge, John Hanna and Jean-Guy Gendron. Before the season ended, some of the fine young prospects, acquired with the Quebec purchase, had made themselves known. There were Simon Nolet and Andre Lacroix. The latter, leading scorer in the AHL who lost out to Nolet when called up to the Flyers, scored six goals and eight assists in 18 games, and added two goals and three assists in the playoffs. Lacroix was not yet 23 years old at the time.

The Flyers also employed 39-year-old defenseman Larry Zeidel, sometimes called the Rock, who had two brief stints with Detroit and one full season with Chicago in the early fifties but had toiled for 16 seasons in the minors with Indianapolis, Edmonton, Hershey, Seattle and Cleveland. A fighter with a reputation as a wild man, he led three different leagues in penalty minutes. Twice at Hershey he went over 200, accruing a total of 293 in 1959–60. His coach there, Frank Mathers, called Zeidel the most intense player he has ever known. If Larry felt he was not in high enough gear when he awakened from his pregame nap, he stoked his fires by playing records of martial music. He psyched himself into such lathers that once, in an anxious effort to get back on the ice, he ripped off the door of the penalty box. Zeidel has the kind of face that made a department store detective suspicious when Larry went tablecloth shopping.

Swarthy, with eyes made flinty by surrounding scar tissue, Zeidel has a face adorned by hundreds of stitch marks. There have been the stick battles as well as the ones with fists. The classic Western League encounter between Zeidel and Jack (Tex) Evans occurred during the 1952–53 season. After breaking their sticks on each other, they continued to attack with the splintered shafts in a bloody brawl that left each with 40 stitches. "Evans hacked me up," remembers Zeidel, "but I hung in there and battled with him. He couldn't put me away. I was swinging and missing. He was swinging and hitting. He carved me up. My home town newspapers (Edmonton) said he wouldn't amount to anything if he didn't watch his temper. His home town papers (Saskatoon) said I was some kind of nut."

When expansion arrived, Zeidel decided to merchandise himself and get a major league position. He spent $150 for a brochure enumerating his abilities as player, coach and executive. Included were 8-by-10 glossies of the Rock, both in uniform and behind a desk, and an affidavit from a doctor stated that Zeidel had the heart of a 20-year-old. He received many answers but no jobs. However, when Van Impe and Watson were training camp holdouts, two of his former bosses, Poile and Allen, called him. When Poile and Cleveland owner Paul Bright couldn't reach an agreement, the enterprising Zeidel set up a three-way conference call and helped put the deal over himself.

Once with the Flyers, Zeidel played his way into the regular defense rotation. "He's 39 now," said Poile. "He's too old to be a hatchet man. But he's a winner. He's been a winner all his life." For the most part Zeidel did stay away from the brawling but he did have his moments. There was a 10-minute incident involving four players after the final buzzer of a Philadelphia-St. Louis game and an altercation quite a bit more ugly on March 7 when the Flyers played Boston in that one "home" game in Toronto.

A vicious stick duel between old-time antagonists Zeidel and Bruins' Eddie Shack left both men's blood-drenched heads in need of sewing. Although he did not indict Shack, Zeidel, the NHL's only Jewish player, claimed the fight was precipitated by a succession of anti-Semitic remarks from the Bruin bench. He accused them of saying that they "wouldn't be satisfied until they put me in a gas chamber," and specified Don Awrey, Gerry Cheevers and Tom Williams as the ringleaders. It was later established that Williams was not in uniform that night, although conceivably he could have been near the ice or could have made the remarks in earlier games. Coach Harry Sinden of the Bruins denied hearing the remarks from the bench and said: "But I don't doubt someone called him 'Jew boy' or something like that on the ice. He was calling [Phil] Esposito 'Wop.' That doesn't mean they are bigots."

On the plane taking the Flyers from Toronto to Quebec, Zeidel told Philadelphia writer Ed Conrad: "Nearly the whole Boston team tried to intimidate me about being the only Jewish player in the league . . . Boston started pulling this kind of stuff when we played them earlier in the season. I didn't let it get me even though it hurt me to hear it.

"It was bad on my part to try and ignore it because things only got worse," he continued. "And they really got bad just before our last game in Boston Garden. That bit about me being a 'Jew boy' is music to my ears. But when they brought up the business of the gas chamber and extermination, I didn't buy it." It turned out that Zeidel's grandparents had been eliminated by the Nazis in just that fashion.

As a result of the fight, Zeidel was suspended for four games and Shack for three. Each was fined $300. Although two Toronto fans at rinkside claimed to have heard the racial slurs, Clarence Campbell swept the matter aside in the manner of a Zamboni machine clearing away snow from a rink surface. Both he and the Flyers' Ed Snider, himself Jewish, announced that the incident had been magnified by the press. After this, Conrad reported, "If you ask Zeidel about it now, he'll tell you he has no comment. 'Sorry,' he'll say. 'I'd rather not talk about it any more.'"

Despite promises from American and Canadian Jewish anti-defamation groups to have the NHL conduct a thorough investigation of the case, it was temporarily forgotten as the Flyers struggled to the pennant, helped by their oldest player, Larry Zeidel. After the regular season the NHL issued an unconvincing whitewash of the episode.

In becoming the first NHL team to finish first with a below .500 percentage (31–32–11), Philadelphia allowed the least goals in the West Division (179—third lowest in the entire league) but were outscored by every team in the league save Oakland. The Flyers tallied only 173 times. Realizing they had to recharge their offense, the Flyers planned to make use of Lacroix, Nolet and Gendron as a unit when they opened their 1968 training camp. They received a severe setback when veteran Gerry Melnyk, a 50-point man obtained from St. Louis, suffered a heart seizure during preseason play and was forced to retire.

Until the advent of the Flyers, Philadelphia's hockey teams had all been minor league except for one year. In 1930 the Pittsburgh Pirates franchise had been bought by prize fighter Benny Leonard and brought to Philadelphia as the Quakers. Their competition was the Arrows, a New York Ranger farm team in the Canadian-American League. Both teams played in the Arena, a building with a small ice surface and a 6,000 seating capacity. The Arrows were first in their minor league while the Quakers were last in the American division of their major league. When the press tried to instigate a match between the two, the Quakers demurred. After all, they figured, it was humiliating enough to be beaten by the NHLers. By the spring of 1931, they had established a record for futility that still stands—fewest wins and points in one season (four wins and four ties in 44 games); and longest losing streak—15 games. After one campaign they quietly quaked away.

The Flyers debut was far more auspicious. If winning in the West Division signaled their arrival as a major league team, the 1968 league meeting underlined and stamped it as official. Philadelphia lost two players in the draft—20-goal winger Bill Sutherland and tough defenseman Jean Gauthier. The teams claiming these men were, respectively, Toronto and Boston.

Instead of improving, the Flyers described a downward spiral. Manager Bud Poile became involved in feuds with some players and Zeidel eventually quit the team when Poile threatened to dispatch him to Quebec of the American League although Zeidel's record clearly indicated he belonged in the NHL.

In time Poile was to cross owner Ed Snider who fired his manager and named coach Keith Allen as a replacement. At the start of the 1969–70 season, Vic Stasiuk, a former NHL forward, was named coach and appeared to be leading the Flyers to a playoff berth when, suddenly, they collapsed in the homestretch and were eliminated on the final weekend of the season.

Bolstered by such young players as Bobby Clarke and Serge Bernier, the Flyers climbed to third place in the spring of 1971 but they were rapidly eliminated in the first round of the Stanley Cup playoffs by the Chicago Black Hawks.

Fred Shero, a former Ranger defenseman who had earned a solid coaching reputation in the New York farm system, particularly with the champion Omaha Knights of the Central League, took over the Flyers' bench controls for 1971–72. On the last day of that season they were beaten out of a playoff spot when Buffalo burned them with a goal in the last four seconds.

Undaunted, Shero rallied the team in 1972–73. Doug Favell came into his own in goal. Clarke continued to increase in stature and value; Rick MacLeish, obtained in the three-cornered Parent deal, became a 50-goal man; rookie Bill Barber scored 30; Gary Dornhoefer and bearded Bill Flett put more bite into the attack; and the Broad Street Bullies or Mad Squad—Dave Schultz, Bob Kelly, Andre Dupont, and Don Saleski—sunk their teeth into enemy flanks as each went over 200 minutes in penalties and the Flyers broke the league record with 1,754 minutes.

Finishing second, they eliminated Minnesota and reached the semifinals of the Stanley Cup for the first time. Unfortunately they ran into the Montreal Canadiens but as the capacity crowds at the Spectrum indicated, the Flyers were the liveliest thing in Philadelphia.

Pittsburgh Penguins

BEFORE A PUCK WAS EVER DROPPED many observers felt that the new Pittsburgh entry in the National Hockey League had lost a face-off. The winning name in the contest to give the team an identifying symbol was Penguins. Coach Red Sullivan's immediate reaction was: "I can see it now. The day after we play a bad game the sportswriters will say, 'They skated like a bunch of nuns.'" Although there were nights during the season when the Penguins exhibited some bad habits, no one advised them to get to a nunnery because the management dressed them in pale blue rather than black and white. The team symbol, a penguin skating along, stick in hand, flowing scarf from neck, was nowhere to be seen on the uniform. Only the word "Pittsburgh" adorned the front of each jersey. (In 1968–69, the Penguin symbol, sans scarf, was added in a new uniform design.)

One partially plausible answer as to why Penguins was chosen is that the Civic Arena, completed in 1961 at the cost of $22,000,000, is called "the Igloo" because of its roof's shape. Whatever the reason, the name of the team only added to the disgruntlement of Pittsburgh's hockey fans, already angry over the loss of the Hornets, their longtime American Hockey League member, who had won both the regular season AHL title and the Calder Cup in 1966–67. Although they were now to see the Howes, Hulls and Beliveaus, the ice fans of Steel City no longer had a team they identified with and had to be won over.

From the midthirties, when John H. Harris bought a franchise in the AHL, the name Hornets had been symbolic of Pittsburgh hockey and a training ground, first for Detroit but later, and more famously, for Toronto Maple Leaf farm hands. When the old Duquesne Gardens on Craig Street was torn down in the 1950s, there was an absence of hockey in Pittsburgh for five years until the Civic Arena opened and the Hornets returned for the 1961–62 season.

The National Hockey League's previous stay in Pittsburgh lasted from the fall of 1925 through the 1929–30 season. The Pirates, who took their name from the National League baseball team, did quite well in their first year, finishing third. In the playoffs they lost to Montreal Maroons 3–1 and tied them 3–3 but were eliminated under the total goals rule, 6–4. In 1926–27 they became part of the American Division and ended up fourth, out of the playoffs, but bounced back the following season to finish third. This time they won a game, beating the Rangers 4–2 after bowing 4–0, but again wound up on the short end of a total goals series 6–4. This was to be their last quest for a Stanley Cup. In 1928–29 the Pirates won nine and tied eight in 44 games, and the next season they won only five and tied three. This led, in 1930–31, to Philadelphia as the Quakers and an even lower estate.

The Pirates goalie for the first three seasons was Hall-of-Famer Roy (Shrimp) Worters, who later went on to star with the New York Americans. Their leading scorers were Hib Milks and Harold Darragh who contributed 71 and 59 goals, respectively, over the five-year span. Lionel Conacher played with them for one season and part of another. Others prominent in the Pittsburgh picture were Harold (Baldy) Cotton, Duke McCurry, Gerald Lowrey, Herb Drury, Tex White, Jesse Spring, Rodger Smith, Ty Arbour, Johnny McKinnon and Odie Cleghorn.

Cotton, of course, later became one of the best known scouts in the history of the game. He hunted ivory for the Boston Bruins and is now with the Minnesota North Stars.

Drury, a fleet forward with the nickname of Monk, was renowned for malaprops as well as his speed. He once announced that he was going to write a letter to "Clader" when he meant President Calder of the NHL. On another occasion he referred to Red Dutton as "that fellow Sutton."

Smith was the father of Desse Smith, a defenseman with the

Bruins, and grandfather of Gary Smith, goaltender for the Oakland Seals and Chicago Black Hawks.

McKinnon, a high-scoring defenseman who had 13- and 10-goal seasons, is the only Pirate to remain in the record book; he is the coholder of the honor, "most goals in one game by a defenseman." On November 19, 1929, he led his team to a 9–5 victory over the Maple Leafs by scoring four times. Oddly enough, Happy Day, the man who shares the record, accomplished his four goals in the very same game.

Cleghorn, who had come down from Canada to lead the Pirates in their first season, is the man who first used three forward lines in a game. He used to throw them on for short stints, thereby establishing a procedure used by coaches to this day.

In their first year in the NHL, the Penguins, unlike the Pirates, did not make the playoffs. They came close enough, however, to make one think that if they had not sustained a series of injuries to key men, they might have sneaked in. The race was that tight.

In the expansion draft of 1967 general manager Jack Riley and coach Red Sullivan sought players with experience and wound up with the oldest club—average age 32. Riley, a popular hockey man who had run the Rochester team of the American League, and then became president of that league before joining the Penguins, explained: "We have a modern building but we do not have a brand new arena as do four of the clubs. A new building excites the fans for a year or two . . . We won the Calder Cup last year. Our fans don't want a building program, they're used to winners. We felt we had to put a quality product on the ice immediately. I'm aware of some of the potential problems, but we tried to select players with pride—good competitors who will go all out. The older players have been winning in hockey in recent years, so that's the way we went."

Three of the important draftees were Earl Ingarfield, Ken Schinkel and Andy Bathgate. All were over 30 and had something else in common. They had played for the New York Rangers where the Penguin coach, Sullivan, had played and coached. In fact, the Pittsburgh roster began to resemble an old Ranger list with defenseman Al MacNeil and forwards Val Fonteyne and Mel Pearson. Players like Noel Price, Billy Dea and Art Stratton had also worn Ranger livery at one time in their careers. When third-round draft choice Larry Jeffrey was traded to New York for forward Paul Andrea, defenseman Dunc McCallum and handyman George Konik, a

Ranger look was really in evidence. To these ex-Rangers, Riley and Sullivan added wingers Ab McDonald, Bob Dillabough and Keith McCreary from Detroit, Boston and Montreal, and defenseman Leo Boivin from Detroit.

Before the 1966 season, Pittsburgh had purchased three defense-men—Ted Lanyon, Dick Mattiussi and Bill Speer—and goaltender Les Binkley from the Cleveland Barons. At that time the Penguins had no farm team of their own so the four were spread around the minors and convened with the rest of the squad at Brantford, Ontario. A hot battle for the two goaling jobs developed among Binkley, rookie Joe Daley, veteran Hank Bassen and amateur Marv Edwards. Bassen, who as a Hornet had led his team to the Calder Cup the previous year, was garnered in a trade with Detroit just before the season opened. He figured to do a job and be colorfully popular at the same time. What hadn't been anticipated was exactly how good Binkley was.

Leslie John Binkley was born in Owen Sound, Ontario, birthplace of another pretty fair netminder, Harry Lumley. When the 1967–68 season commenced he was 32 years old and had put in seven seasons with Cleveland and one with San Diego. In his first two years at Cleveland he played a total of nine games but in the eight of the second year he gave up only 11 goals for a 1.38 average and people started to talk about the amazing trainer of the Barons. Some people believed the myth that he had suddenly developed into a goaler. Actually he had come to Cleveland from the Toledo Mercurys as a backup man and had undertaken training duties as a sideline. In 1961–62 he took over the Cleveland net and had been a regular ever since, winning Rookie of the Year and making the All-Star Team twice in the AHL. A measure of his worth was proven in 1966–67 at San Diego when, with a last place team and a 3.56 average, he made the Second All-Star Team. The bombardment at San Diego, a new team in the Western League that season, prepped him well for what was to come at Pittsburgh. A symbolic scene at Madison Square Garden early in the season was Binkley and his Penguin mates groping along the ice in front on the goal crease for one of Les' contact lenses, lost making a tough save at the final buzzer. Fortunately, the lens was quickly retrieved before it froze into obscurity, and as he left the ice the large crowd gave him a resound-ing ovation. Although the Rangers had just beaten him 6–4, Binkley had shown the fans a major-league performance.

Binkley is a six-footer with agility and guts. In Boston he made 33 saves and shut out the Bruins 1–0. It was one of six zero jobs that tied him for second place in that department with Lorne Worsley and Cesare Maniago behind Ed Giacomin's eight. In playing 54 games he compiled a very solid 2.87 average.

The Penguins were an up and down team from the beginning. Picked by some as the best balanced team in the division and given a good shot at first place, they blew hot on the road and cold at home. Bathgate offered a possible explanation: "We seem to be too tight at home. Maybe we're trying too hard to impress our fans."

Even with their inability to put any long winning streaks together, the Penguins bounced along in fourth place until the St. Louis Blues started rolling in the second half of the season. Schinkel notched a hat trick against Chicago while holding Bobby Hull to one goal, and Bathgate fired three goals in a winning effort against Minneapolis. Then Ingarfield fractured his kneecap. Bathgate, without his old center-ice sidekick, went nine games without a goal. On January 28, Schinkel's ankle stopped a Bobby Orr slapshot and he went to the sidelines with a broken foot.

After two 5–1 defeats by Detroit and St. Louis, Sullivan shook up his lines and the Penguins responded with 5–0 and 5–3 victories over Philadelphia and the St. Louis Blues. "I wasn't surprised by our turnabout," said Red. "I've said all along that we couldn't win with just one or two players but rather it would take a team effort. We don't have that one player or two who can put us over the hump, if you know what I mean. We have to depend on everyone to play real well."

Sullivan was a player who transcended limited skills to become a major leaguer on the intangible qualities often summed up as "guts." Given the last rites after his spleen was ruptured when Doug Harvey speared him in the late 1950s, Sully rebounded to play again and even score 20 goals for the Rangers in 1958–59. As a player he understood completely the meaning of the word "hustle." As a coach, he expected the same kind of effort from his charges. If the Penguins didn't always play well, at least they were trying hard most of the time. Pittsburgh fans in the Igloo began to warm up to them.

When Binkley needed a rest from too much rubber, Bassen took over. The rambunctious redhead, whose wandering tactics cost him goals at times, collided with hard-nosed Jim Roberts of St. Louis some 20 feet from his crease and received a bloody nose for his travels. In the third period he moved behind the net to gather a loose puck and again ran into Roberts. After smacking him with his stick, Hank traded punches with Jim.

At one point, Sullivan commented: "Our checking has been inconsistent." The squat Leo Boivin, sometimes called the Fireplug, did nothing to tarnish his reputation, built in seasons with Toronto, Boston and Detroit, as one of the NHL's authentic body checkers. He also managed to score nine goals, one under his all-time season high. Noel Price, at first the target of boos, finished with a respectable six goals and 27 assists; and George Konik, the one time Teddy Bear, bright Ranger prospect, after some costly mistakes on defense, shifted to forward, scored the goal in the 1–0 victory over the Bruins, lifted the club to a 2–2 tie with the Rangers on a third-period score and developed into an effective penalty killer.

The Penguins received further help from the helmeted forward, Gino Ubriaco, who showed late foot to tally 18 goals, and young centerman Bobby Rivard. Dunc McCallum arrived from Baltimore to shore up the defense but soon fell to the injury jinx. While defenseman Bill Speer showed improvement as the season wore on, center Art Stratton, a leading scorer in the division's first half, tailed off in the second and was traded to Philadelphia for winger Wayne Hicks. As the Penguins made a determined bid to catch Minneapolis and the last playoff spot, Sullivan praised Rivard, Konik and left wing Keith McCreary. Before the 1968–69 season the first two had been shipped elsewhere.

The most crushing blow in the futile pursuit of fourth came in early March when Binkley broke a finger in a 6–6 tie with Oakland. The Penguins blew a big lead and lost a vital point along with their ace goaler. It was to their credit that they kept battling right to the end of the campaign. Binkley, having recovered, returned in time to lead them to victory in three of the last four winning games. When it was all over they had as many wins as the North Stars but two less points. Sullivan praised them: "With all the injuries we've had you've got to give these guys credit. You know, it would have been easy for them to let down; they would have had a natural excuse. But they've skated their hearts out."

Ingarfield scored 15 goals and 37 points in 50 games and Schinkel 14 goals and 39 points in 57. Conceivably, if Pittsburgh had gotten full service from these two they might have made the difference. Val Fonteyne contributed 34 points as well as his usual intangible assets, Billy Dea and Keith McCreary turned in good jobs, and Ab

McDonald scored 22 goals and 43 points. Despite this, towering Alvin was involved in a three-cornered trade of captains with St. Louis and Philadelphia, during the summer of 1968, which saw Lou Angotti come over to Pittsburgh. Riley and Sullivan also went for two digging forwards from Oakland—Charlie Burns and Wally Boyer. To balance the age, they picked up two young operatives from Boston's Oklahoma City farm, forward Jean Pronovost and defenseman John Arbour; and, in a surprise move during training camp, they obtained defenseman Bob Woytowich of Minnesota for a 1972 draft choice, leading some to think that Red and Jack were collecting captains. Ingarfield was named Pitt's captain for 1968–69.

When Hank Bassen announced his retirement it was one thing; when Andy Bathgate left training camp, seven NHL games short of 1,000, it was another. Called "the best seventeenth draft choice in sports history" by Riley, the right wing with the flashing eyes and the smashing shot had engineered a great comeback with the Penguins, leading all West Division scorers and finishing eighteenth in the overall league lists with 20 goals and 39 assists. In the previous season he had managed only eight goals in 60 games with Detroit. After his hat trick against Minnesota, Andy had quipped: "I guess the last one was seven years ago, when I used to be able to skate a little bit."

In 1960–61 Bathgate was in the middle of a brilliant string of seasons with New York Rangers, and he certainly could skate more than "a little bit" despite the fact that his left kneecap was held in place by a steel plate and his right knee was reinforced by a brace whenever he was on the ice. As a Ranger Bathgate was a superstar with a quick, hard, accurate wristshot and a devastating slapshot; precision passes; a stick-handling dexterity that recalled the wizards of an earlier era; and a keen hockey intelligence with which he could ad lib during the most demanding situations. Few who were there will forget a play he made against Chicago at Madison Square Garden in the 1957–58 season. Writer Kenneth Rudeen described it thusly: ". . . the puck squirted out over the blueline from the offensive zone in which the Rangers were putting together an attack. Bathgate chased it, got his stick on it and, facing away from the goal, considered for a split second how to dispose of the defenseman closing in from the rear to his right. He then flicked the puck behind him on a diagonal line from right to left, catching the defenseman flatfooted, whirled around to his left and picked up the puck again, skated in on the goal and, feinting the goalie out of position, scored." Moose Vasko and Glenn Hall were the victims but they couldn't have been any more astounded than the incredulous witnesses in the stands.

While Bathgate could not be described as pugnacious, he was a mean man if you pushed him too far. One Saturday night in New York he pulverized Vic Stasiuk in the first period and again in the third, when the huge Boston forward had the temerity to challenge him again. When Howie Young, in his first go-round as Detroit's bad boy, bugged Bathgate, Andy annihilated him. The reflexes that made the great plays were just as sharp in fisticuffs.

In 1962–63 he set the longest consecutive goal-scoring streak for the modern era—10 games (tied by Bobby Hull in 1968–69); in 1963–64 he compiled the most assists in a season by a right winger —58, a record which stood until Gordie Howe broke it in 1968–69. Fifteen of these were accomplished in 15 games with Toronto after the Rangers had traded him. His critics said he didn't shoot enough and that he wasn't strong enough defensively, weak arguments in the face of one of the best power play men and most productive right wings the NHL has ever seen. He helped Toronto win the Cup in 1964, and his six goals was a strong factor in Detroit's bid to upset Montreal in the 1966 final. For the Penguins, Bathgate, the man who holds all the main Ranger scoring records, was a bright light in a might-have-been season. In the fall of 1968 the Penguins felt his legs no longer had it, and he was waived to Vancouver but returned to finish as Pittsburgh's third scorer in 1970–71.

Despite missing the playoffs there were signs of encouragement in the Penguin nest. Pittsburgh fandom, resentful and skeptical at first, had been won over, and late in the season the club's majority interest was sold to a group of Michigan investors, headed by Donald H. Parsons, board chairman of the Bank of the Commonwealth in Detroit, who announced that the Penguins would remain in Pittsburgh. The only expansion was the placement of a player development club at Amarillo, Texas, of the Central Professional League which was abandoned a year later.

The Michigan group retained as president, Jack E. McGregor, a youthful Pennsylvania state senator with the fresh, eager look of a Junior A hockey player. It had been McGregor, along with Pittsburgh lawyer Pete Block who assembled the men, including representatives from the Heinz and Mellon families, that comprised the group to bring NHL hockey to Pittsburgh. These original investors required help after losing about $700,000 in a disastrous soccer promotion with the now defunct Phantoms of that city. McGregor admitted that the soccer fiasco had been a factor in making the stock available but he also cited "unforeseen expenses—as a for instance, the proposed settlements with the American and Western Hockey Leagues, the figures being far, far greater than anticipated." Before selling to the Detroit financiers, Pittsburgh played off bids from the Atlanta Braves baseball team and the Avon cosmetics company. Early in the 1967–68 season rumors flew to the effect that the Braves were buying in and moving the team to Atlanta the next season. This did not help public relations. When McGregor announced that the deal was off, he said: that he was "sorry in a sense because of my total respect for key management officials in the Braves' corporation and happy in a sense because it helps squash the rumor that the Braves were going to steal the franchise and take it out of town.

"It is absolutely untrue," he added, without a trace of a smile, "that the Braves backed out of this because they didn't like the name 'Penguins.' "

Rumors of a franchise move notwithstanding, the Penguins kept plugging away and actually gained their first playoff berth in April 1970 under the direction of Red Kelly. Pittsburgh moved smartly into the semifinal round before being eliminated by the St. Louis Blues.

Delighted with the play of rookie forward Michel Briere, the Penguins looked forward to 1970–71 until tragedy struck shortly after the 1969–70 season had ended. Briere was seriously injured in an automobile accident in Northern Quebec and never recovered. After a long convalescence, the young player died while the 1971 playoffs were being contested. Without Briere, the Penguins were unable to gain a playoff berth in 1971.

They bounced back to fourth in 1971–72 with the help of emerging young stars Syl Apps, Jr., Bryan Hextall, Jr., Greg Polis, and Jean Pronovost, and older heads like Ken Schinkel, Tim Horton, Ron Schock, and Eddie Shack but in four, closely-contested games they were eliminated by Chicago in the Stanley Cup quarterfinals.

In 1972 Binkley jumped to the Ottawa Nationals, Horton was drafted by Buffalo, and although Al McDonough, obtained from Los Angeles, and Lowell MacDonald, out of retirement after overcoming several knee operations, each scored over 30 goals, Pittsburgh finished fifth. Kelly was fired during the season in favor of Schinkel, who turned in his jersey for the place behind the bench.

The switch failed to charge the Penguins with the necessary juice to overtake St. Louis.

In the 1970s Peter Block returned as part of a group with Thad Potter to take over for the failing Parsons outfit in the management end and Pittsburgh solidified their following. Schinkel, ready to begin his first full term at the controls, hired former NHL defenseman Fred Hucul as defensive coach and the Penguins prepared for their annual scramble toward the third ice floe from the top.

St. Louis Blues

AFTER THE 1967–68 SEASON the *Hockey News* named William Scott Bowman "Coach of the Year." Scotty, then 33, and youngest coach in the league at the time, was certainly deserving of the award as he guided the St. Louis Blues from last place (they were 4-10-2 when he took over behind the bench in late November) to a third place and a berth in the finals of the Stanley Cup.

No less deserving of praise, but not as quick to receive it, was Lynn Patrick, who began the Blues first season as general manager-coach, with Bowman as his assistant in both roles. When Patrick, who started his professional career as a player with the St. Louis Flyers of the old American Hockey Association in the early 1930s, came up to the New York Rangers in 1934–35, he was accused of making it the easy way because he was the boss's son. He was called "Sonja" by the Madison Square Garden gallery long before the appearance of Allan Stanley inspired a more derisive edition of that nickname. But Lynn Patrick made it on his talent, not because he was Lester Patrick's son. He played on the last Ranger Stanley Cup winner and made the All-Star Team.

As a coach, Patrick came within one goal of winning the Cup with the Rangers in 1950. Then he shifted to the Boston Bruins, coaching for four years and holding down the general manager's job for 11 more. At first the Bruins were perennial play-off participants but in the latter third of his administration they became redundant cellar dwellers. Patrick's reputation grew tarnished and the fortunes of his next charges, the Los Angeles Blades of the Western League, did nothing to polish it. When he was hired by the Blues, professional scoffers were quick to say, "That's it for the St. Louis. Patrick's a loser." People inside hockey knew better. The Blues knew they had an astute hockey man.

Patrick had said at the outset that if holding down two jobs was going to hurt the club he would drop one and give his full attention to the other. Things did not immediately change for the better. The Blues lost seven in a row. Then Patrick and Bowman engineered the first of a series of maneuvers that got them rolling. They traded veteran wing man Ron Stewart, who had been one of the early season standouts, and Ron Attwell, to the Rangers for a rugged, defenseman who could also lug the puck, Barclay Plager, and a rangy center, Gordon (Red) Berenson.

The Blues had been playing a close-checking hockey, well supported by Mr. Goalie, Glenn Hall, and the very able Seth Martin, late of the Canadian National team. But they weren't scoring. Berenson helped remedy that. A strong skater with legs like oak posts, the redhead had been a part-time player at Montreal and at New York, where injuries had hampered him the previous season. With the Blues he scored 22 goals and was voted West Division "Player of the Year" by *The Sporting News*.

Next the Blues recalled two unlikely forwards from the Kansas City Blues, their farm in the Central League. One was Frank St. Marseille whose main experience had been three years with the Port Huron Flags of the International League; the other, Tim Ecclestone, acquired from the Rangers right out of their junior team at Kitchener in the Ontario Hockey Association. The slick St. Marseille ended with 16 goals and as many assists in only 57 games, and while Ecclestone's point record was not as impressive, he made a tough adjustment and, at the age of 20, seemed pointed toward stardom.

On December 6 the Blues were still in the wake of the Oakland Seals. Then some of the old guard started to appear. The Blues had been unable to entice their eleventh-round draft choice, former Chicago center Bill (Red) Hay out of retirement, but in December, Richard Winston (Dickie) Moore, author of 256 NHL goals, who hadn't laced a skate since the elimination of the Toronto Maple Leafs from the play-offs in the spring of 1965, came a long way to St. Louis. On December 10 he caged number 257 behind Bruce Gamble. Together with St. Marseille's first NHL goal, earlier in the game, it added up to a 2–1 win over Toronto. Moore did not only help on the ice. Like Bernie Geoffrion with the Rangers the year before, he stoked the competitive fires in the dressing room.

Little by little the pieces began to fit with the momentum of a rapidly forming picture in a jigsaw puzzle. The crafty playmaker, Don (Slip) McKenney, returned from sick bay to center for Moore, and sturdy rookie Gary Sabourin began to make people take notice. By the end of December, St. Louis had eased into fifth.

As January progressed, so did the Blues. The defense, led by captain Alger Arbour, continued to be stingy. The bespectacled puck blocker, often referred to as a "second goalie," had been trapped in the Toronto farm system at Rochester during the 1960s, after six major league years with Detroit, Chicago and Toronto through 1961–62, until freed by expansion. An appreciative Glenn Hall said: "I don't think there's anyone I'd rather have playing in front of me than Arbour. He's the most underrated defenseman in the game. As a defensive defenseman, there just isn't anyone better. Among other things, there is no one better at blocking pucks. Al does it with such perfect timing that it's beautiful to watch. But if I wore glasses as he does, I don't think I'd ever want to drop on my knees in front of someone with a puck on his stick."

Along with Arbour and Barclay Plager, on the St. Louis blue line were the smooth-passing Fred Hucul and the aggressive Noel Picard. Jim Roberts, one of the genuine hard noses of the league, sometimes doubled from his right wing post. Then there was Bob Plager. Not that brother Barclay is any lemon meringue (he led the league in penalty minutes with 153), but Bob, a flakey gladiator, seems to really revel in the back-alley aspects of the game. Although he only compiled 86 minutes during the regular season, he did better in the play-offs, losing out to Barclay by only four minutes, 73 to 69. (Both surpassed the former record of 55, jointly held by Red Horner and Jimmy Orlando.) Once, while on opposing teams in the minors, the two truculent siblings battled it out in a display of misplaced affection. They fought, toe to toe, for five minutes at center ice in one of the most infamous conflagrations in OHA history. After doing an encore in the stands behind the penalty box, they were ready for a postgame reprise. Bob still maintains, "I licked him, fair and square."

But Barclay scoffs: "The day that fat tub could get the better of me hasn't come."

When rabid Robert reported to the Blues training camp in the fall of 1968, one hand was incapacitated. It had been broken in a summer row with younger brother Bill, the defenseman the Blues had just drafted from Minnesota. The thought of three Plagers— and Noel Picard—must have even scared the Blues. Billy was farmed out to Kansas City before the opening game.

When R. Plager was with the Rangers, he reported late one year with an excuse that he had fallen down the side of a mountain. The real cause was found later to have been a barroom brawl in which he stifled a foolish troublemaker. To make up for lost time in getting to camp, he enlisted a special escort in the person of the police chief of his home town of Kapuskasing. During one off season he had reporters convinced that his summer job was as a beer taster in that quaintly named Ontario hamlet. When the put-on was discovered, thanks to press coverage, it was revealed that burly Bob actually drove the brewery's truck.

It was in January that the defense corps added another new, old face. Jean Guy Talbot, drafted from Canadiens by Minnesota, had been traded to Detroit in November. When Bowman claimed him on waivers, he was signing a man who had almost killed him with a stick during a junior game. "That happened in 1951 when I was 17 years old," Bowman remembers. "Talbot fractured my skull and sent me to the hospital with 42 stitches."

The injury ended Bowman's playing days and turned him to coaching at a very early age. In the winter of 1968 both the Blues and Talbot had something to be thankful for. Talbot, a useful utility man, who knew how to kill a penalty, was yet another potion in Bowman's skillful blend of youth and age.

On January 27, in St. Louis, the Blues spotted the Rangers a 3–0 lead in the first period, then roared back to win 4–3, as Berenson tied it and Billy McCreary won it. The other two Blues' goals were fired by Larry Keenan, a forward with a minor league record for scoring and accumulating broken bones and other maladies. Drafted out of the Toronto organization, Keenan had knocked in four scores in the Blues' first six games of the season before fracturing his ankle. He didn't return until almost the New Year, yet managed to collect 12 goals in 40 games. In the play-offs he added four more.

The comeback against the Rangers pushed the Blues' confidence over the restraining line. At the end of the month they were a point up on the Penguins, and by February 7 were tied for third with the Kings. That night, in their home rink, they played one of those games that local buffs will probably talk about for years. With

Boston leading 5–4, Bruins' John McKenzie fired a high, hard shot at Glenn Hall. When the puck rebounded rapidly back toward the blueline, Al Arbour snared it, dashed down the ice and beat goalie Ed Johnston with a low sizzler. St. Louis had tied the score and the Arena was a bedlam. Then referee Bob Sloan decided that McKenzie's shot had been a goal and, therefore, Arbour's could not count. Suddenly 5–5 became 6–4. Bedlam gave way to pandemonium. The crowd of nearly 10,000 staged a throw-in that held up the game for 17 minutes.

Bowman, after seeing the game films, insisted that there had been no Boston goal. The goal judge said he never saw the puck enter the net. As far as the Blues were concerned, the villain in the piece was linesman Brent Casselman, who, as the man nearest the goal, had influenced Sloan's decision.

It would take more than mere officials to stop the Blues and the Canadiens found that out on February 28. Trailing 3–0, St. Louis rallied for three in the last period to salvage a tie. The man who supplied the first-goal spark was none other than the ex-Montreal sniper, Dickie Moore.

On the final weekend of the season the Blues put together back-to-back wins over Minnesota to take third by a point. Two goals in the last two and one-half minutes by the explosive Keenan won the Saturday night game at home; then the Blues went to Minnesota on Sunday, and beat the North Stars on three last-period scores, 5–3.

In order to reach the confrontation with the East Division contender, St. Louis had to claw its way through two seven-game series. If the first four teams had ended the season in a blanket finish, the West Division's part of the quest for Lord Stanley's mug was the season in microcosm. No less than six times did the Blues go into sudden death, three of those occasions being double overtime. Four of the six went their way.

In the Philadelphia series, Keenan won the third game in the second overtime. When they bowed 2–1 in double overtime at home in the sixth game, it looked like it was all over. But Bowman had another ace up his sleeve, a well-worn hole card named Doug Harvey. Hired to coach the Kansas City team, he had steered them into the Central League play-offs but they had been eliminated by Fort Worth and the out-of-shape but rink-wise-beyond-his-considerable years Harvey suddenly found himself in his one hundred thirtieth Stanley Cup game.

It was Dickie Moore who set up St. Marseille on the first goal in the Spectrum on the night of April 18. In the second period, with the score tied, Harvey and Gerry Melnyk assisted dead-eye Keenan for the winner. Berenson's empty-net goal in the last minute of the game iced it.

Back in St. Louis on April 21, it was again Moore and Harvey who played important roles as the Blues skated past the North Stars, 5–3. Moore had a goal and two assists while the 43-year-old Harvey assisted on a game-tying goal. McCreary bagged the eventual winner and Keenan got the insurance tally.

In game two Minnesota bounced back to win on Parker Mac-Donald's overtime goal, 3–2, but Moore and Harvey assisted on the tying goal. Moore garnered the only St. Louis score, unassisted, in the 5–1 defeat of game three. He banged another home as the Blues tied up the series with an overtime win in game four. As they had done during the season in that Canadien game, St. Louis entered the last period trailing by three goals. With only eight minutes and three seconds remaining, Roberts scored on assists by Moore and Ecclestone. Then came Moore's goal from Keenan and Bob Plager a minute later. With 11 seconds to go, Roberts tied it with Barclay Plager's help. One minute and 32 seconds into overtime, Sabourin won it on a pass from Terry Crisp. They had fired 45 shots at Cesare Maniago and had finally worn him down.

Game five again went to overtime and St. Louisans began to think that some madness had possessed their team. It had. Bob Plager had a goal and an assist in this one; Sabourin scored the other regulation time goal; and McCreary counted the winner at 17:27 of the first extra period. After Minnesota had won at home, by their favorite 5–1 score (Sabourin was the lone Blues' marksman), the stage was set for more Missouri mania.

At the St. Louis Arena on Friday, May 3, the Blues and North Stars played through two scoreless periods. Then rookie Walt McKechnie put the Stars in the lead at 16:49 of the third on a pass from Bob McCord, but before St. Louis fans could gnaw completely past their knuckles, the unquenchable Dickie Moore had made it 1–1 at 17:20, aided by Keenan and Barclay Plager. As St. Louis cardiologists stood by en masse, the two teams battled through the first overtime to no decision, with Minnesota having the edge in shots, 14–10. At 2:50 of the second overtime, electricity struck the North Stars in the person of Ron Schock. The tall, blond 23-year-old forward drafted from the Bruins had been a disappointment with only nine goals in 55 games during the season. But on this night he took passes from McCreary and Melnyk, sped in on Maniago and fired his first and only goal of the play-offs. The jubilant patrons almost accomplished with their roar what a tornado had done to the Arena roof in 1959. The unbelievable Blues were in the Stanley Cup final against the Montreal Canadiens!

Even though the Missourians bowed in four straight games to *Les Habitants*, they played with the same great desire that had brought them from last place to West Division play-off champions. Twice they had to be taken into overtime before they could be vanquished. Anyone who had suggested in October that an East-West final might be competitive was accorded more than a raised eyebrow.

In game one, Barclay Plager and Moore gave the Blues a lead until Yvan Cournoyer tied it, and Jacques Lemaire won it in overtime. Game two was decided 1–0 on Serge Savard's third-period goal during a penalty-killing tour with Claude Provost.

Back in Montreal for the third contest, the Blues presented a dilemma for some of the Forum fans. With ex-Canadiens Harvey, Moore, Roberts, Talbot, Berenson, McCreary and Picard in the line-up, mild schizophrenia prevailed. So did the Canadiens. Harvey and Picard helped St. Marseille to score but Cournoyer tied it before the first period ended. Savard, again killing a penalty and the Blues, put the Habs one up at 1:23 of the second, but Berenson knotted with the help of Talbot. Wherever you looked, a Canadien was scoring—even if he was a Blue. The current Canadiens thought they had it wrapped up when Backstrom counted at 11:43 of the third but again the heroic Red Baron, Gordon Berenson, brought the Blues even as he stole the puck from J. C. Tremblay to score at 17:25. In the overtime, Canadiens graphically again demonstrated "sudden death." In game one Lemaire had scored at 1:41; here Bobby Rousseau sunk Dick Duff's rebound at 1:13, after Hall had miraculously thwarted Duff twice from close in.

At this point, no one would have derided the Blues if they were bombed out of the Forum in game four. They had come through 17 play-off encounters with untold pressure on them. It was time to crack. Instead, St. Louis fell behind on Duff's goal in the first period but passed the Canadiens in the second with two of their own. Rookie Craig Cameron, assisted by Arbour and Ecclestone, was the first scorer; Sabourin, fed by another rookie, Gary Veneruzzo, the second. When Montreal rang down the curtain in the third it was defenseman J. C. Tremblay who was atoning for his "sin" of game three. First he assisted on Henri Richard's goal, and then produced

the champagne cork opener on passes from Backstrom and Cournoyer.

In the four games Montreal had outscored St. Louis only by
11–7 although they had outshot them by a 151–81 margin. Only in
the first game had the shots on goal been fairly even, 38–36 for the
Canadiens. Clearly, the hero in defeat had been Glenn Hall, with a
superhuman demonstration that won him the Conn Smythe Trophy
as the Cup's most outstanding player.

To help Hall in the 1968–69 season, the Blues drafted another
ex-Canadien, the colorful Jacques Plante, and brought him out of
the retirement he had been living in since leaving the Rangers at
the end of the 1965 season. Seth Martin had returned to the amateurs, and Dickie Moore had hung them up for the third time. To
pick up the slack on the left side, they obtained Camille Henry,
perhaps the greatest goal scorer, pound for pound (261 goals and
145 pounds through the 1967–68 season) in the game; and Alvin
(Ab) McDonald, a 22-goal scorer as Pittsburgh Penguin captain in
their first season.

In other moves, Bowman became general manager as well as
coach and Patrick assumed, among other responsibilities, the building of a farm system, as managing director. To aid Bowman, Harvey
was brought up to the parent team as player and assistant coach.
Hucul took his place at Kansas City.

Hockey has a heritage in St. Louis. The Arena, built in 1929, has
housed a variety of teams and leagues. In 1934–35 the Ottawa club
brought NHL hockey to the Mound City as the St. Louis Eagles
and then dropped out of the league. They played at the Arena, as
the occupants from 1932, the St. Louis Flyers of the American
Hockey Association, moved, temporarily, to the Winter Garden.
When the Eagles fled, the Flyers flew back in, remaining until 1942
when the war terminated the AHA. In 1944 the Flyers once again
skated in the Arena in the American Hockey League. After nine
seasons they folded.

In 1962 the Syracuse Braves of the Eastern Pro League finished
the season in St. Louis and became the St. Louis Braves. A farm
club of the Black Hawks, they remained until the Blues arrived. A
very progressive organization, headed by Sidney Salomon Jr., chairman of the board and president, and his son Sidney Salomon III,
executive vice-president and league governor, the St. Louis Blues
inherited the only building in the West Division that was not brand
new or built within the previous five-year period. The way in which

they refurbished it, set an example for their dealings with players and public alike.

Sid Salomon Jr. is reported to have more money than some countries, a rich residue no sane prophet could have forecast when Salomon earned $125 a month as a sports writer for the old *St. Louis Times*. That was in 1929, when he was 19. He abandoned journalism for the insurance business, indicating beyond dispute that he should spell his name Solomon.

President Campbell was suitably impressed when Salomon achieved control of the St. Louis franchise. "In Salomon," Campbell said, "we've got a genuine kingmaker. He swung the 1944 Democratic convention to putting Harry Truman on the ballot as the vice-presidential candidate instead of Henry Wallace."

The little old haberdasher from Independence, Missouri, was thus a heartbeat away from the American presidency, which fell to him after Franklin Roosevelt died in 1945.

Salomon maintained his backroom strength as treasurer of the Democratic National Committee in 1950–51, and as chairman of the fund-raising for the successful Kennedy-Johnson campaign in 1960.

As a baseball man, Salomon has served on the board of directors of the Cardinals and the old St. Louis Browns. In 1955 he bought the Syracuse team of the International League and took them to Florida as the Miami Marlins.

As a hockey man, he treated the entire Blues' squad and their families to a two-week vacation at the Salomon's Gold Coast Hotel in Miami right after the play-offs. At the 1968 training camp, Scotty Bowman led the players on an outing to St. Andrew's, in the Maritimes, where they golfed, swam and generally enjoyed themselves on a late summer holiday. Sid Salomon III feels that gestures like this help create a tightly knit, family feeling among the Blues.

Young Salomon, a crack insurance salesman for his father's firm, is just as conscious of making the fans feel at home at the Arena. In their first season, the Blues drew large, enthusiastic crowds. It is said that they drove the St. Louis Hawks of the National Basketball Association to Atlanta. Before the 1968 campaign it was announced that they had tripled their season subscriptions to 9,000. Only 1,000 seats were left for the home opener against Los Angeles despite preoccupation with the World Series under the Gateway Arch. The box office manager told Salomon that if the tickets had been $3, instead of $4 and $2.50 seats, the place would be sold out because he had orders for 1,000 of the $3s that he couldn't fill.

Salomon remedied this by giving 800 of the $4 seats to the first people who requested the $3s. To each ticket he had attached a note informing the buyer that the club was making the extra dollar an opening night present. Then he instructed the box office to fill the other 200 orders with $2.50 seats, a 50¢ refund and a note of apology, an unheard of gesture for a team on top.

The Blues flourished under general manager-coach Scotty Bowman, reaching the Stanley Cup finals in each of its first three years of existence. But the Blues were beaten in four straight games by the Canadiens in 1968 and again in 1969 and whipped in four straight by the Bruins in 1970.

Bowman turned the coaching chores over to defenseman Al Arbour in the fall of 1970 and, this time, the Blues floundered. Realizing that changes were necessary, Bowman traded ace center Red Berenson to Detroit along with Tim Ecclestone for Wayne Connolly and Garry Unger. He also lured Carl Brewer out of retirement and persuaded Al Arbour to play again while he, Bowman, took over the coaching once more.

He coaxed the Blues into a second-place finish in April 1971 but the St. Louis sextet was stunningly upset by the Minnesota North Stars in the first round and, for the first time in the team's history, watched the rest of the playoffs from the sidelines. For a change there was good reason to sing the blues in St. Louis.

The moaning continued into the 1971–72 season until a night in Philadelphia on January 6, 1972. Bowman had left after the last season to coach Les Canadiens and Arbour was once again off the ice and masterminding the Blues as bench coach after Sid Abel and Billy McCreary had failed to make them move.

The team was in fifth place and showing no signs of life. Thrashed by the Rangers, 9–1, on the previous night, they were losing 2–0 to the fourth-place Flyers as the second period ended. Suddenly Arbour was out there on the ice—in his civvies—arguing a call with the referee. As he returned to the stands a fan doused him with beer and a full-scale riot erupted among Blues, fans and police. It lit a Blue flame that burned to a 3–2 St. Louis victory and illuminated a path to the playoffs. This time the third-place Blues ousted the North Stars in seven games, capped by Kevin O'Shea's sudden-death goal, but bowed to Boston in four straight.

The 1972–73 season was not without tribulations before triumph, either. After a tentative start Arbour was removed for Bowman's old buddy Talbot and the Blues eventually huffed and puffed into fourth, three points ahead of the Penguins and Kings. In the quarter-final, however, they ran into the solid Chicago Black Hawks.

In 41-goal man Garry Unger the Blues had an offensive leader; Gary Sabourin remained an important cog; the Plagers, Barclay and Bob, were still bulwarks on defense aided by the terrible-tempered Steve Durbano; and smooth-skating Ab DeMarco, obtained from Rangers, added an offensive arm to the defense and power play. Through 1972–73 the Blues were the only expansion team to never have missed the playoffs. Just prior to the junior draft meetings in May 1973 Chuck Catto, late of the Cleveland Crusaders, was named general manager to replace Sid Abel who left to take the GM job with the new Kansas City entry.

Buffalo Sabres

FOR MANY YEARS one of the strongest minor league cities, Buffalo had attempted to obtain a National Hockey League franchise when the NHL launched its first expansion program in 1967–68. At the time, representatives of the upper New York State metropolis were shunted aside, mostly because Toronto Maple Leafs' interests feared that Buffalo would intrude on the lucrative market developed by the Leafs. But the Toronto organization also realized that there were compensating factors in having the Buffalo team in the majors; not the least of which would be a big, fat, $6,000,000 entrance fee to be paid when the next group of new teams was admitted.

The Buffalo hockey promoters were patient but determined. Seymour H. Knox III, regional vice-president of Domenick & Domenick, members of the New York Stock Exchange, led the New York State contingent into the NHL meetings. He was abetted by his brother, Northrup R. Knox, who at one time was an outstanding goaltender at Yale and later became a court tennis champion for ten years.

The Knox Brothers won their crusade for big league hockey in Buffalo in 1970 when the NHL approved two new franchises; the other going to Vancouver, British Columbia. Many hockey critics believe that the next move by the Knox Brothers was their most pivotal one. They appointed former Maple Leaf general manager–coach Punch Imlach to handle both jobs.

During his tenure in Toronto, Imlach had proven himself a champion-builder but there was considerable doubt about his ability to make the Sabres respectable, especially since talent was becoming harder and harder to find. But there was one salvation, the NHL draft, and Punch came up with a winner when he selected the French-Canadian center Gil Perreault as his first choice.

The six-foot, 195-pound skater had been the talk of Canadian junior hockey for several years. During the 1969–70 season he had scored 51 goals during the regular schedule and then added 34 in 28 playoff games. If the Sabres were to be respectable, Perreault would have to make the difficult adjustment from the junior game to the majors in only one season.

At first there were doubts about Perreault. On October 27, 1970, the Sabres were beaten, 7–2, by Vancouver at the Pacific Coliseum and Gil became the target of abuse from the victors. "I guess we showed them who got the best draft picks," said Mike Corrigan of Vancouver.

Yet, even in defeat Perreault sparkled and his natural ability caught the eye of Vancouver's Andre Boudrias. "Perreault is going to be a good one," Boudrias said. "He works. He doesn't wait for the puck to come to him. And when he gets it, he can go."

Buffalo didn't get going until half of the maiden season was over. By Christmas 1970, the Sabres were last in the NHL's East Division, 16 points behind Vancouver and rather red-faced about the whole thing; all except Imlach who was confident he could turn the team around.

"Once I got the kind of line-up I wanted," said Imlach, "I knew we would be trouble for the rest of the league."

Imlach wasn't whistling Dixie. During the last half of the schedule Buffalo played .500 hockey and closed out the season with eight wins, four losses, and three ties. Just before the close of the schedule, Imlach huddled with his skaters and let them know where they were at, in his estimation.

"You guys are not an expansion team anymore," said Punch. "In our first try we're finishing fifth in the old division and we're ahead of one established club [Detroit]. And we have more points than, or as many as, four expansion outfits. In our first year, remember, I'm surer than ever that my original prediction will come true, that we'll be the first of the new teams to win the Stanley Cup—and a lot sooner than many people think."

Imlach then went about the business of strengthening his club. He obtained Richard Martin, a 71-goal scorer from Montreal, in the draft of overage juniors and decided to make him a left wing on a line with Perreault. Buffalo hockey fans responded to Imlach's enthusiasm, and within a season it was clear that the Sabres would be one of the best drawing cards in the NHL.

"Hockey has gone over tremendously in Buffalo as we knew it would," said Seymour Knox. "Now it's up to us to put together the kind of club our fans deserve."

Imlach tried 36 players during the 1971–72 season. His objective was to reduce the overall age of the club and build with a youth movement. By the final month of the season the oldest forward on the Sabres was captain and center Gerry Meehan and he was only 25.

Wheeling and dealing, Imlach came up with the kind of talented youth that would pay off on a long-term basis. Richard Martin was a star before his rookie season was over but there were others such as Jim Lorentz, Don Luce, and Rene Robert, to name a few.

Perreault, who had won the Calder Trophy as rookie of the year in 1971, emerged as a mature leader. His linemate Martin scored 44 goals while Perreault collected 48 assists, many of which were the result of Martin's scores. They became the "Gold Dust Twins" of Buffalo and fans responded in record droves. Out of 39 home games, 35 were sellouts and it became apparent that within a year it would be virtually impossible to buy a season ticket for Sabres' games.

The strain of producing a contender took its toll on Imlach. In the middle of the 1971–72 season he suffered a heart attack and was sidelined through the end of the campaign. He was ordered to curtail his activities and appointed Joe Crozier, a veteran minor league coach, to relieve him of bench duties. Punch would limit himself to managing the club but never lowered his goals.

"We hope we can pay off this season," said Imlach on the eve of the 1972–73 campaign. "We still aim to be the first expansion team to win the Stanley Cup. And we have to make the playoffs first. We intend to make them this year."

Once again, Punch displayed his brilliance in the hockey market. He obtained eager, veteran defenseman Tim Horton from Pittsburgh in the intraleague draft and Horton played with the enthusiasm of a rookie. In the amateur draft, Imlach came up with defenseman Jim Schoenfeld from the Niagara Falls Flyers and the kid developed into one of the most colorful personalities in Buffalo sports history as well as a gifted defenseman. Rene Robert, plucked from Pittsburgh the previous season, led the team in goals with 39 as he helped form the devastating "French Connection" line with Perreault and Martin.

The results were just as Imlach predicted—almost. In their third season the Sabres *did* gain a playoff berth, beating out his arch-rivals, the Toronto Maple Leafs and the Detroit Red Wings, and they made a healthy run for the Stanley Cup.

Unfortunately, they went up against the East Division champion Montreal Canadiens in the first round. Buffalo lost the best-of-seven series, four games to two, but they gave the proud Canadiens a fright. "We're not likely to meet a better team than that," said Montreal managing director Sam Pollock.

That the Sabres had arrived 'way ahead of time was obvious. "We were fortunate," said Seymour Knox, "that when we were ready to go into the NHL, a man like Imlach was available. He was exactly what we needed, as a general manager, as a coach and as a salesman."

Vancouver Canucks

THE STORY of the Vancouver Canucks' brief life in the National Hockey League can best be described as a build-up to a letdown. When Vancouver entered the NHL in the Fall of 1970 along with the Buffalo Sabres it appeared that the Canucks would be an instant success, commercially and artistically.

Ironically, the club representing one of Canada's largest cities was owned by American interests. A Minnesota-based group called Medicor operated the team with two Americans, Thomas K. Scallen and Lyman D. Walters, in command. Vancouver citizens apparently didn't mind since their main objective then was to get big-league hockey in British Columbia; and that is precisely what Medicor did.

Scallen and Walters picked Norman "Bud" Poile as their manager and the man responsible for building the team. Poile, a former NHL star with Toronto, New York, and Chicago, had been the manager of the Philadelphia Flyers when that team entered the NHL and won the West Division championship in its first season. The Flyers slipped after that and Poile thought he had discovered the reason why.

"Their mistake," said Poile, "was not in concentrating on centers in the draft. Centers are the key to hockey success and without good ones you don't stand a chance."

With that in mind Poile selected big Orland Kurtenbach from the New York Rangers in the draft and Ray Cullen, a Minnesota North Stars journeyman. Having second choice—after Buffalo—in the junior draft, Poile picked Dale Tallon, another center who had played for

the Toronto Marlboros of the Ontario Hockey Association's Junior
A League.

Still another plus for the Canucks was the fact that they owned 52
professional players from their own Western League club as well as
several skaters from the Rochester Americans of the American
League. "I think some of our WHL players can help our NHL
entry," said Poile. "George Gardner, for example, is a major-league
goalie in my opinion. But even then, if they aren't much help, they
give us depth, which is a big asset in itself."

For coach, Poile selected Hal Laycoe, a former NHL defenseman
with the Rangers, Canadiens, and Bruins who had coached 24
games with Los Angeles before being fired in the 1969–70 season.
Laycoe was pleased that Poile had signed big men such as Kurtenbach and defensemen Pat Quinn and John Arbour. "Hitting teams,"
said Laycoe, "are teams with a will to win and that's what we have
to instill in this new team. It may take a while to establish but that
will be our objective."

The Canucks started with a bang. They remained an East Division contender for most of their first season before settling into sixth
place. Their future in April 1971 looked, at the very least, hopeful.

"We ended our first year with nine proven major leaguers," said
Poile, "nine players we can build a playoff contender around. That's
a great deal more than I expected."

Poile was especially pleased with the way Tallon developed and
was delighted with the reception of the fans. In their first season
the Canucks played to 97.8 percent of the capacity at the Pacific
Coliseum and figured to sell out every game in seasons to come.

But the rookie year turned out to be illusionary. All that seemed
good soon would turn bad, although it wasn't apparent until well
into the 1971–72 season. In his second attempt at the draft, Poile
selected Jocelyn Guevremont, a big French-Canadian defenseman,
and Bobby Lalonde, a smallish, high-scoring wing. "Put it all
together," said Poile, "and we're in pretty good shape, with excellent
prospects for the future."

Sadly, for Vancouver fans, the Canucks could not put it all
together. Their scoring was frugal and their goaltending generous
—to the opposition. They finished at the bottom of the East Division
with the worst record in the NHL. Inevitably, heads began to roll.

Laycoe was relieved of the coaching job and replaced by Vic
Stasiuk, a hard-nosed crony of Poile who had previously been dismissed by the Philadelphia Flyers and California Golden Seals. It

was hoped that his aggressive style would be an improvement over the easy-going Laycoe.

Another problem was the arrival of the World Hockey Association which immediately began raiding NHL clubs for talent. The Canucks were as susceptible as any team and lost their "policeman" forward Rosaire Paiement to the Chicago Cougars and goalie Gardner to the Los Angeles Sharks.

Poile never did find an adequate replacement for Paiement but he did insert young Dunc Wilson into Gardner's spot and hoped for the best. "Our scouts told us that of the young goalies available," said Poile, "Dunc was the best."

But Wilson's *joie de vivre* attitude toward life immediately grated coach Stasiuk and almost immediately there was friction between the two diverse personalities. If that wasn't a problem enough, more came with each week for the embattled Poile.

Tallon, who was shifted from defense to forward and back again, became disenchanted with life on the Canucks and made it clear that he wanted to be traded. Wayne Maki, a rugged efficient forward, suffered a brain tumor in mid-season and was hospitalized. Orland Kurtenbach also was sidelined with stomach problems and the Canucks' attack went to pieces.

By mid-season there was a near mutiny over Stasiuk's stewardship during a stopover in Pittsburgh. The testy coach remained in command but it was apparent that his job was in jeopardy unless Vancouver somehow made the playoffs.

But the Canucks never had a chance. They hit bottom again— with a resounding thud. Their captain Kurtenbach scored only nine goals and their leading scorer was a skinny Chicago Black Hawks' reject named Bobby Schmautz.

The strain of managing Vancouver had its effect on Poile who was hospitalized late in the 1972–73 season and advised by doctors to relinquish the managership of the team. He agreed to step down but remained on as one of the Canucks' vice-presidents.

That, however, was the least of the front office woes. On April 13, 1973, Canucks' president Scallen was sentenced to four years in prison after being told he had violated the trust placed in him by the people of British Columbia. The rap against Scallen was that he switched $3,000,000 from one company to another to prevent his Medicor firm from sinking. As one observer put it, "It was theft, but there was no personal gain." Scallen promptly launched an appeal.

The Scallen incident coupled with the uprising against Stasiuk, Poile's sickness, and the general disintegration of Vancouver's hockey team seemed to be the Watergate of British Columbia. While awaiting his appeal, Scallen desperately tried to strengthen his crumbling club but by the autumn of 1973 it appeared to be a project that would take a decade rather than a season.

If there is any solace for the Canucks, it is rooted in the unswerving loyalty of the home crowd. "We have a unique situation in Vancouver," explained Canucks assistant vice-president Babe Pratt. "Every time we lose, we get 50 phone calls from fans wanting to know if any season ticket-holders have cancelled. We have 125 season subscribers in Edmonton, Alberta, and 75 in Calgary, Alberta, who pay to come in by plane for each home game."

Then, a pause and smile: "We can only hope that we don't make the playoffs because it could mean trouble—NHL rules say we have to guarantee 500 tickets to the other club!"

Atlanta Flames

LEGEND HAD IT that the closest Georgians would ever get to ice would be sipping gin-and-tonic. Professional ice hockey never would make it in the Deep South, experts reasoned, because it never had made it. Such thinking helped explain why the admission of the Atlanta Flames to the National Hockey League in 1972–73 was greeted with militant skepticism.

Yet, on October 14, 1972, the 15,078-seat Omni arena opened the major league hockey season in Georgia for the first time, and based on public acclaim Flame-watching will soon replace the gin-and-tonic sipping as the favorite pastime in Atlanta.

Because they entered the NHL along with the New York Islanders in a turbulent hockey year, spiced by the arrival of the World Hockey Association, the Flames were taken lightly by their opponents. Like most expansion teams, they were a ragtag collection of big-league rejects and untried kids directed by Bernie "Boom Boom" Geoffrion whose only other NHL coaching experience ended in disaster.

But they had two assets. Flames president Bill Putnam helped mold the Philadelphia Flyers when that team entered the NHL and came to Atlanta with plenty of experience in team-building. Putnam picked Cliff Fletcher to be his general manager. With a handsome portfolio as a scout. Fletcher was in an excellent position to evaluate what talent was available and his choices were superb.

Fletcher immediately proved his worth by signing most of his available talent while the rival Islanders lost a horde of skaters to the new WHA. "Cliff did a hell of a job, along with the scouts," said Geoffrion. "They went to work right away. That's why we didn't lose any players to the other league."

If Fletcher had the smarts, Geoffrion had the smiles. A member of Hockey's Hall of Fame, he charmed Georgians the moment he set foot in Atlanta. "He became an instant hero," said *The New York Times,* "idolized almost as much as he used to be during his starring days in Montreal."

The Boomer's *joie de vivre* and rampant enthusiasm was infectious even before the 1972–73 season got underway and helped explain why the Flames sold 7,000 season tickets before they ever played a game. But once the season began, Geoffrion's popularity reached new heights.

Unlike their Northern counterparts, the Islanders, Atlanta won lots of games early in the season. They beat the Islanders at Nassau Coliseum on October 7, 1972, and continued playing like a poised, experienced club well past the mid-point of the campaign. After 50 games, the Flames had won 20, lost 22, and tied eight. More important, they were right in the thick of the West Division pennant race.

Geoffrion received most of the credit for the surprise start. His enthusiasm seemed to galvanize the players. "He gave them confidence," said Fletcher.

Geoffrion did it with a distillation of sugar and vinegar. He coddled some and scolded others. "My job," said Geoffrion, "was to mold them together. I spent time with guys who wanted to learn. They knew they had to work or I'd get rid of them. I gave them confidence and stayed with them."

The confidence seeped into the grandstands which grew more and more crowded as the season progressed. By mid-season, 2,000 additional season tickets had been sold. "The people were talking about us in the streets," said Fletcher, "and then coming to watch us. The great start meant thousands more at each game."

There are several theories about hockey's instant appeal in Atlanta. One has it that no matter where the game is played, be it in Canada or Russia, the fans appreciate 60 minutes of solid action. "Hockey has the theatrics of wrestling," wrote Tony Petrella in *The Atlanta Constitution,* "the hitting of a Joe Louis–Max Schmeling fight and the raw excitement of a Georgia Tech–Georgia football game. Give hockey a brand new showplace, an exciting image and the city of Atlanta is ready for hockey."

The Flames didn't make the playoffs in their first season but the fans didn't seem to mind. "The spectators here were great," said Geoffrion. "I've never seen any better, even in Montreal. They cheered when the team came out on the ice and cheered even when we lost. They were fantastic."

Much of the cheering was directed at goalies Phil Myre and Dan Bouchard. "They gave us the best goaltending in the West Division," said Fletcher, "except for Chicago. And I think Bouchard is going to become the best in the business."

Their leading scorer in the first year was an unheralded forward named Bob Leiter, who had bounced around the minors for several years prior to his call to Atlanta. He was aided by Curt Bennett, a huge center who had been obtained from the New York Rangers in mid-season and who seemed destined for stardom in seasons to come.

Curiously, the player from whom the most was expected and the least delivered was Jacques Richard, the Flames number one draft choice, who finished ninth in team scoring. "He had difficulty adjusting to the scene in Atlanta," said Fletcher. "He was only 21 years old and could hardly speak a word of English when he arrived. In a few years he should be one of the league's best scorers."

Whether Richard reaches the superstar plateau or not, there is little doubt that the love affair between Atlanta and ice hockey is here to stay. Before the first season had ended, architects were devising plans to add more seats to handle all the fans who want to see hockey at the Omni.

The hockey fever apparently knows no limits and Atlanta's two newspapers have taken due notice of the enthusiasm. They give the Flames extensive coverage because the townspeople demand it.

"Go to a cocktail party now in Decatur or College Park," wrote Jim Huber in *The Atlanta Journal*, "and you'll likely hear nothing but hockey for hours. Retail and wholesale sporting goods stores have been forced to quickly stock whatever hockey equipment they can find. Flames jerseys sell like hotcakes, street hockey outfits are in serious demand, table hockey games go the first day they're put out. Youngsters are just as likely to be seen swapping Bobby Orr for Yvan Cournoyer in the bubble gum card department as Hank Aaron for three Mickey Mantles."

The ice hockey age has, in fact, conquered the Deep South.

New York Islanders

ALTHOUGH the National Hockey League accepted ten new teams between 1967 and 1972 only one of them emerged as a genuine "clown" club of the ice. That would be the New York Islanders who made their debut in October 1972 and within five months were the laughing stock of major league hockey.

Massive ineptitude was the major problem from top to bottom. Unlike their rival, the Atlanta Flames who entered the league at the same time, the Islanders did not take the World Hockey Association seriously. Before the start of the 1972–73 campaign, the Islanders had lost several first-rate players to the new league including forwards Norm Ferguson, Ted Hampson, and Garry Peters.

But that was just one of the difficulties. For a time during the 1972–73 season it seemed that *everything* the Islanders did would prove to be disastrous in one way or another. They drafted a 20-year-old right wing and then had to give him skating lessons, his style was so awkward. They played an entire game with one of their defensemen, Neil Nicholson, wearing the wrong color helmet (subjecting him to an automatic penalty if the opposition chooses to complain). Another time the Islanders lost a game to Minnesota, 1–0, because they *didn't* complain that Jude Drouin of the North Stars scored the winning goal with an illegal stick. "Someday," commented John Jeansonne of *Newsday*, "this team may provide material for Johnny Carson." The Islanders were so bad, they finished the season with a record 60 defeats.

"We are the cripples of the NHL," said an Islander official before the first calamitous season had ended. "If you saw a cripple walking down the street would you laugh at him?"

Opponents laughed at the Islanders but the fans who paid to see them at Nassau Coliseum in Uniondale, Long Island, treated them with the same affection which New Yorkers once held for the Mets when they were the clowns of major-league baseball.

On October 7, 1972, when NHL hockey made its debut in Long Island, a crowd of 12,221 visited the Coliseum. The Islanders lost that game, 3–2, to Atlanta and lost most of the games thereafter. But the fans didn't mind and by February 1973 it was almost impossible to buy a ticket to an Islander game, they had become so popular. It was hard to explain but there were answers.

"A new breed of hockey fan—dedicated to the proposition that perfection can be boring—discovered hockey at the Nassau Coliseum," wrote Wes Gaffer, hockey writer for *The New York Daily News*. "The frustration that Mets' fans once experienced now resides with the Islanders fans who suffer the same pangs but all agree that there's a better day coming."

The Islanders' difficulties started with owner Roy Boe, owner of the New York Nets of the American Basketball Association. Boe was unfamiliar with hockey management and hired his first coach, Phil Goyette, two months after the rival Flames had hired their coach, Boom Boom Geoffrion.

"Atlanta got a tremendous jump on us," Boe conceded, "there's no doubt about that. But they got their franchise nearly two months before we did."

Boe hired Bill Torrey, who previously had been executive vice-president of the California Golden Seals, as his general manager. Torrey allowed the players to escape to the WHA putting the Islanders in a hole before they even took the ice. Torrey then hired Phil Goyette, who had no previous major league coaching experience, to coach the team. By mid-season Torrey fired Goyette and replaced him with Earl Ingarfield, who had been an Islanders scout.

Despite their top-heavy record, the Islanders did produce some quality performances. Gerry Desjardins, the team's first-string goalie, played competently and often spectacularly during the 1972–73 season and even managed to take a humorous persepctive to his hazardous job.

"I can see pucks in my sleep," said Desjardins. "And when I wake up my wife gives me the shots on goal!"

Billy Harris, the Islanders' top draft choice in 1972, also was a positive force for the team although he slumped badly in mid-season. A husky right wing, Harris then came on strong to score 28 goals and 22 assists and appeared destined for bigger things in future seasons.

"I had hoped we'd do better than we did in your rookie season," said Harris. "But it was a learning year for all of us."

Harris virtually became a *cause celebre* because he was severely criticized in some quarters and just as enthusiastically defended in others. But he was only 21 years old and his most difficult task was adjusting to a life on his own in the metropolis.

"My whole style of living was changed," said Harris, who had lived in Toronto all his life. "I played in every one of our 78 games. That long schedule, the traveling involved, living by myself all combined to make big-league life a lot more strenuous than I expected. You really have to look after yourself.

Ed Westfall, who had come to the Islanders from the 1972 Stanley Cup champion Boston Bruins, played solid two-way hockey for the last-place club when he wasn't sidelined with injuries. After playing for Boston, Westfall found it somewhat difficult making the adjustment to the new team—and the conditions surrounding it.

"We had trouble getting ice time for practices even at home," said Westfall. "We couldn't even get an hour to skate at the Coliseum on our own. You know, just to limber up. They always had to put the basketball floor down or something like that."

In the final weeks of the 1972–73 season the Islanders appeared to play better hockey and were responding more positively to new coach Ingarfield, who, in turn, responded more positively to them than his predecessor, Goyette.

"My job," said Ingarfield, "is to let the players know I'm trying to understand them; that I'm with them. Hockey is an emotional game. I've got to keep their morale up."

The Islanders' confidence was aided by constantly growing crowds. On March 6, 1973 the largest weekday crowd (14,268) in the club's young history jammed the Coliseum to see the Islanders lose, 3–2, to the Montreal Canadiens. Buoyed by the audience, the Islanders outplayed the visitors for two periods before succumbing. It was enough to fill manager Torrey with confidence about the team's future.

"The only thing that really matters now," said Torrey, "is going with the young guys. Our amateur draft has proven to be as good as anybody's in the league and I will stack my scouts against anyone's. The circumstances at this point have forced us to try what players we have and use all of 'em that come our way."

It sounded a lot like the early years of the Mets who eventually went on to win a World Series. Perhaps, the Islanders' day soon will come.

PART THREE
The Players: The Past

The Bentley Brothers

THIRTY YEARS AGO, when the Chicago Black Hawks were in lamentable shape on a practically permanent basis, a wiry shred from Western Canada came to them named Douglas Bentley.

He was small, 142 pounds, and old as hockey rookies are measured, 23, and he had been rejected by three other NHL clubs. Experts representing Toronto, Montreal and Boston unanimously judged Bentley to be too frail. The Hawks, with nothing more to lose anyway, took a chance.

Bentley, cocky and aggressive, survived against heavier opponents with speed and finesse. He put himself in brotherly perspective whenever his smooth style was praised. "You should see Max," he said of his younger sibling. "He's twice as good as I am."

Max arrived in Chicago in the spring of 1940—20 years old, thin, black-haired, an undernourished paperweight. Coach Paul Thompson, perplexed, shipped him to the Chicago farm in Kansas City with instructions "to fatten Max up."

In the fall, fattened to an underwhelming 150 pounds, Max was reunited with Doug on a forward line with the Hawks. They ultimately were allied with Bill Mosienko, a swift right wing from Winnipeg, but not before Max tried to con the Hawks into signing another Bentley brother. "You should see Reg," Max insisted. "He's twice as good as I am."

Coach Thompson did obtain Reg Bentley in 1942 and, for a brief period, the Hawks were the only team with three brothers on one

line. The family compact collapsed, however, when Reg, lacking
the guile of Max and Doug, was shipped back to the bushes.

The Bentleys hit a combined scoring peak in 1942–43, the season
Doug won the scoring title with 73 points and Max third with 70.
World War II intervened and both went away, out of hockey until
1945–46. Max was superb offensively when he came back, able to
win the scoring title in successive seasons—with 61 points in 1945–
46 and 72 in 1946–47.

On November 2, 1947, after winning the Hart Trophy as the most
valuable player in hockey, Max was traded to Toronto in a massive
player deal. The Hawks, needing quantity instead of quality,
swapped Max and rookie Cy Thomas to the Maple Leafs for Bob
Goldham, Gaye Stewart, Gus Bodnar, Ernie Dickens and Bud Poile,
who now presides over the Philadelphia Flyers.

With the Leafs, integrated with athletes superior to the Chicago
forces, Max helped Toronto win three Stanley Cups in four years.
But his headiest moment was as a Hawk, in 1943, when Chicago
subdued the Rangers 10–1. Max knocked down seven points, four
goals and three assists, scoring all the goals in one period, a NHL
record.

The Bentleys were elusive targets, but meaty marksmen constantly aimed at them. Johnny Gottselig, coaching the Hawks in
1946, would complain: "It's the same damn story every winter.
Nobody is fast enough to catch 'em, so they try to knock 'em out.
Something's gotta be done to protect the Bentleys."

Something, on occasion, was done by the ogres in the Chicago
line-up. Johnny Mariucci, a defenseman who used to extract teeth
in the Bierman fashion as a football player at the University of
Minnesota, constantly policed the Bentley tormentors. Sometimes
the Bentleys themselves retaliated, to the intense delight of Eddie
Froelich, the Chicago trainer.

Froelich would say, "Remember the time Doug got his teeth
knocked out?" and then he'd be into one of those tales of hockey
mayhem. "We're playing Toronto and in the first period Doug
tangles with Gus Bodnar. That sonofabitch Bodnar rammed his stick
down Doug's throat. Mouth looked awful. Four teeth knocked out.
Bleeding like a stuck hog. I fixed him up best I could." Froelich
basked in an old bloody memory. "When the next period began,
Doug insisted on playing. He did play, in the second period and
the last one. After each period, he come back vomiting blood." Glory

is often gory, Eddie Froelich said. "Talk about guts! Doug had 'em in spades!"

Max Bentley, squeamish in contrast to his brother, was hockey's leading hypochondriac. He always announced he felt wretched. Joseph Cavanaugh Farrell, formerly the relentless publicist of the Hawks, constantly supplied the press with bulletins on Max's delicate health. "Max always suspects he's got cancer, kidney trouble or a bum ticker," Farrell reported. "If they named a new disease tomorrow, Max would catch it by nightfall." Farrell then told reporters, "Come into the dressing room and I'll show you how sick Max is."

In the dressing room, within Max's view, Farrell would elaborately slip two cough drops into his mouth. Max, scrambling over littered equipment, rushed to Farrell's side. "Gimme some of those," he said plaintively. "I'm in terrible shape."

"One winter," Farrell related, "Max was sure he had cancer. There was a brown spot on his lip. So Eddie Froelich gave him some harmless sugar pills. Max came in after the game and the spot was gone. We told him the phony pills must have cured him."

"No," Max argued. "It's gone back to my throat. I don't feel so good."

Mr. Farrell reached his punch line. "I'll tell you how sick he was: that night the little loogan scored three goals!"

The Bentleys were raised in the Saskatchewan hamlet of Delisle, where their father was a storekeeper. Five brothers in the family of 13 grew up to play for the same senior team in Alberta 33 years ago—Max, Doug, Reg, Scoop and Roy Bentley all members one winter of the Drumheller Miners.

Max and Doug eventually played for New York Rangers in the early fifties when they were on the far slope of their slick careers. Doug at last turned to coaching in the minor leagues, at Saskatoon, Edmonton and Charlotte, North Carolina. But in retirement, Max claimed that hockey hasn't offered him any employment at the executive level. He farms at Delisle, and gambles on horses and, at 49, hopes he'll get a coaching offer.

In 1972, after a long bout with cancer, Doug died in Saskatoon, Saskatchewan.

Frank Brimsek

ONLY TWO BOSTON GOALKEEPERS have won the Vezina Trophy as the best players at their position—Cecil (Tiny) Thompson, who won it four times between 1930 and 1938, and Frank Brimsek, who took it twice. The last time for Brimsek was 28 seasons ago, in 1941–42.

By then it was fashionable to call him Kid Zero and, when he matured, Mr. Zero. The appellation was justly earned: he shut out enemy shooters in six of the first eight games he played for the Bruins. Harold Kaese, the Boston columnist, was notably impressed. Mr. Kaese wrote, after Brimsek was the acrobatic hub of Stanley Cup triumphs in 1938–39 and 1940–41: "If all the pucks stopped by Frigid Frankie were stuck together, they would make a solid rubber hose, three inches in diameter, long enough to reach from Boston to his home in Eveleth, Minnesota."

Brimsek was taciturn and remote when he came up to replace Thompson, up through Eveleth High School, St. Cloud, Minnesota, Teacher's College and Providence Reds of the American League. He made the Boston varsity in late November, 1938, after Thompson was sold to Detroit Red Wings. "Nobody thought Brimsek could replace Thompson," said Win Green, the club's trainer, in a reflective moment years later. "What a mistake that was!"

Art Ross was not making many mistakes as the Boston manager in those years, and at training camp he personally tested both goalers. He shot 25 pucks from the whites-of-their-eyes range of 10 feet at Thompson, and scored six times. He fired 25 at Brimsek from the same distance and did not score once. "The kid had the fastest hands I ever saw," Ross testified. "Like lightning."

Brimsek played his first game for the Bruins in Montreal on December 1, 1938. They were beaten, 2–0. He played his second game in Chicago on December 4 and won 5–0.

The next game was in the Boston Garden, before loud witnesses not inclined to salute any kid who had deprived them of one of their favorites, Thompson. "The crowd was so quiet that first night," Brimsek remembers, "that I could hear them breathe and feel their cold eyes on my back." He showed them, and Chicago, the fast hands of a pickpocket. He smothered the Black Hawks 2–0, his second consecutive shut-out. On December 11 he made it three in a row with a 3–0 conquest of New York Rangers.

The descriptive overworked in the frantic Boston press was "sensational," gaudy hyperbole fenced in with exclamation marks. Would anyone ever score on Kid Zero?

The Rangers reduced Brimsek back to the ranks of mere mortals by beating him for two goals on December 13, but the Bruins won 3–2. He had frustrated rival scorers for 231 minutes and 54 seconds. Then he reeled off another shutout string of 220 minutes and 24 seconds against Montreal Canadiens, Detroit and the New York Americans. In the space of three weeks the busher from Eveleth had experts asking whatever became of Tiny Thompson?

Brimsek yielded 65 goals in the 41 games he played in his rookie season and accomplished 10 shutouts. Naturally he won the Vezina as the stingiest goalkeeper and the Calder Trophy as the league's superior freshman.

His shutout sequences were not records. Alex Connell, a fireman who specialized in putting out blazes for the Ottawa Senators, shut out the opposition for 446 minutes, nine seconds in 1927–28. Connell had six consecutive shutouts during his memorable span. His task was easier than Brimsek's, however, because forward passing was not allowed in the attacking zone in Connell's time.

Brimsek looked nerveless, face impassive, conversation monosyllabic. He seemed stoic, in the fashion of his Czech parents. But his mood was all mask, a ruse that did not escape Coach Lester Patrick of the Rangers. "Where do they get that Frigid Frankie stuff?" Patrick demanded. "He's nervous and high strung. His words spill out of him. He's a bundle of nerves, but they still call him Frigid Frankie! Such claptrap!"

Brimsek was in many ways a hockey hypochondriac to match

Max Bentley, a contemporary outpatient with Chicago and Toronto. Both had an old maid's fussiness about their health. "I've got a cold," Brimsek frequently complained before games to the trainer. "My head aches. My throat is sore. I think I'm catching the damn flu." Other players, aware of his complaints, were assured whenever Brimsek complained. Any time he talked like a basket case in the dressing room, he was feverishly good on the ice. He talked like a physical wreck, but in his first six seasons he missed only one game. That trouble was also in his head—he had a broken nose.

Brimsek served two years in the Coast Guard during World War II, then returned to play for Boston until 1950. He wasn't as good as he was before the war but neither were his teammates. He retired to run a sporting goods store in Virginia, Minnesota, finished at 36 as a clay pigeon who went looking for bullet shots.

Brimsek was elected to the Hall of Fame in 1966, one of few Americans to enter a lodge that is essentially Canadian property. He would tell his Canadian associates, smiling small, "You're just a bunch of lousy foreigners."

The Kraut Line

MILTON CONRAD SCHMIDT sounded subdued after Robert Bauer's funeral in 1964: "Bobby was our team . . . my right arm."

Schmidt was 46 then, three years younger than Bauer, on his way to a second term as general manager of the Bruins. After Bauer succumbed to a heart attack, Schmidt felt more alone than at any other time in his adult life.

Bauer's story was also the story of Schmidt and Woodrow Dumart, whose ample girth gained him recognition as Porky. They were associates on Boston's Kraut Line, the distinguished forwards in the halcyon era of the Bruins 30 years ago. They rank as the commanding unit in the decade between the decline of Toronto's Kid Line of Conacher–Primeau–Jackson in the middle Thirties and the formation of Montreal's Punch Line of Blake–Lach–Richard immediately after World War II.

Dumart played left wing with a hard shot, one of the heavy shots of all time, up there with the cannonading of Babe Dye and Charlie Conacher. Schmidt was the center, a full-throttle style of attacker, his ample nose stuck out like a bent prow. Bauer was the right wing, compact and clever along the boards, considered a smooth playmaker around the goal.

The story of the Krauts has a touch of those incredibly heroic novels that the older generations were saturated with in childhood. "They had the ring of *The Rover Boys in Andorra, The Golden Boys on Center Court at Wimbledon,* and so on," Herbert Warren Wind wrote. "They were the stuff of devoted boyhood chums scaling the heights together, all for one and one for all."

Bauer, Schmidt and Dumart first were allied in the winter of 1934–35 on a junior team called the Green Shirts in Kitchener, an industrial town 65 miles west of Toronto. Albert (Battleship) Leduc, a venerable Montreal defenseman, later christened them the Sauerkrauts when he coached them at Providence.

Leduc's inspiration was simple. They all had German ancestors, born as they were in the twin sauerkraut settlements of Kitchener–Waterloo. Kitchener was originally called Berlin, but World War I prompted an unsubtle change to the name of a British field marshal. History tried to repeat in the second rash of patriotism that broke out during World War II. A Boston newspaper temporarily tagged the Kraut Line the Kitchener Kids, but it never caught on. They stayed the Krauts.

Schmidt and Dumart became teammates for the first time when they played for Kitchener in the Ontario Hockey League, a junior league for players under 21. In their third year, 1934–35, they were joined by Bauer. He had been attending St. Michael's College in Toronto, where professional scouts began to woo him.

Boston beat Toronto to Bauer and signed him in the spring of 1935. Dumart also contracted with the Bruins, after Art Ross personally scouted him. Bauer and Dumart touted Schmidt so lavishly that the crusty Boston manager invited him to training camp the next September. Schmidt, 17, was politely receptive. "I appreciate the invitation very much," Schmidt wrote Ross. "I will immediately get a job to pay my way to your camp in Hershey."

Ross was nearly blind before he died, with nothing to laugh about, but he could still smile about Schmidt's naïveté. "Schmidtty didn't know that the club paid a player's training-camp expenses."

Schmidt was drainpipe thin in his first pro camp, sent home to fatten his 125-pound frame. The next season, made robust by Kitchener's country cooking, he was linked again on a line with Bauer and Dumart on the Boston farm in Providence.

They arrived in Boston to stay in 1937–38, and the next four years were the good old days that Bruin fans still revere. Bauer, Schmidt and Dumart, precise and imaginative, were vital to a club that finished first four successive times and won the Stanley Cup twice. In 1942 they enlisted, as a trio, in the Royal Canadian Air Force.

In their last game before leaving for service, the Krauts combined for eight scoring points in an 8–1 drubbing of Montreal Canadiens.

At the finish, players of both teams plucked them up and carried them off while the organist in the Boston Garden played "Auld Lang Syne." Nostalgia was thicker than sour cream whenever Bauer recalled the moment. "The ovation, at the height of my youth, sort of grabbed me."

They returned to Boston as a line after three years of service in Europe, hardly soon enough to suit Art Ross. The Bruins were toothless when the men went away, targets for derision from a hooting Boston crowd. "Hey, Ross," a fan yelled during one wartime stoning, "where the hell's your power play?"

Ross bit off a frustrated reply, "In England, France and Germany, you slacker!"

The Krauts played together for two seasons after the war, before Bauer retired. He was the only NHL player to quit after a season in which he scored 30 goals, the equivalent of hitting .350.

Dumart was an active player until 1954, when he was 37. The previous spring, in a Stanley Cup semifinal upset of the favored Detroit Red Wings, Dumart checked the Wings' great Howe with a bill collector's vigilance. He retired to work for Bauer's skate company and continue living next door to Schmidt in the Boston suburb of Needham.

Schmidt hung on as a player until 1955, but before that there was a memorable moment in Boston during Schmidt–Dumart Night on March 18, 1952. Bauer abandoned his retirement for one game to play with his pals, old pals. Chicago Black Hawks were the opposition.

Schmidt had 199 goals at the time and poetic justice demanded that he get his number 200 in alliance with Bauer and Dumart.

Early in the game there was a splendid Hollywood serving of corn. Bauer, unsteady on his skates, passed the puck to Dumart at center ice. Dumart walked in and fired. There was a rebound and Schmidt pounced on the loose puck. He drove it past the sprawling goalie. Dumart dived into the net to retrieve the puck as the souvenir of Schmidt's 200th goal. Pure joy swept the Boston galleries. Then there was a hush for the old announcement Boston fans hadn't heard since Bauer's retirement in 1947—"Boston goal by Schmidt, assists from Dumart and Bauer!"

Memories are made of that, Milt Schmidt says. He was the core of the Krauts, to be sure, three times the all-star center, the league's leading scorer in 1939–40, the most valuable player in the NHL in 1950–51. "Schmidt was the fastest playmaker of all time," Art Ross insisted. "I mean no player ever skated at the tilt he did and was still able to make a play." His formidable truck-collision style left him with badges of brutality—broken ribs, a broken jaw, a shattered nose, damaged knees and a wry neck. "He hit," Conn Smythe used to say, "to hurt."

Lynn Patrick set up the definitive Schmidt anecdote in 1955, after he was elevated to general manager and Schmidt replaced him as coach. The conversation switched to hockey after a round of golf. "Schmidt will never be as successful as I was as coach," Patrick volunteered to a small group in the locker room. Patrick is notoriously unegoistic and his listeners, particularly Schmidt, were startled to hear his apparent boasting. "That's true," Patrick repeated. "Schmidtty will never be anywhere as successful a coach as I was." He paused to charge his glass. "He'll never be able to look down the bench when the team's in trouble and holler, as I could, 'Milt, get out there!' "

Joe Malone

IT IS NORMAL in this world, and particularly in the toy existence of sport, to beat the drums for the coming thing, and to forget the thing that has slipped into the shadows.

Shakespeare had Ulysses say:

> . . . To have done is to hang
> Quite out of fashion, like a rusty mail
> In monumental mock'ry. . . .
> . . . The welcome ever smiles,
> And farewell goes out sighing. . . .
> *Troilus and Cressida*, III, iii

Today Philip Anthony Esposito of the Boston Bruins is the big rhythm in the National Hockey League, set to the music of three straight seasons of more than 50 goals, including one in which he popped 76 in 78 games.

There will be other superb shooters after Esposito, other muscular melodies to fascinate hockey fans. But chances are there will never be in the game again the sort of productive player that Joe Malone was in the medieval winter of 1917–18.

Malone was stocky, black-haired and 27 years old in the last winter of World War I. He played for the Montreal Canadiens on a forward line, joined with Newsy Lalonde at center and Didier Pitre on right wing. His slick accomplices also included Bert Corbeau, Jack Laviolette, Louis Berlinquette and Georges Vezina, the tall goaler whose distinguished name survives on the trophy awarded annually to the outstanding goalkeeper in the NHL.

The NHL then contained four teams—the Canadiens and Wanderers from Montreal, the Toronto Arenas and the Ottawa Senators. The schedule was a mere 22 games, or slightly longer than the exhibition series each modern team plays in preparation for a 76-game grind.

Malone struck in clusters. He scored five goals in his first game, then repeated the feat in two subsequent games. Today, in the frantic era of constant attack, it is a major story when a player scores five times in one game during a prolonged season. Bobby Rousseau was the last to fire five with such multiple accuracy, for Montreal Canadiens in a 9–3 conquest of Detroit Red Wings on February 1, 1964. Then, on November 7, 1968, Red Berenson scored six for St. Louis against Philadelphia.

Malone scored in 14 consecutive games, and finished the schedule with 44 goals in 20 games. He missed one game, he remembers, because the arena of the rival Montreal Wanderers burned down. He missed another for reasons that escaped his recollection—"either I was hurt or drunk, can't remember which."

Malone's mark was therefore 44 goals in 18 games, or roughly 2.44 goals per game. People who ordinarily took scant interest in hockey were asking in 1918 what this Malone was like, this Irish critter who beat goalkeepers as if he owned them.

"Handsome, good-looking, polished," were the descriptives Frank Selke applied to Malone in his book of recollections, *Behind The Cheering.* "Joe," Selke said, "could make some of Hollywood's glamour boys look undistinguished by comparison."

Malone was 79, retired nine years from his career as a tool designer, when he died May 14, 1969, in the Montreal suburb of St. Laurent, Quebec. There was a hint of brogue around the scalloped edges of his conversation. "Maybe I should have scored more than 44 goals, the amount of time I spent on the ice that year," he said. "In those days the regulars played perhaps 50 minutes a game." Years come and go for ancient athletes as shadows on a window pane. Every time Malone runs a picture through his mind, he leaves a little more on memory's cutting-room floor. But his ability to score in bunches stands out sharp as a skate blade. "One time," he remembers, "I got nine goals in a Stanley Cup game. In 1913 it was."

Malone was in the high time of life as captain of the Quebec

Bulldogs. He embarrassed the Sydney, Nova Scotia, Millionaires with nine goals in a game the Bulldogs won 14–3 on March 8, 1913. In another game, in 1920, he ruined the Toronto St. Pats with seven goals, a record still acknowledged by NHL mathematicians.

"I guess today's game is faster," an admission from one not wishing to sound like a professional oldtimer. "It's faster because the players are fresher, the way they change lines every two minutes." Malone insisted, however, that the present entertainment lacks some of the skills exhibited in the past. "There was more individual play in my time . . . not so scrambly, and not so many rebounds."

He played professionally for 16 seasons, from 1909 to 1924, with Quebec, Waterloo (Ontario), Canadiens and Hamilton Tigers, and then he was gone, retired just before the era of large crowds and bigger money. He was unique and he is worth remembering, as hockey historian Charles Coleman did in *The Trail of the Stanley Cup*. Coleman's all-star selections, based on massive statistical research of 1,200 players in 10 leagues, pegged Malone as one of three superior forwards in the 34 seasons between 1893 and 1926. His all-star compatriots were Clint Benedict, goal; Sprague Cleghorn and Ernie (Moose) Johnson, defence; Newsy Lalonde, rover; Frank Nighbor and Russell Bowie, forwards.

Howie Morenz

NO DISCUSSION of hockey's greatest players ever gets off the ice until some oldtimer, perhaps a King Clancy or a Newsy Lalonde, has said, "I mean—next to Howie Morenz, who was the greatest?" Then the argument can really get going on Maurice Richard and Gordie Howe and Bobby Hull and the others. But the Morenz legend keeps growing decades after his death, kept green in the memories of men who saw him in his stirring prime. Their fondest fiction may be no better than the truth, for the truth is that he was the most idolized player in Montreal hockey history— paramount in a city that has been flashily represented by stars like Richard and Doug Harvey and Lalonde and Jean Beliveau.

Morenz leaps across the screen of remembrance in the *bleu-blanc-rouge* of Les Canadiens, number 7 on his back and the puck at the end of his stick as he skates swiftly over the bright ice of Montreal's old Forum. First, winding up, Morenz circles his own goal. Then a little pushing hop tips off his charge down the ice. He gains speed as a stocky blur, long striding, grabbing the Montreal spectators to their feet and keeping them there, howling. He drives to the enemy blueline and, rising to the noisy crescendo, hurls his wiry body past the two defensemen who would impede him. Then, a quick final feint at the goalkeeper, a quick shot into the vacant net—goal! Morenz has scored! Delighted partisans rain the ice with joyous debris, programs, peanuts, hats, rubbers. Greater love had no fan than in sacrificing his rubbers for a Morenz goal, because Montreal is not exactly a town where snow and slush are unknown.

"I seen 'em all score goals," King Clancy insists. "Howe deftly, knocking everybody down with those windshield-wiper elbows. Richard coming in mad, guys piled all over him. Hull, booming a slapshot . . ." Clancy pauses for emphasis. "But I *never* saw anybody score like Morenz on a furious rush down center."

Morenz arrived in Montreal in 1923, up from the Ontario railroad center of Stratford, 45 minutes northwest of Toronto. Sports writers, groping for gaudy adjectives, soon dubbed him the Stratford Streak. "But, boys," he advised them amiably, "I was really born in the village of Mitchell." That intelligence prompted them to call him, naturally, the Mitchell Meteor. Before his first professional season ended, with the Canadiens winning the Stanley Cup, his assortment of descriptive tags included Hurtling Howie, the Canadien Catapult, the Marvel of Hockey, and, clumsily, the Phantom of the Ice.

Elmer Ferguson was a young sports writer for the *Montreal Herald* then, and the one-time dean of Canadian press boxes, Ferguson remembered, "When Howie skated full speed, everyone else on the ice seemed to be skating backward."

Off the ice, Morenz was just as fast. His behavior was cut to fit a line in the corny old "Face on the Barroom Floor": ". . . When he had cash to treat the gang, his hand was never slow."

He could, the fiction goes, shoot golf in the 70s. He was feverishly addicted to gambling on horses, so consumed by the game that he once tore up a winning parimutuel ticket, returned to the track at night, fell to all fours and searched until he found the winning scraps. He played a ukulele, not well. He wore spats. He was a lively, sophisticated athlete in sophisticated Montreal, where gambling, drinking and simpler, more elemental hobbies are easily pursued.

The Canadiens won the Stanley Cup three times in the 12 seasons Morenz played for them, and twice—in 1927–28 and 1930–31—he won the NHL scoring championship. In 1927–28, he scored 40 goals in a 44-game schedule.

His name sounded French-Canadian, but it was not. His ancestry was German-Swiss. But he possessed the flaming temperament typical of flamboyant Frenchmen—a peppery competitor, not the baleful blowtop that Rocket Richard was in a later generation of Canadiens.

One night in Boston, against the Bruins of the late twenties, Morenz faced off for the puck against Ralph (Cooney) Weiland. The puck wedged between their sticks, then bounced into the air. Weiland tapped it behind Morenz with his hand and it dropped behind Howie. Weiland pounced on the puck and, unchecked, got loose to score the winning goal.

Several hours later, in Boston's Hotel Manger, Elmer Ferguson heard an urgent knock on his door. Ferguson had finished his story for the *Montreal Herald* and, half asleep, answered the door. It was 4 A.M.

"What the hell you doing up at this hour?" he greeted Morenz.

"I haven't been to bed," Morenz said.

"So where have you been?"

"Out," Morenz said, not smiling. "Out walking."

"Walking where?" Ferguson wondered.

"Just up and down. Up and down the streets. I lost the game, didn't I?"

"Don't be silly," Ferguson said, "It was just another game and the whole team lost it."

Morenz refused to be consoled. "No. Weiland got by me on that face-off. He beat me."

Ferguson used up an hour, he recalls, trying to convince Morenz that losing nights are for sleep.

Morenz carried his ukulele on road trips, crooning away the train rides with mellow melodies like "If I Had a Girl Like You." The Montreal girl he married in 1926 was Mary MacKay, who bore him two sons and a daughter. One son, Howie, Jr., played amateur hockey in Montreal, but did not have the competitive stature to cut it with the pros. Morenz's daughter, Marlene, grew up to be the wife of Bernard (Boom Boom) Geoffrion, a former Montreal star and ex-coach of the New York Rangers.

His surpassing talent absorbed, in the middle twenties, all the alcohol rubs Morenz gave it. He spent one Saturday afternoon, before a game, consuming quarts of beer and exotic limburger cheese with onions at Elmer Ferguson's house. Ferguson finally told him, "You stink and you're full of beer. You'll never play hockey tonight."

Morenz laughed. And he played. He scored three goals; and, later, mentioned to the somewhat surprised Ferguson: "New scoring method. First I breathe on the goaler, then I shoot 'er in!"

One goaler, the late Roy Worters of the deceased New York

Americans, testified: "He's some wild wind, that number 7 of Canadiens. To me, he's just a blur—77777!"

Morenz had small, swift allies, Aurel Joliat on his left wing, Billy Boucher on his right. Georges Vezina, the Chicoutimi Cucumber, died of tuberculosis in 1926, but the capable George Hainsworth followed him into the net. Battleship Leduc and Sylvio Mantha protected the defense. The other forwards included Pit Lepine, Art Gagne, Armond Mondou and, later, Johnny Gagnon, the Little Black Cat.

Morenz was the commanding star, *"L'homme-éclair,"* the top man in any language. The collective cry for these Flying Frenchmen was the Gallically gleeful *"Les Canadiens sont la!"*

Speed was the strength of Morenz's game and he began to lose it in the early thirties, lose it to reckless skating and fast living. The Canadiens won the Stanley Cup in the spring of 1930 and again in 1931. Morenz won the Hart Trophy as the most valuable player in the NHL in 1931 and 1932, a prize first awarded to him in 1928.

His goal production sank from 14 in 1932–33 to eight in 1933–34, and then Canadiens swapped him to Chicago Black Hawks. Sentimentalists insisted the trade broke Morenz's heart, although that seemed to be slicing it a bit thick. He was not wounded enough to reject the contract for $12,500 which the late Leo Dandurand obtained for him from the Black Hawks.

Dandurand was the cunning owner of the Canadiens, and he protested, "The fans were starting to boo Howie in Montreal, and booing was the one thing he couldn't stand. I really did him a favor by sending him to Chicago."

The record does not support Dandurand. Morenz was neither very successful nor very contented in Chicago. The Black Hawks of that era played tight, defensive hockey and Morenz was constantly in the unseemly position of home-run hitter ordered to bunt.

One night, after the visiting Canadiens had beaten the Hawks in Chicago, Major Frederic McLaughlin stomped through the dressing room. He was the eccentric coffee baron who owned the Hawks since their admission to the NHL in 1926. McLaughlin strode toward Morenz and pointed an accusing finger at him. "You," McLaughlin shouted, "cost us this game!" Morenz looked up, unsmiling, said nothing. The next season he was shipped to New York Rangers in exchange for Glenn Brydson, an uninspired journeyman. He did not regain his old flair with the Rangers, although the Broadway Blueshirts were geared to his style of constant attack.

Leo Dandurand sold the Canadiens in 1936, sold them to operate a race track in New Orleans. Cecil Hart, hired as manager by the new group, attempted to rehabilitate the Habitants by rescuing Morenz from New York.

Morenz appeared to recover his former exuberance in the old surroundings. He was a vigorous, balding figure between Joliat and Gagnon in the early part of the 1936–37 season, and the Canadiens began to revisit old glory.

Short glory, though. On January 28, 1937, playing against the Black Hawks in Montreal, Morenz charged toward the Chicago net in the first period. He veered to the left side of the goal, hurtling into the stick of Andy Blair, a tall Chicago rearguard. Then Morenz crashed into the boards, his left foot thrust into the wood. He fell and, while falling, Blair's defense partner skated into him. Four bones in his left leg were smashed when Earl Siebert hit him. He was carried to the Montreal dressing room, placed on a rubbing table and given a cigarette. "I'm all through," between painful puffs, "all finished." Someone cursed Siebert. Morenz looked up, wincing. "Don't blame Siebert. It was an accident. My skate caught."

The bones were set at Hospital St. Luc and Morenz appeared to be recovering in the months after the accident. Affable streams of visitors poured sociable slugs of whisky into him, loudly seconding his motion, "I'll be back next year."

On March 8, more than five weeks after the fracture, Morenz stumbled out of his hospital bed to the bathroom. He fell on the floor. An embolism stopped his heart, killing him instantly.

Three days later, his coffin was taken to the Forum and rested on boards at center ice. His teammates stood near the casket as an honor guard while a Presbyterian minister conducted the funeral service. There were 10,000 mourners in the arena and 15,000 more, silent and bareheaded, stood on the streets outside. He was buried on the snowy slopes of Mount Royal, the peak that dominates the Montreal skyline.

Long after, working as an information officer for the Canadian National Railway in Ottawa, Aurel Joliat would say it for all of hockey's oldtimers: "Morenz was something that was only once."

The Patricks, Hockey's Royal Family

AT FRANK PATRICK'S FUNERAL, in Vancouver, British Columbia, on July 2, 1960, the Reverend R. R. Cunningham sketched an analogy: "I stood not long ago in a huge forest in the British Columbia interior," Reverend Cunningham told the mourners. "Of a sudden, I came to a clearing where loggers had felled many large trees. Only gaps remained where these great firs had stood." Now death, the minister said, had felled the Patricks. Only gaps remain. Lester Patrick, 76 and two years older than Frank, had succumbed to remorseless disease a month earlier in Victoria.

The minister's metaphor was apt. The Patricks took hockey out of the honky-tonk and moved it into the salons of the big cities on the continent. The game grew respectable in their image. "The Patricks are hockey's Royal Family," Frank Selke once said, in a poetic moment when he was running the Montreal Canadiens.

By that gauge, Lester was the crowned head of the family. His sons, Murray and Lynn, played for him in the late Thirties when he commanded the New York Rangers. They would later coach and manage the Rangers at different times, Murray (or Muzz) replacing Lynn in 1952, after Lynn shifted to the Boston Bruins. Muzz now directs special events for Madison Square Garden in New York, but Lynn remains in the NHL as general manager of the St. Louis Blues.

Frank Patrick's son Joe, never involved in organized hockey, is in the brokerage business in New York.

The Hall of Fame preserves the elder Patricks' claim to whatever immortality hockey has to offer. Lester and Frank were the first to introduce artificial ice plants to Canada, at Vancouver and Victoria in 1911. The Vancouver arena, largest in Canada at the time with 10,000 seats, cost $175,000. Frank was the first promoter to put numbers on a player's sweater. He conceived the lucrative play-off system that has been copied by every sport including major league baseball. He and Lester were prominent in professional hockey's first far-flung expansion, selling their interest in five Western League teams to NHL operators in 1926 for $272,000. The modern rule-book is another monument to Frank's inventive sense. He introduced bluelines, the forward pass, the goal crease, the penalty shot. The NHL still uses 22 of the rules he devised.

Alcoholic indiscretions ultimately cost Frank his position in hockey, positions of management in Boston and the NHL office in the early thirties. In the last 15 years of his life, retired in Vancouver, he exhibited a philosophical humility.

"I'm not afraid of death," he would tell those who came to visit him in St. Paul's Hospital. It could be the opening paragraph of the best story a fellow ever read or a writer ever wrote.

Frank sat in a blue robe, gray, with a lived-in face. He talked with the wine of words long aged in the cellars of thought.

"There are two ways to look at death," he said. "One way is to believe that life is infinite . . . maybe it is . . . it is difficult to believe that a Creator who made such a lovely thing as life would not allow it to go on after death." He sketched the thought slowly. He had come to understand that in the act of dying a man often rips the mask from his face and reveals the small creature of God.

Then Frank said: "But on the other hand, if there is nothing after death, we can't do anything about it. So there's no point in worrying about something we can't help."

The Patricks drifted apart in the last years they lived, but when young—as boys in Drummondville, Quebec, as undergraduates at McGill University—they were as close as brothers can be. Frank had justifiable pride in his older, taller brother, Lester. He was particularly eloquent in the French-Canadian patois of Quebec, and a friend once chided Frank about Lester's ease in French: "Your brother Lester sure speaks better French than you do."

"Yes," replied Frank, not raising his voice. "And he speaks better English, too."

Walter (Babe) Pratt, the blithe old defenseman of the Rangers of 35 years ago, remembers the language Lester used as coach of the Broadway Blueshirts. "He was the greatest coach a team ever had when you were losing," Pratt said. "He never got on you and made it any worse. But when you were winning"—Pratt winced from an ancient verbal lash—"when you were winning, Lester was the toughest boss that ever lived. He couldn't stomach us making any mental lapses."

Pratt was paid more after he was traded to Toronto, and he played better. Lester was amazed. "How come," he asked Pratt one day, "you didn't play as well for me in New York?"

Pratt shut one eye in a slow wink. "Lester, I'm now being paid enough to eat on. I'm finally getting the wrinkles out of my belly."

That wasn't Lester Patrick, not totally. He wasn't altogether a bloodless old tightwad. He was tough and human and canny, stubborn and calculating and proud and humorous and clever, complete in three dimensions. The late Walter Brown would testify, when he was president of Boston Bruins: "I'd sooner have Lester's handshake than all the documents a lawyer can conceive."

Lester's most illustrious moment occurred April 7, 1928, the night he defiantly tended goal for Rangers in a Stanley Cup game after Lorne Chabot was hurt. It is generally forgotten that he had substituted in the nets 24 years before, briefly replacing Doug Morrison of the Brandon, Manitoba, Wheat Kings in a game Brandon lost 6–3 to Ottawa Silver Seven. Patrick stopped one shot before Morrison, who had been penalized, returned to the game.

On April 7, 1928, however, the circumstances were frantically different. Lester was 44 then and had not fired a shot in anger for several years. The Rangers, whom he coached from the bench, were behind Montreal Maroons one game to none in the best-of-five Cup final. Early in the second period of the second game, scored tied 0–0, a backhand drive by Montreal's Nelson Stewart knocked out Chabot. He was rushed to a hospital for repairs to his wounded left eye. Teams did not employ second-string goalkeepers, and Patrick sought permission to use Alex Connell, the Ottawa netminder who attended the game. Eddie Gerard, the Maroons' recalcitrant manager, refused. Patrick then asked for Hughie McCormick, the goalie for London, Ontario, Tecumsehs in the Canadian Pro League. Gerard, adamant, said no.

Patrick was a gaunt, aroused figure in the New York dressing room, white-haired and red-tempered. "The hell with Gerard! I'll go in and play goal myself!" The Rangers were startled. Lester play goal? That gray old man? It would be 30 years before Johnny Bower of Toronto Maple Leafs would prove, beyond ridicule, that old folks could play goal in the NHL at 44. "Listen!" Patrick told his troops. "I'll stop the pucks if you'll backcheck to stop those bloody rebounds!" He pulled on Chabot's bulky pants; too wide. He stuck his feet into Chabot's skates; too big. Only two words seemed to describe New York's hopes: Too bad.

"Steady, now," Patrick said to himself. "Forget the crowd. Don't play fancy. Just stop the puck."

Referee Mike Rodden dropped the puck and Russ Oatman got it for Montreal. He shot it past Lester's spacious ears. Bill Phillips drove the first Montreal shot on Patrick. He caught it. Oatman drove another on Patrick's pads. No goal. Jimmy Ward and Babe Siebert tested Lester, but the second period ended the way it began: 0–0.

The Rangers received a fortunate break early in the third period. Bill Cook wafted a long shot at Clint Benedict in the Montreal goal, and the bemused Benedict muffed it. Rangers 1, Maroons 0. Then Nels Stewart challenged the New York defense. Nobody challenged with such blowtorch intensity in those days. Stewart was a Bobby Hull confined to a much shorter schedule. Stewart cruised through Ching Johnson and Taffy Abel on the New York defense. He fired a harsh shot which deflected off Patrick's pads. Johnson took a penalty. Stewart shot again and Patrick repulsed it with his stick. The next time Stewart reflected his nickname of Ol' Poison. He faked a shot, forced Patrick to his knees, then lifted the puck into the net. Maroons 1, Rangers 1.

The score remained tied for the rest of the third period, in spite of efforts by Phillips, Stewart, Ward, Hooley Smith and Red Dutton to untie it. Sudden-death overtime was required. Stewart snared the face-off and aimed a drive at Patrick's head. Dunc Munro fired from outside the defense. Stewart pulled the trigger three more times. Then, after 7:05 of overtime, Johnson broke away for New York. He closed on Benedict, shifted, and passed to Frank Boucher. In a set-up situation like that, Boucher was inclined to come up bingo. His goal reprieved Rangers, and Patrick, 2–1.

The Rangers subsequently won the series and their first Stanley Cup, three games to two. Somebody named Joe Miller, from Ottawa, replaced Chabot and the immensely relieved Patrick in the last three games.

Lester was inclined, late in his life, to play down his pinch-goaling. "I stopped maybe six hard shots altogether. The boys back-checked terrifically to save the old man." But newspaper files suggest that Lester was giving himself the worst of it. Andy O'Brien, checking moldering editions of the *Montreal Star*, discovered that Patrick stopped 15 shots described as "dangerous," held Maroons scoreless three times when New York had a player in the penalty box, and stopped Stewart five times.

The performance at least impressed Stewart, who admitted before he died: "The old white-haired bastard was terrific."

Babe Pratt

ASSISTANT to the vice-president of the Vancouver Canucks Walter Pratt, known as Babe, is a welcome sight on his infrequent visits to Toronto and New York, cities where, 35 years ago, he lived it heavy and walked it big.

Pratt is a retired but not noticeably retiring hockey player, gone from the National League for 19 years. It is reassuring to discover that life as a lumberman on the west coast of British Columbia has not rendered him less articulate than he used to be. No change toward silence had been feared, or possible.

Babe was, as a player, a huge, splendid athlete with a long, dry throat. He roamed the defense for the Rangers, the Maple Leafs and Boston Bruins, blithe and irreverent, the mayor of Fun City. In retirement, in New Westminster, British Columbia, he went dry.

Chiefly to get Pratt started, which is less difficult than, say, landing on the moon, reporters sometimes suggest that players of his generation were scandalously underpaid. "Underpaid!" he says, in the high tenor trumpet of a wounded elephant. "Listen: when I played for Lester Patrick in New York, he wouldn't give a worm to a blind bird!"

Patrick, with a snug, careful grip on the bankroll, gave Pratt $2,500 a season when he came up from Philadelphia Ramblers. It was chicken feed, and not very high-grade chicken feed at that, compared to modern NHL salaries, which average $18,200. Pratt would say of Patrick, often within the Old Fox's hearing, that "Lester isn't close or tight, but he's damned adjacent!"

Pratt was similarly discreet after he was traded to Toronto in

1942 for Hank Goldup and the late Dudley (Red) Garrett. His new superior was Conn Smythe, the supercharged Leaf proprietor with a smoking-volcano personality.

Smythe's dressing-room addresses were sprinkled, Pratt recalls, with pleasant little unprintables.

"Conn was an exhorter, full of impassioned pep-talks. Before one game he gave us the old win-it-for-my-daddy bit."

Smythe was in the center of the dressing quarters, Pratt says, exhorting his troops. "Gentlemen, my dear old daddy is down in the dumps! He's dying! Nothing would save him better than for the Leafs to go out there and fight, fight, fight! Win, win, win for my dear old daddy!"

The Leafs did not win. They got slathered in one of those museum pieces, 11 to 0, or something equally atrocious. Afterward, Sweeney Schriner, the smooth left wing, addressed Pratt in mock solemnity. "Yessir, Babe, we sure knocked off Smythe's old man tonight."

Another morning Smythe harangued the Leafs after a particularly grievous slump. "You guys remind me of two racehorses I own," he began. "Sir Marlboro was fast out of the starting gate, like this hockey club. He was a front-runner, good until they turned in the bend for home."

Smythe's voice was shot through with disgust. "But in the stretch Sir Marlboro faded, forced back with the also-rans!"

Smythe fixed his glittering gaze on Pratt. "But Shoeless Joe, my second horse—aha! What a horse! He'd start slowly and then come on, and on, and when it counted he'd lunge and stick his nose in front to win!"

There was an exultant note in Smythe's triumphant tone. "Gentlemen, that second horse was MY kind of hockey club!"

There was a moment's silence after Smythe finished, only a moment. Then Pratt turned to Bob Davidson, who was sitting beside him, head down, staring at the floor.

"Which end of the lousy horse are you?" Pratt muttered.

Jim Coleman, when he wrote amusing essays for the *Toronto Globe and Mail*, identified Pratt as the Honest Brakeman. It was Coleman's hilarious contention that two box cars were stolen one night when Pratt, employed as a youth in the Winnipeg railroad yards, was supposed to be standing guard.

Pratt was always vocally aware of how much he was worth, even if general managers disagreed. He won the Hart Trophy as the most valuable player in hockey in 1943–44, and went to training camp seeking a raise to $7,000. Clarence (Hap) Day, then Toronto's manager, refused the demand.

Pratt ultimately signed, hollering protests, for $6,500. Then he informed Thomas (Windy) O'Neill, his roommate: "Okay, if they want to pay me for half a season, that's what they'll get. I'll be the only guy in the history of hockey to get $6,500 for half a year."

O'Neill, now a lawyer in Toronto, remembers: "That's about how it was. Babe was nothing until Christmas, always out carousing, sometimes stiff at practice. Halfway through the season he straightened out."

"Okay, Windy," he told O'Neill in early January. "Now I start to play."

"You never saw a guy stand the league on its ear in the last half of 1944–45 like Babe did," O'Neill insists. "He gave Flash Hollett of Detroit a whale of a run for high-scoring defenseman and finally beat him."

Pratt's blithe tendencies ultimately caused his expulsion from the NHL. He was briefly barred in the middle of the 1945–46 season for gambling; or, as league President Mervyn (Red) Dutton phrased it, "for conduct prejudicial to the welfare of hockey." Dutton reported that Pratt was friendly with gamblers and was suspected of breaking the NHL rule which forbids players to bet on the outcome of games. He said there was no evidence that Pratt was betting against the Leafs. "When I confronted him with evidence, he admitted he had been gambling. He said he never wagered against the Leafs, but did tell me he had been offered a bribe to throw a game. He said he rejected the bribe, and I believe him."

Smythe may also have believed Pratt, but that did not stop him from selling his tarnished star to Boston on June 19, 1946. Pratt played 31 games for the Bruins in 1946–47, then drifted to Hershey and Cleveland before moving to British Columbia in 1950 as playing coach of the New Westminster Royals.

Historians insist the late Ed Wildey of Toronto was the first hockey coach to remove his goalkeeper for a sixth attacker late in a game. Wildey guided a teen-age team called Young Rangers and, about 45 years ago, he pulled his goalie near the end of a playoff game. Young Rangers pressed a six-man offense and tied the score, thus adding a fresh gambit to hockey strategy.

In 1950 Pratt resorted to audacity that would make even the inventive Mr. Wildey revolve in his tomb. New Westminster was in dreadful shape against the Vancouver Canucks, behind 6–2 with 14 minutes to play. At that juncture Pratt decided his goalkeeper wasn't doing New Westminster much good anyhow, so he junked the man for a sixth forward. The rash gesture worked. New Westminster's goal was unprotected for almost 14 minutes while Pratt flung six attackers into the Vancouver zone. The Royals scored four goals to gain a 6–6 tie.

One of Pratt's several charms is that he was a take-a-chance coach, unhampered by caution. When he pulled his goalie with 14 minutes to play . . . when he kidded Lester Patrick's celebrated talent for embracing nickels . . . when he joined Windy O'Neill in committing dawn attacks on Mother Machree before Stanley Cup games . . . when he asked the Bentley brothers, Doug and Max, which one of them posed for the Indian head on the Chicago sweaters, he was exercising a gift that has been nearly unique in hockey—that of burlesquing the game and its Establishment, with the skill of a satirical comic, while playing it as well as any defenseman ever played it.

In recent years, mellowed after the gambling incident, Conn Smythe has testified: "Pratt may be the best defenseman I ever had." Playing skill alone was enough to put him in the Hall of Fame in June 1966. For many even better reasons, the Babe belongs there.

Maurice Richard:
The Rocket's Red Glare

MAURICE RICHARD, revered as The Rocket, goes around hockey today, signing autographs and talking, playing in oldtimers' games, a retired hockey player. He is 52, combative fires partially stoked after more than a dozen seasons of retirement from Montreal Canadiens.

But fans and writers are delighted to discover the Rocket's red glare was not extinguished when he abandoned the Canadiens. He offers opinions at the drop of a question mark; none of them is guarded or hampered by caution.

The authors asked him if the erstwhile hero of French Canadian hockey, the elegant Jean Beliveau, could be considered a superstar in the NHL galaxy. "No," Richard replied, frank and forthright. "Beliveau turned pro too late to rate consideration as an all-time all-star."

Beliveau did not join the NHL mercenaries until he was 23, relatively old for a rookie. He couldn't afford to become a professional, for the incontestable reason that the Quebec Aces paid him $20,000 a year to remain amateur.

Richard claims to regret only one thing in the 18 years he played with an impacted passion. Just once, he says, he would like to have won an individual scoring title. He won a fierce success in every other respect. Until Gordon Howe surpassed him, in 1963, he scored more goals, 544, than any player who previously poured sweat. Until Bobby Hull scored 54 goals in 1965–66, Richard scored the most goals in a single season, 50 in 1944–45. He was the all-star right wing eight times.

Richard's name never led all the rest in total points, and that sour knowledge curdles his thoughts. He was second five times, twice by a single point. "The NHL give only one trophy," he complains. "They give it to the man who score the mos' points. Every year they should also give a trophy to the man who score the mos' goals." On that basis, Richard would have won a scoring trophy five times, for achieving the most goals in five different seasons.

Richard had his best chance for a scoring championship in 1954–55, the year of the infamous Richard Riots in downtown Montreal. He led teammate Bernard Geoffrion, who now scouts for New York Rangers, by four points with three games left in the schedule.

Then Richard displayed the violence of his affections toward Harold Laycoe of the Boston Bruins and a neutral party named Cliff Thompson, a linesman. With his stick, Richard carved intricate patterns on Laycoe's startled expression. With his fists, he hung a blue forget-me-not under Thompson's eye. Clarence Campbell, the NHL president, surveyed the wreckage of Laycoe and Thompson and suspended Richard for the remainder of the season. In the last three games Geoffrion scored five points to beat Richard in the scoring race, 75 to 74.

There were subsequent demonstrations, sufficiently grimy to provide the NHL with its most soiled historical footnote. Campbell was hooted and abused in the Montreal Forum. Riot squads mopped up the streets.

Richard makes a little joke whenever he mentions Hal Laycoe and Cliff Thompson today. "The year after I beat them," he says, "they both retired."

The Rocket's problems with Campbell extended off the ice, when he was a sports writer. For several years, while he played, he wrote a column on the side for a French-language paper in Montreal. He never used it to wage much peace. One day, like Zola, Richard came out strongly for Truth: the typewriter turned into a flaming spear in his hands. "*J'accuse!*" the Rocket wrote, and went on to say many bold, belligerent things about the conduct of the NHL under Campbell's jurisdiction. He would call a spade a bleeding, rust-pitted shovel, Richard said, even if it cost him his job in hockey. All it cost him, as it turned out, was his job as a columnist. Campbell, a Rhodes scholar, could read French.

Richard was silenced in print for the balance of his playing career, but he did not have to like it. Years later he was on the same plane with Campbell as they flew to Boston for a sport celebrities dinner. Asked if, on such occasions, he and the president spoke to each other, Richard replied, in the old dour, intimidating way, "Some. Maybe two words."

The Rocket's antipathy toward hockey's commissioner dates from March 17, 1955, the explosive night of the Richard Riots. Montreal's short hockey fuse was ignited at 9:11 P.M. that night, when a tear gas bomb exploded in the Forum. The detonation occurred as 16,000 fans watched the Canadiens battle Detroit's Red Wings; the game was forfeited to Detroit after the first period, the Wings leading 4–1. Sidney Katz, an editor for *Maclean's* magazine, wrote of the bomb throwing: "It touched off the most destructive and frenzied riot in the history of Canadian sport."

Hundreds of the fans had come to the game in an ugly mood, angry at Campbell, seeking vindication for Richard. During the first period they directed their abuse at Campbell, who has two seats at one end of the Forum. *"Va-t'en*, Campbell! Scram, Campbell!" The insults were accompanied by a strafing of the president and his secretary, Miss Phyllis King, with decadent fruit, ripe eggs, pickled pigs feet and empty bottles.

Miss King, who later became Mrs. Campbell, had expected trouble. After Richard's suspension was announced, she answered threatening phone calls at NHL headquarters in the Sun Life Building in downtown Montreal.

One of the first callers advised, "Tell Campbell I'm an undertaker and he'll be needing me in a few days."

Another threatened, "I'm no crank, but I'm going to blow your place up!"

Scores of women, Miss King subsequently said, bawled on the phone. One of them ran up a long-distance bill from Toronto pleading with Campbell to cancel the suspension.

Campbell's callers ran the range of uncomplimentary epithets from "dictator," "sick," "coward," "German," "little pig," "big pig," "face of a snake," to "sloven," "yellow face," "large bowl of soup," and "Judas."

Campbell, an English-Canadian, received hundreds of letters from French-Canadians accusing him of racial bias toward their Gallic demigod. One missive said, "If Richard's name was Richardson you would have given a different verdict. You, Campbell, are not as good as any French-Canadian around. I was at the morgue this morning to look at a body after an accident. I only wish you had been on the slab, but don't worry—you will be soon."

Another suggested, "The Frenchmen have always been slaves and suckers and it's a pleasure for you to see others' blood run."

Another, equally peevish, wrote, "You British animal! Why did your vile ancestors set foot on our lovely land? Go back to where you came from—England and hell!"

The lunatic fringe of the Canadien nationalist element were uncommonly bitter to Campbell, who had indeed spent time in England, but only as a Rhodes scholar at Oxford and an officer in the Canadian army. In the addled fashion of misdirected minorities, some of Richard's fans regarded him as a special champion of their race. In him they saw a hero of overpowering strength who smites down his, and their, persecutors. In their deep emotional self-identification they experienced a surge of triumph in their own vanity. Some sports fans attend wrestling matches for much the same gratification: Good Guy subduing Bad Guy.

There was, at the time, abundant evidence that Richard held a peculiar place in the affections of French Canada. In 1954 when Montrealers were asked by the Canadian Broadcasting Corporation to nominate three personalities to appear on a television program on New Year's Eve, they voted for Richard, Cardinal Léger and Mayor Jean Drapeau.

Within three weeks after Richard began writing a column for the weekly paper, *Le Samedi-Dimanche*, its circulation increased by 18,000.

Once, when he was dining in a private club with Ken Reardon, then a vice-president of the Canadiens, a group of French businessmen at the next table passed a plate and presented Richard with $100.

Camil DesRoches, formerly an obliging publicist for Canadiens, once admitted, rather wistfully, "But Richard is not the Pope."

"No," said Frank Selke, formerly managing director of the team. "He is God."

This was the background to the Richard Riot on March 17, 1955, the sort of rebellion one New York sociologist has defined as "a device for indulging ourselves in a kind of temporary insanity by all going crazy together." It is an accurate description of what happened in the five hours after the bomb was thrown in the Forum. Perhaps 10,000 fans, demonstrators and gawkers massed around the outside of the arena. There were overtones of lynch rule about to become law: "Kill Campbell! Kill Campbell!"

The windows of passing street cars were smashed and, for no discernible reason, cab drivers were yanked from their vehicles and assaulted. Bricks, chunks of ice and unopened bottles of beer were thrown through the Forum windows. The berserk herd upset corner newsstands, doused them in oil and left them burning.

Then the mob moved eastward down St. Catherine Street, the artery feeding Montreal's main shopping district. A swath of destruction cut through 15 blocks, the stuff of a wartime air blitz. Display windows were smashed and looters hurried off with everything portable—jewelry, clothes, clocks, radios and cameras.

The cost of the riot, when it was added up, would have paid Bobby Hull's salary for at least part of a season: an estimated $30,000 worth of damage due to looting and vandalism; 12 policemen and 25 civilians injured; eight police cars, several street cars and taxis damaged. Thomas Leggett, Montreal's director of police, confessed later, "It was the worst night I've had in 33 years as a policeman."

The *Montreal Star* said of the unhinged binge, "Nothing remains but shame." The *Toronto Star* commented, "It's savagery which attacks the fundamentals of civilized behaviour." The riot also made headlines in papers from Los Angeles to London, England. "Ice hockey is rough," observed the *London News Chronicle*, "but it is now a matter of grim record that Canadian players are spring lambs compared to those who support them." A Dutch newspaper, obviously using a garbled story, hung out the headline: STADIUM WRECKED, 27 DEAD, 100 WOUNDED.

Campbell was asked, long after, why he decided to attend the game? It never occurred to him to do anything else, he said. "If I failed to go I'd have been branded as a coward. In any case, I'm a season ticketholder and had a right to go. I also felt the police would protect me."

The police were not much protection, obliged as they were to handle the demonstrations outside the Forum. Inside, when Campbell was recognized, the missile pitchers zeroed in on Miss King and him. Miss King was wearing a brown otter coat and a white straw hat decorated with a large black flower, an unfortunate ensemble. "The hat," she said, "made a clear target." Her hat was soon knocked off with a well-aimed rubber. Campbell's green fedora was spattered with the aromatic juices of oranges, eggs and tomatoes. But Campbell refused to budge, tight-lipped, trying to carry on his customary practice of making notes on the refereeing in a black notebook. His only nervous gesture was reaching for a handkerchief and tucking it in his sleeve.

After the first period, one André Robinson, 26, confronted Campbell and, without uttering a word, squashed two large tomatoes on the president's chest. Robinson fled down the steps but was apprehended by police.

The authorities did not catch whoever pitched the tear gas bomb, but the pitcher may have done Campbell a favor. As the thick, burning fumes spread out, the mob momentarily forgot Campbell and clawed toward the fresh air outside. Campbell and Miss King sought refuge in the Forum's first-aid clinic, 70 feet from their seats. At the height of the exodus, with tears streaming down everyone's face, a comic at the organ high in the loft played "My Heart Cries for You."

By the end of the riot, at 3 A.M. on March 18, 1955, the police had arrested 70 suspects. One-third were under 18 and were sent home with their parents. The rest were transferred to Montreal's central police headquarters. They were a gay group, as it were, talking hockey to cool off from their rowdy excitements. At 7 A.M. a guard came in and announced, incorrectly, that Campbell had resigned. The arrested characters cheered and broke out into gratified song.

Judge Emmett J. McManamy, addressing the offenders in court later in the morning, chided the subdued rioters. "Last night's riot," he said, "brings home to the people of Montreal a terrible lesson of the narrow margin between order and disorder. It must never happen again." Several of the men seemed near tears as the judge spoke. "All those who participated in the riot are not before the court, but those who are must accept the responsibility." Following a remand, the rioters were fined a trifling $25 each and required to post a bond of $100 to keep the peace for one year.

André Robinson, the young man who squashed the tomatoes on Campbell's shirt, was typical of the misguided fools who made an inflamed mob. He had a job as a railroad clerk and had never previously been in trouble. "I had nothing against Campbell," Robinson testified later, "but when I saw him at the game I got madder and madder about Richard's suspension. It was our hero Campbell was crucifying."

Robinson's experiences indicated clearly the malignance many Montrealers expressed toward Campbell. One French-speaking millionaire told his lawyer: "Find that young man who smeared the tomatoes on Campbell and look after him. I'll pay all the costs, even if they come to a million dollars."

Robinson became a one-day hero. He was the recipient of flowers, clothes, radios, cuff links and a gold wrist watch from friends after he was designated the "star" of the Canadiens-Detroit game on the sports page of a Montreal newspaper. He received sympathetic letters, many from women wanting his autograph and picture.

The mood of most Montrealers after the riot was a mixture of shame and regret. Richard made a short radio speech that was designed to defuse any further unkempt behavior. "Do no more harm," he advised. "Get behind the team in the play-offs. I will take my punishment and come back next year and help the club win the Cup."

There was no more violence, but Richard did not lessen his combative intensity in the five remaining years of his career. He never adopted the philosophy of winning some games and losing others, shrugging it off, and going out and having a steak and a beer when he lost.

One night, in a friendly game against a team from Johnstown, Pennsylvania, the Canadiens were requested to take it easy on the bushers. They all complied, except Richard. He scored seven goals in one period. "I can only play one way," he explained. "The hard way."

Eddie Shore

ANY HOCKEY FAN over 40 years old has an unofficial option to utter the bromide, "They don't make players the way they used to." Whoever makes the statement is automatically correct. With each decade the style of play has changed and, naturally, the players have adapted with the times. Howie Morenz, the Montreal Canadiens' ace of the Thirties hardly resembled in skating, shooting or stickhandling Montreal's leader in the Sixties, Jean Beliveau. The changes, however, have been more in style than personality.

But when it comes to the unique psyche of the oldtimer, nobody represents the rugged pioneer-type better than Eddie Shore. A product of the Western Canadian prairie, Shore began developing his own Bunyanesque legend while toiling on his family's farm in the province of Saskatchewan. He toughened himself taming wild horses, herding cattle and performing other chores of the typical Western Canadian farmer but he managed early in life to handle jobs that just about any other man would consider too difficult. By the time he had reached his late teens Eddie Shore was a hard man and, if the term could be applied to a human, he came close to resembling some fictitious personage thoroughly resistible to injury.

Like most Western Canadian youngsters, he learned to skate as soon as he could walk and he soon translated his energies to the hockey rinks. The results, as expected, were extraordinary. He dominated every league he played in with a combination of strong skating, masterful stickhandling and relentless energy. Shore was an intense human even then and largely self-taught. He clinically examined his style, ferreted out the flaws and then diligently went about the business of overcoming them.

It was inevitable that Shore would become a professional hockey player and just as certain that he would become one of the very best. There are some analysts who today contend that Shore was unquestionably the most accomplished man to lace on a pair of skates. At the very least the point is debatable but there is no question that he was one of the best, one of the most durable and, by far, the most bizarre star ever to grace the NHL rinks.

He also was one of the most hated players and, later, one of the most hated managers and owners of a hockey team and, perhaps, also one of the most beloved to another segment of players and fans. Rather than casually itemize and gloss over his feats it would be easier to understand the character of Shore, not to mention his abilities, by citing a few symbolic episodes.

Shore joined the Boston Bruins in 1926 as a defenseman and immediately displayed a superiority that was to awe hockey fans for nearly two decades. Seven times chosen as a member of the NHL's All-Star Team, four times voted its most valuable player, Shore truly was "the Babe Ruth of Hockey." It went without saying that Shore was one of the first players inducted into the Hockey Hall of Fame. If Ruth built the Yankee Stadium, Shore *made* the National Hockey League. He could skate faster than most forwards, hit harder than any defenseman and, at a time when hockey was making its pitch as a big-time sport in the United States, he became the sport's leading drawing card.

Between 1926 and 1940 Shore brought to the NHL rinks a brand of rough-and-tumble that has never been equaled. He antagonized fans, fought opponents and stirred more controversy than any other man in the game with the possible exception of Maurice the Rocket Richard. Opponents often teamed up into twos and threes just to nail Shore. Sometimes they got him but, always, he rebounded to excel again. He managed to acquire more than 900 stitches in his face and body, fractures of his back, hip and collarbone and a mouth with every tooth knocked out. His nose had been broken 14 times and his jaw had been cracked five times. But, most significant, when Shore played, the crowds came out to see him and he made it a point never, if at all possible, to let them down. Nothing proves this statement better than an episode that took place early in January 1929.

The Bruins, who, thanks to Shore, were to finish in first place in the NHL's American Division, and win the Stanley Cup, had a game scheduled with the Montreal Maroons at the Montreal Forum, on January 3, 1929. As was the custom in the Twenties, Thirties and Forties, hockey teams travelled exclusively by train. When the Bruins had a game scheduled in Montreal they generally departed one night before the game on a train that arrived in the French-Canadian metropolis the following morning.

So, on January 2 the Bruins had all arrived on the Pullman in North Station ready to depart. That is, all but one—Eddie Shore. It wasn't customary for Shore to pull any pranks or slip into a situation where he would miss a hockey game but this time he was fouled up by an accident in downtown Boston that snarled traffic and delayed the taxicab that was taking him to the railroad terminal, and when he arrived it was to see the last car of the train pull away from the tunnel and head toward Montreal.

Under the circumstances, Shore had few alternatives. He could simply miss the game. Or, he could try the other limited means of transportation to Montreal; a once-in-a-while airplane or an automobile. He tried to arrange for a flight but was advised that what little plane service there was had been cancelled because of a severe sleet storm that was developing. Shore phoned several of his friends, and a wealthy acquaintance decided to offer him his limousine and a chauffeur.

By now the sleet storm was in full blast and was rapidly taking on all aspects of a blizzard but Shore couldn't have cared less. The chauffeur called for him at 11:30 P.M. and the two began the 350-mile drive to Montreal over ramshackle roads that meandered around and over New England mountains.

Accustomed as he was to city driving under fair conditions, the chauffeur carefully drove the car at speeds that varied between three and five miles per hour. Shore was impatient and implored the man to accelerate. "The man apologized," Shore remembered during an interview about the incident, "and said he didn't have chains and did not like driving in the winter. The poor fellow urged me to turn back to Boston."

That was out of the question. Moments later, when the car skidded to the side and just missed falling into a ditch, Shore insisted that the chauffeur give up the wheel and let him drive. This, he gladly did. The Bruin defenseman then came upon an all-night service station, purchased tire chains and continued northward. By then the sleet storm had thickened into a blizzard of blinding proportions. Snow caked on either side of the lone windshield wiper and, within minutes, the wiper blade froze solid to the glass. "I couldn't see out of the window," Shore admitted, "so I removed the top half of the windshield."

Exposed to the blasts of the icy wind, Shore nevertheless started the car again and was gratified that, at least, he could make out the sides of the road. The pair continued across the Massachusetts border and up into the perilous mountains of New Hampshire. "At about 5 A.M.," said Shore, "we began losing traction. The tire chains had worn out."

At this point it appeared that the luck of Eddie Shore had run its course. But, no, as he skidded around a curve, he detected the flickering lights of a road-workers' camp. There was a gas station, too. Shore dashed out of the car, awakened the attendant, bought gas and a new set of tire chains. This eased the peril but didn't eliminate it altogether. The car proceeded to skid off the road four times between the gas station and the Canadian border but, each time, Shore and the chauffeur managed to get it back on the highway again.

By early afternoon of the following day Shore had tired to the point of near collapse. When the second pair of chains fell off at 3 P.M. he stopped the car and ordered the chauffeur to take over the wheel. He told the nervous driver to stay in the middle of the road and run the car at no less than 12 miles per hour. But the moment Shore dozed off the chauffeur lost control of the big car and crashed it into a deep ditch. Again, luck was with them. They were uninjured and the car was not damaged.

This time Shore hiked a mile to a farmhouse for help. "I paid $8 for a team of horses," he recalled, "harnessed the horses and pulled the car out of the ditch. We weren't too far from Montreal and I thought we'd make it in time if I could keep the car on the road."

At 5:30 P.M. Shore drove up to the Windsor Hotel, the Bruins' headquarters. He staggered into the lobby and nearly collapsed. "He was in no condition to play hockey," said Art Ross, then manager of the Bruins. "His eyes were bloodshot, his face frostbitten and windburned, his fingers bent and set like claws after gripping the wheel so long. And he couldn't walk straight. I figure his legs were almost paralyzed from hitting the brake and clutch."

But Shore was determined to play that night. He ate the traditional pregame steak dinner and ignored Ross's orders to go to sleep. As a concession, he decided to take a short nap, and it required several glasses of cold water over the face before he could be revived to go to the Forum.

Needless to say Ross was determined not to let Shore play, but he finally decided to let him get on the ice.

The game was rough and fast. The powerful Maroons penetrated Boston's defense often, but Shore always helped repulse them. Once he smashed Hooley Smith to the ice with a vicious bodycheck and drew the game's first penalty. Ross considered benching him at this point but changed his mind. When the penalty had elapsed Shore jumped on the ice and appeared stronger than ever. Shortly before the halfway point in the second period he skated behind his net to retrieve the puck. He faked one Montreal player, picked up speed at center ice and swerved to the left when he reached the Maroons' blue line.

Shore sped around the last defenseman and shot the puck, low into the right corner of the net at 8:20 of the second period. With only the respite of another two-minute penalty—this one in the third period—Shore played the entire game. The Bruins won the contest, 1–0, on the defenseman's goal.

Although he was a defenseman and, in those days, it was an unwritten rule that defensemen remained at or near their blue line instead of launching offensive rushes, Shore broke the rule constantly. He took advantage of his great skating strides and managed to score 12 goals and seven assists for 19 points in the 1928–29 season to place sixth in scoring in the American Division of the NHL, ahead of such shooting notables as Bill Cook of the Rangers and Herbie Lewis of the Red Wings.

But his scoring ability never quite overshadowed his defensive work, which covered the spectrum. He could pokecheck and hookcheck with extreme finesse and, most of all, he could bodycheck with great ferocity. For the most part Shore hit his opponents cleanly—there was no need to do otherwise because his clean checks were devastating—but the check for which he is best remembered was, to the view of most observers, on the other side of the rule book. It was a block he threw at Ace Bailey, a Toronto Maple Leaf forward, during the 1933–34 season. The repercussions from the Shore–Bailey Incident, as it has come to be known, were severe and, for a time, threatened to end Shore's career, damage the reputation of hockey and result in the death of Bailey. It remains one of the most controversial episodes in the history of the game.

The Bruins were playing host to the Maple Leafs; Shore, who had been suffering through a slump, was on the ice when Bailey was expertly "killing" a Toronto penalty by adroitly stickhandling all over the ice. Finally, Bailey lofted the puck into Bruin territory and Shore captured it. Leaf defenseman King Clancy couldn't stop Shore, but his stick rapped Shore in the skate and disrupted his momentum so that Shore fell and lost the puck.

Bailey dropped back into Clancy's position and was facing the Boston net as Shore got to his feet near the Toronto net. He picked up speed, but as he neared Bailey and Red Horner, both of whom were unaware that Shore was behind them, he moved straight for Bailey—some observers argue that he mistook Bailey for Clancy— and hit him amidships. "He struck Bailey across the kidneys with his right shoulder," wrote Frank Selke, Sr. in his book *Behind The Cheering*. Selke, who then was an official of the Toronto team, watched the action from the press box. "He hit him with such force that it upended Bailey in a backward somersault . . . All of us in the press box heard a crack you might compare to the sound you remember from boyhood days of cracking a pumpkin with a baseball bat. Bailey was lying on the blue line, with his head turned sideways, as though his neck were broken. His knees were raised, legs twitching ominously."

Red Horner skated over to Shore and detected what he thought was a smile on the defenseman's face. He walloped Shore with a right uppercut. "As he fell," said Selke, "with his body rigid and straight as a board, Shore's head struck the ice, splitting open. In an instant, he was circled by a pool of blood about three feet in diameter."

Shore eventually recovered to play again. Bailey hovered near death for several days, then, miraculously—the Leafs had even completed funeral arrangements—recovered. He never played hockey again but he did confront Shore once more on the ice on February 14, 1934, at Maple Leaf Gardens in Toronto. The Leafs had arranged a benefit game with an All-Star Team chosen from all of the other teams. Prior to the opening face-off, Shore, who played for the All-Stars, shook hands with Bailey at center ice.

Shore returned to the Bruin line-up and continued to play an excellent brand of hockey while losing none of his recklessness nor his independence. Shore had long since convinced himself that he knew more about the world than most people, not the least of whom were doctors. Once after a collision Shore's left ear was mashed to such an extent doctors advised him he would have one ear for the rest of his days. "They all said just what the club doctor had told me—it was not possible to save the ear. Just before office hours for the day ended, I ran across a fellow who was more encouraging. He asked me what type of anesthetic I wanted. I told him just to give me a small mirror. That way, I could watch the kind of stitching he did. I made him change the very last stitch. If I had not done that, he'd have left a scar. I told him I was just a farm boy who did not want his looks messed up."

In the late thirties Shore realized his playing career was nearing its completion. He was traded by the Bruins to the New York Americans and began considering the ownership of a team. In 1940 he sunk his bankroll into the Springfield team of the American League and became its president, owner, manager and, quite often over the years, its coach. If Shore was unique as a player he became even more unusual as an owner. Immediately, he developed into the most bizarre owner the sport has known.

Shore remained in charge of the Springfield club until the 1966-67 season when a most unusual incident developed, his hockey team threatened to go on strike in rebellion against Shore's unusual tactics. How could anyone believe a man would open a training camp by ordering two dozen rugged hockey players to tap dance in the hotel lobby? Or execute delicate ballet steps on ice? Would any ordinary coach tape a player's hand to his stick? Or work out day after day with players despite four near-fatal heart attacks? Is it conceivable that a club owner would instruct players' wives to avoid disturbing their husbands during slumps in the interests of a winning team? Is it conceivable, either, that a man would actually lock a referee out of his dressing room as punishment for "poor" officiating? Or order his players to make popcorn, blow up balloons and sell programs when they were not in the game?

"You better believe it happened with Shore," said defenseman Don Johns, who once played for him. "Once Eddie told me he knew why I wasn't a better hockey player. I'm always willing to learn. So I said, 'Okay, Ed, what's wrong with me?' Know what he says? 'You're not combing your hair right,' he says. He told me to part it on the other side. That way it would help me 'cause I'd have something to think about."

Johns was struck dumb at the opening of training camp when Shore beckoned to a rookie while other players stopped to see what Eddie was up to this time. "He wanted the boy to skate with his legs closer," said Johns, "so he pulled out a piece of cord and tied the kid's legs together and told him to skate. Did you ever try to skate with your legs tied with a rope?"

Another time, Johns was immobilized on a hospital bed suffering a 40-stitch cut in his leg. The phone rang. It was Shore. "Mis-ter Johns," he says, "you ought to be ready to play pretty soon."

" 'But Eddie,' I told him, 'I can't even turn my leg . . .' Next thing I knew he hung up. For a minute I thought maybe I was babying myself. So I called the doc and told him to look at the leg. He did and told me I'd be crazy if I got out of bed in the next couple of days."

By the end of the week, Johns was released from the hospital and reported to Shore, who occupied a modest office in the Eastern States Coliseum, the rink he leased in Springfield, Massachusetts. "Mis-ter Johns," Shore ordered, "You're playing tonight."

"He played me for three minutes," says Johns, "and then suspended me for a week. 'When I played hockey,' he told me, 'I once had 100 stitches in the leg and I was out only three—no, two-and-a-half days.' "

After a few weeks, Johns had become numbed by Shore's critiques. Johns' feet were wrong, Shore said, he wasn't shooting correctly or bending properly and so on, ad nauseum. One day, when Johns was about to quit, Shore pointed at him. "Mis-ter Johns," he said. "What did you do wrong this time?"

Exasperated, Johns said, "I guess I wasn't skating right, or my hands were too close to the stick. . . ."

"Bul-loney," Shore said, "you're doing nothing wrong."

Johns considered himself rather fortunate since he was sent to Baltimore after only a year in Springfield. Others curse the day they were told to report.

Billy McCreary, of the St. Louis Blues, once declared that Shore was so tight he'd make Jack Benny seem like the last of the great spenders. "We were on strict budgets with Shore. He allowed us to tip taxi drivers 15 cents. After a while, we got so well known around the league, none of the cabbies wanted to pick us up. . . . That was bad enough. But some guys had a bonus clause in their contracts. If they got, say, 30 goals, they'd get more money. So a guy would be comin' close to 30 near the end of the season. Does he make it? No! Shore would sit him out of the last five games so he couldn't score any more. And if you think I'm joking, just ask any player who skated for Shore."

Still, when polling members of the Shore Alumni Association, a fellow can find as many admirers of the "Old Man" as critics. Everybody agrees though, that Shore was the wildest, most learned hockey man in the world.

One graduate of the Springfield Indians, goaltender Don Simmons, said Shore's techniques left him limp from shock. "I'll never forget how Eddie hated to see his goaltenders fall to the ice. If he got a player and that poor sap fell down to block a shot Shore'd get a piece of twine and tie the goalie's arms to the crossbar of the net. Then he'd dare him to fall."

Shore once ordered Simmons into his office. Don had been in a slump and, naturally, feared the worst. But Eddie was convinced Simmons had developed a mental block against goaltending. He suggested the kid return to his home in Port Colborne, Ontario, for a rest. "He told me to go home to my mother. 'Help her around the house,' he said. 'That'll take your mind off hockey. While you're at it, find a studio and take some dancing lessons.'"

Simmons was astonished soon after he returned. In a tense game between Cleveland and Springfield, referee Frank Udvari called a penalty against the Indians that so enraged Shore he ordered his entire team off the ice with the exception of Simmons. Udvari pulled his watch. "You got 10 seconds to ice a team," the referee said, "or I drop the puck." Shore ignored the threat.

Udvari dropped the puck and five Cleveland players charged at Simmons. So amazed were the attackers at this unheard-of scoring opportunity, they fought among themselves over who would take the shot. Finally, Bo Elik of Cleveland shot and missed. Three succeeding shots went wild and Simmons fell on the puck, stopping play. Finally, Shore sent his team back on the ice.

Although Shore suffered four heart attacks, he continued to indulge in arguments and even suggested a fight with opposing players. Such combat was relatively simple since the Coliseum's penalty box was directly across the aisle from the Springfield bench. All Shore had to do was walk a few feet to the penalty box.

On one such walk a few years ago, Shore unnerved his doctor. Aldo Guidolin, the tough Baltimore defenseman-coach, was penalized after man-handling several Springfield players. As Guidolin stepped into the penalty box, Shore charged him. "If I was 20 years younger, I'd knock the dickens outa you," said Shore. "That didn't satisfy him 'cause we beat 'em in overtime," said Guidolin. "So after the game, he ran down to the announcer's box, turned on the loudspeaker and called the referee every name in the book. You could hear it all over the rink."

An alumnus of Shore's 1959 Springfield club, Guidolin shudders when he recalls the hours of grim instruction with Eddie. "He harped on three points," says Guidolin. "He wanted the hands two feet apart on the stick, the feet 11 inches apart on the ice, and he wanted you to skate in a sort of sitting position. You had to do it exactly right or be in big trouble."

Guidolin discovered this one morning during practice. He had just completed what he considered a perfect pass that resulted in a goal. What's more he had skated at top speed while doing it. Then he heard the whistle and saw Shore motion to him. "Mis-ter Guidolin," he said, "do you know what you did wrong?"

"The pass was perfect," said Guidolin. "I was in the sitting position. My hands were on the stick. What more do you want?"

"Mis-ter Guidolin," Shore replied, "your legs were two inches too far apart."

Outlandish as Shore's ideas of stance and technique may first appear, they are well-grounded in physiological theory developed and harbored in his encyclopedic mind. "Studying under Shore is like getting your doctorate in hockey science," said Detroit defenseman Kent Douglas. "The Old Man taught me things about the game nobody else ever mentioned. He showed me you don't have to hit a man real hard—just to get a piece of him. He showed me how to maneuver a man 'til he's off balance. Then you take the puck away from him."

When Douglas complained about being overweight, Shore stayed up nights analyzing the problem. Finally, he had the solution. "You're drinking too much water," Eddie said. Douglas eliminated excess water from his diet, lost weight, gained speed and stamina and won the American League's outstanding defenseman's trophy.

Shore startled Aldo Guidolin and a dozen other players when he ordered them to try several dance routines. But Eddie could see nothing to be surprised about. Not when his lesson made all the sense in the world. "Tap dancing," Shore explained, "improves balance, and balance is the foundation of an athlete's ability. From balance he obtains power and maneuverability. I want a player to move forward, backward, one side or the other without actually taking a step, just shifting his balance. Add those up each time he has to make a move during a game and he's saving himself a tremendous amount of energy."

Eddie's severest critics were members of the "Black Aces," players out of the line-up due to injury, illness or Shore's desire to bench them. However, they often were compelled to work considerably harder than regular members of the team. They were forced to do such odd jobs as paint arena seats, sell programs, make popcorn, and blow up hundreds of balloons before ice shows. Once, when some Aces were particularly angry, they gave Shore a special lesson in balance. It happened when Eddie—he never ordered anyone to do a job he wouldn't do himself—was changing light bulbs in the Coliseum's high ceiling. To do this, he had to climb a platform that players on ice pushed from bulb to bulb. At one point, Shore was hanging on to an overhead cable with one hand, screwing in a bulb with the other, when someone "accidentally" pushed the tower from under him. "He was just hanging there from the cables like a trapeze artist," says a former Ace. "The fellows finally got around to pushing the platform back so he could get down."

According to several men, Shore treated his coaches the same way he treated his Black Aces. Pat Egan, a former Springfield coach, reportedly painted the arena seats, scraped the ice and even—get this—repaired Shore's house.

Opposing coaches suffered too, when they played in Springfield. When King Clancy was coaching Cincinnati, Shore said he'd allow Clancy use of the Coliseum ice for morning practice. The Coliseum is a barn-like structure with a seating capacity of 5,600 and rows of windows near the ceiling at either side of the ice. Late in the morning the sun beams through the windows, giving the rink its only natural light and warmth. But this, of course, is contingent on the sun coming out.

"We got on the ice at nine in the morning," said Emile Francis, who was then playing for Cincinnati. "The place was dark, so I asked Clancy to get the lights on. Just then, Shore comes by. 'Hey Eddie,' Clancy yells, 'how about giving us some light for practice?' Shore yells back, 'Wait a half hour 'til the sun rises and comes through the windows. Then you'll have plenty of light.'"

At the game the next night, Clancy climbed over the boards, marched solemnly across the ice, and presented Shore with a lantern.

Shore has managed to antagonize almost every coach and manager in the league, but none more than Jackie Gordon, general manager-coach of the Cleveland Barons. In February, 1960 Gordon was coaching Cleveland. The Cleveland club was at Springfield when Shore suffered a fit of pique after referee Lou Farelli disallowed a Springfield goal, although goal judge Bill Tebone had flashed the red light signifying the point. Gordon couldn't believe it when Eddie reacted by removing Tebone from his post behind the net. Shore said if the referee could overrule the goal judge, there was no point in having one. Gordon insisted the least Shore could do was appoint a new judge. Farelli ordered Shore to comply, but Eddie wouldn't hear of it. The referee resumed the game—minus one very important official.

"I did not pull out the goal judge," Shore has insisted. "He saw the puck go in and put the light on. The referee would not take his decision. So the judge said, 'I seen the puck go in. If they think I'm a liar, I don't want the job.' So he walked away.

"The referee asked me to put in another judge. I said, 'This man is honest. If I put in another man, it would be like calling the first man a liar and a cheat.' I told the referee: 'Either he goes back in there or else you won't have a goal judge.'"

Ultimately, league president Richard Canning fined Shore $2,000 for the stunt. Eddie suffered a heart attack shortly thereafter. "When he had the attack," an American League official said, "we decided not to press him for the money. And never have."

The other side of Shore was as hidden from the public as the far side of the moon. He was steel on the outside, but soft as cotton candy underneath. But he never talked about it. You had to talk to Shore's friends to learn he donated thousands of dollars to cover hospital expenses when Doug McMurdy's son was seriously injured. Nor would Eddie tell you how fast he gave Bill Sweeney $1,000 to pull him out of a financial jam. Or of his other acts of benevolence.

Eddie's bizarre behavior reached in many directions, including the world of medicine. He always fancied himself an amateur doctor, trainer and psychologist and insists he twice cured himself of cancer. "He went on a special starvation diet," says veteran defenseman Larry Zeidel, "and says he eventually passed it out of his system."

Eddie himself doesn't care to discuss the bouts with cancer. "All I can say," he once said, "is three specialists gave me only six months to live and that was in 1940."

Shore passed his medicinal advice on to his players, and sometimes his cure-or-else diagnosis disagreed with the patients. Eddie once told Ken Schinkel he was suffering from yellow jaundice. "The Old Man gave me his special 'Marlet Treatment,' said Schinkel.

"It's a laxative made up of oils. I was scared of it so I took only half of what I was supposed to. I lost 12 pounds in no time, so I cut it out. I think if I'd have taken the whole business it would've been suicide."

Shore always was a favorite topic of conversation in the other AHL cities, particularly where he had made a trade. "How does he get away with it?" people want to know. Hockey men marveled at Shore's deal with Toronto several years ago when he sent defenseman Kent Douglas to the NHL club for five players and a foothold in Toronto's Metropolitan League.

Sports writers recalled the time Shore made a man-for-man swap but was tormented at the last minute over what he considered a slight discrepancy in the players' worth. Eddie finally agreed to the trade, with one condition—the other team had to throw in a brand new goal net to complete the transaction.

The raps against Shore's trading tactics were his excessive demands, which often killed deals and buried the promising players in the minors. Shore asked high prices because he believed he deserved them. In a sense, he did. He gave his life for hockey yet he never was fully compensated for the millions of dollars he drew for the NHL when he was the league's leading player. What's more, he invested more of his time instructing young hockey players than all the hockey owners put together multiplied tenfold. And he built what was a feeble Springfield franchise into a hockey power. No owner could match Shore's claim of putting every cent he made out of hockey back into the sport.

Following the players' strike in 1966–67, Shore sold the Springfield players to the Los Angeles Kings of the NHL's West Division. The player uprising was one of the few setbacks he ever suffered and cost him dearly in the area of prestige. His sense of paranoia also was heightened. "I'll tell you what's the matter," he once declared. "Shore has always been in the wrong. He doesn't mean to be but he gets in people's bad graces. He's been outspoken even if it hurts. But his shoulders are fairly broad."

With Eddie, it has been almost impossible to separate the truth from fiction. His life and his legend have become interwoven. His bizarre behavior has become embellished in the stories about him, no doubt, but the stories have roots in basic truths. "Most of us are a little crazy one way or another," Eddie Shore explained. "Some of us admit it. As for me, I'm not sorry about anything I've done in my life."

Cyclone Taylor

A MAN IS NOTORIOUS when many things are said about him by many people, but when many things both true and untrue are said about him—when a mythology springs up around him—the man is truly famous. You couldn't have a Baconian theory or a Marlowe explanation for any less a man than Shakespeare. When several thousand people spend many years doing word tricks and picture puzzles to prove that somebody's stuff was written by somebody else, the somebody of the first part is somebody indeed.

Fred W. (Cyclone) Taylor, near 90 and retired in Vancouver, British Columbia, has come to impress the hockey community that way. He is an old defenseman who has not bounced a bodycheck for 50 years, but more stories, more lies and more honest fiction are told about him than any of his ancient contemporaries, living or dead—all in his honor, all as a tribute. He is the beau ideal of the hardened-artery set.

People will tell you matter-of-factly, in rinks and bars and club cars, that Taylor once scored a goal for the Renfrew (Ontario) Creamery Kings after skating backwards through an entire team of bewildered Ottawa Silver Sevens. It is a splendid thought, though incorrect and technically ridiculous. It has been repeated by no less an esteemed citizen than Miss Charlotte Whitton, formerly the spinster mayor of the Canadian capital of Ottawa and unflinching advocate of a Petticoat Party. Miss Whitton claimed to have seen Taylor score the goal skating backwards, in 1910, and related it in a magazine article years later, after she became aware of the fees

THE PLAYERS

Milt Schmidt, former coach and general manager of Boston Bruins, near the end of his playing career in 1954. *(Courtesy of Dick Beddoes)*

The Stratford Streak—Howie Morenz. *(Courtesy of Stan Fischler)*

Scorer of three goals in 21 seconds: Bill Mosienko of the "Pony Line." *(Courtesy of the New York Rangers)*

Rocket Richard, former Montreal superstar, retired since 1960.
(*Courtesy of Dick Beddoes*)

Usher restrains fan trying to punch NHL president Clarence Campbell during Richard Riot in Montreal Forum on March 17, 1955. Montreal partisans rioted in the Forum, smashed windows and looted stores after Campbell suspended Richard for hitting a linesman. (*Courtesy of Dick Beddoes*)

This is 1957 picture of, from left, Fred (Cyclone) Taylor, Maurice (Rocket) Richard and Lester (Silver Fox) Patrick.

(Courtesy of Dick Beddoes)

Lester Patrick (second from left) receiving scroll representing election to the International Hockey Hall of Fame. Ranger president John Reed Kilpatrick is directly to his right.

(Courtesy of Stan Fischler)

Bill Cook, Ranger star of the twenties and thirties.
(Courtesy of the New York Rangers)

Francis (King) Clancy, former Toronto defenseman, wit and member of the Hockey Hall of Fame.
(Courtesy of Dick Beddoes)

Boston superstar Bobby Orr, six-time winner of the Norris Trophy. *(Photo: Terry Foley)*

Glenn Hall retired after 18 seasons with Detroit, Chicago and St. Louis.

(Courtesy of Dick Beddoes)

Stan Mikita, Chicago Black Hawks' all-star center, the only player in NHL history to win the Ross, Hart and Byng Trophies simultaneously. He did it in two consecutive seasons, 1966–67 and 1967–68.

(Photo: Terry Foley)

All-time superstar—Gordie Howe.
(*Courtesy of Stan Fischler*)

Former Chicago Black Hawk ace Bobby Hull, player-coach of the Winnipeg Jets of the WHA. The Golden Jet, despite missing 15 games at the start of the 1972–73 season because of a court injunction, scored 51 goals and 52 assists to finish fifth in the scoring race. He led his team to first place in the WHA's West Division and into the finals of the World Cup before bowing to the New England Whalers. (*Courtesy* Hockey Spectator)

The Big M—Frank Mahovlich—in full flight down the left boards. After early stardom in Toronto and rejuvenation in Detroit, Mahovlich reached even greater heights with Montreal Canadiens' Stanley Cup winners of 1971 and 1973.
(*Photo: Terry Foley*)

All-time NHL shutout king, Terry Sawchuk. (*Courtesy of the New York Rangers*)

The China Wall—Johnny Bower.
*(Courtesy of
the New York Rangers)*

Defense star Doug Harvey in the
uniform of his fourth NHL team,
the St. Louis Blues.
(Courtesy of the St. Louis Blues)

paid for broadcasting such myths. She testified: "Taylor, with superb protection from his teammates, took a pass from behind the Renfrew goal and speedily but nonchalantly skated backwards the length of the rink, for good measure circled the Ottawa goal, swung around and scored, still skating backwards."

Miss Whitton's rococo account is highly untrue, according to Taylor, who is still perhaps the best source to consult on the feat. But they do not tell lies or believe myths about just anyone, which speaks well for Taylor's enduring and mythological quality. A good book published by the NHL in 1967 called *The Trail of the Stanley Cup*, by Charles L. Coleman, a retired mining engineer, demolished the myth perpetrated by Miss Whitton and other suspect eye-witnesses.

Taylor had deserted Ottawa to play for Renfrew, for more money, and his defection guaranteed a warm reaction when the Creamery Kings played their first game in Ottawa in the winter of 1910. Ottawa fans were further stimulated, in a hot, vituperative way, when the sports page of the *Ottawa Citizen* published a derisive jibe allegedly uttered by Taylor. They read, on February 11, 1910: WILL TAYLOR SCORE? "Early this week Fred Taylor made a crack while in the *Citizen* office, in the presence of witnesses, that he would skate through the Ottawa defense backward and score a goal. Although he was joking, it seems to have got around and been taken seriously. At any rate a fan has posted $100 at the King Edward Hotel, to bet that Taylor doesn't score in any way, shape or form."

More than 7,000 spectators—the biggest crowd to attend a hockey game in Ottawa to that time, bigger than many crowds in the expansion cities of the National League 57 years later—jammed the Ottawa arena on February 12, 1910. Taylor was greeted with decayed lemons and strafed with empty whisky bottles when he skated out for his first shift.

He played a strong game, according to Ottawa newspaper reports, described as a standout beside Frank Patrick on the Renfrew defense. After three regulation periods, the score was tied 5–5. In a subsequent 10-minute overtime period, Ottawa scored three times for an 8–5 triumph. "Taylor scintillated with his rushes," the *Ottawa Citizen* reported, "but the Ottawa defense was impregnable and he never got one clear shot on the Ottawa goal."

That evidence should kill the fiction about Taylor scoring a goal while skating backwards, but it still is told as fact when the hockey ancients coagulate to dip their beaks into a watering hole. The myth's persistence shows that Taylor was a natural born hitching post for legends.

In recent years one of the men who talked about Taylor most was one who knew him best in the old days, when life was young for both of them. The late Frank Patrick told interviewers, shortly before his death in Vancouver, British Columbia, in 1960, that he hated to sound like a professional old-timer, but he wondered if there could ever be another star like the Cyclone Taylor of 1915?

Not a single player in the NHL today, not even the venerable John Bower, old warrior of Toronto Maple Leafs, was born that wartime spring when Taylor laid hold of a Stanley Cup final for the Vancouver Millionaires and simply ripped it apart. He was the principal Vancouver mercenary in subduing the Ottawa Senators after formidable Senators like Clint Benedict and Art Ross and Punch Broadbent had gone barreling through Eastern Canada without serious opposition.

By the time Vancouver had won the Stanley Cup in three consecutive games, by scores of 6–2, 8–3 and 12–3, Taylor was, for the moment, the most famous character in Canada. People who had seen him were trying to describe a chesty man with sinewy arms, a muffin face and a skin infield springing up where his hair used to be. They told how he seemed to blur in full flight and what a stickhandler he was, how he scored six goals in three games by plunging through the Ottawa defense and feinting Benedict, the embarrassed goalkeeper, out of his intimate apparel.

"Cyc Taylor could do it all," Frank Patrick would say, long after. "He could stickhandle. Rag the puck. Score. And skate . . ." Patrick groped for words to describe the Taylor who filled the old black headlines. ". . . Taylor could skate, like a Cyclone raging out of hell."

Ontario newspapers, soon after 1900, tagged Taylor with assorted labels—the Listowel Flash, the Listowel Thunderbolt, the Listowel Whirlwind. He did not arrive in the tiny community until his family moved there when he was five. He had been born in the village of Tara, where vital statistics in the courthouse record: "June 23, 1885, born to Archibald and May Taylor, their fourth child, a son— Frederick Wellington Taylor, eight pounds, three ounces."

He was a star for the Listowel Mintos at 13. He moved up to the Listowel Juniors, then advanced to Portage La Prairie in the Manitoba Senior League in 1905, when he was 20. He transferred from the Canadian prairies to Houghton Portage Lakes, a Michigan team in the International Hockey League.

In 1908 Taylor was lured to Ottawa for $1,000 from the Silver Seven and a steady job with the Canadian immigration department. In his first game he won the appellation Cyclone, a descriptive that ranks with the most colorful in Canadian sport. He scored five goals as the Silver Seven ruined the Montreal Wanderers, the prevailing Stanley Cup champions, entrancing 6,500 Ottawa partisans. Malcolm Price, sports editor of the old *Ottawa Free Press*, was inspired to hyperbolic heights of purple prose.

"Taylor was sensational," Price wrote. "They used to call him the Whirlwind of the International League, but he has become the Cyclone of the Eastern Canada League." It was a nickname that stuck with historians, and came down in company with other *noms de* superstars—Cyclone, Big Train, Stratford Streak and the Rocket.

A year later, sniffing the crisp, exciting smell of money exuding out of Renfrew in the Ottawa Valley, Taylor bolted the Silver Seven. He signed with the Creamery Kings on October 31, 1909. On that date, the golden age of hockey was ushered in when Renfrew offered, and Taylor promptly accepted, the unheard of contract of $5,250 for one season. A season in that Neanderthal era comprised 12 scheduled games, plus another six or eight in playoffs.

The amount was the most money ever paid a Canadian athlete to that time, and remained the top annual wage among hockey players for 25 years. The date is hardly ever mentioned as a turning point for Canadian history, but there are reasons why it should not be forgotten. It introduced an Ice Age when an unlettered Canadian, playing hockey, could earn more playing a game in the winter than the Prime Minister of Canada is paid in a year, even if the Prime Minister offered to sweep out the dressing room of Toronto Maple Leafs on the side. It put the late Charlie Conacher of the Leafs of 30 years ago in a position to know millionaires, and to become a millionaire himself. It brought the word "superstar" into the language. It made possible the National League pension plan, considered one of the finest old-age securities.

Taylor today pays lip-service to all the platitudes. "Of course I recommend hockey as a career, but it shouldn't be allowed to interfere with a young man's education." Then he reflects on the average sum paid to NHL players, about $20,000, and the $80,000 earned by some of the stars. "But when you get money like that, and a good pension, maybe you don't need much education."

He doesn't look like a legend—stumpy, bald, old—but he says people constantly assure him that he is. People still tell him they saw him score skating backwards, in Ottawa and Winnipeg and Vancouver.

It didn't happen, at any time in any rink, but that is the sort of effect Cyclone Taylor had upon spectators. You have to be good to become mythological.

The Present

Johnny Bower: Oldest Guy in Fastest Game

JOHN WILLIAM BOWER, who played goal in the first Stanley Cup game ever played, and beat one-eyed Frank McGee out of the winning score in overtime ("I got my great toe to a low drive," said the goaler later; "It was a high shot that the old coot got his kisser in front of," said McGee, before going off to die in World War I; "Bower pounced on a loose puck from a pile-up," reported Mike Rodden, an antique referee), is constantly plagued with questions about his advanced age.

There is uncommon marveling at the venerable athlete whom Punch Imlach, ex-coach of Toronto's Maple Leafs, reveres as "the oldest guy in the fastest game with the most pressure." When questions are asked, Bower answers with a dignity befitting a moldering landmark: "My biggest thrill was sticking in the big league. You don't expect to stick when you're 33, like I was." The part of this speech that catches the ear is "33, like I was." It illustrates the stately logic by which public monuments like Bower and Satchel Paige are dated. It reminds observers that it was a mere 11 years ago, in 1958, that Bower broke into the NHL to stay.

He was then, as he says, 33; and, as Coach Imlach said whenever the matter came up, Bower had been 33 for a good many years. Bower humors the kidders with serenity, but one year he went to a Toronto training camp armed with a birth certificate. The document stated that he was born on November 8, 1924. He presented his natal credential to Imlach, and Toronto's noble curator said: "So you were born in 1924, eh?"

"Yes, sir."

"But you also insist you joined the Canadian army in 1939?" Imlach pressed.

"That's right."

The coachly genius pounced with his usual alacrity. "Then that means you were only 15. Just a wet-nosed kid when you were allowed to enlist." Imlach, himself a second lieutenant (retired), went after a triumphant punch line. "I knew the army was stupid," he said, "but not that stupid."

Bower is inclined to say, in the tolerance of maturity, that he was restricted so long in the minors because the NHL was loaded with efficient goalkeepers. That is half the story on the long frustration of his big-league ambitions. There is another, lesser-known half.

Bower came from the Cleveland Barons to tend nets for the forlorn New York Rangers in 1953–54, good enough to limit enemy shooters to 2.6 goals a game. The next year the Rangers rewarded him by banishing him to their Western farm in Vancouver, British Columbia. Lorne Worsley replaced him in New York.

There was a shift in the New York front office in 1955–56, involving installation of Murray Patrick as general manager. Phil Watson, easily riled, was hired as coach. At training camp, as usual, Bower and Worsley competed for the goalkeeping job.

Patrick nagged at Watson to decide whom he should keep, and Watson kept postponing his decision. Bower, he thought, was no worse than even with the younger Worsley.

One night, after the Rangers played an exhibition game in Providence, Rhode Island, Patrick told Watson: "Worsley is your goalie. Bower stays right here."

"What gives?" Watson demanded. "I'd practically decided on Bower."

"Bower stays in Providence," Patrick insisted. "And don't ask why, Phil. There's politics in everything." By politics Patrick meant a deal with the Providence management for future players and favors. Bower was the pawn, shuffled to Providence with scant regard for his NHL aspirations.

He played in Providence two seasons, elected the most valuable mercenary in the American League each season. He returned to Cleveland for the 1957–58 season where, in deference to his impeding of rival forwards earlier in his career, he was called the Great Wall of China. He was at an age when few athletes are liberated from the limbo of the minors.

Bower was at last sprung from the bushes by an odd turn. Billy Reay was the Toronto coach in the spring of 1958, on the hot seat as leader of the only Maple Leaf team to finish last in the NHL. Reay wanted, among other personnel, a goalie to replace Ed Chadwick. He went to Alberta, planning to buy Al Rollins, an NHL veteran then playing for Calgary Stampeders. Reay caught Rollins in a Western League play-off game against Vancouver and saw him get stoned for four goals, or six—a brutal performance, in any case. Reay, appalled, retreated to Toronto, muttering to himself: "That kills it. I'm going to buy Bower from Cleveland. He's two years older than Rollins, but no matter how old he is, he's got to be better than Rollins looked."

Bower was rising 34, or more, when Reay rescued him from hockey obscurity. It is one of the ironies that Reay was fired before Bower could prove the wisdom of his purchase. But if Al Rollins had been more proficient one night 11 years ago in Calgary, Bower might never have had the chance to make Imlach resemble a genius.

In 11 seasons in the NHL, Bower has won the Vezina Trophy once on his own merit and shared it once in partnership with Terry Sawchuk. He played a dominating role in four Stanley Cup championships, three of them in succession between 1961 and 1964.

In games or practice, Bower behaves with perspiring agility. He defends his area with short, desperate, skidding moves from side to side, breaking up close-in plays with the best stick check among goalers in the NHL, bent in a familiar crouch, bulky and alert.

Bower is the beau ideal of the old folks set, but he is not precisely unique. Toronto had become haven for the athletic ancient— Allan Stanley, George Armstrong, Tim Horton, Marcel Pronovost, Red Kelly, Terry Sawchuk. Perhaps Plato had a reason why people can survive into athletic dotage in hockey. "He who is of a calm and happy nature will hardly feel the pressure of age," the Greek philosopher said, "but to him who is of an opposite disposition, youth and age are equally a burden."

Punch Imlach suspects any introduction of serene philosophy into a sport where he places a premium on sweat. "How d'you measure athletic deterioration?" Imlach challenged. "It's different for everybody." He explained with some colloquial sweatshirt rhetoric: "Good ones like Bower last because they have so far back to go. Guys who are fringe players don't last on account they don't have much talent margin to go back on."

Bower, an essentially simple man, did not have any mystical

reason for his ability to survive in a fast, tense game commonly regarded as a pastime for the young. "Maybe it's being fit that keeps my reflexes good," he said. "In the summers I run maybe four miles a day."

An incredulous listener once said: "Four miles? You mean like a guy preparing for a big fight?"

"Yes. And a lot of the times I'll run it in my bare feet. That toughens my feet so the skates don't hurt me when I put 'em on in training camp."

Bower's teammates insisted that his survival was a product of perspiration. Dave Keon, a moppet of 29, does not hold with one theory in the NHL about luck riding with Bower. "You know what luck is in Bower's case?" Keon says. "That's when a lot of preparedness and a little good fortune meet."

Large rosters—two goalkeepers, plus 18 others—is one easily perceived reason for the doddering to play beyond their years. Few goalkeepers are required to play the full 76-game schedule any more; Bower was in roughly half of the Toronto games in 1967–68, splitting the duties with 30-year-old Bruce Gamble. But a year later he seemed to have lost his touch once and for all.

Benches full of personnel are also geared to preserving the pensioners by constant substitution. Few players are obligated to work more than 35 minutes in a 60-minute game, on the ice for two- or three-minute stretches, then rested for the same period.

The rare performers like Gordon Howe are gifted with muscular, wear-ever physiques. The Detroit superstar was one of those naturals, like DiMaggio or Hemingway. He played the longest number of seasons any man has ever played in the NHL.

Some experts contend that players formerly retired too soon, victims of the old wives' contention that a man cannot prolong an athletic career past 30. Conn Smythe, once the pungent proprietor of the Toronto franchise, insists many of his superior players quit before the rocking chair really beckoned. "Take Syl Apps," Smythe says of a Toronto star of the mid-forties. "This was a clean-living athlete who could have endured five or eight more years, but he retired at 31 after reading a lot of crap about 30 being too old for hockey."

Under Imlach, any Toronto player under 30 was considered a callow youth, hardly case-hardened enough to enter the old folks home. That theory was never better served than in the last minute of the last game of the 1967 Stanley Cup final, when Imlach sent out his oldest players to defend a 2–1 lead against Montreal Canadiens.

He had Stanley, 41, Horton, 37, Armstrong, 37, Kelly, 40, and Bob Pulford, 31, in front of Terry Sawchuk, the 37-year-old goalkeeper standing in for Bower, who was injured. These venerable heirlooms not only protected the lead; they added to it with a goal that secured Toronto's fourth Stanley Cup in six years.

So it's a young man's world, eh, and youth will be served? Maybe, but there is fireside comfort in a senior citizen like John Bower for those who sometimes weary of what James Russell Lowell called "the elbowing self-conceit of youth."

Bower played only one game in the 1969–70 season, allowing five goals. It was the signal to the grand warrior that he had had enough of the big-league competition. He finally retired to become a coach and scout for the Maple Leafs, secure in the knowledge that the NHL has seen few competitors like him.

Rod Gilbert

OF ALL THE LATTER-DAY HOCKEY STARS none has endured the constant physical torment that has plagued Rod Gilbert since—and even before—he became a member of the New York Rangers. Despite two broken backs Gilbert has emerged in the late sixties as the heir apparent to such erstwhile Ranger aces as Bill Cook, Bryan Hextall, Andy Bathgate and Cecil Dillon, all right wings.

That Gilbert was able to prevail is a tribute to both his own perseverance and grim determination and the Rangers' obsessive conviction that he could become an exceptional hockey player. The fact that the New Yorkers also were desperate for a high scorer after Bathgate was traded to Toronto in February 1964 played an important part in the Ranger investment in Gilbert.

Rod differed from his predecessors mainly because of his size and deportment. At five feet, nine inches, 175 pounds, he was relatively small. His baby face added to the image of fragility and his policy of pacifism on ice confirmed the fact that he would be more the pushed than pusher. Normally this would guarantee failure for the majority of forwards. To succeed in the NHL, according to the Gordie Howe theory, a forward must be aggressive and at least fight opponents to a stand-off. But Gilbert, who is the antithesis of the fighter, managed to survive by distilling three key ingredients—speed, guile and an extraordinary scoring sense. In short, he knew where to be at the right time.

By 1969 it had become apparent that he had clearly overcome

the damage to his back and along with his boyhood chum, Jean Ratelle, was among the most potent and consistent Ranger scorers. If he was to fulfill the total image expected of him he would, in time, become the leader of the Rangers, something he had not been in the years of his ascendancy. But in those formative seasons Gilbert had good cause to be more concerned with his own problems than those of his team.

His woes began long before he became a regular in the NHL. In the spring of 1961, when he was a 19-year-old playing for the Guelph Royals, an amateur team sponsored by the Rangers, he tripped over a piece of cardboard that had been thrown on the ice by a fan. His body hurtled into the wooden sideboards, the force of the blow breaking his back. When he was sent to the Mayo Clinic in Rochester, Minnesota, for corrective surgery there were grave doubts that he'd be able to play hockey again. Gilbert, however, insisted that the complicated operation take place and the Rangers, of course, endorsed the idea in the hopes that he would eventually graduate to the pros.

To repair the fractured fourth and fifth vertebrae in the lumbar region of his lower spine surgeons removed four inches of bone from the tibia of his left leg and grafted the bone as a coupling to hold the vertebrae together. At this point Gilbert's blood failed to coagulate as expected. Pus drained into his leg and back. The infection in his leg reached such grave dimensions that doctors prepared to amputate the leg; a decision, if carried out, that would have ended his hockey career. At this point the condition took a sudden and dramatic turn for the better. Amputation plans were dismissed and, within nine weeks, Gilbert was released from the hospital.

After a lengthy period of recuperation Gilbert engineered the first of what was to be a series of comebacks. The Rangers assigned him to the Kitchener Rangers in the now defunct Eastern Professional League. He played 21 games for them late in the 1961–62 season and scored 12 goals and 11 assists for 23 points. The scoring total was less impressive than his ability to return to hockey with no apparent physical or mental blocks. The Rangers had observed his progress with unusual care. Once it became obvious he was capable of playing the next question was whether he would be able to endure the stress of NHL combat should the call be made.

While Rod was completing his season with Kitchener the Rangers were advancing into the Stanley Cup semi-final round with the Toronto Maple Leafs. After two games—and two losses to the Leafs

—the Ranger casualty list was alarmingly long. The club was particularly weak on the forward line where both Camille Henry and Ken Schinkel were suffering serious injuries. As a result Ranger general manager Murray (Muzz) Patrick phoned Gilbert at Kitchener and ordered him to New York. Less than a year after he had undergone corrective surgery he was playing in hockey's world series.

Few raw rookies ever made a more impressive debut than Gilbert that night at Madison Square Garden in New York. "At first," Rod recalled, "I never expected to play. Why should they have used a rookie in such an important playoff game? In fact Muzz Patrick didn't tell me I'd dress until a half hour before game time." Logic, however, has never been an important element in hockey. Blended together, the limited talents of Gilbert, Dave Balon and Johnny Wilson sparkled for the Rangers who upset Toronto, 5–4. Wilson scored two goals, Balon got one and Gilbert was the architect on Balon's goal which proved to be the winner.

Gilbert, of course, had swiftly become the talk of New York, and it was imperative that Coach Doug Harvey start him with Balon and Wilson in the fourth game of the series. There was a capacity crowd of 15,925 spectators at the Garden that night. They had come to see a playoff game but also to determine whether there really was anything to this Gilbert kid. Certainly, he didn't look impressive. Standing next to his opposing wing, Frank (Big M) Mahovlich, Gilbert appeared lilliputian in comparison, but once the game began he became increasingly more evident.

The Leafs won the opening face-off and sent the puck into Ranger zone but Balon retrieved it and drilled it into Maple Leaf ice. The puck ricocheted off the end boards, off a Ranger stick, off a Toronto stick and onto the stick of Gilbert. At exactly 41 seconds of the first period of his second play-off game Gilbert slid the puck past goalie Johnny Bower and the Rangers were ahead, 1–0.

Midway in the same period Balon and Wilson collaborated on a rush. Gilbert drifted behind. The puck bounced back and forth between Balon and Wilson, then it was dropped to Rod. A second later it had flashed past Bower and now the score was 2–0 for the Rangers. The Leafs scored a goal in the third period to draw within a goal of the Rangers but less than three minutes later Gilbert fed a pass to Balon who fooled Bower and the Rangers won the game, 4–2. When Rod returned to the bench after the Balon goal he nudged Patrick. "Muzz," he said, "do me a favor and give me a kick in the pants so I know I'm not dreaming." Patrick obliged.

Gilbert's astonishing production continued on into the fifth game. The Rangers were behind, 2–1, late in the third period when Rod teamed with Al Langlois to put Earl Ingarfield in the clear for the tying goal at 12:31 that sent the game into sudden-death overtime. The Leafs eventually won on a disputed goal at 4:23 of the second sudden death period. Toronto won the semifinal round, 4–2, but Gilbert had won a berth on the Rangers. "He showed me," said Patrick, "that he has the makings of an NHL star."

However, there were some key "ifs." It already had become obvious that Rod was reluctant to meet the challenge of intimidating defensemen. Better prospects than him had been run out of the league after impressive starts. The subtle suggestion that such a fate could befall Gilbert was implicit in coach Harvey's guarded appraisal: "He handles himself well but it's too early to tell. The test will come after he's been up for a while."

Gilbert's first full season (1962–63) as a Ranger was unimpressive from an artistic viewpoint. He scored only 11 goals and 20 assists and trailed far behind Kent Douglas of Toronto in voting for the rookie-of-the-year award. But he did manage to play in all of the Rangers' 70 games despite his aching back—and it still was aching. "Even though I had had the operation," he said at the time, "it was necessary for me to wear a special back brace. Once I tried to play without the brace I found I got tired right away." The brace was a huge white corset consisting of heavy fiber and leather draped over thin tongues of steel extending from Gilbert's chest to his hips. Trainer Frank Paice would tighten the vise for Rod before every game to a point where breathing would be almost impossible. "It was necessary," said Rod, "for me to stand up on the bench during the rest just so I could catch my breath."

Always there was the threat of an attack from one of the enemy's more hostile defensemen. "You expect that in hockey," Gilbert observed. "The other teams knew there was something wrong so they'd take a run at me. But that didn't bother me. I was made to be a hockey player."

To some the remark could be discarded as a bromide of the business. But there was a metaphysical air about Gilbert that transcended the norm. He apparently believed there was a destiny to fulfill and mummifying brace and all he began his ascendancy in

1963–64, his second full season in the NHL. He amassed 24 goals and 40 assists to more than double his goal and point output of the previous year. He increased his goal production to 25 in the 1964–65 season although he collected three fewer assists. By the spring of 1965 he was doing so well even the champion Montreal Canadiens expressed an interest in trading for him but the feeling was not mutual. "I've spent my entire career with the Rangers so far," he replied, "and I hope I can play another 20 years with them."

If one is convinced that professional sport is a callous operation oblivious to personal sensitivities then the Rangers should have discarded Gilbert for a healthy forward. Unknown to the Montreal club but known to the New York officials Gilbert's back fusion was deteriorating. It was obvious that if he was to continue playing hockey he would have to succumb to another operation. And, if he succumbed to another operation there was every chance it would fail and he would be finished; the investment completely wasted. But, in one of those rare instances of loyalty to the athlete-serf, the Rangers decided to retain Gilbert and gamble on his eventual recovery.

No date had been set for the new surgery and St. Clare's Hospital, New York, was furthest from Rod's mind that balmy afternoon in August 1965 as he guided his outboard motorboat to shore at his parents' lakeside summer cottage in St. Gabriel de Brandon Quebec. As the prow of the boat slid along the sand Rod leaped over the side and began pulling the outboard from the water. Suddenly, a bolt of pain shot up his back. He shrugged off the attack and hoped the pain would subside. But by next morning he found it almost impossible to lift himself out of bed. He phoned Emile Francis, who had replaced Muzz Patrick as general manager of the Rangers, and was ordered to New York for an examination.

This time Dr. Kazuo (Yana) Yanigasawa, the Rangers' team physician who, to the players has a Messianic quality about him, examined Gilbert. "You need another operation," Dr. Yanigasawa said. "If you can stand the pain you play out the season. Or you can have the operation now and miss the entire season. It's your decision."

Despite the gravity of the situation he maintained an outward calm. Rod made his decision to play. "There really was no choice," he explained. "When you love hockey as much as I do, you play and take your chances." But training camp was a gruelling experience for him, and the day the Rangers opened their season on October

24, 1965, Gilbert was lying on his back in St. Clare's Hospital. He had played in the All-Star Game a few days earlier in Montreal and, during a turn on the ice, felt a twinge in his back. He had to be helped to the train taking him to New York and barely could move when it arrived in Grand Central Station. Dr. Yanigasawa diagnosed the injury as a muscle spasm in the area of his broken back but said that Rod would be able to play within two weeks. "What bothered me most," said Gilbert as he lay on the hospital bed, "is that I had played 212 straight games as a Ranger and now the streak was broken."

Soon he returned and almost immediately he was battered from all sides. Once, Bobby Baun, who then was playing defense for the Toronto Maple Leafs, nailed Gilbert with such force he sent Rod careening into the boards. When Gilbert's wind returned he crawled to the bench where trainer Frank Paice removed his jersey. The crash had forced the heavy metal brace into his hip bone, badly bruising the hip. The pain was so intense it felt as if a bayonet was stuck in his side. But Gilbert insisted on playing and, somehow, managed to continue without missing a game until January 1966. "If I'm knocked unconscious," he said with that curious mixture of cornball and conviction, "I take pride in always leaping back into action."

In January 1966 the Ranger brass ordered Gilbert to stop playing and prepare for the second back operation. The decision was hardly philanthropic. The team was depressing and was perilously close to elimination from a play-off berth. It was obvious that the already handicapped Gilbert couldn't help them anymore. "Rod has been playing under tremendous strain," said Francis, "and we've been fortunate to have his services for half a year. But we have to go along with the doctor and do what's best for Rod."

What was "best for Rod" was spinal fusion surgery which would correct what physicians call "pseudoarthrosis." Hundreds of body-checks had loosened the coupling between his fourth and fifth vertebrae; the coupling that was made by the Mayo Clinic doctors. "I wasn't so upset before the first operation," Gilbert made clear. "I hadn't been in the pros. I hadn't tasted the glory. If things didn't work out I knew I could go to college. But the second time was different. I had been in the limelight and I liked it. There was no place to go if there was no hockey. There was no guarantee I'd be back to normal after the operation but I had to do it because I couldn't keep playing with that brace on my back."

Two days later the operation was described as a complete success but Gilbert didn't believe it. "I was convinced," he said later, "that my hockey career was over. For the first week I was just lying on my stomach. It was like an eternity. Then they would put me on my back. Two nurses had to slowly edge me on my side and took such a long time to turn me over. After that my parents came to visit me from Montreal and it was a disaster. I hadn't eaten since the operation—can you imagine going a whole week without eating?—and I couldn't talk. I was in bad shape. When Emile Francis came to see me I couldn't even talk to him."

Eventually, the pain subsided, the wound healed and Gilbert returned to Montreal for the decisive convalescence. When Gilbert showed up at training camp in Kingston, Ontario, on September 20, 1966, he showed no signs of ill health. "The only thing that ached," he mentioned, "were the muscles from not playing so long. Otherwise, I was loose. There was no pain and, for the first time in years, I felt complete freedom."

It was apparent that the Gilbert renaissance was underway. He maneuvered capably in training camp and on October 22, 1966, scored a three-goal hat trick against Toronto, the first time he ever scored three goals in one NHL game. The second operation was so successful—or, so it seemed—he glibly dismissed questions about his controversial back problems. "What back?" he would reply. "I don't remember a thing about it. All the misery and agony faded into the background on the ice. Now I'm convinced it never happened. I never want to remember again."

But he couldn't escape the spectre of another broken back. Late in the 1966–67 season the Rangers were playing a game against the Bruins in Boston Garden. It was cold and damp in the rink and while Gilbert sat on the bench he began to experience a gnawing pain in his back again. He was convinced he was in trouble again, and this time the trouble could spell *finis*.

Dr. Yanigasawa's examination failed to detect any flaws in Gilbert's back. The diagnosis was that the Ranger star was suffering from a "cold in the back," an explanation that convinced nobody, not even Gilbert. He was advised he could continue playing provided that he wear a thick blanket over his jersey while he sat on the bench. Gilbert agreed but nothing he did on the ice changed the opinions of those who believed he was through. His goal production was drastically curbed and he finished the season with 28 scores, considerably less than was expected of him in midseason. But he did score two goals and two assists in four play-off games against Montreal, a factor that revived hopes for 1967–68.

Skeptics were given a severe setback as soon as Gilbert hit the ice. The blanket as well as the back brace had been discarded. Liberated from the encumberances, Gilbert moved right up to the top ten in the scoring race after a brief early-season slump. At one point he was contending for the scoring championship and recorded some significant goals. Likewise, his buddy Ratelle, survived a similar back operation, rejoined Gilbert and enjoyed a superb season.

In a game at the Montreal Forum on February 24, 1968, Gilbert scored four goals against the Canadiens and fired 16 shots on goal, an NHL record. During the Stanley Cup East Division semifinal round against the Chicago Black Hawks Rod scored two goals within six seconds at Chicago Stadium. He finished the season in fifth place among scorers, with 29 goals and 48 assists for 77 points, and led the Rangers in play-off scoring with five goals in six games.

One by one Gilbert has surmounted obstacles and emerged as one of the premier forwards in the NHL. Maurice (Rocket) Richard, one of hockey's most prolific scorers, said Gilbert is capable of a 45-goal season. In 1971–72 he scored 43, almost matching the prophecy.

Critics have argued that Gilbert is far from the complete hockey player. They have fingered him for weak defensive play, have pointed out that he's not as aggressive as a high-scoring forward should be, have criticized him for using a curved banana blade stick and slapping the puck at times when he should use the traditional wristshot. But Gilbert has disagreed and so has his manager. "If you tell Rod not to slap the puck," Francis has answered, "it's like telling Bobby Hull to stop slapping. Rod's slapshot is a great weapon; the kind you don't discourage an offensive player from using."

Because of his unusual sequence of back problems, his spectacular start with the Rangers and the results expected of him Gilbert has sometimes won headlines not commensurate with his ability. He has yet to win a scoring championship or a league trophy. His team has yet to finish first or win the Stanley Cup. As such, Gilbert cannot be classified as a superstar. But he is an exceptional one, and any athlete who can survive two broken backs and return to the battle certainly deserves marks for gumption. When he can make a come-back and be one of the best he is, as Gilbert put it in his own words, "the luckiest guy in the world."

Glenn Hall

GLENN HENRY HALL prefers the solitude of rocking on the veranda of a cottage beside a lake west of Edmonton, Alberta, and cold beer. "Who needs goalkeeping?" is what he wants to know.

He often played hockey as though in agony, frequently distressed to the point of vomiting before games, then going out and guarding goal like a demented acrobat. In 1972, he rejected an offer to play goal for the Alberta Oilers.

Hall hates noise and the attendant idiocies of hockey with such vehemence that he once confided to Louis Cauz, the distinguished hockey correspondent of the *Toronto Globe and Mail*: "All I want to do is stand out in the middle of that 160 acres I've got near Edmonton and holler 'Screw you! Screw you! Screw you!' 'til I'm good and hoarse and hear the 'You! You! You!' echo back across the field."

For all his distaste, Hall survived 18 seasons in the NHL at Detroit, Chicago and St. Louis, three times winner of the Vezina Trophy as the best at his position, 11 times selected to one or other of the All-Star Teams. He was designated Mr. Goalie in Chicago, a quaint tag that did not prevent the Black Hawks from dumping him into the expansion draft in the summer of 1967.

Hall was eagerly grabbed by Lynn Patrick, then general manager of the St. Louis Blues. "Hall always held out on Chicago every fall because he said he had a barn to paint," Patrick said. "Well, I'll tell you how much I want him. I'll go out and help him paint the blessed barn."

Only Patrick, who is not offended by Anglo-Saxon epithets, did not say blessed. Nor did he have to dig out his paint brush and become a Picasso of the prairies. He did, however, have to inflict plenty of green from the Blues upon the reluctant goalkeeper.

Hall is generally reported to have signed his first contract with St. Louis for $47,500, the largest salary ever paid a goaler for a single season. The national debt of Yucatan is smaller.

Money cannot always immunize a professional against the fear of mediocrity in himself, which is why many NHL goalkeepers have prematurely abandoned the game. Tension frays their lives. For instance, Bill Durnan won the Vezina Trophy six times in seven seasons in the Forties, but Durnan quit Montreal Canadiens before shell shock got him. "The pay was good," he says, "but the wear and tear is more than I could take. The tension was almost as bad as the stitches used to sew up cuts."

Muzz Patrick would say, when he coached New York Rangers: "A goalie just stands there, seemingly impassive but actually boiling inside. They even play a different game than anyone else. The closest approach in another sport might be the catcher in baseball. But still, he does things that are baseball—goes up to hit, chases fouls and so on. In hockey, a goalie does nothing that other players do. Except for his sweater, he even dresses differently right down to his skates."

The late Wilf Cude, who tended nets for Detroit Red Wings and Montreal Canadiens 35 years ago, endured nerves and injuries before suddenly deciding to retire. "I was having my afternoon steak before a game," Cude told Trent Frayne, a Canadian magazine writer. "I poured a hell of a lot of ketchup on it. I'd just started to eat the steak when my wife Beulah made some casual remark about a trivial subject. For no good reason, I picked up my steak and threw it at her."

Cude said his wife ducked and the steak slapped against the wall. "The ketchup splattered and the steak hung there on the wall. Slowly it began to peel, and I stared at it. Between the time that steak hit the wall and then hit the floor, I decided I'd been a touchy goalkeeper long enough. By the time it landed, I'd retired."

Hall says, "I'd sometimes ask myself what the hell I'm doing in hockey? But it was the only way I could support my family." There is a hint of a smile on his gaunt features. "If I could support my four kids some other way, you can bet I wouldn't be playing goal."

But when he can no longer keep goal, he indeed will not remain in hockey in any executive job. "No coaching for me," Hall disclaims. "You'd have to put up with sports writers and fans, always saying something nice. I've never been diplomatic."

Hall's fits of nervousness were apparent when he came up to Detroit from Edmonton in 1954 to win the Calder Trophy as the outstanding rookie. Bob Goldham, a veteran on the Detroit defense, frankly advised him, "Hell, rook, it's going to get worse before it gets better."

Hall insists that it *did* get worse, although conditions were not wretched enough to prevent him from playing 502 successive games between 1955–56 and 1962–63. Once he did threaten to quit, half-way through his first season in St. Louis, convinced that he was fighting the puck.

"Oh, my God, Glenn!" Coach Scotty Bowman said, "why don't you talk to the team doctor?"

Hall, pale and tormented, did consult Dr. J. G. Probstein, the physician in charge of restoring the Blues. Hall mentioned how hockey was chewing him up emotionally.

"So no job's perfect," Dr. Probstein said. "Suppose you go back to the farm. You'd still worry there. You'd worry that the barn was going to burn down. You'd worry that the tractor was going to run over your kids."

"You make farming sound worse than hockey," Hall said.

"All I'm saying," the doctor said, "is that you're a born worrier. You'd worry whether you were in a barn or a rink. But in a rink you can worry for more money."

Hall remained, perhaps doubtfully, defending the St. Louis goal with the agile ferocity of the entire Green Bay football club. He was the defensive hub of a team that won the first championship of the expansion division. "Goalies are a breed apart," Blues' coach Bowman maintains, "and Hall is apart from the breed."

Glenn Henry Hall, 38, did not, by his own admission, want to play in the expanded NHL; but St. Louis would have been less respectable in expansion if he hadn't been on the ice oftener than the puck.

After five years of expansion Hall, 43, still was playing for St. Louis. His former goaltending partner, Jacques Plante, had been dispatched by the Blues to Toronto, clearly suggesting that, at least to St. Louis moguls, Hall was the more valuable goaltender. But after the Blues' first-round elimination in the 1971 playoffs Hall's playing days were ended.

Doug Harvey

BEFORE THE BOBBY ORR ERA there was no question among hockey seers but that Douglas Norman Harvey was the best of the modern defensemen.

Long after he was considered "over the hill," Harvey excelled for the St. Louis Blues through the 1968–69 season. His bland, round face overlapped into a bulldog's jowls. His midriff was overblown to the point where his waist was an imaginary line. Once, a reporter was overheard to criticize Harvey's obesity.

William (Scotty) Bowman, the young, intense general manager and coach of the Blues, was listening. "I don't care what Doug weighs, or how old he is," Bowman said. "He can still help us, like he did in the playoffs in the first year of expansion."

In the first year of the expanded NHL, in 1967–68, the Blues won the West Division championship with Harvey as a 43-year-old recruit on defense. He had come up from Kansas City, where he coached and played for the St. Louis farm club in the Central Pro League.

There were subsequent changes in the Blues' executive suite with Bowman adding the onerous general manager's job to his coaching duties. He brought Harvey, 10 years his senior, back to the big time as his assistant.

By then the long boyhood was over for Harvey and his playing skills were tarnished. He had become a vagabond since leaving Montreal Canadiens eight years earlier, first to New York, then hard-panning through the minors in St. Paul, Quebec, Baltimore and Pittsburgh.

It was fashionable, in the newspapers and the arenas, to mourn him as an old athlete who had dozed unaware past his bus stop. Why shouldn't a man tire of an art he has mastered, if that is the way it happens with him, and quit to run a bar and wear a business suit and ponder his memories?

What made the stubbornness difficult to fathom in Harvey's case is his place in hockey. He was a consummate craftsman, perhaps unmatched among defensemen of our time for union of style, wisdom and strength. He won the James Norris Memorial Trophy seven times as the best defenseman in the game; he was elected an all-star 11 times.

Toe Blake coached Harvey in Montreal in the late fifties, during one tyrannical span from 1955 to 1960 when Canadiens won the Stanley Cup for five successive seasons. Harvey was distinguished then as the hub of Montreal's smothering power play, associated with Boom Boom Geoffrion, Jean Beliveau, Rocket Richard and Richard Winston Moore.

"No player puts my heart in my mouth as often as Doug," Blake said. "But I've learned to swallow in silence. His style is casual, but it works. He makes few mistakes and, 99 per cent of the time, correctly anticipates the play or pass." Blake added the definitive estimate of the most imposing NHL defenseman since the slightly immortal Eddie Shore: "Doug plays defense in a rocking chair."

Harvey began playing it professionally in 1947, after rejecting an offer from the Boston Braves to play baseball. He had used up two summers in the Border Baseball League at Ottawa, once leading all batsmen with an average of .351.

Before that, in the last massive global war, he spent 16 months as a gunner on a Canadian merchant ship in the North Atlantic.

The high time professionally for Harvey was the fifties—unhurried on the ice, popular off it, casually capable on a team where temperaments are not customarily cool. But when he hit the far slope of his career, and kept playing, hockey's rigid group-think suggested there was something not quite respectable in a player refusing to admit he has been caught by age. His persistence, the purists insisted, made a mockery of The Game.

Harvey was amused by the concern for his decrepit state. He did not view his demotion to the minors as a cold, brown experience for the big-league and bright-lights guy he used to be. "The money's not the best in the American League," he said, unperturbed. "But it's not the worst either."

Harvey became a nomad in 1964, when the NHL governors made him a free agent in return for his long service. Such gestures are rare because many sportsmen discard nothing as long as they suspect there is some wheat left in the husk.

He coached New York Rangers to brief success for one season, sufficiently gifted at leadership to guide them into an uncommon appearance in the Stanley Cup playoffs. Critics wondered why he abandoned the executive end of the pastime for service among the yeomanry? "Aw, what the hell," he said. "When I was a coach, I couldn't be one of the boys. This way, if I want a beer with 'em, I get a beer."

There is a whimsical quality to this fellow, a nimble satirical sense which makes him uncomfortable in the role of boss. In 1966–67, during Harvey's employment with the Baltimore Clippers, the Springfield Indians rebelled against the sweat-shop tactics of Shore, the irascible, eccentric owner. One morning, at a Baltimore practice, Harvey led the Clippers on a two-minute sympathy sitdown.

Before leaving Baltimore, Harvey made a certain amount of comic history. He appeared at a black-tie sports banquet in a top hat, cummerbund, tails, and tattered white running shoes. Sort of dead end, to the end.

Gordie Howe

THERE HAS NEVER BEEN a better player than Gordie Howe although there have been better scorers, better defensive players, harder shots and more adroit—although not by much—stickhandlers. Nobody, however, combined the arts of shooting, scoring, stickhandling and *all* other hockey skills to the degree Howe did. During his reign, which began in the 1946–47 season, Howe clearly established himself as the most accomplished player of hockey's modern era. Of course, there is no way of knowing just how he would have handled himself in the twenties and thirties when passing and stickhandling dominated the game and speed was underplayed. But Howe always had been the very best in the very skills that predominated in earlier eras. That he was able to dominate the fifties and sixties is a tribute to his amazing versatility, seemingly inexhaustable energy and the ability to adapt to a new style of hockey, which is just what has been dispensed in the late sixties. The fact that he scored 44 goals and 103 points in 1968–69 testifies to his amazing longevity. His 59 assists set a new record for right wings.

The record book provides the most definitive testimony to Howe's claim as hockey's greatest star. He scored more goals and more assists than any man in the history of hockey. He played more seasons (25) than anybody and won more individual trophies than any of his opponents. The choice award is the Hart Trophy as the league's most valuable player. He won that six times which is two more than Eddie Shore, the excellent Boston Bruins defenseman, could accomplish. Shore is runner-up to Howe in that department.

Howe is only one of two players to have won the NHL's Lester Patrick Trophy "for outstanding service to hockey in the United States." The Patrick Trophy simply added to the traffic jam in Howe's trophy room. He won the Art Ross Trophy as the league's leading scorer six times, more than any other player, past or present. Each year the Red Wings present awards to their own and each year Howe won most of them. There were those who believed Howe could continue as one of the top players in hockey until he reached the age of 45 in 1973. This was based on several interesting possibilities. First, there was Howe's durability. Second, his obsessive love of hockey. Third, his natural ability. Fourth, the declining level of competency in the NHL. And, fifth, the fact that Howie savored the idea of playing the game when one or both of his sons, Mark and Marty, were old enough and competent enough to join him as a teammate on the Red Wings. In 1972–73 both were members of the Toronto Marlboros—Mark a forward and Marty a defenseman—and seemed destined to follow their father to the NHL. Then the Houston Aeros of the WHA, unrestricted by the NHL agreement with the CAHA not to draft under-20-year-olds, signed the brothers for the kind of big money prevalent today in pro sports. Then Gordie, disgruntled as a non-consulted VP with the Red Wings, decided to come out of retirement for the long Houston green but also for his long-stated ambition to play one season with his sons.

"He's likely the greatest hockey player that ever played," said Bobby Hull during the 1967–68 season, "or likely ever will play." There's special significance to Hull's statement. It was made during a season when Howe reached the age of 40 and Hull 29. Hull was, supposedly, at the zenith of his career, Howe in the twilight. Yet, Howe completely overshadowed his younger opponent. He played a full schedule of 74 games. Hull played 71. Howe scored 82 points to finish third in the scoring race only five points from the top. Hull finished sixth, seven points behind Howe. While Gordie Howe talked about remaining in hockey until his sons are old enough to join him, Bobby Hull talked about retiring to his cattle farm. "Obviously," said one observer, "there's a great difference in desire between the two stars."

It is conceivable that nobody has wanted to play the game of hockey more than Howe. If this were not the case he wouldn't have played in 1968–69 at the age of 41 and he wouldn't have played in 1950–51 after suffering an injury that came within a gossamer length of ending his life.

On March 28, 1950, the Red Wings were engaged in a bitter Stanley Cup semifinal round with their traditional enemies, the Toronto Maple Leafs. Howe, who just then was emerging as one of the brightest talents in the NHL, launched an attack for Detroit in the third period of the opening game. The puck was recaptured by the Leafs who drove into Detroit territory. Howe doubled back to thwart the attack. As Howe swerved to check Ted Kennedy, the Leaf player sidestepped him and Howe plummeted at full speed into the wooden sideboards. The resulting concussion was so serious that a brain specialist was rushed to the hospital and an operation was immediately ordered to relieve pressure on Howe's brain. In a typical Howe gesture while being wheeled into the operating room, he mumbled to manager Jack Adams, "I'm sorry I couldn't help you more tonight."

The operation temporarily saved Howe's life but he lingered on the lip of death for several days. His mother was flown in from her home in Saskatchewan to be at his side for what many believed would be his last hours. But Howe pulled through the crisis while the Red Wings and Maple Leafs bludgeoned each other in one of hockey's most vicious series. Naturally, Howe's injury became a *cause célèbre* with the Detroit club charging that Kennedy deliberately—and subtly—shoved the butt end of his stick into Howe a split second before the Detroit player dived into the boards. The Leafs, particularly Kennedy, claimed that no such thing happened and Toronto's assertions were later substantiated after NHL President Clarence Campbell conducted a thorough investigation of the incident. As for Howe, he contributed little evidence to support the charges leveled by his teammates and the Red Wing management. "To this day," he said during an interview in 1966, "I can't remember what happened that night I got hurt. All I can recall is chasing Kennedy and trying to get the puck away from him . . . I don't even remember going into the boards."

Howe always had been a truculent type but those close to him contend that the Kennedy incident reshaped his philosophy about NHL hockey. When he returned to the Red Wings the following season—although it had been thought he might never play hockey again—he developed into a devastatingly aggressive forward. Word soon got around the NHL player grapevine that it would be most imprudent and unhealthy to annoy Gordie Howe. Those who did found themselves groping for consciousness on the ice, bruised and sometimes bleeding. At first the mean side of Howe went unnoticed by the spectators but players who suffered from his in-fighting privately confided that Howe had become a mean hockey player.

The one player who, perhaps, can best attest to Howe's meanness and ability as a fighter is Lou Fontinato, a defenseman with the New York Rangers during the late fifties. For a time Fontinato roamed the ice with the reputation as one of the NHL's hardest bodycheckers and best fighters. He tested Howe several times and, to everyone's surprise, thumped Howe without noticeable backlash. One night in Madison Square Garden, Howe and Fontinato clashed again. They separated and now Fontinato was skating up ice with Howe in pursuit. Seconds later, Fontinato was bleeding from the ear. In fact, his ear was nearly clipped off by some mysterious swoop of a stick. Doctors managed to sew the loose parts back on but Fontinato hadn't learned his lesson.

Once again the Red Wings and Rangers clashed on Garden ice. This time Howe and Eddie Shack of the Rangers collided behind the net. They fenced with their sticks as other players intervened. Fontinato, who had been stationed 60 feet away at the blue line, rushed into the fracas and began tossing punches at Howe who, until then, had been concentrating on Shack. Howe absorbed the flurry of blows thrown by Fontinato without any damage and without retreating. Then, with the same cool calculation he would use in setting up a goal, he chop, chop, chopped Fontinato apart with a series of short jabs to the face. The potency of Howe's fists was so awesome that linesmen who normally would have pried apart the combatants stayed on the periphery out of danger.

Finally, when Fontinato's face was smeared with blood, his nose broken and at a right angle to his face, Howe was pulled away from his foe and unquestionably was the heavyweight champion of the NHL. The incident, which within the hockey world was important and treated as such, received international attention when *Life* magazine carried a full-page spread of the bout and the bloodied and demolished face of Lou Fontinato. The humiliation of Fontinato had a lasting effect on all NHL players and particularly Fontinato. He lost his air of braggadocio. His aggressiveness gone, he lost his value to the Rangers and eventually was traded to Montreal where his career abruptly ended when he suffered a broken neck in a collision with Vic Hadfield of the Rangers.

Howe never mellowed. If anything he became more dangerous as he got older and his pace slowed. In December 1965 he was accused of spearing Lou Angotti of the Rangers in an episode that nearly cost Angotti the sight in his left eye. "It's a shame such a great hockey player as Howe has to use his stick the way he does," said Emile Francis, general manager and coach of the Rangers. "Sometimes he carries it like a spear."

Such allegations never made a very deep impression on Howe. His answer to critics has been, "Hockey is a man's game." And that's that. Of course, the fact that he has been hockey's greatest drawing card for more years than any other player has helped deflect the criticism with his scoring stick. On October 16, 1946, he scored the first goal of his NHL career against Turk Broda of the Toronto Maple Leafs. On February 17, 1951, he scored his one hundredth goal. The goalie was Gerry McNeil of the Canadiens. On February 15, 1953, he scored number 200. The victim was Al Rollins of the Black Hawks. On February 7, 1956, Rollins was the goalie when Howe scored his three hundredth. On December 13, 1958, he beat Jacques Plante in the Montreal net for number 400. On March 14, 1962, Lorne (Gump) Worsley was the Ranger goalie when Howe scored his five hundredth goal.

The goal that most critics consider the most important of Howe's career was scored on November 10, 1963, when he beat Charlie Hodge in the Canadiens' net. Howe was playing game number 1,132 for the Red Wings and his goal number 545, breaking the all-time goal-scoring record held by Maurice (Rocket) Richard of Montreal. To say the least, the goal detonated a major controversy. The proud Richard had scored his 544 goals in only 978 games, 154 fewer than Howe required. Richard insisted that his record be kept on the books with an asterisk next to it just as baseball officials had done when Roger Maris hit 61 home runs, breaking Babe Ruth's record.

NHL President Clarence Campbell summarily rejected Richard's request but the furor lingered on. Richard, who never was known for his diffidence on or off the ice, raised some abrasive questions about Howe's competence in relation to his own: "Howe is a better all-round player than I was, but I never thought he was too good a money player . . . I don't remember Howe scoring many game-winning goals . . . It always looked as though he would even be a greater player if he hustled more."

Richard's arguments were punctured by seasoned observers.

Campbell immediately produced statistics showing that Howe even then held the league record for game-winning goals—96. Richard had 83. As for Howe's image of nonhustling, it was merely a deception, partly a ploy, partly a link to his laconic background. He was raised in Floral, a tiny suburb of Saskatoon, Saskatchewan and, despite decades in the metropolis of Detroit, has remained a small-town westerner, drawling and taking his time about life. When he originally signed a contract with the Red Wings he insisted then that Jack Adams throw in a new Detroit jacket as a bonus. Adams forgot about his promise and Howe quit the team until Adams questioned him, was reminded about the "bonus" and, since then, Howe has never held out for a better contract.

His laconic behavior on ice often lulls the opposition into thinking he's too tired to make a play or too disinterested. Howe, of course, measures his movements. A key to his longevity was his refusal to waste energy unnecessarily. When an opening developed, he'd move and often faster than anybody else on the ice. His skating style is what the pros call "strong." He has perfect balance and, as such, is difficult to upend. His strength is Promethean by hockey standards. He could carry the puck with one hand on the stick while warding off an opponent with the other. No other player in the NHL but Howe is an ambidextrous shooter. And, while today's forward now relies so heavily on the slapshot, Howe remains a traditionalist, using a straight blade instead of a curved banana blade. His quick wristshot has remained the most effective scoring weapon, per shot, in hockey.

The shot is only a segment of the Howe arsenal. His strength is manifest in various ways. For years he has outmuscled opponents and wrested the puck from them in the corners from which goal-scoring passes were delivered. Or, he would camp in front of the net, seemingly impervious to the pushing and shoving of rival defensemen. In the 1965–66 season Howe suffered through 13 games without a goal but managed to break the slump by outpushing his rivals. His longtime teammate, Alex Delvecchio remembered the episode. "It was against the Rangers in New York. A shot—in fact I fired the puck—bounched off the seat of his pants past Jacques Plante into the Ranger net. That was muscle. The fact the puck went in off the seat of his pants is incidental. He was in the right place at the right time and he was shoving three guys out of the way. Each year he'll pick up nine or 10 goals that way, just with strength, bulling his way through or past rival players."

There always has been the threat that Howe suddenly would lose his touch, his speed, his shot. When he was 33 years old and in the midst of a goal famine a hockey writer thought he detected the beginning of the end for Howe. The writer dispatched a note to a magazine editor suggesting a story titled: "Is Gordie Howe Washed Up?" The editor was intrigued with the idea and replied: "I like it, but let's wait a year and be sure." Seven years later they were still waiting, but, naturally, with each season Howe's strength ebbs just a little and his speed diminishes just a little more.

When he reached the age of 40 on March 31, 1968, Howe allowed that playing was becoming more difficult for him than it ever had been, that it often felt more like work than play. From time to time the Red Wings experimented with Howe, moving him back to defense. Usually, he performed creditably at the position but the experiment was quickly abandoned when the Red Wings needed goals. The man confronted with the problem of preserving Howe and keeping the Detroit club in play-off contention was Sid Abel, general manager of the Red Wings. According to Abel, Howe's future is directly related to his psyche. "Should Howe's goal production ever fall off to a point where he had only one goal by mid-season," Abel has said, "and wasn't getting any chances around the net, then I would consider shifting him back to defense. That's because he's a big guy and to take advantage of his experience. However, I don't think that day will come because I think that the fun would have gone out of hockey for Gordie and he would quit."

In some ways the fun began to disappear as far back as the 1966–67 season. The Red Wings finished fifth that year, far out of contention for the Stanley Cup play-offs. A season later, in the first year of expansion to the West Coast, the Red Wings again were out of it, only this time they were dead last in the six-team East Division of the NHL. Some of those close to Howe contend that the dismal record of the Red Wings depressed him more than his own accomplishments buoyed him. They also pointed out that the gregarious Howe missed many of his old Red Wing cronies.

Abel believed he found the tonic for reviving Howe late in the 1967–68 season when he acquired Frank (Big M) Mahovlich from the Toronto Maple Leafs. During the last month of the season Howe and Mahovlich meshed their gears so well it appeared that Detroit might just have found the key to its renaissance and, more important, the source of Howe's revival. In 1968–69 the line of Howe,

Mahovlich and Delvecchio enjoyed a bountiful season, but the Red Wings finished out of the playoffs—in fifth place—once more.

That Howe was healthy enough and competent enough to remain in the NHL into the 1970s is irrelevant to any analysis of the man. What matters, of course, is the fact that he has been the most complete hockey player the game has known. If he trespassed over the line of rulebook decorum it was only because hockey often is ruled by a jungle law and Gordie Howe, more than anyone, had a strong survival instinct. He managed to retain all of the classical skills that make hockey a complicated art while adjusting to the slambang style of the late sixties that has often rendered it a kaleidoscope of speed and smash. His durability speaks for itself and his accomplishments eloquently underline the assertion that he is, was and always will be recognized as hockey's greatest star.

The most significant problem Gordie Howe has raised for the future of professional hockey in years to come is that there will never be another one like him.

Bobby Hull

IN THE LATE WINTER of 1966 interest in Robert Marvin Hull's drive to a season's record for goals scored in the National Hockey League demonstrated how a single exceptional performer can fascinate the public and rouse the imagination of thousands who have no personal enthusiasm for his field.

Hull scored number 51 in the cavernous Chicago Stadium on March 12, 1966, a slapshot from 30 feet that beat Cesare Maniago, the lanky goalkeeper for New York Rangers. The red light signifying goal inspired more than 20,000 zealots in the Stadium to outrageous joy. They littered the ice with debris that ranged from hats—both men's and women's—to toilet-paper confetti. Hull skated slowly through the din to the Chicago bench and, whimsically, picked up one of the more ludicrous hats. He dragged it on over the skin patch that has sprung up where his blond hair used to be.

He was Hull and he was laughing because no one in all the years had scored more goals in a single big-league season. Rocket Richard, who thrived on violence, pegged the mark at 50 in the wartime season of 1944–45. Bernard Geoffrion tied it in 1960–61. Hull matched it in 1961–62.

Everybody seemed delighted when the Hereford hero of the Hawks crashed through the 50-goal barrier. Not since William Tell blasted an apple off his son's brow had any shooting operation attracted such attention from so many people who do not watch hockey normally, or care about it.

Extraordinary performances in any occupation generally have this effect. When Babe Ruth was slamming baseballs into oblivion in 1927, he drew tens of thousands of customers who were not baseball fans, as such, but went to see a man whose like, they believed, would not pass this way again. It was much the same eight years ago, when Roger Maris exhibited Ruth's likeness in a power charge to 61 home runs. As Maris slugged toward Ruth's 60, crowds swelled wherever the New York Yankees played.

And so with Hull in the winter of 1965–66. After the great ghost hunt ended, the most striking aspect of it all was how hockey fans got emotionally involved. Perhaps the individual who preserved a sense of proportion best was Hull himself. On the ice he was abused and hounded by opponents dedicated to stopping him by all means short of homicide. Off the ice he was badgered ceaselessly by fans, the press, radio, TV, press agents, promoters. Only on rare occasions did Hull let his temper slip, and then it was due to some especially outrageous question or repeated references to "pressure," with the implication he was choking up.

"But of course you were under pressure," one of the authors said to him after number 51 was in the records.

"Of course," Hull said simply. "You can't want something very bad, and be held up getting it, without feeling a weight on you."

After almost every game the Black Hawks play, Hull, constantly the last man to leave the dressing room, is mobbed by autographiends in every rink in the league. He is unceasingly obliging.

One Saturday night after a game in Toronto, surrounded by perhaps 200 fans, Hull bent to sign a program shyly offered by a young girl of 10. "What's your first name?" he asked.

"Catherine," she said.

Hull flashed his high-beam smile. "How do you spell it? With a C or a K?"

She said with a C and he signed, in flowing script, "Best wishes, Catherine—Bobby Hull."

How do you spell it? With a C or K? Of such thoughtful gestures are public relations made.

One of the games played by Hull's acquaintances revolves around that old corny line from a television program: Will the real Bobby Hull please stand up?

Is he the boisterous beer drinker who, with some Chicago playmates, got involved with a bush-league hoodlum in a bar near Comiskey Park, where the White Sox play?

"We were sitting around having a few," Hull remembers, "and this guy comes up and gets pretty obnoxious."

At last Hull advised the intruder to get lost. When he replied impolitely, Hull reached across the table, grabbed the man's tie and twisted it into a choking noose. "Then I corked him one. He pitched forward and I slammed his head down on the table. The last I see of him, he's crawling out the door on his hands and knees."

Hull later discovered that the character was a small-time gunsel who carried a weapon. "I've never," with a mock shudder, "been back to that bar since."

Or is he the lusty family man who escaped a hasty marriage at 18 to ultimately link with Joanne, a former figure skater who has been his wife and the mother of his four bouncy children? Theirs is a lively domestic routine. He comes home after a long practice, after weary sessions with his business agent, and he is growling. Joanne fights back.

Hull marches out of the house, fuming. She locks the door. He puts one burly shoulder to it and heaves it off the hinges. "Oh, it gets a little loud sometimes," Hull says, the big grin on him.

"You tell 'em, Star," Joanne says, smiling.

Or is he what physiologists have called him, perfect mesomorph? He has the physical credentials for it, two inches under six feet, 195 pounds, biceps like the fender of a truck.

To thousands, he is the greatest hockey player of the time, maybe the most imposing superstar of all the years, certainly the game's biggest box office. One of the pure pleasures of a hockey fan's life is watching Hull play. He is one of hockey's excitements and has been since he came to Chicago, in 1957.

Hull is frequently on the ice more than the referee, there for regular shifts on left wing, on the point for power plays, out to kill penalties when the Hawks are shy a man.

He is a powerful skater—an ice-bound Fred Astaire he has been called—idling fluently, then surging into overdrive as a chorus of sound comes out of the crowd, a predictable, irrepressible reaction to Hull on a big night, rising with him in a long, drawn-out OOOHH.

He possesses the slapshot as no one has, the home-run drive delivered at 118.3 miles per hour, rising from the curve of the exaggerated banana blade on his stick. His wristshot, fired with a mere flick of his thick wrists, has been timed at a trifling 100.7 miles an hour.

Or is he the Hull of Bobby Hull Enterprises, a muscular product merchandised by slick public relations counselors? He endorses products for Ford, hockey equipment for Levy Industries, barbed wire for Monova, sportswear for Jantzen. There is a Bobby Hull book, a Bobby Hull syndicated sports column, a Bobby Hull table hockey game.

"If he's not a millionaire now," says Lester Stanford, his business manager, "we'll soon make him one."

To his mother—a calm, ample woman—Hull is her fifth child of 11, born in Point Anne, Ontario, a small town attached to a cement plant about 130 miles east of Toronto on the north shore of Lake Ontario. "The population of Point Anne," his sister Judy says, "is about 1,000 if you count the dogs. It's about 100 if you don't."

Hull's father, a foreman in the cement plant, was a robust amateur player who listened when the Hawks sought his 11-year-old son, Robert Marvin. When the boy was 11 the Hawks shipped him to Hespeler, Ontario, 170 miles from home, to board with strangers, attend a strange school, and play for one of Chicago's Junior B farm clubs. The Hawks rewarded him with $5 a week.

"I wrote him every day," his mother has said. "But I didn't tell Robert much about what was happening at Point Anne because I was afraid of making him homesick."

He was homesick, as he indicated in one return letter. "Gee, Mom, keep all those notes coming with nothing in them."

He is the Hull who went from that primitive start to Junior A hockey in St. Catharines, Ontario, and, then at 18, to the Hawks. He never played a minute in the minors.

Or is he, as those closest to him assert, the Hull who is more at home with Hereford cattle on a remote farm than with a hockey stick in the large, bright arenas of the continent?

The real Hull is perhaps that one, the owner of one of Canada's major herds of polled Herefords, a heavy investor in land near Picton, a small town not far from Point Anne. His summer work includes playing pat-a-cake with 100-pound bales of hay, flung into barns for winter feed. Hull reads cattle catalogues the way gambling addicts consume the racing form, or evangelists vacuum up the Bible. The word is avid. Every autumn, with his partner Ralph Richards, he conducts a sale of breeding stock in the ramshackle Picton Fairgrounds.

The real Hull is the one wearing a cowboy hat and manure on his cattleman's boots and gently advising gawking youngsters, "Don't

try and milk the bull." He is all farmer after the auctioneer has
gaveled down the last cow, and the buyers have gone away, and
he and Ralph Richards are musing on proceeds from the sale. Then,
in response to bawling stock that is demanding room service out in
the yard, Hull tells Richards, "Okay, let's get those freeloaders
watered and fed."

Frank Mahovlich

EVERY SPORT has it lead tragedian and the NHL is no exception.

Frank Mahovlich, who symbolizes the tragic figure in big-time professional hockey, appeared never to reach far enough. Whatever he grasped during his long stewardship with the Toronto Maple Leafs from 1957 through 1968 when he was traded to Detroit never satisfied his critics.

More than any NHL notable, Mahovlich was the antihero. It has been his misfortune that hockey's multitude of fans cast him in a different role but neither his personality nor his playing could avert the inevitable collision. As a result Mahovlich never fulfilled the demands made of him and twice in his career suffered what most observers would describe as nervous breakdowns directly attributable to his hockey dilemmas.

To begin with Mahovlich entered the NHL on a tidal wave of press clippings touting him as an extraordinary left wing. At six foot, one inch, 200 pounds he had the superstructure of an impregnable forward. Add to that a shot that burst like a cannon and long strides that immediately could thrust him past a defenseman and there was the theoretically perfect scorer. The youngster from Northern Ontario confirmed his early enthusiastic notices by winning the Calder Memorial Trophy as rookie of the year in 1958. For the next two seasons his achievements leveled off but give him time, they said, give him time.

At last, in November 1960, Frank Mahovlich, who had been

dubbed the Big M, suddenly ignited and in a matter of weeks became the most explosive force in hockey. The emerging phenomena was apparent to all who saw it. On November 5, 1960, the Leafs were playing the Rangers on Toronto ice. On a play midway in the game Mahovlich rushed toward the New York goal like a comet, sped around white-jerseyed opponents as if they were tenpins and briskly shot the puck past goalie Jack McCartan. Mahovlich had scored four goals and helped win the game for Toronto.

At that time the devastating Maurice (Rocket) Richard of the Montreal Canadiens held the NHL goal-scoring record of 50 goals in a season. Now, Frank (Big M) Mahovlich was making serious overtures to break that record. By late December 1960 Mahovlich had scored 29 goals in 32 games and oddsmakers were quoting even money that the 23-year-old would create a new record. As the season neared its end Mahovlich lifted his total to 48 but he could not score the necessary two to reach 50. More significant was the fact that in the final weeks of the season Mahovlich appeared to falter. He scored only one goal in five play-off games and now the pattern was slowly developing—Mahovlich inspired florid fanfares but produced with less than the expected eloquence.

Further confounding analysts was the mystifying personality of Mahovlich. Hypersensitive to both critics and coaches, Big M was given to brooding first over coach Billy Reay and then general manager coach Punch Imlach. "He got into a feud with Reay," a Toronto writer explained. "Frank had been injured but Reay insisted on dressing him. Mahovlich resented it, lost respect for Reay and wouldn't play for him."

The Mahovlich–Reay feud was resolved when Reay was fired and replaced by Imlach, himself a truculent, insensitive man who, at first, proved to be a catalyst for Mahovlich. Imlach appeared to understand the young man. "If you kick him," Imlach once observed, "you get nothing. He thinks you're being unfair to him. The only thing to do is take advantage of his ability when he's playing his best."

Imlach's crusty nature began corroding relations between coach and player in a manner that was to be repeated on other occasions with other players. It is credible that Mahovlich would have failed earlier in his career if in February 1959 the Leafs hadn't acquired Leonard (Red) Kelly from the Detroit Red Wings. A defenseman all his NHL career, Kelly promptly was converted to center by Imlach in an act of strategic genius that also inadvertently evolved as a gem of a psychological boost for Mahovlich. "I feel comfortable on a line with Red," he explained. "He added experience and a calming influence to our line. He even had a psychological effect on me because I suddenly felt more confident." Under Kelly's guidance, Mahovlich developed a booming slapshot. Catapulted by Kelly's passes, he was able to outflank the enemy defenses and execute his dazzling stick fakes against goalies.

Big M's increased production begot attention; and attention begot careful probing. In time opponents began detecting weaknesses in Mahovlich's armor that proved to be fateful in seasons to come. They discovered that if he was hit hard early in a game he tended to quit for the rest of the evening. They also learned that he was prone to brooding. Once, after an incongruous fight with tiny Henri Richard of the Montreal Canadiens, Mahovlich mentioned that he was in a *cul de sac*.

"What's the point of my fighting with a little guy like that," he said. "I have five inches on him. If I beat him I'm a bully and if I lose I'm a bum. I'll fight anytime but to me it's a waste of time and energy. Swinging the arms takes a lot out of a guy. By the time a guy's through fighting he doesn't have any power left to score."

The statements were significant in the light of developments. To the fan it appeared that Mahovlich *always* seemed more concerned with conserving his energy than expending it. In the seasons after his 48-goal year fans at Maple Leaf Gardens began demanding a 50-goal year from Mahovlich. They began what eventually became a routine of booing him no matter how well he played on Toronto ice. Big M, in turn, became cynical. "I ignore the cheers and the boos," he once declared. "When I go good, they come over to me in the dressing room and say 'You played a great game, Frank,' and when I'm bad, they don't talk to me."

Yet, hockey's professional businessmen still appreciated him. In the early sixties the Chicago Black Hawk management offered what, until then, was the most fantastic sum—$1,000,000—for a hockey player. Jim Norris, then president of the Black Hawks, scribbled on the check: "Payment in full for player Frank Mahovlich." To this day, doubt has been cast on the integrity of the offer. Some critics have charged that it was nothing but a publicity stunt. Others pointed out that Norris was slightly inebriated at the time; when he sobered up the deal was canceled. Majority opinion, however, is that Norris made the offer in good faith on the grounds that he could afford to part with the money and the potential of a team featuring

Mahovlich on left wing on one line and Bobby Hull on left wing on another.

The offer underlined Big M's worth and, not surprisingly, resulted in a new nickname for him, "The Million Dollar Hockey Player." It was axiomatic that the publicity did Mahovlich infinitely more harm than good and was the prelude to his ultimate downfall with the Leafs. Fans reasoned that if the player was worth a million he should produce commensurately on ice. No doubt Big M's boss, Imlach, had the same idea. Certainly Mahovlich didn't. He became more and more divorced from Imlach. Where once the two could communicate, now there was a barrier between them and, as the seasons passed, the barrier became more and more impenetrable. This was tragic for both Imlach and Mahovlich because at one point they understood and appreciated each other. In 1960, for example, Imlach recalled the time Mahovlich visited his office and suggested a line change. "It made sense," the general manager-coach said, "so I decided to take his advice.

"After that he developed a new self-confidence. He no longer was a kid. Until then he kept everything inside himself; never said too much. But after that talk he became vitally interested in the team. Instead of sitting back and brooding to himself he began to take over. He'd give a guy hell if the guy did something stupid on the ice. This maturity made him twice the player he was last season."

Imlach's carping—which penetrated the psyches of less sensitive Maple Leafs—disturbed Mahovlich. He found it less and less easy to chat with the boss. His marriage seemed to stabilize him and he appeared to be leveling off to a plateau just under that of the league scoring leaders when his life became shrouded in secrecy during the early part of the 1964–65 season.

On November 12, 1964, Mahovlich was admitted to a Toronto hospital under strict security. Hospital bulletins remained suitably vague for several weeks although rumors indicated that he was suffering from a nervous ailment. Big M remained hospitalized until early December amid speculation that he might never play again. The reason, observers guessed, was that hockey was too traumatic an experience for him. His wife, Marie, hinted about the torment during her husband's convalescence in December 1964. "He's such a shy and reticent guy. It bothers him even if he has to speak in public. It might be all right for a movie star or actor, they can handle it, but not Frank."

Mahovlich returned to the lineup later in December and finished the season with the Leafs. He appeared to have shaken the *Welt-schmerz* and scored 32 goals in the 1965–66 season, which was a most creditable effort. From that point on his play deteriorated. It is meaningful that the deterioration closely paralleled the growing sense of dissension on the Maple Leaf team. If Mahovlich was having trouble with Imlach so were other players. Defenseman Carl Brewer, a former all-star, quit the team. Others, such as Bob Pulford, Bob Baun and Kent Douglas feuded with Imlach. Baun and Douglas were traded prior to the 1967–68 season but Mahovlich remained. Then, it happened again! Early in the 1967–68 season Mahovlich fell prey to the nervous disorder. He walked off the Leaf train following an especially successful game at Maple Leaf Gardens in which he starred but was booed at the finish.

This time there was little left to the imagination of probers. Mahovlich was distraught. He would return, of course, but the possibilities of a rapprochement with Imlach were negligible. Late in the 1967–68 season, when Mahovlich had amassed only 19 goals, Imlach tacitly conceded he had failed in the noble Mahovlich project. After weeks of intensive negotiations the Leafs finally traded Mahovlich to the Detroit Red Wings along with Pete Stemkowski and Garry Unger and, in return, obtained center Norm Ullman and forwards Floyd Smith and Paul Henderson.

The Red Wings, without actually saying it, believed it was Imlach who caused the imperfection in Big M's motor. They reasoned that in the relaxed atmosphere of the Detroit dressing room he would respond with better hockey. They also hoped that by teaming Frank with his younger brother, the gregarious Pete, Big M would finally emerge from his psychological cocoon.

Almost immediately a change was evident. Playing on a line with Gordie Howe and Alex Delvecchio, he scored seven goals in the final weeks of the season to finish with a total of 26. He also scored the goals 300 and 301 of his NHL career on March 24, 1968, a feat matched only by Gordie Howe, Maurice Richard, Jean Beliveau, Bobby Hull, Bernie Geoffrion, Ted Lindsay, Alex Delvecchio, Andy Bathgate, Norm Ullman and Nels Stewart. There were some who believed that this was, in effect, a hockey rebirth of Frank Mahovlich and one that should have happened more than a decade earlier because when Big M was a youth in Schumacher, Ontario, he had intended to pursue a career with the same Red Wings he had finally joined at the age of 30.

"My school team had Red Wing jerseys," Mahovlich once

reminisced, "so, naturally, I rooted for them." At the time Big M played for the Schumacher Lions, a town club unaffiliated with any NHL team. The Wings figured they could acquire him by sponsoring the whole team, which they did. But before sponsorship became official the Leafs wooed him to Toronto. The Detroit organization never forgave the Leafs for the loss and this must have been a factor in their quest for him in 1968.

"We wanted to send Frank to high school in Hamilton and have him play for our junior team there," admitted Jimmy Skinner, former Red Wing coach who had been on Big M's trail at the time. "Then the Leafs became interested. They learned that Frank's father was an ardent Roman Catholic and they had a priest from St. Michael's College interview him and offer to send the boy to St. Mike's if he'd sign with the Leafs." He played for St. Michael's teams in the Ontario Hockey Association Junior B and then Junior A divisions. He was voted to the All-Star Team in 1956–57 and won the Red Tilson Trophy as the league's most valuable player. He became a Leaf regular in the 1957–58 season, which is precisely when his troubles began.

A typical appraisal was made by Harry Howell, the veteran defenseman: "He's the toughest man in the league to stop. Players like Henri Richard get by on speed but don't have Mahovlich's strength. Bobby Hull has power but doesn't have Big M's great reach or shift. Jean Beliveau can stickhandle but he doesn't have Mahovlich's speed."

And so it went. Everybody believed in Mahovlich, it seemed, except Frank himself. Even on nights when he dominated the play he seemed uncertain of himself. Once, during a game at Madison Square Garden in New York, he assisted on the first Leaf goal and scored the third and winning goal in a 3–2 victory over the Rangers. After the game—and this, his greatest season when he scored 48 goals—a reporter asked him if he had found himself as a hockey player.

"Not really," he said thoughtfully. "I don't really think I know myself completely or that I'll know when I'll fulfill my potential. Maybe it'll take three or four years, maybe never."

He was asked if he enjoyed hockey.

"You mean do I do it just for the fun of it like they say Gordie Howe does? I like it. Y'know, Howe didn't find himself right away. Maybe I'll grow up the way Howe did."

Ironically, he never matched Howe's efforts; at least not as a

Maple Leaf. But, as a Red Wing, playing with Howe, there is a possibility that he could extend his reach. "Sometimes," he once put it wistfully, "I think it's possible for me to go all the way."

He did make great strides in the next two seasons. In 1968–69, playing on a line with Gordie Howe and Alex Delvecchio, Mahovlich scored 44 goals and 29 assists. A season later his record was an equally commendable 38 goals and 32 assists, proving beyond any doubt that Big M's departure from Toronto was one of the best things that ever happened to him—or the NHL. But his Detroit stewardship ended in the 1970–71 season when he was traded to the Montreal Canadiens. Teamed with brother Peter, Big M played some of his best hockey ever and was a star for the Canadiens in their Cup triumphs, emerging as the record-breaking, leading scorer of the 1971 playoffs and a potent force in the 1973 victory.

For Frank Mahovlich, hockey was once again fun.

Stan Mikita

A REPORTER, attempting humor, put it to Stan Mikita not long ago in a paraphrase of a popular ad: "When you're number 2, Stanley, I guess you try harder."

Mikita has a quick sense of the ridiculous, but saw no fun in the crack. "No man ever considers himself number 2 in anything," he said, not smiling. And added, in a tone of voice that shut the lid on the subject: "Especially not me."

Mikita, the slick, dark center of Chicago Black Hawks, is considered number 1 in many expert appraisals, with ample reason. "He is the best player in the NHL," Punch Imlach has contended for years. "I wish I had him."

His credentials are imposing: top points producer in four of the five seasons between 1963–64 and 1967–68; all-star center six times in the seven seasons between 1961–62 and 1967–68; the only player to win the Hart Trophy, the Lady Byng Trophy and the Art Ross Trophy in the same year, and he did it twice in a row: in 1966–67 and 1967–68.

The Hart is awarded to the player picked the most valuable to his team, in memory of Cecil Hart, former Canadiens coach. The Lady Byng is granted to the player who best combines hockey talent with exemplary behavior, first presented in 1925 by the wife of a former Governor-General of Canada. The Art Ross, given by the late, irascible manager of Boston Bruins in 1947, is automatically won by the player who leads the league in scoring points.

But in spite of Mikita's professional dominance, he was second behind Robert Marvin Hull on the scorecards of hero worshippers. His celebrated teammate made more money, got higher headlines, received louder adulation.

Mikita professed an awareness of being forced to play Lou Gehrig to Hull's Babe Ruth, a throwback in comparisons to the ogres of the New York Yankee wrecking crew, 40 years ago.

He was careful to clear the record on one perennial story out of Chicago, however. "It's not true, that stuff about Bob and me feuding. I'm not jealous, like they say, about him getting most of the publicity."

Mikita's publicity has been much more favorable in recent seasons, in direct ratio to his improved manners on the ice. Before the 1966–67 season, he led NHL centers in penalties for six consecutive years. He behaved like an original dead end kid who required calendars to add up the time he spent in the penalty box—154 minutes, or more than two and a half games in 1964–65.

The descriptive most often used, in his unruly period, was chippy. Allan (Sam) Stanley, when he played defense for Toronto, said of Mikita: "Give Stan a little jab and he'll react immediately. Most players wait for a chance to retaliate, but Mikita'll hit you back in the same motion. He's ornery."

Stanley, who weighs 195 pounds, confessed to some admiration for Mikita, who is a wiry 163: "Mikita may look small, but there are no small men in the NHL. There are no small men, I mean, who aren't men."

In 1966–67 Mikita abandoned truculence to become a model of propriety. He reduced his sinning to 12 minutes that season, to 14 in 1967–68 but went up to 52, for him a modest figure, in 1968–69. The Gallic tag hung on him by Montreal fans, *Le Petit Diable*, became passé; he was still small, but no longer a devil.

It nettled him when the hockey press kept asking if he was surprised at his transformation into a relative Good Guy. "Give a guy credit when he does something," just a hint, just the edge of the knife showing. "No, I'm not surprised I won the Byng two years straight. I behaved. But the Hart, the one for the most valuable, that's the trophy I wanted."

Mikita won $11,500 in bonuses in each year he swept hockey's three major individual prizes. Once, after World War II, he thought $11,500 was all the money in the world.

He was eight, in 1948, when his parents let him go from Sokolce, Czechoslovakia, to be adopted by an uncle and aunt in St. Catharines,

Ontario. He did not realize then, in the emotional wrench of a child leaving home, that his parents were doing him a material favor.

Born to an impoverished family, he was christened Stanislas Gvoth. His father worked in a textile factory, his mother in the fields. The Communists gained control of Czechoslovakia in 1948 and the Gvoths decided it was best for their son's future to send him away, out of the country if possible.

It was possible; a childless uncle and aunt from Canada, Joe and Anna Mikita, visited the Gvoths in Sokolce. They were delighted to adopt their nephew.

"I really wanted to leave, at first," he remembers. "But when I got to the station in Prague, and saw the train ready to pull out without my father and mother, I wrapped my arms around a telephone pole and cried." His recollections of the journey are poignant. "Every inch of the train ride I plotted to jump off and go home." The plots were foiled by his vigilant uncle, and he arrived in St. Catharines near Christmas, 1948. One day, below his new family's apartment, Mikita saw small boys playing hockey in the street. He joined them, hesitant, defiant, scared. He had skated on double runners in Czechoslovakia but hockey, as these kids were playing it, was a strange, fast game.

He understood no English, but one of the kids gave him a stick and tried to explain the game. He accepted the stick and, when one of the boys tried to get past him, he rendered an example of his subsequent professional behavior. He hit the boy with the club.

"My first words of English were hockey words," Mikita says. "Puck, stick and goal."

The hardness comes on him, remembering. "I learned other words in school in St. Catharines like DP. Dirty foreigner." Then, the old dregs of a vivid bitterness, "DP and foreigner, they sounded like swear words to me, and I guess they *were*."

He stubs out a cigarette, a trifle irritated. "Sure, I fought in the streets. Who wouldn't? I've been fighting all my life."

He fought up through minor hockey in St. Catharines, up to the Teepees, Chicago's principal junior farm. From there, in 1959–60, he joined the Hawks.

For several seasons he was the pivot between Ken Wharram and Doug Mohns, who were called the Scooter Line by Coach Billy Reay because "they were so mercurial." The Scooters became permanently disrupted at the start of the 1969–70 season when Wharram suffered a heart attack which caused his premature retirement from hockey.

With Wharram gone, Mikita nevertheless continued to excel. He scored 39 goals and 47 assists to finish third in scoring during the 1969–70 season behind Bobby Orr and Phil Esposito. In 1970–71, troubled by a bad back, he registered 24 goals and 48 assists for 72 points, and continued to star with 65 and 83 points in the next two years.

He often thinks, in his maturity, about the security of his young daughter, Meg, and son, Scott. One summer he was asked if he could do what his parents thought they had to do—let him go when he was eight?

He stared, and felt for the right expression. "I go into little Meg's room at night," Stan Mikita said, "and I look down at her. A little kid, innocent. Could I give her up?" Vehemence underlined his murmur. "Let her go, I ask myself. No way. No . . . way."

Bobby Orr

ONE DAY Phil Esposito was excused from a workout of the Boston Bruins at the old Boston Garden. He was excused because he complained of a slight leg injury.

Esposito, who has the soulful eyes of a Cuban bandit, hung around the rink to witness his playmates submit to a heavy drill prescribed by Coach Harry Sinden. He formerly played center for Chicago Black Hawks, on a line with Bobby Hull. During a lull in the drill, Bobby Orr called to the malingering Esposito: "Hey, Hull practiced every day, didn't he? Didn't he make you practice with him?"

"You're right," Esposito agreed casually. "But there are no Hulls on this team."

The remark was not quite accurate, as Pete Axthelm noted in *Sports Illustrated*. Orr, who was 23 in March 1971, approached the super-star status of Hull or Stan Mikita or Gordie Howe before he had been two years in the NHL.

The comely defenseman was rookie of the year when he was 19, and one mercenary offered a gaudy forecast of Orr's potential at the annual NHL awards luncheon in 1967. Harry Howell, who presided over the New York Rangers' defense, received the James Norris Trophy that day as the league's best defenseman. Howell exhibited a graceful touch when he stood up to accept his prize. "I'm glad I won the James Norris Trophy this year, because"—he nodded toward Boston's prodigy—"because in 10 years it will be the Bobby Orr trophy."

The next year, in his sophomore season, Orr won the Norris knick-knack and won it again in 1969. By then he was realizing the profes-

262

sional potential that Canadian writers anticipated in their breathless appraisals before he was 16. *Maclean's* magazine, a Canadian periodical, spilled all over itself with a cover story on Orr, the 166-pound juvenile. The gushing text ran: "He is a swift powerful skater with instant acceleration, instinctive anticipation, a quick accurate shot, remarkable composure, and unrelenting ambition, a solemn dedication, humility, modesty, and a fondness for his parents, and his brothers and sisters that often turns his eyes moist." That subdued description made the crew-cut youth seem a glorious combination of Paul Bunyan, Gordie Howe and St. Francis of Assisi. Others subsequently sought to improve on the modest list of Orr's attributes.

Leighton (Hap) Emms, who generally managed the Bruins in Orr's freshman season, claimed he would not trade Orr even-up for the entire Toronto team. Milt Schmidt, who replaced Emms, insisted he would not take $2,000,000 for Orr. "Bobby's worth at least that to Boston," Schmidt insisted, "because he's the kind of player the Bruins can build around for 20 years."

The last year Orr played junior, for Oshawa Generals in the Ontario Hockey Association, ads in the Oshawa newspaper quietly advised: "See Boston's $1,000,000 Prospect Bobby Orr!" The ads obviously were not written by Milt Schmidt.

During the play-offs in the spring of 1967, the ads threatened the fans: "Probably Your Last Chance to See BOBBY ORR Play Junior Hockey." It *was* the last time, after contractual arrangements made by Orr's crafty lawyer, R. Alan Eagleson, the executive director of the militant NHL Players' Association. The negotiations between Emms and Eagleson were rancorous, but agreement was reached after Emms capitulated more than Eagleson did. Orr signed a two-year pact, with a bonus, for a reported $50,000; Eagleson privately confided to the authors that the figure was closer to $70,000.

Orr certified his potential to such an extent in his first two seasons that Eagleson, with his eye on the main chance, blandly announced he would seek to make his client the first $100,000-a-year hockey player. The Bruins, perhaps reluctantly, did pelt Orr/Eagleson with banknotes until Eagleson, rising from the couch, pronounced himself satisfied.

The respective parties, not particularly anxious to give the internal revenue agents any answers they don't know, were vague on the details of Orr's contract. Part of the deal obliged Orr to work 12 months a year for the Bruins, engaged in public relations when he isn't playing hockey. There was a deferred income clause, which guarantees Orr a remuneration after he is finished as player. His income for playing hockey was about $47,000 a year, exceeded by only a few, all of whom had been around longer. Howe received more than $70,000 a year from Detroit, and Hull probably got $85,000 from Chicago. Glenn Hall, the highest paid goalie, apparently was in the $48,000 class in St. Louis. By 1971 Orr's salary was more than $100,000 a year.

Orr was born 160 miles north of Toronto, in Parry Sound, where male members begin skating before they are weaned. Bobby learned to control the puck on the frozen sound, for the incontestable reason that you don't get to play much in the winter scrambles unless you grab the puck and keep it.

Before he was six, Orr was playing organized hockey as a Minor Squirt. He was a Squirt at six, then moved through the age brackets of Peewees and Bantams. NHL scouts, constantly sleuthing the snowbanks for immature prospects, stumbled on him when he was 12.

Orr was playing for Parry Sound in a Peewee play-off game against Gananoque, 300 miles away, near the Quebec border. A Montreal scout was there with Wren Blair, then a Boston bird dog and now the chatty general manager of the Minnesota North Stars. "I was there to watch a couple of Gananoque boys called Eaton and Higgins," Blair recalls. "Soon's I saw this Parry Sound kid in droopy pants in charge of the game, I forgot Eaton and Higgins." The Bruins, full of largesse, ordered Blair to Parry Sound as soon as his first enthusiastic report on Orr was read. He was instructed to donate $1,000 to the town's hockey program.

The Bruins, pressed by covetous representatives of Toronto, Montreal and Chicago, offered Orr a contract, under pro hockey's quaint child labor laws. He was 14 when Blair suggested a Junior A tryout. The NHL, at last heeding public criticism in Canada, has since allowed its prospects to ripen a little longer. In the expansion program the draft age has been raised to 20.

His parents, Doug and Arva Orr, agreed to let him go, reluctantly, after the Bruins contrived a deal that included $2,800 for Mr. Orr. The father, not much older than Gordie Howe, is modestly rewarded as a crate loader for Canadian Industries, Ltd., an explosives company. "Bobby was only 14," Doug Orr says, "but I felt he had a right to make up his own mind about Boston."

On Labor Day seven years ago, while his parents watched, Bobby signed a Boston Junior A card on the kitchen table of the family's old stucco home. Wren Blair, also watching, took him away to play for the Oshawa Generals, 25 miles east of Toronto.

He was almost an immediate star playing against boys four and five years older, and more mature. His talent seemed instinctive: constantly in clear spots, drawing the puck as a magnet to him. Some of what he has is physical: smooth, bursting-style skating, a baleful shot from the point.

"He runs the game," Milt Schmidt contends, "like Doug Harvey used to for Montreal. He presides over an attack." "They say only one other person in Parry Sound could skate faster," Doug Orr says. "Me." The father also attracted the hockey scouts, in 1942, when he was 17. But there was a war on, and he joined Canadian Navy, and when he was discharged four years later, a family of five began to arrive. The chance he had at 17 was gone by the time he was 21.

Both Orrs, Doug and Bobby, inherited their athletic ability from Doug's father, Robert Orr, for whom Bobby was named. The grandfather was a professional soccer player in Ireland before he emigrated to Parry Sound. "I think granddad only saw me play once," Bobby says. "That was the time I scored my first Junior goal. It made him sort of happy."

Boston's budding demigod has a self-effacing stance, as though unaware of his hockey stature. He is good, and probably knows it, but he makes a habit of not showing it.

One summer, when Howe was making a personal appearance in Parry Sound, he stood outside a store signing autographs. The crowd of youngsters parted at one juncture and Orr approached Howe, shyly. "Hi, Gord." He handed Howe a slip of paper, "Could I have your autograph, please?"

The exchange might have been the other way around, based on Orr's performance in 1970. He was winner of the Hart Trophy, Norris Trophy and the Conn Smythe Trophy. His astonishing 33 goals and 87 assists for 120 points marked the first time a defenseman ever led the NHL in scoring and his 87 assists set a new NHL record, and he continued setting records in the 1970–71 campaign.

Orr not only was rewriting the record book, he was establishing a totally new style for the seventies. His mode was a perfect combination of defense and offense; a blend that suggested the position of "rover," which was a part of hockey when it was a seven-man game at the turn of the century.

There no longer is any question about Orr's greatness. All that remains is to discern whether he is the greatest player of all time.

Terry Sawchuk

TERRANCE GORDON (TERRY) SAWCHUK suffered through one of the most tragic lives possible for a man who was regarded as the master of his trade—major-league goaltending.

He had 103 shutouts after 20 seasons in the NHL, at Detroit, Boston, Detroit again, Toronto, Los Angeles, Detroit for a third time and, finally, in the 1969–70 season at New York. No other big-league goalkeeper has blanked the opposition more times, and the only man who is close, like Sawchuk, is dead. George Hainsworth retired in 1937 with 94 shutouts.

Despite his success on the ice Sawchuk seemed to suffer more mental anguish than most athletes. His final demise, in the spring of 1970, symbolized Sawchuk's misfortune. He had a dispute with Rangers' teammate Ron Stewart. While the two were engaged in "horseplay" on the lawn in front of the apartment they shared Sawchuk allegedly fell over a barbecue grill. He was rushed to the hospital with internal injuries. Three operations failed to relieve him and he died on Memorial Day weekend, 1970, at the age of 40, his demise still regarded as a mystery to many hockey observers.

Terry learned his hockey as a youth in the East Kildonan sector of Winnipeg, Manitoba. He was a chubby kid who wore his nickname Butch as a badge of juvenile toughness.

He inherited goalkeeping pads when he was 10, after an older brother died of a heart attack. When he was 12, a baseball accident left his right arm two inches shorter than the left and the elbow joint so stiff that he cannot touch his right shoulder with his right hand.

There was a fanatic persistence about Sawchuk's drive toward an NHL career. He refused to attend movies as a child, lest the glare hurt his eyes. He avoided reading schoolbooks for the same reason.

Professional success came early. Sawchuk was rookie of the year in the old United States League at 18, rookie of the year in the American League at 19, rookie of the year in the NHL at 21. That tri-cornered feat makes him the only goalie in history to score a hat trick.

In 1952, when Detroit swept the Stanley Cup in eight consecutive games, Sawchuk achieved four shutouts and yielded five goals, a trifling 0.62 goals per game.

Throughout his career he was dogged by misfortune. In 1948 his right eyeball required three stitches to shut a slash from a stick. His appendix kicked up a holler and burst. In 1953 he suffered chest injuries in a car crash. In 1954 there were rumors he might retire because of eye trouble. In 1955 he received the worst wound of all— he was traded to Boston, where the hockey fans and sporting press are uncommonly frantic.

Then in 1957, in the middle of the season, Sawchuk abruptly quit the Bruins. His cobra-quick reflexes had begun to fray. He discovered that high-power hockey can be a high-power nuisance. He caught mononucleosis, which is an impressive collection of syllables meaning a virus in the blood. Mononucleosis is best described as an ultra virus. Victims feel like their white corpuscles and red corpuscles have chosen up sides and are playing roughhouse hockey in their veins.

Sawchuk was traded back to Detroit in 1957, but the Red Wings got less Sawchuk than they had before. His weight dropped from 215 pounds to 167. Psychologists probed the dark recesses of his psyche and found a man standing on the edge of an emotional abyss, harried by flying pucks and a persecution complex.

In 1966, two years after he was drafted by Toronto Maple Leafs, Sawchuk needed an operation to fuse two damaged vertebrae in his spine. His wife had endured considerable time in hospital having their seven children. "We are," Sawchuck said, making a small joke, "the sort of people who make health insurance popular."

Sawchuk's single commanding performance probably occurred on April 15, 1967, in the fifth game of a tense Stanley Cup semifinal between the Leafs and Chicago Black Hawks. He replaced a shaky Johnny Bower in the second period with the best-of-seven series tied 2–2 in games, and this fifth game snarled 2–2 in goals.

The Hawks, playing in the noisy cavern of Chicago Stadium, pressed in the first two minutes of the second period, boisterous

action boiling around Sawchuk. Bobby Hull pivoted 15 feet to Sawchuk's left, almost parallel to the goal, a practically impossible angle
from which to score. Hull shot, high and hard. The puck struck
Sawchuk's left shoulder and knocked him down. Other players
skated around the Toronto net—the Leafs in some chagrin, the
Hawks curious.

Pierre Pilote, then the Chicago captain, crafty, canny, got out his
barbs. "How'd you feel, Terry? You should of let it go, Terry.
Might've been a goal."

Bob Haggert, the Toronto trainer, skidded across the ice from
the Toronto bench to Sawchuk. "Where'd you get it?"

Sawchuk, on his knees, "On my bad shoulder."

Haggert, leaning down, "Think you're all right?"

Sawchuk stood up, reaching around for his stick and gloves, a
little defiant: "I stopped the damn shot, didn't I?"

It is now a hallowed story, a footnote in clutch exhibitions, how
Sawchuk stopped 36 shots in Toronto's 4–2 conquest, frustrated the
most insatiable shooters in the game, shut them out with the rem-
nants of a young Sawchuk: down the glove, out the arm, over the
stick, up the glove, shutting off the daylight the shooters thought
they saw—all a kind of desperate epileptic action.

At least one aroused witness, Toronto coach Punch Imlach, insisted Sawchuk's was the most monumental stand in goal since
Horatius of Roman legend denied those people access to a bridge.
"Like that guy Horatio," Imlach said, in gaudy tribute. ". . . Fantastic!"

Sawchuk sat in his damp underwear for a long time after such
games, head down, hands cupped around a can of Coke, absorbing
what he had done. Comment came out of him heavily, the way it
does when fatigue catches up and removes, even for winners, the
jubilation.

He was the most stylish goaler extant, but refused the adjective
"disciplined" for his style in a big game. "That's not the word," he
said with a wan smile, after beating Hull and the Hawks. "I'm
scared every time they get near me."

He put much down to luck: "I'm lucky I can walk after the spinal
fusion, let alone skate." Or: "I'm lucky when the puck hits me, and
stays out."

Sawchuk was not the exulting kind, but even he was impressed
with his defiance of the Hawks on April 15, 1967. I'd like to leave
hockey like that," he said softly. "In good style."

He was traded to Los Angeles in 1967 and played mediocre hockey in the 1967–68 season. He returned to Detroit the next year, and although he lowered his average to a respectable figure, he appeared in only 13 games. Before the 1969–70 season, the New York Rangers acquired him, but he was undecided whether he would report or retire. Seemingly, for Sawchuk, the glory had ended.

However, he was persuaded by Rangers general manager-coach Emile Francis to try once more, and Terry agreed. It was thought that Sawchuk would play 15 to 20 games and thus relieve regular Ed Giacomin. But Sawchuk had lost his touch. He played only eight regular season games and even though he did register one shutout it was apparent Sawchuk was washed up.

The glory had, in fact, ended.

PART FOUR
The Game

The Biggest Fight

FIST FIGHTS, stick-swinging duels, mass brawls and wrestling matches are as much a part of hockey as goals and assists. At the turn of the century stickhandlers were clubbing each other with the same ferocity that Eddie Shack and Larry Zeidel displayed at Maple Leaf Gardens in Toronto when they stick-dueled each other to bloody pulps in March 1968.

Fights are an inevitable consequence of a game that legalizes most forms of body contact. Since there often is a fine line between the legitimate and illegitimate contact, rule infractions constantly occur. When they occur—and the referee overlooks them—the offended player almost automatically seeks retribution and the roots of a fight have been planted. Usually the battles involve individuals although there often are situations when an entire team will wage a war with another team until the season has ended and the grudge is buried—usually until the next season.

Isolating an individual battle as a classic is difficult because there have been so many unusual ones. The Zeidel–Shack stick-swinging episode was matched in the fifties when Bernie (Boom Boom) Geoffrion of the Montreal Canadiens clubbed Ron Murphy of the Rangers into submission with his stick. In the thirties Nels Crutchfield of the Montreal Maroons nearly decapitated Bill Cook in a similarly vicious stick-swinging match.

Mass brawls have been even more apparent. Full-scale riots involving the Chicago Black Hawks and Toronto Maple Leafs or Philadelphia Flyers and St. Louis Blues seem more serious because of the high penalty totals than they actually were as far as damage done. But the mass brawl that combined all the elements and which goes down as hockey's greatest fight involved the Rangers and the Canadiens. It started this way:

Kenny Reardon, the rambunctious Montreal Canadiens defenseman, had one thing in mind as he stickhandled across Madison Square Garden ice on the night of March 16, 1947—freeze the puck. "Dick Irvin, our coach, had bawled the hell outa me for losing the puck and the game last time we were in New York," says Reardon, now living in Montreal. "I wasn't goin' to let it happen again."

Montreal was leading the Rangers 4–3 with only 32 seconds left in the game. If the powerful visitors could hold the lead they'd clinch first place and a new prize of $1,000 for each player the NHL was giving away that year. The downtrodden Rangers, on the other hand, needed the win to stave off elimination from a play-off berth.

As hockey games go, this one was especially ripe for mayhem. Freshman referee George Hayes already had earned a reputation for being overly tolerant of rule violations. Furthermore, the teams had been nurturing individual and collective hatreds all season. A few were unleashed the previous night when Montreal beat the Rangers 1–0 at the Forum. Others exploded in the second period of the game when Reardon and Maurice Richard of Montreal squared off with Bill Juzda and Bryan Hextall of the Rangers.

"They were out to get Richard and Reardon," charged Dick Irvin, the frenetic Canadiens coach, "in order to ruin them for the playoffs. We already had killed the Rangers' chances for the play-offs so they wanted revenge." Reardon, who in 1946 had declared war on Ranger fans by personally slugging a promenade customer, agreed with his coach. "But," adds Reardon, "I couldn't afford a fight in that last minute. I wanted to stay out of trouble."

As Reardon cruised over the blue line his overwhelming desire to nurse the puck got the best of him and he committed an egregious hockey sin—he fixed his eyes on the black rubber disk and forgot to look where he was going. The next thing he knew Bryan Hextall's hip loomed menacingly in front of him. Reardon bounced off Hextall like a pinball right into Cal Gardner's waiting stick which obligingly bludgeoned Reardon across the mouth. "My upper lip," Ken says, "felt as if it had been sawed off my face."

Reardon finally was revived by Dr. Vincent Nardiello and escorted to the Garden's medical room along a route that might well have been a minefield. His chief obstacles included the Rangers' bench, three rows of hostile fans and an alleyway heavily populated with anti-Montreal guerrillas. As Reardon passed the Rangers' bench Phil Watson suggested that Kenny's mangled lip was not nearly punishment enough for him. Reardon bolted for Watson but a policeman intervened. Then up popped a balding fan brandishing a fist. "Reardon," he shouted, "I've been waiting a long time for you to get it. You louse."

"That did it," Reardon says. "I swung my stick at him—then a cop grabbed me from behind and I fell." The disturbance aroused the Rangers who rose from their seats out of natural curiosity. From a distant vantage point of the Montreal bench across the ice it appeared that the entire New York team was preparing to pounce upon Reardon.

"Get the hell over there," implored Irvin, standing on his bench. And the Flying Frenchmen poured over the boards like GIs at Normandy. When the first platoon reached the front they were somewhat dismayed to find that the Rangers had not laid a stick on Reardon. Instead of retreating peaceably the Canadiens began brawling with the fans. A posse of special police tried to disperse the mob but they would have had a better chance teaming a herd of rhinos. And so, round 1 of what the *New York Times* called "the grandest mass riot in the local history of the NHL" had begun.

Montreal captain Butch Bouchard, who led the stampede, clouted the bald-headed spectator with his stick while goalie Bill Durnan and Maurice Richard sought other prospective victims. The sight of their defenseless followers being manhandled by the stick-swinging enemy disturbed the Rangers. Finally, somebody in the blue-shirted ranks yelled "Charge!" and the counterattack (and what turned out to be the real battle) was underway.

Within seconds the Rangers wiped out Montreal's beachhead, forcing the invaders to regroup at center ice, where four main events were in progress. (1) Maurice Richard versus Bill Juzda; (2) Bill Moe versus Bill Durnan; (3) Hal Laycoe versus Leo Lamoureux; (4) Butch Bouchard versus Bryan Hextall. The Marquis of Queensbury would have sanctioned the Moe–Durnan and Laycoe–Lamoureux bouts, but the others were strictly back-alley affairs.

Moe, who had been ordered not to play because of a shoulder injury, floored the heavily padded Durnan with a roundhouse right. Laycoe and Lamoureux flailed away at each other in a fierce toe-to-

toe encounter that ended only because the belligerents were too tired to throw another punch.

Meanwhile, Richard broke his stick over Juzda's head, snapping the shaft in two. Juzda arose slowly, like a Frankenstein monster, and tackled Richard, bringing him down violently. In another precinct, Bouchard ripped Hextall's stick away from him and flattened him with a punch. Having dispensed with Durnan, Moe cracked a stick over Bouchard's head and Butch didn't even seem to notice that he had been hit.

One of the more bizarre preliminary bouts involved Murph Chamberlain of Montreal and Joe Cooper of the Rangers. When Murph missed a wild uppercut, Cooper replied with a sizzling right that catapulted Chamberlain clear over the sideboards and deposited him in a front row seat. Juzda then excused himself from Richard, picked up a stray stick and poleaxed Buddy O'Connor, breaking his jaw. "It became an almost endless fight," wrote Bill Wittig in the *New York Sun*. "No sooner was one group of players quieted down than another would start at it again. In one span there were 15 fights going on between the players and not even eight Garden policemen could restore order."

At this point organist Gladys Goodding lit into "The Star Spangled Banner" but judging by the reaction she might well have been playing "Broadway Boogaloo." Peacemakers were as contemptuously regarded as the enemy. When Frank Boucher offered to mediate the Ken Mosdell–Edgar Laprade dispute, Mosdell murderously swung his stick at Boucher, causing the Ranger manager to seek asylum behind the dasher board.

The only players to escape unblemished were the normally violent Phil Watson of the Rangers and George Allen of Montreal. Watson says it wasn't an accident. "I grabbed hold of Allen," Watson explains, "and said, 'Look, George, what's the sense of getting all tangled up? Whaddya say we stand on the side and watch this one?' He said okay, so we did. It was the best fight we ever saw."

The *brouhaha* lasted 20 minutes, the armistice finally induced by mass exhaustion. When it came time to report the offenders, referee Hayes obviously suffered a fit of compassion—he handed out only three penalties, 10-minute misconducts to Richard, Juzda and Chamberlain.

The last half-minute was not without incident either. Tony Leswick of the Rangers, looking more like a Bengal Lancer, attempted to impale Durnan while the usually pacific Ab DeMarco erupted

THE GAME

Left wing Steve Vickers, the first New York Ranger to win the Calder Trophy since Camille Henry in 1954. Despite missing 17 games with a knee injury Vickers, en route to his rookie award, scored 30 goals in 1972-73, including back-to-back hat tricks. (*Courtesy of New York Rangers*)

Bill Hicke, first president of the World Hockey Association's Players' Union.
(Courtesy of Stan Fischler)

Smooth-skating, slick-shifting Gil Perreault, ace puck-handling center of the Buffalo Sabres, won the Calder Trophy in 1971 and followed it with the Lady Byng in 1973. With Richard Martin and Rene Robert he helped form the "French Connection" line which terrorized NHL goaltenders for 105 goals and 243 scoring points in 1972-73. (*Vincent P. Claps*)

A GAME IN THE LIFE:
ROD GILBERT

Flashing into the attacking zone.

Following through on the big slap-shot.

Receiving congratulations after a scoring play.

Sprawling unconscious after a collision.

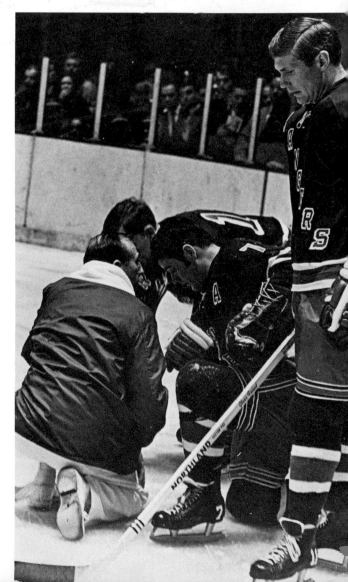

"What city are you in and who are we playing?"
(Courtesy of Orazio Belfiore)

With the move of his older brother Bobby to the Winnipeg Jets of the WHA, Dennis Hull chalked up a career high of 90 points in 1972-73 in assuming new leadership duties with the Chicago Black Hawks. Dennis, author of one of the hardest, if not the hardest, shots in hockey, had potted 210 goals through 1972-73. *(Daniel S. Baliotti)*

Rangers' All Star defenseman Brad Park makes sure that Bruins' Derek Sanderson goes nowhere. Scene typifies New York's squelching of Boston in five games in 1973 Stanley Cup quarter-final. Note Sanderson's number 27. He couldn't regain his old 16 when he returned to Bruins from Philadelphia Blazers of WHA. *(Photo: Roberto Borea)*

Two of the world's finest athletes —Jesse Owens (left), and Gordie Howe, who signed with the Houston Aeros in the summer of 1973 at age 45.

(Photo by Shirley Fischler)

Lou Fontinato, New York Rangers' strong man of the 1950s and one of the reasons they made the playoffs three years running after a long drought. Fontinato led the league in penalty minutes as a member of the Rangers and also when he was with Montreal Canadiens. A neck injury, suffered in a collision in a game against the Rangers, prematurely ended his career.
(Courtesy of Stan Fischler)

"The Roadrunner," Yvan Cournoyer (12) and Jacques Lemaire (25), two of the Montreal Canadiens' super-shooters. Cournoyer with 15 goals set a new scoring record in the Stanley Cup playoffs of 1973. He scored 40 goals during the regular season in 1972–73 while Lemaire netted 45. Rangers' stylish Jean Ratelle (at right) also broke the 40 mark by one in the same season.
(Photo: Terry Foley)

Here's Tony Leswick in a typical situation. He's mixing it with Howie Meeker of the Maple Leafs (15) and appears to be getting the worst of it. Win or lose, Tony always came back for more, though. George Hayes is the linesman; Turk Broda, the goalie.
(Courtesy of Stan Fischler)

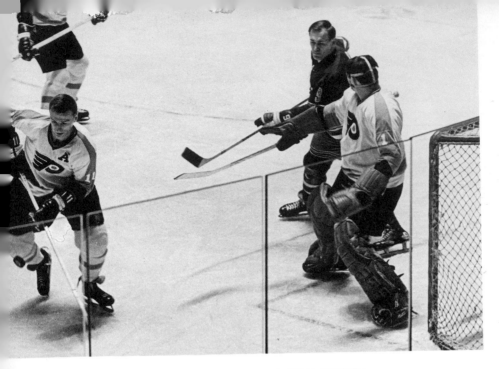

HOW A HOCKEY FIGHT STARTS

Collision in front of net: Reggie Fleming, New York Ranger forward (dark jersey);
Doug Favell, Philadelphia Flyer goalie (light jersey).

Sticks high.

Sticks up.

Sticks down, gloves off.

Players down.

The ice clears.
(*Courtesy of Orazio Belfiore*)

John Ferguson (left), modern ogre of Montreal Canadiens, swings roundhouse right at Bob Nevin of the New York Rangers. Ferguson hung up his skates—and gloves—after the 1970–71 season. At the same time, Nevin was traded to Minnesota.

(Courtesy of Dick Beddoes)

against Mosdell. As the final buzzer sounded police averted another great war by immediately herding the players to their dressing rooms.

Montreal won 4–3 and, but for one man, the Canadiens toasted their victory (and escape from Manhattan) on the train all the way home. That one disconsolate man was Kenny Reardon, who needed 14 stitches to close his lip. But it wasn't the injury that bothered Reardon.

"I was the guy who started the damn fight," Reardon remembered, "but, believe it or not, I never saw it. Right after the cop knocked me down I got up and walked to the clinic. I didn't find out about the fight until the game was over and the guys came into the bloody room all cut. Sorta burns me up. I coulda had a great time!"

The Dawson City Challenge

OTTAWA'S SILVER SEVEN dominated the Stanley Cup championships in the all-conquering fashion of the modern Montreal Canadiens, retaining Lord Stanley's old basin against seven challenges from 1902 through 1905.

One of the Silver Seven conquests was the most comic in Cup history, achieved in 1905 against a bizarre group called the Dawson City Klondikers. This roistering squad was composed of itinerant players nobody in hockey had ever heard of—anonymous athletes who might have admitted, under pressure, that they had never heard of themselves.

Dawson City was the hub of the Klondike mining region of the Yukon, major watering hole on the Trail of '98 for Robert Service characters like Sam Magee and Dangerous Dan McGrew. The Klondikers were adventurers from scattered sections of Canada, lured north by the exciting romance of gold. The romance had worn thin when the gold turned out to be a brassy mirage, and the Klondikers wanted out, back to civilization. They coaxed a rich prospector named Colonel Joe Boyle to finance the road trip— 4,400 miles by bicycle, dog sled, stage coach, boat and train.

Their names are preserved in old newspaper files, and cemeteries. Albert Forest from Three Rivers, Quebec, was the 17-year-old goalkeeper, youngest player in Stanley Cup history. His rowdy associates were Jim Johnston, point, from Ottawa; Dr. Randy McLennan, cover point (an Ice Age hockey term for defense), from Cornwall, Ontario; Norm Watts, right wing, from Aylmer, Quebec;

George Kennedy, left wing, and Hector Smith, center, from West Selkirk, Manitoba; Dave Fairburn, rover, from Portage la Prairie, Manitoba; and A. N. Martin, a spare from Ottawa. Enroute, through Winnipeg, they recruited a Lorne Hannay from Brandon, Manitoba, to play cover point.

The Klondikers left Dawson City on December 19, 1904, some of them running behind dog teams and "waving to gay crowds lining the route." The community's resolute population, now about 1,000, was then estimated at 150,000. The journey, longest road trip in hockey annals, consumed 23 days. Modern travelers, hastened by planes, can make it in 10 hours.

"The first day," the *Ottawa Journal* reported, "the Klondikers covered 46 miles, the second 41. The third day saw some of them struggling to cover 36 miles, some suffering with blistered feet. To proceed, these had to remove their boots. It may give an idea of the hardship they faced when it is recorded that temperature went down to 20 degrees below zero during the mush from Dawson City to Skagway."

Skagway, on the southern coast of Alaska, was the only exit from the Yukon to the "outside." The Klondikers missed their boat connections by two hours and were forced to wait five days for another vessel headed south to Seattle. "We had one practice while we waited," the *Journal* quoted one Klondiker. "It was a rink 40 feet by 50, half of it covered with sand which dulled our skates."

They finally left Skagway on New Year's Eve on a scow called the S. S. Dolphin, bound for Seattle. From there, they traveled 200 miles north by train to Vancouver, then caught a Canadian Pacific mainliner east to Ottawa.

From the bleak British Columbia mountain town of Field, one Klondiker reported: "The only accommodation afforded us on the train for training purposes is the smoking room with a floor eight feet square. Exclusive rights have been granted us in this respect on account of the passengers being few and no smokers among them. Skipping is the principal exercise indulged in, and, owing to two not being able to conveniently train at one time, the quarters are in use most of the day." The quote may have been spurious. Most hockey players could not put three sentences together in that articulate fashion after a four-year cram course in English at Yale.

The Klondikers reached Ottawa on January 12, 1905, a day before the first of the their best-of-three games challenge. They were bivouacked at the sporty Russell Hotel, where high-octane beverages and low-tone ladies were in abundant supply.

Their opponents included several of the prominent players of the time—Harry Westwick, Art Moore, Harvey Pulford, Alf Smith, Dave Finnie, Fred White and Frank McGee, considered to be hockey's first superstar.

"Hysterical" was the *Ottawa Journal's* adjective for "the surging crowds" that attended the first game in Dey's Gladstone Avenue Rink. Earl Grey, the Canadian Governor-General who later awarded a trophy in his name for the football championship of Canada, was in the crush of 2,200 witnesses. They saw Yukon invaders gaudily dressed in "uniforms of black and gold stripes with white knickers and striped stockings."

There was no other color. Ottawa won 9–2 and the Klondikers won blunt criticism in the *Journal*: "The visitors were clearly outclassed. It is true that they hardly had time to get in shape, but the form they showed was the most mediocre kind."

Norm Watts, the rambunctious right wing of the Klondikers, behaved like an early-day John Ferguson or Ted Green. He caressed Art Moore with his club viciously enough to open a four-stitch cut on the scalp of the Ottawa defenseman.

The celebrated McGee only scored once in the first game and, afterward, the Klondikers expressed belligerence. The pugnacious Watt, helping himself to a free lunch at Sam Cassidy's saloon, demanded, "Who the hell's McGee? He don't look like much."

McGee was a chunky blond center, bereft of one eye because of an accident suffered before he joined the Silver Seven. In the second game against Dawson City, on January 16, 1905, he was, as they boast of Robert Marvin Hull today, something else. McGee scored 14 goals in a 23–2 slathering of the inept Klondikers, eight of them in succession in a space of eight minutes and 20 seconds. He scored three—his sixth, seventh and eighth—in 90 seconds, and four in 140 seconds, records unmatched for Stanley Cup play. No one else ever scored 14 times in any professional game. McGee's hockey career was brief, embracing only four seasons with Ottawa between 1902 and 1906. He volunteered for the Canadian army in World War I, where he was killed in France in 1916.

The Klondikers, in losing the second game of their ridiculous challenge 23–2, sank in the limbo of hockey history without leaving a trace. Their notorious safari cost Colonel Boyle, their amiable sponsor, $3,000.

The Fastest Three

IT WAS DIFFICULT to determine whether the 1951–52 season was more traumatic for the New York Rangers or the Chicago Black Hawks. The Black Hawks finished last, 23 points out of a play-off berth. The Rangers finished fifth, seven points behind the fourth-place Boston Bruins. But the Chicago club had some consolation—it placed one player, Bill Mosienko—among the top 10 NHL scorers. Mosienko, who had gained fame as a linemate of Max and Doug Bentley in Chicago's halcyon years, finished seventh in scoring, one point behind Montreal's Bernie (Boom Boom) Geoffrion. The highest Ranger scorer was Ed Slowinski, buried in sixteenth position.

The absolute despair of the Rangers and Black Hawks was reflected in the audience at Madison Square Garden on the night of March 23, 1952. The huge arena was less than half-filled when the teams lined up for the opening face-off of what was to be the last game of the season for both clubs. So decimated by injuries were the Rangers that they were unable to dress either of their two goalers, Chuck Rayner or Emile Francis. Instead, they pressed into service Lorne Anderson, a young goaltender who had played for the New York Rovers, the Rangers' farm team in the senior amateur Eastern Hockey League.

Anderson, who was average in minor league competition, appeared jittery when the game began. Soon after the opening face-off the Black Hawks' first line of Mosienko, Gus Bodnar and George Gee moved the puck into Ranger zone. Mosienko sent a pass to defenseman Bill Gadsby who spotted Bodnar near the net. He relayed a pass to his teammate and Bodnar scored on Anderson only 44 seconds after the game had begun.

But the Ranger defense steadied in front of the kid goalie and the New York forwards responded with three goals in the first period and two in the second. By the time Ed Slowinski had scored for the Rangers at 3:37 of the final period New York had built up a commanding 6–2 lead and appeared certain of ending the season on a reasonably pleasant note. In the meantime Anderson had calmed somewhat and appeared capable of containing the visitors in the final 15 minutes of play.

Normally, a last-place visiting team could be expected to coast through the last period of a game it was losing by a big score but the Black Hawks' scoring leader, Mosienko, already had calculated that if he was to make a name for himself, permanently, it would be a good idea to make a grand effort against the Rangers. Three days before the final game, Mosienko was in Toronto visiting a friend. "We were thumbing through the record book," he remembered later. "I remarked how nice it would be to have my name in there with some of the hockey greats."

Mosienko, however, was not making much progress against the Rangers. At the six-minute mark of the last period he had only one assist to show for himself when he joined Bodnar and Gee on the ice again.

"I remember it like it was last night," said Mosienko. "Suddenly Gus got me the puck in center ice, I went in around Hy Buller on the New York defense, on top of the goalkeeper." Unknown to most fans, Buller was playing despite a cracked ankle. He had decided to play in a bid to set an all-time Ranger scoring record for defensemen. Mosienko shot the puck along the ice to Anderson's right side. It disappeared into the net at 6:09. "That was my twenty-ninth goal of the year, so I reached into the net for the puck as a souvenir. Right off the face-off, Bodnar got me the puck again. I slipped around Buller again and moved right in on Anderson."

Mosienko slid the puck in the same place, along the ice to Anderson's right. Anderson appeared unprepared for the quick shot. The puck flew by him before he could make his move and it was in the net. The time was 6:20, exactly 11 seconds after the first goal. The score was now New York 6, Chicago 4. "That was my thirtieth goal, so I dove into the net for that puck. On the face-off, Bodnar shoveled the puck to Gee. I'm flying along the right and Gee passed to me. Somehow, I got around Buller again."

The crowd, which had taken only a perfunctory interest in the proceedings, suddenly took note. Few realized that the fastest two goals had been scored in four seconds by Nels Stewart of the Montreal Maroons on January 3, 1931 at Montreal. Or, that the record for the fastest three goals had been set by Carl Liscombe of the Detroit Red Wings. He accomplished the feat in 1:04 in 1938 against the Black Hawks. The team record for fastest three goals was 24 seconds set by Hooley Smith, Babe Siebert and Dave Trottier of the Maroons in 1932.

There was no question but that the Mosienko line would remain on the ice again. The Rangers, who still held a two-goal lead and were concerned about an end-of-season win, tightened their defense as they prepared for the face-off. But, again, the Black Hawks won the draw and the puck fell on the stick of Gee.

"Georgie was on the left wing," said Mosienko. "When he got control of the puck he began moving toward the blue line. As he reached the blue line, I made my move. He saw me cutting over the line and he laid a perfect pass on my stick." Then Mosienko switched tactics when he confronted Anderson a third time. He drew the goaler out, and, certain Anderson would be looking for a shot on the ice to the right, flipped the puck into the top righthand corner. Time: 6:30.

Mosienko was about to skate to center ice for the face-off when Jim Peters, a teammate, caught him in a sweaty embrace. "Hey! You better grab that puck, too! I think you've got a record!"

"So," Mosienko recalls, "I fished after the third puck." Then he was struck by the recollection of one that got away. "The funny thing is that about 45 seconds later, I was in alone again. I faked Anderson out of position, had an open goal to hit—and shot wide."

So instead of four goals in 66 seconds, Mosie was stuck with three in 21. It is one of the old scenes that he runs through the projector of reminiscence whenever he appears for oldtimers' games that are amiable winter diversions in Canada. "Like they say," Mosienko said, "I caught lightning in a beer bottle."

The Fix That Failed

FRANCIS MICHAEL (KING) CLANCY is the NHL's original good-humor man, with the built-in public relations of a Pope John. There is a perpetual high-beam grin on his map-of-Ireland mug, sort of like everybody's benign uncle who shows up at family reunions a little bombed.

Clancy retired as a defenseman with Toronto Maple Leafs in 1937, but he never strayed far from Maple Leaf Gardens. He was Punch Imlach's loyal subaltern for 10 years, a cajoling buffer between the players and the perverse Imlach.

"Did you ever hear how I tried to fix it for Convey to be a star?" Clancy will ask enchanted listeners, and then he's off spinning a yarn about a caper that failed.

The late Eddie (Cowboy) Convey had been a Leaf, not especially formidable on left wing, and he was sent away to the New York Americans in 1933. The Americans would demote him to the minors, but not before his old Toronto pals tried to keep him in the big league.

One night the Americans visited Toronto, and, the whisper went, Convey needed a big game to survive in the NHL. Clancy's concern prompted him to conspire with Charlie Conacher, the large, blunt right wing, and Lorne Chabot, the tall, dour goalkeeper. "Look," Clancy told them before the game, "if we get a few goals up, let's make it easy for Convey. Let's help him score a couple."

The Leafs romped ahead 4–0 in the first period, far enough in front for Convey to get his chance—with Clancy's skilled collusion.

Convey got off the Americans' bench in the second period and, for a hilarious few minutes, it was as though the stage had been manipulated. He was on against Conacher on the Toronto forward line, Clancy on the Toronto defense, Chabot in the Toronto goal.

"Now!" Clancy muttered to Conacher as Convey skated down the wing. Conacher obligingly fell down to let him through. Convey hit the Toronto blue line, where Clancy conveniently neglected to check him. Convey walked in on Chabot, who didn't move. He had a clear shot at an open side of the net—and drove the puck wide.

"One more chance!" Clancy called to Conacher and Chabot and, soon, the Cowboy again came riding down the wing. Conacher faked a bodycheck, and missed. Clancy stumbled and fell down. Convey swept in on the stationary Chabot, who left one side of the goal unprotected. Convey boomed a drive, high into the seats.

"One more time!" Clancy commanded and Convey got it, the next time he appeared on the ice. "Let him through!" Clancy shouted at Conacher, who let Convey sail past. He escaped Clancy's bogus check.

Clancy is up now, aping the Convey of many years ago. "He flew by me, really danglin', and went cruisin' in on Chabot, who was ready to step aside. He took careful aim and shot. Chabot fell to let the whole goal open, and whap! Convey hit him right in the Adam's apple with the puck! Down he went, chokin' and gaggin'!"

Conacher skated back to help Clancy assist the distressed Chabot. "Any more of this," Chabot said, when he could speak, "and Convey'll kill me!"

"I guess we better knock off fakin' for him," Clancy suggested.

"Right," Conacher said, not concealing his disgust. "Screw Convey!"

Three years later, in the Stanley Cup playoffs, Clancy instigated a Toronto win against the imposing Boston Bruins. It was a celebrated caper with absolutely no fake in it.

The clubs were matched in a short two-game series, total goals to count. The Bruins won the first game 3–0 in Boston and in the second, in Toronto, they scored another goal in the first period.

Leafs went off for the first intermission, sullen and agitated, behind 4–0 on the round. There is a one-seat bathroom off the main dressing quarters in Maple Leaf Gardens, and Conacher wandered into it for a cigarette. Clancy was there ahead of him, camped on the only available seat.

"Get off there!" Conacher grumbled.

"Get off!" Clancy said, in a bristly brogue. "What the hell d'you mean, get off? I'll not be gettin' off for anybody who's waltzin' around like you are tonight."

Conacher, the big Toronto shooter, had been restricted in the series by a Boston tormentor, followed around like a busted garter by Red Beattie. He complained to Clancy about Beattie's nagging attention. Clancy turned solicitous and stood up. "Well, now, sit down and I'll tell you how to handle Beattie." Conacher sat down, taking consoling puffs of a cigarette, and Clancy perched on his knee.

"Why don't you go out and belt Beattie?" Clancy asked. "Give it good to the sneaky bastard."

"I'd get a penalty," Conacher said.

"So what's a penalty?" asked Clancy, who later became a referee. "Look, I'll get the puck and pass it to you just when Beattie's near you. When he gets close, whack him!"

Conacher obeyed the instructions of his Irish playmate. He jammed an elbow into Beattie's flushed features but Odie Cleghorn, a tolerant referee, overlooked the foul.

A few minutes later Clancy tripped Eddie Shore, the meat and sinew of the Boston team. Cleghorn also missed that infraction, to Shore's very vocal chagrin: "Trip, Odie! I was tripped!"

Clancy, skating in malicious circles, stimulated Shore's wrath. "The man's blind, Eddie! He's robbin' you, sure as hell! Look how he blew the call on Beattie!"

Then Red Horner, a few minutes later, deflected a shot from Art Jackson past Tiny Thompson in the Boston goal. The Bruins, led by Shore, clamored around Cleghorn, vehement in their insistence that Horner had been illegally standing inside the goal crease.

Clancy's urchin sense of opportunity stoked the turmoil. "Eddie," he bawled at Shore, "what a lousy decision! You're bein' robbed blind! Blind!"

Shore's temper came untied. He shot the puck at Cleghorn, hitting that distinguished gentleman in the middle of his ample rear.

"You're gone!" the referee hollered. "That'll cost you a two-minute penalty!"

Injustice fanned Shore's indignation. He picked up the puck and pitched it into a delighted Toronto crowd.

"And that'll be 10 minutes more!" the referee said, as he added a misconduct penalty to the minor.

While Shore was gone, fuming, the Leafs scored four goals to grab a 5–4 lead on the round. They kept scoring after he returned, finally winning the game, 8–3, and the series 8–6. Conacher scored three goals and assisted on two others, but on most scorecards Clancy was responsible for needling the Bruins into elimination.

The Funniest Guy

HOCKEY FANS of the sixties and seventies will never see the likes of Jean Baptiste Pusie, easily the clown prince of the ice. His reign was during the thirties when madcap escapades were tolerated by the hockey brass and decorum was not necessarily considered a worthwhile attribute of a stickhandler. It was an era when Charlie Conacher of the Toronto Maple Leafs could get away with hanging his tiny teammate, King Clancy, out of the window of a New York hotel by his feet and when heavyweight bootleggers such as Big Bill Dwyer could own a hockey team (the New York Americans) without the NHL suffering any compunctions.

It was an era when Frank Boucher and Ching Johnson of the Rangers could commandeer a Toronto trolley car in the wee hours of the morning and, by "tipping" the motorman with some alcohol, cruise the various routes of the Queen City without second thoughts. Hockey still had the pioneer brashness to it. The game was not long out of the Canadian sticks and many of the players wore their naïveté with a charm that would only invite scorn and reproach in the mod sixties.

The business of hockey was then a game and often a silly one. There was a time when Colonel John Hammond, the naïve president of the Rangers, thought it would be a good idea if he obtained Eddie Shore from the Boston Bruins. It was a reasonable wish since Shore happened to be the best defenseman in the league at the time. In exchange Colonel Hammond ordered his manager, Lester Patrick, to offer Myles Lane, a young defenseman with considerably less ability than Shore. Hammond's idea was that the Bruins would want Lane because he was a native of the Boston area and graduated from Dartmouth College.

Patrick, realizing he was in the midst of a silly bid, nevertheless wired Art Ross, manager of the Bruins and made the proposition— Lane for Shore.

A day later, Ross wired Patrick with a message that has since become legendary: "You are so many Myles from Shore you need a life preserver." In time Shore was to be a teammate of Jean Pusie and the combine was one of the weirdest in hockey's history; the severe, unsmiling Shore and the irrepressible Pusie.

A husky French-Canadian defenseman with an immense ego and a clipped English accent, Pusie made his debut in the autumn of 1930 at the Montreal Canadiens' training camp.

Coach Cecil Hart was startled when the 20-year-old rookie entered his office, introduced himself, vigorously pumped his hand and unequivocally declared: "Meestair 'art. Pewsee weel be zee greates' . . . 'ockey playairs like me weel make dis game pop-u-lair."

Hart admired the youngster's off-ice exuberance but he detected two egregious flaws in his playing technique. Pusie's heavy shot worked only when he had ample time to lower his head for a protracted wind-up. And his stickhandling was predicated on the notion that opponents were never closer than 10 feet from him. When Jean Baptiste skated, his eye remained glued to the puck.

"Ship him to London for seasoning," Hart suggested to manager Leo Dandurand, "and see what happens."

Pusie was suitably depressed when he joined the London Tecumsehs of the International League but confident that he'd be an NHL star. "I weel show dem," he assured coach Clem Loughlin. "Dey make beeg mistake."

In his first home game Pusie was fed a lead pass and broke into the clear. This was a perfect opportunity for Jean Baptiste to fire his unusual shot. He wound up in the classic style and hit the puck so hard it yanked the goalie's mitt from his hand. Both puck and glove sailed into the net.

Before the goalie could move, Pusie dove into the cage, retrieved the glove and presented it to the goaltender with a low bow. He held his opponent's bare hand up to the crowd, carefully counted the fingers and said, "Dey are all dere. You are luck-y." He replaced the glove and condescendingly patted the goalie on the back.

"Pusie then leisurely strutted to center ice, a veritable one-man parade, and the audience went wild," said the late Bill Roche, assistant sports editor of the *London Advertiser*. "Verdi's 'Triumphal March' would have been ideal for him."

Pusie's opening night exploits were so liberally recounted that London's arena was jammed for the next game. The crowd had come to see Jean Baptiste and when the home team was awarded a penalty shot, fans demanded that Pusie take it. "I had no choice," said coach Loughlin, "he already owned the joint."

Only Pusie and the opposing goaltender remained on the ice. For a few seconds Jean Baptiste remained sphinx-like in the center of the rink, glaring wide-eyed at his enemy. Suddenly, he let out a shriek and dashed frantically toward the net. When he reached the penalty shot line, he drew back his stick. The goalie tensed for the shot but Pusie never fired. He stopped short, spraying the goalie with ice shavings. Then, placing stick and gloves on the ice, he skated to the netminder, courteously shook hands and returned to center ice.

Again Jean Baptiste began his rush, wound up for the shot and, this time fired. But Pusie had miscalculated. The puck dribbled off his stick and lazily rolled to the goal line, an absurdly easy stop. The goalie, however, was so mesmerized by Pusie's overture, he remained transfixed as the puck rolled past him into the net.

"Pusie dashed to the goalkeeper, who was still stupefied," said Roche, "and kissed him on both cheeks. That woke him up. He grabbed his stick and went for Pusie's head. Too late. Pusie was already strutting back to center ice on his way to fame as a hockey comic."

One day he told Loughlin he had a plan for reviving hockey interest in Buffalo. "Okay," said Loughlin, "but remember, no penalties." Pusie had perfected a dying-swan act in which he would check an opponent lightly and then rebound several yards to the ice, hopeful of drawing a penalty. When he executed the play against Buffalo, the referee failed to blow his whistle. This enraged Jean Baptiste. "You knock Pewsee down," he roared at the aston-ished Buffalo player, "I get you." Jean Baptiste leaped at his man, the opponent swung back and soon both benches emptied. Within minutes, more than 400 fans were on the ice flailing away. A bat-talion of police had to be summoned to quell the riot.

Following his season at London, Pusie moved to Regina in the Western Canada League. His most notable performance that season was a bit of philanthropy during a game that Pusie's team was winning 18–0, every goal having been scored by Jean Baptiste. With just minutes remaining, Pusie began another rush. Only this time he abruptly wheeled at center ice, skated back toward the Regina goaltender and fired the puck into his own net. "Sorry," he explained, "I feel bad about dat poor team."

Despite his shennanigans, Pusie still was aiming for an NHL berth. In 1932–33 he led the Western League in scoring while playing for Vancouver. The New York Rangers purchased him but the best he could do was score two assists in 19 games. "As a character, he was wonderful," recalled Frank Boucher, a member of the Rangers at the time, "but he didn't have enough ability."

A year later he was acquired by the Boston Bruins, played a few games and was dispatched to their farm club, the Bruin Cubs. Pusie startled officials one night when he disappeared from the penalty box after being served a major and misconduct penalty. The referee stopped the game and search parties were organized to find Jean Baptiste. "We looked high and low," said Walter Brown, president of the Bruins. "Nobody could ever find him."

Eventually, Pusie was discovered strolling down a Garden runway. He was peeling an orange. "Whass de fuss," he wondered, "over a leetle ting like takin' a walk? Zee penalty bench—eet was too 'ard."

Pusie not only fancied himself a great hockey player but also an extraordinary fighter. Between seasons he decided to put his pugilistic talents to use and signed for a bout at Halifax with Tiger Warrington, a light heavyweight. "Pusie was knocked out in 24 seconds of the first round," said Muzz Patrick, vice president of the Rangers and onetime amateur heavyweight champion of Canada. "But he wasn't the least upset."

When a heckler needled Pusie about the knockout, he blandly replied: "Sure t'ing I got beat—but I 'ave de bes' 'til den."

Pusie's lifelong ambition to play in Montreal finally was realized in 1935 when the Canadiens purchased him from Boston. He scored two assists but was remembered for other things. "The players weren't fond of him," said Elmer Ferguson, columnist of the *Montreal Star*. "He had a bad habit of never taking a bath. He was a crazy sonofagun, and not good enough for the NHL."

Jean Baptiste wound up with St. Louis in the American Association, as garrulous as ever. At times he defied everyone on the ice—including his own teammates—and then challenged any or all of the fans to battle. When the club was winning, he'd grow a beard and often comb his hair in the midst of a game or pause to chat with the fans.

Once, in an important game, Pusie found himself stranded on the blue line, the lone defenseman, confronted by a four-man rush. He looked pleadingly at the crowd, gazed at the onrushing skaters and executed a play which, perhaps, was never seen in hockey, before or since. "He dropped his stick," said Jack Riley, manager of the Pittsburgh Penguins, "lifted his hands in surrender and fell to his knees." Then, the opponents stickhandled past the ostrich-like Pusie and scored easily.

After the Canadiens dropped him, it became apparent, even to optimistic Jean Baptiste, that he was a failure. His comedy became overly conscious, strained and sad.

"He was at his best," said Roche, "in the early days when his stuff was spontaneous. He finally carried things too far and got into trouble tangling with the fans and the police."

Pusie retired in 1942 and died of a heart attack in Montreal on April 23, 1946. He was 43.

"You really had to be in the rink to believe what he did," said Boucher. "His split-second timing and crazy face movements were as good as a vaudevillian. But in the end, you'd have to say he was a tragic guy. Too bad. If he was half as good on the ice as he was funny, he'd be in the Hall of Fame.

The Gambling Scandal

THREE PLAYERS have been banished from the National Hockey League for life, one for gross assault of a referee and two for consorting with gamblers.

Billy Couture, whose name was pruned to Coutu and pronounced Coo-chee, was the first to be expelled. He was a crude, tough defenseman who came out of Sault Ste. Marie, Ontario, to play for Montreal Canadiens, Hamilton Tigers and Boston Bruins.

Coutu was 34, practically finished, when he formed part of an abrasive Boston defense against Ottawa Senators in the Stanley Cup final of 1926–27. His roistering contemporaries on the Boston blueline were Sprague Cleghorn, Lionel Hitchman and Eddie Shore.

The last game of the series, which Ottawa won, was played in Ottawa on April 13, 1927. Coutu's expulsion from the sport followed his vigorous belting of Gerry LaFlamme, an unfortunate referee. Frank Calder, the frugal league president, also fined Coutu a modest $100 for his part in the dispute. Four others—Hooley Smith and George (Buck) Boucher of Ottawa, Hitchman and Jim Herberts of Boston—were fined for attempting to remove heads from bodies, hatchet style.

Coutu, still alive at 76 in Sault Ste. Marie, recalls the incident with no particular rancor. He spends his nights, perhaps to atone for past sins, in a policeman's uniform. "I'm a constable," he says, "on the night shift at the F. J. Davey Home for the Aged."

Coutu insists he was only following instructions the night he was permanently excused from the NHL. "Art Ross," he says, "started the whole thing." Ross was the Boston manager in 1927 and not unknown for defiance of authority. Coutu claims he didn't blame Ross at the time because he didn't want to hurt Ross while he lived. "He's dead now, bless his soul," Coutu says. "So I guess I can talk. Tell it how it was, like they say.

"Anyway, we're getting a raw deal in Ottawa this night, so Art called us together. 'Start a commotion,' he told us, 'and make sure the referee is in the middle.'

"Well, we had one dandy fight. Players on both teams were in on it. I was nearest the referee, so I let him have it. LaFlamme was his name. He's dead now, too, poor fellow."

Remorse was not one of Coutu's emotions when he played, on the testimony of King Clancy, who opposed him with Ottawa in the 1926–27 play-offs. "Coutu'd wield his stick like a razor," Clancy maintains. "He'd just as soon cut your heart out with it."

It is probable that Coutu would have been allowed back in the NHL if he had not been at the tag end of his career. His beating of LaFlamme, brutal as it was, was no worse than much of the gang-land morality that mottled hockey 40 years ago. There has been gossip, from time to time, about gambling on games by players in the NHL, at least since the spring of 1928.

Montreal Canadiens were eliminated in the first round of the Stanley Cup play-offs that year, beaten three goals to two by Montreal Maroons in a two-game, total-goals-to-count series. The first game was tied 2–2; Maroons won the second 1–0.

Howie Morenz, a fierce competitor, failed to score for Canadiens and was anonymously abused afterward. He received phone calls accusing him of throwing the series. No one, perhaps not even Morenz, took the calls seriously.

In 1946, in Toronto, Babe Pratt was suspended for 16 days for admitting he bet on games involving the Maple Leafs. Mervyn (Red) Dutton, then the NHL president, reinstated Pratt after failing to discover evidence Pratt bet against the Leafs. The Establishment seemed to agree that Pratt's indiscretion was merely a boyish caper and, 20 years later, elected him to the Hall of Fame.

Billy Taylor and Don Gallinger were banished to the Hall of Infamy in 1948 for deeds partially similar to Pratt's. They were expelled for life on March 9, 1948, and remain outcasts to this moment. The terse explanation of Clarence Campbell, in office as NHL president less than two years, was "life suspensions for conduct detrimental to hockey and for associating with a known gambler."

Gallinger was 22 at the time, a center for the Boston Bruins, considered one of the postwar hubs of the team. Taylor was 29, a slick center grown shopworn after several seasons with Toronto, Detroit, Boston and New York. They were roommates when Taylor played for the Bruins.

Campbell has always kept the charges against both men confidential, a situation that Taylor prefers. Gallinger, more loquacious, has tried to have his banishment lifted. Six years ago, in an absorbing, controversial series of articles, Gallinger told his story to Scott Young of the *Toronto Globe and Mail*. "I don't deny it," Gallinger told Young. "I did bet against the Bruins in a few games."

Originally Gallinger did deny his implication when the gambling story broke in February 1948. He denied it to Art Ross, the Boston manager, and to Campbell when the president interviewed players on every NHL team. About 18 months later, on October 9, 1949, Gallinger confessed to Campbell in an emotional meeting in the Royal York Hotel in Toronto. He told Campbell substantially the same thing he revealed to Scott Young 14 years afterward.

The NHL, through complicity with the Detroit police department, obtained evidence on the gambling activities by illegal wiretapping. The wiretap provided records of phone calls made by Gallinger and Taylor to James Tamer, a Detroit gambler and paroled bank robber.

"My bets varied from $250 to $1,000 a game," Gallinger admitted. "My instructions from the guy," presumably meaning Tamer, "were to bet on what I knew of the team's attitude and our injuries." He began to bet, Gallinger said, in December 1947, three months before the incident became scandal. He insisted only eight or nine games were involved. "There was a game I wagered on when we were going into Chicago to play the Black Hawks. We had some injuries, so I bet $1,000 we would lose. So we went out and won 4–2 and I blew the bet."

Clarence Campbell had one word for such wagers. "Despicable!" the commissioner said.

Gallinger said he asked Campbell to keep his 1949 confession confidential in deference to his father, who couldn't believe his son was involved in the cynical business of betting against his own team. Campbell complied with the request.

After his father died, in 1951, Gallinger made requests for reinstatement. Character testimonials on his behalf were made to the NHL governors in 1955 by clergymen, Canadian senators, and by

Bobby Bauer, a distinguished Bruin who had played in Boston with Gallinger. One governor, not identified by Campbell, said after Gallinger's appeal in 1955: "Although as a Christian I forgive him for his dereliction, and as a man I admire him for his attempt to rehabilitate himself, as a person entrusted with a portion of the stewardship of major-league hockey I cannot possibly bring myself to believe that he should be reinstated."

Senator W. D. Euler of Kitchener, Ontario, responded as one of Gallinger's rehabilitation sponsors. "The NHL's justice," he said, "is not tempered with mercy."

Gallinger—described as "big, talkative, obsessed and courageous" by Scott Young—came to believe Campbell was responsible for his lifetime blackball. "He made it a personal thing against me," Gallinger said.

Gallinger's reason for seeking reinstatement as late as 1963 was to provide some respectability for the summer hockey school he hoped to run at his resort in the Muskoka holiday area of Ontario. Young's stance was clearly on Gallinger's side; even some murderers, he argued, get parole from their lifetime sentences.

Conn Smythe brought Taylor to the big league after Taylor's prodigal feats as a junior with the Oshawa Generals 30 years ago. He was the outspoken leader of the Leafs when Gallinger strayed in Boston.

Smythe's attitude remains inflexible, although he has been out of hockey for 10 years. He turns thumbs down in a flamboyant gesture whenever Gallinger's name is mentioned. "Keep him where he is!"

Young wrote hockey with flair and understanding, but his editorial campaign on Gallinger's behalf was not particularly appreciated by NHL authorities. He said Gallinger's obsession with clearing his name could be enough to put him in a mental institution. "The only thing that will put Gallinger in a mental institution," Campbell retorted, "is Young dragging out this story again."

The trumpet of publicity did not force an easing of the penalty, but it did prompt a blowing of Campbell's celebrated cool. "If Scott Young was on fire," the president said, "I wouldn't spit on him!"

Finally, late in the summer of 1970 the NHL governors relented and voted to reinstate both Taylor and Gallinger. Taylor immediately returned to hockey by getting a coaching job with an amateur team in Ontario.

The Longest Game

IN 1935–36 the National Hockey League was still divided into two sections, a Canadian Division including the Montreal Maroons, Toronto Maple Leafs, New York Americans and Montreal Canadiens, and an American Division including the Detroit Red Wings, Boston Bruins, Chicago Black Hawks and New York Rangers. The Maroons finished first in the Canadian Division and the Red Wings were the American Division champions. According to the system of the day, the two first-place teams would meet in the opening round of the Stanley Cup play-offs.

Judging by their respective records, which were almost identical, the Maroons and Red Wings would be in for a difficult series with bookmakers at a loss as to whom to list as the favorites. The opening game of the series at the Montreal Forum on March 24, 1936, proved how evenly matched they were.

Led by Hooley Smith, Baldy Northcott and Jimmy Ward, the Maroons presented one of the most formidable attacks in the league. Detroit, however, was strong up front, too. The Red Wings' first line of Marty Barry, Herbie Lewis and Larry Aurie had an impressive season with Barry winning the scoring championship in the American Division.

Despite the notable scorers on both teams three periods of play elapsed without either club scoring a goal. This meant sudden-death overtime; the first team to score winning the game. Although the Forum crowd was excited about the prospect of sudden death there was some reason to suspect this might be an exceptionally long night. For one thing the teams were getting excellent goaltending from Normie Smith in the Red Wing cage and Lorne Chabot of the Maroons. For another, there was precedent for a marathon match. On April 4, 1932, the Toronto Maple Leafs and Boston Bruins played past 1 A.M. in what had been the longest NHL game on record.

By the time the Maroons and Red Wings had played through the second overtime without a goal the crowd began to get restless. The players, of course, were laboring on badly chopped ice that didn't have the benefit of modern resurfacing machines in vogue today. Nevertheless, they plodded on past midnight with no end in sight.

When the sixth period began a cascade of cheers went up from the previously numbed crowd. Perhaps they hoped to inspire the Maroons to a spirited rush and a score but this didn't happen. Neither team scored and the teams moved into the seventh period as a handful of fans streamed to the exits.

Despite the hour, the majority of spectators remained in their seats. By now the monumental contest became an obsession with both players and fans and everyone seemed determined to see it through to a conclusion, no matter what happened. Nothing very much happened in the seventh period but the eighth—or fifth sudden death—period loomed as the decisive one.

Near the end of the period Marty Barry, the Red Wings' accomplished center, was approaching collapse. With what energy he had at his command, Barry sent a pass to Herbie Lewis that catapulted his wing into the clear for a play on goal. He moved into striking distance and released a hard shot that obviously beat goalie Lorne Chabot. As Lewis prepared to raise his stick in the traditional victory salute he heard the puck clang off the goal post. It rebounded harmlessly to the corner where Hooley Smith retrieved it and began a counterattack with as much danger as Lewis' play.

Smith was accompanied on his rush by Baldy Northcott. There was a choice, either Smith could make the play himself, using Northcott as a decoy, or he could try the pass. At first, Smith cut sharply toward the net, giving the impression he would go it alone. But, at this precise moment, he skimmed the puck to Northcott who shot hard at the Red Wing net. However, Normie Smith anticipated the play, caught the puck on his pad and steered it to teammate Doug Young who reversed the field.

Now, it appeared that each team was bent on wild kamikaze attacks in the hopes of bringing the game to a sudden end. Young raced along the boards until he reached Maroon territory. Then, he fired wildly but the puck suddenly hit Maroon defenseman Lionel Conacher's skate and changed direction, sliding straight for an empty side of the net. It appeared to be equidistant between Young and goalie Chabot. The Red Wing skater lunged for it but before he could get his stick on the rubber Chabot smothered it with his glove. Shortly thereafter the period ended and the teams had completed eight scoreless periods of play.

Four minutes and 46 seconds after the ninth period began, the teams had broken the longest-game record set by Toronto and Boston and, still, there was no end in sight. It was past 2 A.M. and many of the spectators were fighting to keep their eyes open, not wanting to miss the decisive goal if it ever was to be scored.

By this time the veterans of both teams were fatigued beyond recovery. It was essential to employ the players with the most stamina and, naturally, those with even a smidgen of energy remaining were the inexperienced younger skaters. One of them was Modere (Mud) Bruneteau, a native of St. Boniface, Manitoba, who had just one season ago played for the Wings' minor league team, the Detroit Olympics. He was the youngest man in the longest game, equipped, Jack Adams believed, with the strongest legs. Adams was the Detroit coach and he remembered, before he died last year: "The game settled into an endurance test, hour after hour. One o'clock came, and then 2 A.M., and by now the ice was a chipped, brutal mess. At 2:25 I looked along our bench for the strongest legs and I scrambled the lines to send out Syd Howe, Hec Kilrea and Bruneteau."

As a rookie on a loaded first-place club, Bruneteau saw very little action during the season and scored only two goals while achieving no assists for a grand total of two points. But he was young and at the 12-minute mark of the ninth period, Mud Bruneteau was in a lot better shape than most of his teammates or opponents.

Adams' instructions were typically explicit. "Boys, let's get some sleep. It's now or never!"

Bruneteau surrounded the puck in the Detroit zone and passed it to Kilrea. They challenged the Montreal defense, Kilrea faking a return pass, then sliding it across the blueline. Bruneteau cut behind the defense and retrieved the puck. "Thank God," he says, "Chabot fell down as I drove it in the net. It was the funniest thing. The puck just stuck there in the twine and didn't fall on the ice."

There was a dispute when the goal judge neglected to flash his red light, but Referee Nels Stewart arbitrated. "You bloody right it's a goal!" Stewart announced, and put up his hand as a signal. After 116 minutes and 30 seconds of overtime the Red Wings had defeated the Maroons, 1–0.

There was a wild, capering anticlimax. Bruneteau's sweater was removed, not delicately, by his relieved associates. One fan thrust a $20 bill on Bruneteau as he left the ice. Other exuberants reached for their wallets. "There I was, my stick under one arm and my gloves under another, and," laughing, "I grabbed money in every direction!"

When he reached the Detroit dressing room, Bruneteau tossed a bundle of bills on a rubbing table. "Count it," he told Honey Walker, the trainer, "and split it for the gang." The windfall was gratifying for professionals in a depression year: $22 for each member of the Wings, including Adams, Walker and the stickboy.

Mud Bruneteau's shot went into the net at 16:30 of the sixth overtime or 2:25 A.M. Eastern Standard Time. Normie Smith, who was playing in his first Stanley Cup game was limp when it was over. He had stopped 90 shots in all. "We were all pretty much all in," Smith recalled years later, "but very happy."

Meanwhile, Bruneteau sat on his bed in Montreal's genteel Windsor Hotel near 5 A.M. on March 25, 1936, still unwinding from a Stanley Cup playoff that he had won for Detroit Red Wings less than three hours before. He was about to undress after a beer celebration when there was a knock on the door. He sat very still, not caring to be disturbed. The knocker persisted. Finally Bruneteau let his visitor in, somewhat startled to recognize the Montreal goalkeeper he had beaten to end the weary marathon. Lorne Chabot, dark eyes staring under a thicket of black brows, had come to call.

"Sorry to bother you, kid," Chabot said, "but you forgot something when you left the rink." Then, handing Bruneteau a puck, "Maybe you'd like to have this souvenir of the goal you scored."

Bruneteau mused on the long-gone moment last summer, 53 now, operator of a bar in Omaha, Nebraska. Chabot has been dead for several years. "Can you imagine that such a great man as him would do such a thing for a rookie? I remember him standing there in the door, big, handsome guy with a kind of fat-looking face. I felt, I guess, funny. He came in and we sat on the bed, and talked for a long time."

Bruneteau was a journeyman, mutely remote from stardom until one goal left him with reverberating notoriety. Afterward, apart from 35 goals scored in the wartime season of 1943–44, he was undistinguished.

"The publicity has never ended," he says, in the cool of his Omaha oasis. "It could've happened to a lot of guys who were better players. I was just another guy named Joe."

Adams' gratification paused short of hoping prolonged games would become habitual. "Rotten ice produced rotten hockey that was torture for the players and boring for the fans. I knew the NHL had to do something."

Adams discovered what to do in the spring of 1938, when the Red Wings and Montreal Canadiens toured Europe. "I noticed one night at an ice show that the attendants swept the surface with sheepskin brushes and then flooded it before the next show." He recommended ice-flooding between periods to the NHL governors, and in 1940–41 resurfacing became mandatory. "That legislation speeded up play, because it meant the players didn't have to skate through slush late in the game. It convinced me that there'll never be any approach to Bruneteau's overtime record. There are too many shots and too much wide-open play to permit long stretches with no goals."

The impetus gained from the Red Wings' marathon opening-game win was enough to lift the Red Wings to a three-straight play-off victory over the Maroons and a four-game win over the Toronto Maple Leafs for the Stanley Cup. Smith, the alter hero of the marathon match, lost both trophies he had hoped to obtain as souvenirs.

His goalie stick was autographed by every member of the Red Wings but somehow wound up in the hands of a Judge John Scallen. "I also was supposed to get half the puck that was in play at the finish of the game," said Smith, "but I don't know what became of that."

Nor did he get his name inscribed in the record book that lists the longest game. That honor was bestowed on Modere (Mud) Bruneteau, the rookie who had scored only two goals all season.

The Octopus Pitcher

VISITORS TO DETROIT during the Stanley Cup play-offs are gratified to witness the rare pitching form of Pete, the Octopus Pitcher.

Mankind is grimly returning to the ape state, but the determined march is sometimes relieved by rare cashews like Pete who are unafraid to act, as the charming colloquialism goes, a little milky in the filbert. Pete's surname is Cusimano—the swarthy, stocky scion of an old Sicilian family, in the coffee-selling game in Detroit. His peculiar avocation is pitching octopi into hockey rinks.

Cusimano's quaint expression of affection for the Red Wings was revealed in 1952, during Detroit's all-conquering dominance. They swept the semifinal series in four games, the minimum number, and were subduing Montreal's Canadiens three games to none in the final when the Cusimano family struck for the first time.

"My dad was in the fish and poultry business," Pete tells interviewers. "My brother Jerry and me helped him and often, after work, we'd go to the Red Wing games." They fervently hoped that Detroit would win the Cup in 1952 in eight consecutive games, a tyrannical sweep of Lord Stanley's old birdbath. Before the eighth game, Jerry Cusimano suggested: "Why don't we throw an octopus on the ice for good luck? It's got eight legs, and that might be a good omen for eight straight wins."

It was done, on April 15, 1952. Jerry Cusimano wound up and flung the eight-armed seafood in the Detroit Olympia. The octopus omen may or may not have been significant, but the odor was. "You

302

ever smelt a half-boiled octopus?" Pete Cusimano once demanded of a startled reporter. "It ain't exactly Chanel No. 5, y'know."

It ain't exactly what Frank Udvari, the referee, wanted for company that night, either. Cusimano relishes the recollection: "You should have seen how Udvari jumped when he saw our first octopus!"

The Wings responded to the Cusimanos' grand gesture by leaping all over the Canadiens. They won 3–0, their eighth triumph in eight play-off contests in 1952.

Since then, whenever the Wings have a play-off crisis, Pete Cusimano stays loose with an octopus coiling and squirming in the bullpen. He has thrown his high, hard, spitting-horrible pitch at least once in every Detroit series in the last 15 play-offs. The octopi pitched by Pete are three-pound missiles, partially boiled to turn them a deep crimson, very sticky. And, as he gaily testifies, "they don't exactly come up smelling like cherry custard." His brother Jerry is no longer active in the Cusimano hockey hobby; he was killed several years ago in a car crash.

Enchanted reporters have asked Peter, "So what kind of a motion do you use to toss an octopus? Overhand? Three-quarters sidearm? Like a shot putter, or what?"

Cusimano stands up to demonstrate. Peering in toward the plate, looking for the catcher's signal, scowling, he does indeed resemble Don Drysdale of the Los Angeles Dodgers. "You grip the thing in the palm of your hand," he explains. "You pick out your target. Then you rear back and heave it like you would a hand grenade. You got to keep your elbow stiff to get the best distance."

"You ever pick out any special targets?" he was once asked.

"Not always." He preened as a man several months gone with a swelling sense of destiny. "I look on the whole ice surface as my strike zone. But one time . . ."

"Yes?"

"One time I got hot at Ted Kennedy of Toronto. He'd been having a big series against the Wings. Scoring a lot of goals and scragging a lot of our guys. So during a beef, when they're all standing around arguing, I decide to let him have it." Pause. "Only I hit another Toronto player."

"Yeah?"

"Yeah. Vic Lynn was standing right beside Kennedy and HE got the octopus. Splat in the kisser."

Historians claim it riled Lynn's considerable temper. He was a redneck from Saskatoon who took offense at the drop of a dirty look.

Cusimano's boyish quirk has made him an odd celebrity among Detroit's hockey crowds. One night he was sitting near a priest and his friend.

"Psst, Father," the friend whispered. "You're sitting close to the celebrated octopus pitcher."

"Oh, no!" the clergyman said, amazed.

During the game Cusimano let fly, directing the octopus at Referee Bill Friday. Missed, but not by much.

"I'd have hit him, Father," Cusimano said, "if you'd have blessed the octopus."

"No," the priest said. "Not necessarily."

The Tough Guys

WHEN the late Edouard (Newsy) Lalonde was 82 he navigated about Montreal with a cane, hobbled by age and reduced to, of all things, bowling. It was difficult to remember that in his time, 50 years earlier, Ladonde could buckle a swash with any ruffian alive.

Hockey was essentially a mug's racket in the Neanderthal years before 1930, populated with logging-camp roughnecks who could drink an opponent's blood at body temperature, or near there. It was natural, therefore, for Lalonde to pick seven ogres from his era when he selected 11 for his "all-time, meanest, toughest team."

He preened a little when he made the selections for Andy O'Brien of *Weekend Magazine*. "Of course, for these splendid chaps, there can only be one coach." Smiling blandly, "Me."

Lalonde's career spanned 21 seasons, from 1906 to 1925, divided among seven teams—Cornwall, Ontario; Toronto; Renfrew, Ontario; Montreal Canadiens; Vancouver Millionaires; Saskatoon Sheiks; and New York Americans. He spilled enough corpuscles to gratify any blood bank on the continent.

Lalonde's verray *parfit gentil* knights are:

GOAL:
Paddy Moran—Quebec Bulldogs, 1902–17.
DEFENSE:
Joe Hall—Quebec, Montreal Canadiens, 1904–19.
Sprague Cleghorn—Montreal, Boston Bruins, 1911–26.
Eddie Shore—Edmonton Eskimos, Boston, 1926–40.
Lou Fontinato—New York Rangers, Montreal, 1955–63.

FORWARDS:
Leo Labine—Boston, Detroit Red Wings, 1951–62.
Bill Ezinicki—Toronto Maple Leafs, Boston, 1944–45, 1951–52.
Ted Lindsay—Detroit, Chicago Blackhawks, 1944–45, 1964–65.
Cully Wilson—Toronto, Seattle Metropolitans, Calgary Tigers, 1913–26.
Bill Cook—Saskatoon Sheiks, New York, 1922–38.
Ken Randall—Toronto, New York Americans, 1925–35.

Lalonde appraised Moran, who died in 1966 at 89: "Paddy was in a class by himself at chopping at the toes of opposing forwards who dared get near him. If he didn't disturb you that way, he'd rile you by spitting tobacco juice in your eye."

Newsy had special personal reasons for picking Joe Hall among his rearguard rowdies. One night Hall, viciously swinging his stick, practically severed Lalonde's windpipe. In a subsequent skirmish, Lalonde made the retaliatory gesture of smashing Hall's collarbone.

Sprague Cleghorn, who was 66 when he died in 1956, made the all-time meanies on merit. He admitted to disabling three players one night in Ottawa and was arrested in 1921 in Toronto for attempting to detach Lalonde's comely skull from the rest of him. "I pleaded before the judge on behalf of Sprague," Lalonde remembered, "and he got off with a $200 fine." Lalonde's tolerant turning of the other cheek seemed an uncommon reaction to a Hessian who attempted to make him the main event at a funeral.

Cleghorn, undeterred, stick-whipped Lionel Hitchman of Ottawa Senators so severely in 1923 that his own manager, Leo Dandurand of Montreal Canadiens, fined him $200. "All told," Cleghorn said, not long before he died, "I figure I was in 50 stretcher-case fights."

Eddie Shore qualifies for Lalonde's Loogans on constant rambunctious merit, notably the night in Boston when he crosschecked Ace Bailey of Toronto with sufficient wickedness to end Bailey's career.

Fontinato's mayhem was relatively modern, ended six years ago after he broke his neck in Montreal. "Leapin' Lou wins his recognition honestly enough," Lalonde said. "The 202 minutes he served in penalties in 1955–56 was a record until Howie Young took 273 for Detroit in 1962–63."

Young, later employed by Chicago, showed credentials coarse

enough to make all-time tough, but his muscular mischief has not been consistent. He became more loveable after he abandoned inflammatory beverages.

Lalonde stationed Bill Ezinicki at center on his first larruping line, between Leo Labine and Robert Theodore Blake Lindsay. Labine qualified because his tendency toward needling often provoked ill-tempered opponents into penalties.

Together and apart, Lindsay and Ezinicki made a certain amount of soiled NHL history. Lalonde applauds their brawl in 1951 as "a positive gem." Lindsay, then a Detroit left wing allied with Sid Abel and Gordie Howe, shoved Ezinicki, who had been traded from Toronto to Boston. Ezinicki swiped at Lindsay's forehead with his stick. Lindsay clubbed Ezinicki on the head, opening a gash that required 11 stitches to close. Ezinicki, berserk, ran into a right-hand punch delivered by Lindsay and fell backward on his head. He lost one tooth and needed 19 stitches to shut the assorted wounds on his head. Lindsay was fined $300 by NHL President Clarence Campbell and suspended for three games.

"Cheap at double the price," Lindsay muttered.

"There's only been one other case," Lalonde insisted, "where as much damage has been done by one man to another as Lindsay did to Ezinicki. That was when Dick Irvin assaulted Cully Wilson in Western Canada." Wilson, playing for Calgary Tigers in 1925, playfully crosschecked Irvin's teeth into his tongue. Irvin, a Regina center who later coached in Toronto, Montreal and Chicago, didn't like it much. Wilson was assessed a five-minute major penalty, but Irvin considered the rebuke too mild. He later skated by the penalty box and, flailing his stick as a bludgeon, knocked Wilson cold. "Cully," Lalonde claims, "needed enough stitches in him to weave an Indian blanket."

The retribution may have been deserved, on behalf of others whom Wilson had tormented. In 1919, he hit the smooth, clean Mickey Mackay of Vancouver Millionaires with enough viciousness to shatter Mackay's jaw. He missed all of the next season while his mandible healed.

Wilson's slaughterhouse style qualifies him to play center on Lalonde's second line, between Bill Cook and Ken Randall. Cook, still rawboned at 73, is considered the heavyweight champion among NHL right wings. Randall, a boisterous member of the Americans, was a frequent adversary of rival werewolves.

Randall was particularly fond of quarreling with Nels Stewart, a surly, gifted redneck who played for Montreal Maroons 35 years ago. One night in New York, furious at Randall's jabbing, Stewart refused to yield his position to a substitute.

"Beat it back to the bench, you!" Stewart said. "I want to give it to that sonofabitch Randall!"

Newsy Lalonde recognized the give-it-to-'em instincts of contemporary choirboys like John Ferguson of Montreal Canadiens and the three Plager brothers of St. Louis Blues. "Those boys have good, dirty habits," Lalonde said, sighing. "But it just costs too much in league fines to be a meanie today."

The Worst Goalie

BECAUSE OF THE VERY NATURE of the job—cumbersome padding, space limitations around the net and incessant pounding from attackers—goaltending is both a traumatic and yet, ironically, hilarious profession. Over the years some of the NHL's most accomplished goaltenders have fallen victim of frazzled nerves. Often, it happened when they were heavily bombarded while receiving light protection from inferior defenses. Other times, though, goaltenders on supremely capable teams suffered nervous attacks and were compelled to quit.

Bill Durnan, one of the most highly regarded goalies, walked out on a strong Montreal Canadiens club in the late forties for just that reason. Frankie (Mister Zero) Brimsek went to pieces after being traded from the Boston Bruins to the Chicago Black Hawks in the same era. A few years later Terry Sawchuk, regarded by some experts as the greatest goaltender in NHL annals, left the Bruins in the lurch by departing from the team in midseason. More recently, Roger Crozier, considerably younger than the others, stopped playing for the Detroit Red Wings, because of excessive nervous tension. After a respite, Crozier returned to the line-up.

Some have wanted to quit but for various reasons remained and suffered through the agony. Glenn Hall who starred for years with the Detroit Red Wings, Chicago Black Hawks and St. Louis Blues, was so affected by the excitement he admittedly vomited prior to many games he played. "The game," Hall once told writer Roger Kahn, "is 60 minutes of hell."

Hall's colleague, Ed Giacomin of the New York Rangers, allowed that the 118-mile-an-hour slap shots of Bobby Hull left him mesmerized. Instead of chancing a breakdown of his crack goalie, Ranger general manager Emile Francis benched Giacomin when the Black Hawks played for several games in the 1967–68 season and inserted spare goalie, Don Simmons, in what developed as a reasonably effective method of sparing Giacomin's nerves.

These examples represent the extreme end of the pole. At the other corner are the goaltenders who practically immunized themselves to the hullabaloo that surrounds their job. Walter (Turk) Broda, who played for the Toronto Maple Leafs in the late thirties and forties, was a gregarious type, less inclined to worry than most of his counterparts. Likewise, Lorne (Gump) Worsley, the rotund goalie for the New York Rangers and Montreal Canadiens, had a similar cool that helped him surmount the tensions of the season until 1968–69 when his nerves became frayed because of jet plane travel.

But, in all hockey history, no goalie ever portrayed the character of the imperturbable ice sphinx better than Steve Buzinski. And nobody ever did it under more difficult circumstances. Buzinski was signed by the New York Rangers shortly after the United States had entered World War II and the well of hockey players had nearly run dry. His attitude was unusual to say the least and unrealistic to say the most. But he was a very special character and the Hall of Famers who were confronted with him found him a great source of amusement.

Unfortunately, Buzinski took himself seriously. For years after he departed the league—almost as quickly as he entered—he steadfastly denied the stories told about him but Ranger officials insisted they happened, starting just prior to the 1942–43 season.

Lester Patrick, New York Rangers manager, sat numb behind his Madison Square Garden desk. It was October 1942, training camp was just a week away and Patrick, for the first time in his lengthy career, did not have a goalkeeper in his club.

Under ordinary circumstances this would have been an incredible state of affairs, but October 1942 was not a normal month. At least not for the National Hockey League. Canada had been involved in World War II since 1939 and most NHL stars already were in service. Of all the clubs, the Rangers were hardest hit. More than half of Patrick's 1942–43 first-place team was in uniform, including goaltender Jim Henry.

Patrick called Frank Boucher, the coach, into his office. "Frankie," he exclaimed, "what are we going to do for a goaltender?"

Boucher was no less puzzled. "Only one thing we can do, Lester," Boucher replied. "Comb every blessed town in Canada."

The message went out to Ranger scouts across the Dominion: "Find a goaltender." Three days later, Patrick received a wire from scout Al Ritchie in Saskatchewan. "HAVE YOUR MAN. WILL REPORT NEXT WEEK. HIS NAME: STEVE BUZINSKI."

When the Rangers opened training camp in Winnipeg, Manitoba, neither Patrick nor Boucher knew very much about Buzinski, the most important man on their team. They had heard that he was a grain and cereal expert with the Dominion Experimental Station and a goaltender with an amateur team known as the Swift Current, Saskatchewan, Intermediates.

Buzinski was late arriving at camp. When he finally did make it to the Winnipeg Amphitheater the Rangers already were on the ice holding a practice skate. "He startled everybody," Boucher recently recalled. "I remember seeing a wee fellow with a black helmet. He was so small all I could see was his head and shoulders over the sideboards. At first I imagined he was a lad who cleaned the ice after the workout. I couldn't help laughing to myself until he climbed the dasher—he just about made it over—and skated to the net. 'Oh, my God,' I said to myself, 'this couldn't be.' But it was. Steve Buzinski had arrived."

He was a little man, thin and with extremely bowed legs. He wore a pair of tattered goalie pads that curved around his limbs like cowboys' chaps. "When you looked at him," Boucher said, "you felt the poor fellow was shot full of holes." But the Rangers were in no position to quibble—there weren't any challengers. Buzinski was awarded the job by default.

New York opened the season on October 31, at Maple Leaf Gardens in Toronto, and were beaten 7–2. "Steve Buzinski," the Associated Press wrote, "looked flimsy on a couple of Leaf goals." Flimsy, perhaps. But he did betray an asset, a rare sense of humor.

Midway in the game Bob Davidson of Toronto caromed a shot off Buzinski's forehead during a scramble around the cage. The puck inflicted a harmless cut. But, as soon as the goalie detected a spot of blood, he swooned to the ice in a dead faint. The Rangers charged at the referee.

"Give Davidson a major penalty for high-sticking," demanded the Rangers' Ott Heller, who was standing over the prostrate Buzinski.

"Take gas," shouted Davidson, "he got hit with the puck."

"Stick," wailed Heller.

"Puck," snapped Davidson.

Suddenly, Buzinski opened his eyes, raised his head, and bellowed at the referee: "I got hit with the stick." And in the same motion, closed his eyes and resumed his reclining position on the ice.

Next stop was Detroit. This time the Rangers lost 12–5. Carl Liscombe of the Red Wings scored three goals and four assists for a new league record. This feat impressed everyone with the possible exception of Buzinski who marveled at his own goalkeeping skills. When the Wings were leading 7–1, Liscombe fired a shot from center ice. It was considerably wide of the net but Buzinski made a desperate lunge and caught it in the webbing of his mitt. Then he nonchalantly tossed it into the corner of the rink as teammate Bryan Hextall skated by. "Hex," Buzinski said, with the confidence of a 10-year man, "it's just like pickin' cherries off a tree."

Minutes later Buzinski gloved another high one. This time a Red Wing skated in front of him, a maneuver which pleased the goaltender no end because it gave him an opportunity to kibitz with his opponent. Buzinski bobbed and weaved like a welterweight, quipped with the Red Wing and, in the same motion, tossed the puck into the corner—the corner of the net.

Despite the nonsense, Patrick was not about to give up on his rookie, although he had allowed 32 goals in four games. "It isn't fair to pass judgement on Steve after such a short time," Patrick insisted. "Remember, Charlie Gardiner was murdered in his first four games. Then Charlie started to improve and developed into one of the greatest goaltenders in history."

Buzinski was inclined to agree. When a reporter inquired about the difference between big league hockey and the Swift Current Intermediates, Steve was surprised. "No difference at all," he replied. "Same as back home. Only difference I notice is that the rinks are classier and there are more people than I'm accustomed to see in one game."

But the facts indicated otherwise. On the weekend of November 16, the Rangers were beaten twice by Boston and Buzinski appeared to be turning punchy from all the rubber hurled at him.

"Steve showed a new technique," said Dan Daniel in the *New York World-Telegram*. "He adopted the falling system. Persuaded that he who drops over the disk need not have fears of it being elsewhere, Buzinski spent more time on the ice than a mackerel in cold storage."

After the ninth game, the Rangers were in last place and even Patrick was ready to concede that Buzinski was not a major leaguer. Coincidentally some of the Rangers heard that Jimmy Franks, a goalie of proven ability, was available. They threatened a mutiny unless Patrick replaced Buzinski with Franks. Patrick agreed.

"I'm not hitting Buz below the belt," explained Phil Watson after the change, "because considering his experience, or lack of it, he did a marvelous job. But his newness in NHL play was disconcerting to us."

Franks became Ranger goaltender but Patrick kept Buzinski on the payroll. "He was a refreshing prairie boy," Boucher explained, "always good for laughs. We simply listed him as a member of our public relations department."

But deep down, Patrick believed that Buzinski had talent. He was willing to wait and so was Steve. "He just sat around and played cards and got paid," said Alfie Pike. "No matter what we said to Lester, he wouldn't get rid of Buzinski."

One afternoon the Rangers' farm team, the New York Rovers, asked Patrick to lend them a few players to round out a scrimmage. Pike agreed to go and Patrick suggested to Buzinski that he could use some practice. "Go along with Alfie," Patrick said. Patrick's was a quiet command that never tolerated rebuff.

Buzinski, who was enjoying his public relations job, was surprised at the request. "He looked up at Lester," Pike recalled, "and said, 'Gee, I'd like to help you out, Mr. Patrick, but I've got a lot of letters to write.'"

On the following day Buzinski was on a train to Swift Current. He had a one-way ticket.

"We were sorry to see him go," said Boucher, "kind of missed the little guy. Granted he was one of the worst goalies in NHL history, but also one of the funniest."

PART FIVE

Controversies

The Governors

HOCKEY has always been a sport of the rowdy and the rough-neck, its business at the National League level often conducted with a brass-knuckles gentility.

Perhaps the willful men who own the game today are more couth than their predecessors. They are a trifle less inclined to the vulgar, a word the oldtimers used to mistake for color.

The league customarily is not appalled by the morals of its governors, otherwise known as team owners or presidents.

Witness the case of the late James Norris, Jr., the former partner of Arthur Wirtz in operating the Chicago Black Hawks. Norris was also chief tentacle of Octopus, Inc., colloquial title of the International Boxing Club. As such, he was investigated by the Senate Interstate and Foreign Commerce Committee.

The senators were fascinated by names in their Norris file such as Golfbag Sam Hunt (a Capone alumnus), and Sh'h (the sobriquet of a racetrack fink), and, above all, the late Frankie Carbo, a well-dressed figure of mystery who was twice tried for murder (one conviction, one hung jury).

The clubby group that votes people into the Hockey Hall of Fame coolly ignored the Norris dossier and ultimately installed Big Jim in the museum of old muscle on Toronto's lakefront.

The clubby group that votes in the Hall of Fame elections is, in fact, a partisan extension of the NHL establishment, composed of 10 or 12 old retainers and writers and broadcasters beholden to the NHL.

Still, the Establishment is disturbed by the tarnishing of the NHL's image by two governors found guilty of theft and fraud in the early 1970s.

Harold Ballard, the hearty 76-percent owner of the Toronto Maple Leafs, was sentenced to three years in prison in Ontario in October, 1972, on charges of fraud and theft involving roughly $205,000. Ballard was eligible for parole within a year and received his first weekend pass from a minimum security jail at Millhaven, Ontario, six months after his term began.

Thomas Kane Scallen, who controlled 70 percent of Vancouver Canucks through the Medical Investment Corporation in Minneapolis, was sentenced to four years in the penitentiary on charges of stealing $3,000,000 from Northwest Sports Enterprises, the corporate title of the Canucks.

Scallen was released on $25,000 bail in the spring of 1973 pending an appeal, which was scheduled in the fall of that year.

Ballard and the late Stafford Smythe, allied with a Toronto publisher named John Bassett, purchased 60 percent of the Maple Leaf Gardens in 1961. They purchased the old Cashbox on Toronto's Carlton Street from Smythe's father, Conn Smythe, the prickly founder of the franchise.

Bassett made the partnership a trio, but the real alliance was between Smythe and Ballard.

"We're like Mike and Ike," Ballard used to say. "You could write a story about us and call it the 'Gold Dust Twins.'"

Events from 1969 to 1973 turned the Gold Dust to cheap tin. In July, 1969, Smythe and Ballard were charged with income tax evasion. The case dragged through the courts until finally, in the fall of 1971, Smythe was ordered to stand trial.

They were also arrested on June 18, 1971, and charged with fraud and theft involving $478,000 from the Gardens. Evidence at Ballard's trial in the summer of 1972 established that much of the money was used to build a mansion in the exotic Toronto borough of Etobicoke for Smythe and to renovate Ballard's Elizabethan-style home in the same borough.

When the income-tax scandal broke in 1969, Smythe and Ballard were detached from their respective portfolios as president and vice-president of the Gardens. The deciding vote in their ouster was cast by their old buddy Bassett, who was then chairman of the board.

They returned to power in December, 1970, after Bassett discovered he could not purchase enough stock to outvote the Ballard-Smythe bloc. On September 1, 1971, Smythe and Ballard achieved 76 percent control of the Gardens by buying Bassett's 196,200 shares for $5,403,450.

Six weeks later, suddenly, Smythe died from complications following emergency surgery to repair a bleeding ulcer. Ballard was not inclined to believe the reason given on the death certificate.

"Staff just drank himself to death," Ballard would say. "I'll bet his liver was filled up like a sponge."

Smythe's death, at 50, removed him from the jurisdiction of the courts. He probably had the worst public relations of any prominent citizen in Canada, and Ballard's friends are inclined to believe that antipathy toward Smythe was carried over in the Crown's case against Pal Hal.

NHL rules apparently provide that no person with a prison record can be a league governor. But, through his incarceration, Ballard remained the governor representing the Maple Leafs, as it were, in absentia. His surrogate was the older of his two sons, William Owen, a budding lawyer trusted with Ballard's power of attorney.

Ballard, after Staff Smythe died, rarely mentioned his deceased partner by name. "All my troubles," he said, "were caused by The Other Guy."

He laughed when a Toronto sportswriter told him, "Okay, we'll forget Gold Dust Twins as the title of a book and call your story 'Fat Harold and the Other Guy.' "

There was a sick sort of laughter in the joke prevalent in the Canadian jockstrap set as 1972 wound down. The ideal Christmas gift for a man who has everything, macabre wits were saying, was a set of license plates made by Harold Ballard.

On April 12, 1973, Tom Scallen was sentenced to four years after Mr. Justice Harry McKay told him he had violated the trust placed in him by the people of British Columbia.

Justice McKay said that deterrence to others was the main factor in the sentence. The public, he said, must be protected from those who would profit at its expense by acting in defiance of the laws of the country.

The judge imposed concurrent four-year terms for each of the offenses of which Scallen was convicted. These were theft of $3,000,000 from the Canucks and making a false prospectus in connection with a public issue of shares and debentures in the club. Scallen's conviction followed 26 hours of deliberation by a jury.

Mr. Justice McKay said the evidence and the jury's verdict established that Scallen acted deliberately and fraudulently.

He said Scallen used his position of trust in a public company to induce the general public to purchase the shares and had invited the public to join in "the exciting project of bringing NHL hockey to Vancouver."

The jury found, the judge said, that rather than intending to use the public's money in the manner represented, for the benefit of Northwest Sports, Scallen had already decided to divert $3,000,000 to pay a debt of Medicor's in the United States.

"In fairness I must say it was never suggested in evidence that you intended to permanently deprive Northwest of the money," the judge said. He said the deprivation was temporary and the money eventually returned, after "much scurrying around the country," by Scallen. He said this did not change the fact that Scallen had placed in serious jeopardy $3,000,000 invested by the public in Northwest.

Mr. Justice McKay said he was taking into account Scallen's previous good character. "I have great sympathy for you just as I would have for any man of your capabilities who has brought himself into this position. But sympathy must not deter me from what I must do, which is to state that deterrence is the main factor in my decision."

The first mortgage on the Canucks, in effect, was held by a group of the club's directors, led by Coleman Hall.

Hall is considered persona non grata by members of the NHL establishment such as president Clarence Campbell, but a syndicate led by Hall seemed in the spring of 1973 the most likely to relieve the impoverished Scallen of the Canucks.

The most artistic and least disreputable of three Canadian teams in the NHL, the Montreal Canadiens were sold by the Molson brewers to the Bronfman distillers on December 30, 1971.

A group presided over by Montreal lawyer Jacques Courtois purchased approximately 700,000 of the 1,025,000 shares for an estimated $15,000,000. The purchase included the Canadian Arena Company, which owns and operates the Montreal Forum and the Canadiens.

David Molson and his brothers, William and Peter, bought controlling interest in the company in 1968 from their cousins, Senator Hartland de M. Molson and T. H. P. Molson. Senator Molson bought the team from the late Senator Donat Raymond in 1957.

Courtois is president of the new Montreal hierarchy and the

team's NHL governor. His partners include Edward and Peter Bronfman, through companies controlled by them, the Bank of Nova Scotia, and Baton Broadcasting Ltd.

John Bassett, a former major shareholder in Toronto Maple Leafs, holds controlling interest in Baton Broadcasting. Courtois is a partner in the Montreal law firm of Chisholm, Smith, Davis, Anglin, Laing, Weldon and Courtois, and a director of the Bank of Nova Scotia.

Molson said only one main condition was attached to the surprising sale of Canadiens. "We insisted we would never sell to Americans," he said. "Only to Montrealers or Quebeckers."

Others perceived the unceasing French-English rift in Quebec as the reason for Molson's abandoning hockey.

"David Molson was in some disfavor in Montreal," Harold Ballard said in Toronto. "He was not a carbon copy of Staff Smythe exactly, but he did look down his nose at some people below him. He thought they should bow and scrape to him."

Ballard claimed anti-English sentiment had Molson "over a barrel. There have been cops around David's box at the Forum and around his home. He told me once that he was afraid of getting knocked off."

The line of succession has remained fairly constant in the four pre-expansion NHL clubs in the United States. The lofty, sometimes surly Bruce Norris continues to manipulate the Detroit Red Wings as his late brother Jim and father did before him.

Bill Wirtz, with the image of a smooth, swinging hipster, replaced Jim Norris as the governor representing Chicago. He is the son of Arthur Wirtz, a burly imposing man whose partnership with Jim Norris once included control of the IBC; hockey teams in Detroit, Chicago, and New York; and pieces of arenas in St. Louis, Omaha, Indianopolis and Cincinnati.

Another Wirtz heir, Mike, was customarily a massive companion of Big Jim at hockey conclaves, more or less present as a caddy. When Big Jim desired a drink, Mike would get it. When Big Jim desired a cigaret, Mike would strike the match.

Bill Jennings, a tall, gray, urbane attorney, represents the New York Rangers. He is a power broker in the NHL, allied with Norris, Wirtz, and Jack Cooke of Los Angeles, but lost prestige among his peers when it was discovered in April 1973 that he attempted to arrange merger discussions with the World Hockey Association.

Francis Weston Adams, considered shrewd and calculating in

Boston and less so elsewhere in the league, voted for the Bruins when the governors decided to rearrange civilization by expanding to 12 teams in 1967. In 1969 he put his son, Weston, Jr., in nominal control of the Bruins.

Weston, Sr., inherited a major share of the Boston club from his father, Charles Francis Adams, and once played a static, but well-meaning game of goal for Harvard University. He was the goaltender for the third-team scrubs. Weston, Sr., died in the winter of 1973 about the time the Storer Broadcasting Company bought control of the Bruins.

Jack Cooke, ever ready to rattle and roll, has operated Los Angeles Kings since expansion, slowed perceptibly by a heart attack during the 1972–73 season.

The Knox brothers, Seymour and Northrup, so wealthy that their collective first names should be Fort, allowed Punch Imlach to build the Buffalo Sabres into a playoff contender in their third season.

Walter Bush and his partners, including the well-connected Gordon Ritz, provide the Minnesota North Stars with a solid corporate base. Bush has been mentioned as a possible successor to Clarence Campbell as NHL president, but a more likely choice is James D. Cullen, secretary and general counsel of the St. Louis Blues.

The Blues are controlled by the Salomon family, made rich through insurance. Sid Salomon III, a frustrated goalkeeper, represents St. Louis at gubernatorial meetings but is less of a heavyweight than his politically savvy father, Sid Jr., a prominent Missouri Democrat.

"Let me tell you about Sid the Third," Lynn Patrick said, when he was assembling the first St. Louis team in 1967. "The first thing he wanted me to do was buy him a set of goalpads."

Peter H. Block, a dilettante among his peers, is governor for the Pittsburgh Penguins. He was part of a Pittsburgh syndicate, including the wealthy Thayer R. Potter, which assumed responsibility for the Penguins in 1970 after the financial empire of Donald Parsons of Detroit collapsed.

Thin, tense Edward M. Snider pilots the Philadelphia Flyers at the executive level, saved from plunging down an open manhole in hockey matters by general manager Keith Allen, who always skates with his head up.

Roy Boe, whose wife was successful in the dressmaking game in New York, is the most fashionable NHL governor from the point of view of exorbitant tabs. He was assessed $6,000,000 for admittance to the NHL as owner of the New York Islanders and dunned $5,000,000 more by the New York Rangers as indemnification for moving into what the Rangers arbitrarily considered their territory.

The stylish William Putnam, who would make an impressive candidate to replace Clarence Campbell, led the Omni group in control of the Atlanta Flames. Their board of directors includes the only black at an executive level in the NHL, Herman J. Russell. Putnam was previously connected with the Philadelphia Flyers and, before that, associated with Jack Cooke in shifting the Minneapolis Lakers of the National Basketball Association from Minnesota to Los Angeles. He departed before the 1973-74 season.

Oakland remains the colossal failure of the NHL, the Golden Seals controlled most recently by the noisy, impulsive Charles Finley. Through a succession of owners and coaches and general managers, the Seals remain the laughable property in the NHL zoo. That they were saddled with Finley seems appropriate. As owner of the Oakland Athletics in the American Baseball League, his favorite employee is a mule, Charlie O.

The Referees

THE MOST THANKLESS OCCUPATION in sports is refereeing hockey games, or calling balls and strikes, or arbitrating football's relentless debates. It is a mug's racket.

"You're supposed to be completely impartial," says Ian (Scotty) Morrison, chief of officials in the National Hockey League. "But the abuse you take from partial players and coaches makes the job sometimes impossible."

Morrison could have added "abuse from owners" as well, but did not, being a prudent man who has a strong sense of self-preservation. He knows the NHL proprietors run the game to suit their self-enlightened whims.

Roy Alvin (Red) Storey testified, after he resigned as the league's senior referee in 1959, "One governor once told me that 'We own this league and, by God, you'll run it the way we tell you to!'"

Storey would not identify the governor but it might have been Constantine Falkland Cary Smythe, the scrappy Celtic terrier who exhibited totalitarian tendencies when he operated Toronto Maple Leafs.

Frederick James (Mickey) Ion, who died in 1964 in a nursing home in Redmond, Washington, was the patron saint of referees. His hide was sufficiently rhinoceros to blunt the shafts directed at policemen. "Tough is the only way to referee," Ion said a few years before his death. "I used to tell young referees breaking in with me to remember one thing. Remember, I told 'em, from the time the game starts until the time it ends, you and I are the only sane men in the rink." At the end, Ion was a pale remnant of the referee who once was a vivid figure. Both of his legs were cut off below the groin as a concession to phlebitis.

But he had the conviction, as a lacrosse player in British Columbia 60 years ago, that the best and most natural retort to an adversary was a punch in the snoot. He refereed in the old Western Canada Hockey League run by Lester and Frank Patrick and, after 30 years, ended his career in 1942 as referee-in-chief of the NHL.

Ion was lively at 77, sharp as aged cheddar. Sarcasms dripped from his lips when he compared officiating in his time against refereeing today. "We used to run a game with one or two referees," he said. "Now they have a referee and two linesmen cluttering up the ice. The linesmen skate like they're on crutches. And in those striped shirts they wear, they look like jailbirds. Oh, shit!" Ion would display, with a seasoned vanity, a scrapbook that contained "my national anthem"—an anonymous bit of doggerel, very shaggy:

> Whose eagle eye can follow the puck
>   Through all its dizzy flight?
> Who has to know? Not trust to luck
>   But must be always right:
>   It's MICKEY!
>
> When the going is tough and the boys get rough,
>   Who rules with an iron hand?
>   MICKEY!
>
> With the home crowd sore and raising a roar
>   Who has to show his hand?
>   MICKEY!
>
> In the vicious mix of whirling sticks
>   With calm, ever roving eye,
> Mid strife and hustle of hard-fought tussle
>   There's MICKEY standing by.

Visitors to the nursing home could read other tributes preserved in old newspaper clippings. One testimonial, uttered by King Clancy, claimed "Nothing but ice water ran through Ion's veins."

There was a story about an intense dispute between Ion and Toe Blake, when Blake was a young player with Montreal Canadiens. Ion had nailed Blake with a two-minute minor penalty and Blake skated to purgatory, not gracefully. "I can't tell you what I want to tell you," he muttered, "because you'd raise the penalty. But you can guess what I'm thinking!"

Ion pounced. "I have guessed," he told Blake, "and for that you get five minutes. Nobody's going to think obscenities like that about me!"

In the so-called halcyon days, 45 years ago, referees wore a large letter R on the chest of their jerseys. One night Ion was in charge of a game between Toronto and an Ottawa team managed by the volatile Tommy Gorman. Gorman grew exercised at penalties that Ion assessed the belligerent Ottawa players. "You know what R stands for?" Gorman hollered at one frustrated juncture. "It stands for 'robber'!"

Ion chuckled at the recollection. "I ran Gorman out of the rink for that crack," he said. "Oh, how I ran him!"

Latter-day referees are more sensitive to barbs, some of them inclined to think $12,000 to $16,000 a season is not worth the criticism heard from their superiors. Vern Buffey struck back verbally in the venerable Mickey Ion manner. Buffey was gagged by Morrison, the referee-in-chief, after complaining of abuse from coaches and governors during the Stanley Cup play-offs in 1967. Buffey was the victim of a quaint condition called rabbit ears. Rabbit ears, as the authors understand it, is an ailment that causes the patient to hear too much. It cannot be cured with salves and embrocations; kindness does not help much.

Buffey's condition was worsened by George Imlach's version of the Chinese water torture. Imlach, the Toronto coach gifted with a flair for lofty sportsmanship applied the torture into the referee's rabbit ears . . . drip . . . profanity . . . drip . . . profanity . . . drip . . . profanity . . . drip . . . profanity . . . drip . . . profanity . . . ad-drip-infinitum. There is a devilish perversity to Imlach's ear-washing. So much profanity drips into the referee's rabbit ears that the poor wretch becomes four-letter-word logged, broken down so far that he may give Imlach's team the breaks.

Morrison, tracking down the abuses, asked Buffey: "What do you hear?"

"From coaches like Mr. Imlach," Buffey said, "we hear insults and cuss words. From rubes-come-recently like Mr. Jennings of New York, we hear slurs on our honesty and integrity. Oh, it is brutal!"

"Well, don't hear insults and cuss words!" Morrison said waspishly, on behalf of the Establishment. "Control your ears! Hear what you need to hear—such as interesting out-of-town phone numbers, advice to the lovelorn and plots against the government. Pick and choose, man! Pick and choose!"

The authors want to say, on the basis of a frivolous study of the disease, that Morrison's recommendation is no way to treat rabbit ears, especially in hockey. In hockey, the victim is completely unable to hear a kind word—even if a player or coach or owner is sloppy or drunk enough to let one fall in a referee's hearing, and, naturally, no player or coach or owner is ever that sloppy or drunk.

The truth is, that sufferers from rabbit ears can hear nothing but abuse; that is the pathology of rabbit ears. Scotty Morrison might as well tell a victim of galloping garrulity, such as president Bill Jennings of New York's Rangers, not to babble incessantly.

The only way a rabbit-ears man can relieve himself is to throw all the loudmouth bums out of the rink, or defy the ban against talking back, as Buffey did. Buffey's rebuttal was directed at Jennings on behalf of John Ashley, a gray, embattled colleague whom Jennings had described as an "incompetent bush leaguer." However, the ban is spelled out in a confidential Manual of Instructions issued to NHL officials: "Refrain from using insulting, abusive or vulgar language to spectators regardless of the provocation offered by them—it is much better not to have rabbit ears . . ."

Red Storey, before his abrupt retirement, maintained warm, constant feuds with several club executives. One of his liveliest antagonists was Colonel W. A. H. MacBrien, former chairman of the board of Toronto Maple Leafs.

"Any time there was a game in Toronto," Storey claims, "MacBrien was the pepperiest partisan in the house."

One night Colonel MacBrien was sharing his box with the late Lord Alexander of Tunis, then the Governor-General of Canada. The box was just above the penalty timekeeper's table, where Storey had to skate to report rule infractions.

After one penalty against Toronto, Colonel MacBrien rushed out of his seat and handed the startled Storey a rulebook. When the period ended, Storey clumped down a ramp past the colonel's box. He leaned across Lord Alexander and, with an urchin's sense of humor, said, "Look, you old buzz saw, when you're sitting next to a gentleman try to act like one."

"That," Storey says, "got a good guffaw out of the Governor-General."

There were not as many laughs for referees in Chicago Stadium, which, every hockey night, is a vast loony bin on Lake Michigan. Storey once asked an official of the Black Hawks when they were going to start throwing out the thugs. "You kidding?" the official said. "We've had so much trouble gettings fans in here that we aren't about to start throwing them out."

Several years ago, their hockey patronage pegged at sell-out proportions, the Hawks hired a growling guarantee against obstreperous clients. They imported a muscular police dog from their farm team in St. Louis. The dog, Bruno, is kept penned in the basement, occasionally being led into the crowded lobbies to let demonstrative citizens know there is a carnivorous canine ready to nibble on human hambones.

NHL President Campbell came to the league as a referee in 1938, up from a law office in Edmonton. He had distinguished himself at the University of Alberta by winning a Rhodes scholarship to Oxford.

One night, during untidy combat between Boston and Montreal Maroons, Dit Clapper of the Bruins hung a blue forget-me-not under Campbell's eye. Pugnacity was not Clapper's major trait, but he was irritated when Dave Trottier of the Maroons thrust the butt end of a stick into his face. The infraction was not detected by Referee Campbell; Clapper, retaliating, knocked Trottier down and piled on him.

Campbell skated to the struggling pair, whistle skirling. "Clapper," Campbell announced, voice raised, "you're a dirty sonofabitch!"

Clapper was amazed to hear coarse language from a Rhodes scholar. He demanded, "What did you say?"

Campbell reiterated his estimate of Clapper. "I said you're a dirty sonofabitch!"

Clapper did not give Campbell a chance to say it a third time. He delivered a fist full of knuckles to the referee's startled expression, knocking him back into the delighted players grouped behind them.

Clapper was banished from the game and subsequently fined $100, a trivial rebuke for striking an official. Campbell saved him from stiffer retribution in a report to Frank Calder, then president of the NHL. "I was talking loud," Campbell admitted, "when I should have been throwing them into the penalty box." Campbell has been similarly fair, in the opinion of many referees, as the game's czar.

Some governors, in their calmer moments, have vindicated the judgment of the league's officials. Conn Smythe would wire Red Storey, almost in imploring terms: "You've done as much for hockey as any one man. You can do more. Please stay with the game."

Nine years later, in Maple Leaf Gardens, Smythe's son Stafford pitched a program at Art Skov, another troubled referee. Skov did not like it much, hardly inclined to turn the other cheek. "You're a big man, Mr. Smythe," he said, quite riled. "Why don't you grow up?"

The junior Smythe laughed, but at least one professional did not consider the incident amusing. Tommy Ivan, the manager of Chicago Black Hawks, said: "It's high time we laid off downgrading the referees in public. We better take stock of our popping off." Ivan added, thoughtfully, "A poor devil like Skov is supposed to be perfect, but the only man who ever was perfect was hung on a cross."

The World Hockey Association

IN JANUARY 1971 the very last thing a National Hockey League club owner, player, or fan would have dreamed possible was creation of a second major professional league to challenge the solidly entrenched, enormously powerful and wealthy NHL.

It was 1917 when the NHL was born and since then it has withstood the few challenges to its claim as *the* big hockey league. In March 1932 the American Hockey League, then regarded as a minor league, made an unsuccessful bid to challenge the NHL for the Stanley Cup.

As hockey grew more and more popular in the years following World War II, Al Leader, president of the Western Hockey League, had dreams of improving the quality of play in his organization and eventually establishing it as a second major league which would compete on a level with the NHL. At the time the WHL teams had working agreements with the NHL. If the WHL was to try to make the jump it would have to break with its wealthy cousins.

An insightful Canadian, Leader urged his owners to unite in defiance of the NHL and gamble on his idea that the two leagues eventually could co-exist on a major-league level. But the WHL owners wavered, buckled, and opted for the status quo; a decision they later were to deeply regret. Once the WHL bosses had capitulated it appeared that the NHL had the big-league ice to itself for an eternity. But this was not to be the case.

On a brisk, bright afternoon in January 1971 a chubby little promoter named Dennis Murphy and a slim blonde attorney, Gary

Davidson, were involved in a long-distance telephone call. Murphy, then general manager of the Floridians of the American Basketball Association, was a man of boundless energy and creativity who once had been mayor of the 68,000 citizens of Buena Park, California.

Davidson, a graduate of UCLA Law School, had been a founding partner in the ABA. He had been a four-sport letterman in football, baseball, basketball, and track in high school and had become an ardent tennis player. He knew nothing and cared less about hockey —until Murphy phoned.

"The National Hockey League has had the run of things," said Murphy. "It's about time we formed a league and took a run at them."

Surprised but not astonished, Davidson said he needed time to think about it. In March 1971 he decided that his portly pal had something there after all. They convened and decided that their first objective would be a feasibility study to determine whether there was room for another major league of hockey.

Within three months they were persuaded there was room, and the articles of incorporation were filed in Delaware on June 10, 1971, for the World Hockey Association. The pair then began a series of flights crisscrossing North America in search of backers. Their first break came when Los Angeles tax expert Charles Abrahams, who negotiated for dozens of hockey players, endorsed the Murphy-Davidson plan.

"Don't sign anything but a one-year contract," Abrahams warned his clients, "a new hockey league is on the horizon and you may be able to make a lot more money in it than in the NHL."

Since Murphy and Davidson were short on hockey know-how, they needed a Canadian contact who could direct them to the right people. Their objective was fulfilled by Walt Marlow, a sportswriter for the Los Angeles *Herald-Examiner*, who directed them to red-headed Bill Hunter, who long had been active promoting junior hockey in Edmonton, Alberta.

A galvanic personality, Hunter was intrigued with the idea of fighting the NHL. He knew hockey people throughout Western Canada; lots of people, and he jumped on the WHA bandwagon. As events later unfolded, Hunter proved to be a pivotal figure because he knew a man named Ben Hatskin who was round like Murphy and just as gutsy; and richer.

Hatskin once had played professional football for the Winnipeg

Blue Bombers, then went to work for his father's paper box business and then began making more and more money until he became a millionaire. Somewhere along the way he bought a stable of race-horses but discovered they didn't provide him with the kind of kicks owning professional athletes might, so he bought himself a junior hockey team, the Winnipeg Jets. Hunter knew all this when he phoned Hatskin with some surprising news. "Ben," said Hunter, "come on out to Calgary. I got these two fellas here from California who want to start another hockey league."

Hatskin had been intrigued for several reasons but mostly because he had been thinking of applying for an NHL franchise and only a month before Hunter had called he inquired about the price of a new NHL team. "About $7,000,000," NHL president Campbell told Hatskin. Ben thought that that was too expensive.

Hatskin was even more fascinated when he met Murphy and Davidson and he agreed to fly down to Los Angeles on September 23, 1971, when discussions about formation of the league became more serious. This time Davidson was asking $25,000 each from the prospective franchise owners. At first Hatskin wavered but he came through as did Hunter and a chap from Calgary named Bob Brownridge who also was a millionaire.

"If we hadn't gotten Hunter, Brownridge, and Hatskin," said Murphy, "it would have been unlikely the league would have survived beyond that point."

Hunter was important because of his limitless hockey contacts. Hatskin and Brownridge were vital because of their money. By now the WHA concept was out in the open and was openly scorned by the NHL, its hirelings and friends. Davidson and Murphy were unconcerned. They had lined up interested parties in New York, Miami, San Francisco, Dayton, Chicago, Los Angeles, St. Paul, Winnipeg, Calgary, and Edmonton.

By October 1971, the WHA was producing a chain-reaction of new stories to compete with the opening of the NHL season. One of the biggest was delivered on October 20 when Davidson announced that the WHA would operate without a reserve clause or "any substitute therefor, such as an option clause," in all player contracts.

On November 1, 1971, the WHA made its first big splash with the national media following two days of meetings at the Americana Hotel in New York. It was then that the WHA was formally organized and, following a gala luncheon, Davidson, Murphy, and Hunter told the audience that the new league was "here to stay."

Only a handful in the audience took them seriously. The skeptics said there were too many problems. Many of the cities had inadequate arenas. Others were in relatively small metropolitan areas. But mostly the question was asked: "Where are they going to get players?"

Without saying so, the WHA owners made it abundantly clear they intended to get them from the NHL. At one of the meetings each owner put four players on his negotiation list. "I hope nobody else has Bobby Hull," said Hatskin, "because I've got his name on my list." Then, a warning to his colleagues: "Don't any of you try for Bobby. I can get him and you can't."

Later, Hatskin confided that his bravado was not fully supported by the facts. "I wasn't sure I could get Hull. But I had to show confidence."

It was precisely Hatskin's and Hunter's brand of confidence that inspired several of the other less confident franchise holders. Shortly after the Manhattan meetings Steve Arnold, who had been a partner in the sports representation firm of Pro Sports, Inc., was signed as WHA director of player personnel. Lee Meade, former sports editor of *The Denver Post*, was named public relations director.

A month later the first former NHL employee signed with the new league when Vern Buffey signed as referee-in-chief. In the meantime, Hatskin was doing what few people ever thought he would do; he went after Bobby Hull. They met at the Hotel Vancouver when the Chicago Black Hawks were on a road trip in the British Columbia metropolis. Hatskin offered the Golden Jet $1,000,000 for five years. "I just pulled the figure out of my head," Hatskin later confessed. "The figure $1,000,000 always gets a lot of attention."

Hull was privately enthused because he had experienced several annoying contract problems with the Black Hawks front office. But he also was cautious. "Let's wait on it," said Hull who then contacted his financial adviser Harvey S. Wineberg.

"If Hatskin is serious," said Wineberg, "you'll hear from him again."

He did but Hull referred Hatskin to Wineberg. The financial adviser wanted more money for his client. By February 1972 the figure had climbed to $2,000,000, and was still climbing.

Davidson and Murphy were also busy, trying to consolidate the franchises; which was not easy. The Dayton franchise was switched to Houston; San Francisco was moved to Quebec City; and Milwaukee dropped out of the picture altogether. But the biggest noise of all was heard on February 27, 1972, when Toronto Maple Leafs goaltender Bernie Parent jetted to Miami to announce that he was going to leave the NHL and sign with the Screaming Eagles. For the first time, the NHL was in a state of shock.

The fact that Parent, one of the NHL's best young goaltenders, would dare leave his team in mid-season, fly down to Florida, and announce he was prepared to quit the NHL suddenly lent more credence to the rumors that Bobby Hull, in fact, was thinking of leaving the NHL, too.

"I'd like to stay in Chicago," said Hull, "but I don't expect the Wirtzes (owners of the Black Hawks) to match the offer Winnipeg is making. The new league might need me a lot more than the Black Hawks will."

Hatskin wanted help in landing an ace like Hull and asked his partners to chip in enough money to cover the first $1,000,000 which he'd deliver to Hull. They agreed and also added $100,000 apiece for a war chest. All except for Miami which suddenly pulled out of the league leaving the owners as numbed as they had been enthused when Parent said he'd play for the Screaming Eagles. Another blow followed when Calgary also took its walking papers. Suddenly, the WHA appeared too wobbly for words and enough words were being printed suggesting that the Davidson-Murphy bubble was about to burst.

Undaunted, they kept building. Donald Regan has been brought in as legal counsel, Max Muhleman as head of WHA Properties Company, and Ed Fitkin as assistant to the president. Nobody realized it at the time but the worst was over. In May 1972 the New York Raiders signed a lease to play their games at Madison Square Garden and a month later Philadelphia, with Bernie Parent signed, replaced Miami.

By now the WHA had become a byword to hockey fans and the talk of the continent. In its June 19, 1972, issue, *Sports Illustrated* magazine featured Bobby Hull on its cover wearing a Black Hawks uniform with an accompanying caption: "THE MAN THEY WANT TO STEAL."

In the article that followed, "Hockey's Turn to Wage a War," the question of Hull's potential switch was amply debated. It concluded with Hull's basic statement: "The name of the game now is money."

The Black Hawks finally sensed trouble; big trouble, and offered Hull $1,000,000 for five years. It was too little, too late. Hatskin had produced a 40-page contract which included $1,000,000 for Hull to sign; $250,000 a year for five years as player or, if he wished, as player-coach; $100,000 a year for another five years as a Jets' front office executive. All it needed was Wineberg's seal of approval. "It's a fantastic contract," the adviser told Hull and that was all Bobby had to hear.

On June 27, 1972, Hull rode a Rolls Royce through St. Paul, Minnesota, to autograph the WHA portion of his contract for the first $1,000,000. Then the motorcade headed for the airport, where a chartered airliner took Bobby, his family, Hatskin, and Wineberg to Winnipeg for a tumultuous celebration. "I have no regrets about leaving Chicago," said Hull. "The whole thing has made me wonder what the hell the Black Hawks were thinking. They must have thought I was bluffing or they must have been gambling that the Winnipeg offer would fall through."

Hull's signing opened the floodgates and, one by one, other NHL players moved to the new league. Larry Pleau left the Montreal Canadiens for the New England Whalers; Andre Lacroix left Chicago Black Hawks for the Philadelphia Blazers; George Gardner quit the Vancouver Canucks for the Los Angeles Sharks.

Davidson and Murphy completed their end of the franchise work when Nick Mileti, whose bid to put Cleveland into the NHL had been rejected, was granted the 12th WHA franchise. Mileti promptly hustled for players and signed Gerry Cheevers of the Stanley Cup champion Boston Bruins who also had lost Johnny McKenzie to the Philadelphia Blazers.

In July 1972, the Quebec Nordiques signed defenseman J. C. Tremblay who had been a Montreal Canadiens fixture, and New England captured Bruins defenseman Ted Green. But the biggest contract of all was signed by Derek Sanderson, the Bruin, who jumped to Philadelphia for an estimated $2,325,000. The skirmishing wth the NHL was over. The war was on.

When Rosaire Paiement left the Vancouver Canucks for the WHA's Chicago Cougars, Canucks manager Bud Poile warned that his club would go to court to retrieve Paiement. "We have instructed our lawyers to go ahead and pursue the legal aspect of Paiement's contract," said Poile. "Let's test the contract and find out if it's good or not. This is the one we should hang our hat on. Losing a Paiement would be a very harmful thing to our hockey club."

At issue was the NHL's reserve clause and the question of whether or not it bound a player to the NHL if an NHL club wanted to re-sign the player. Following Poile's declaration a series of suits and countersuits were launched by the battling leagues. The prize plum was Hull. The NHL sought to prevent him from playing; the WHA wanted him on the ice.

While other WHA owners wrung their hands in anxiety, Hatskin seemed amused. At one time, he had 13 lawsuits on his hands. "They sue us," he said, "and I sue them. Then I sue them and they sue me back. Someone's up one suit but I'm not sure who it is."

The NHL succeeded in harassing Hull enough to legally keep him off-ice for the first 15 games of the season and thereby dealt a severe body blow to the new league. When the courts finally gave Hull the green light to join the Jets the WHA season was a month old, but Bobby's magnetism was apparent. In his first game on WHA ice at Quebec City he attracted the largest crowd of the year, 10,126. Wherever Hull went, the gate soared. "I figure Bobby meant at least 1,500 tickets for each game," said Hatskin.

Hull was something special. Derek Sanderson wasn't. The former Bruin was a bust in Philadelphia where small crowds were turning out to see the Blazers. "The people aren't buying my act," said Sanderson.

Using their ABA experience as a guide, Davidson and Murphy anticipated first-year franchise problems. The first arose in New York where owners Richard Wood and Seymour Siegel encountered financial difficulties compelling the league to take over and operate the Raiders. In Philadelphia owner Bernard Brown dismissed team president James Cooper and sought to unload the expensive Sanderson who had been hospitalized and played in only eight games.

When Sanderson attempted to return to the team he was ordered out of uniform. After several weeks of haggling, Brown and Sanderson's attorney Bob Woolf arranged an agreement whereby Sanderson would be paid $1,000,000 to leave the Blazers, which he did. Shortly thereafter, Sanderson signed a new contract with the Boston Bruins.

By mid-season New England, Quebec City, and Winnipeg had emerged as the strongest franchises. The Minnesota Fighting Saints showed an attendance spurt after the new year when a new rink opened in St. Paul. Houston and Los Angeles attracted surprisingly large crowds and Chicago, despite an inferior team, occasionally drew respectable numbers to its games at the Amphitheater. Likewise, the Raiders, after a weak start, caught on in New York City. Ottawa, Edmonton, and Philadelphia were the biggest disappointments.

On the positive side, the WHA was able to sign network television contracts with the Columbia Broadcasting System and the Canadian Broadcasting Corporation and the league received considerable coverage in newspapers and magazines.

Because of his late start, Hull lagged behind the scoring leaders for most of the season. The big surprise was Ron Ward, a Vancouver castoff, who emerged as the league's leading scorer with the New York Raiders until the final week of the season when Lacroix edged him for the points championship.

The other former NHL stars—Cheevers, Tremblay, Green, and Parent—played superbly for their respective teams and when the WHA's regular schedule had ended on April 1, 1973, the new league had attracted more than 2,000,000 fans to its 12 arenas.

"I think we're two or three years ahead of the ABA right now," said Davidson. "As for our television deal with CBS, the money isn't that good right now but we're ten times better off than the American Football League at a comparable time. We got exposure and that's the most important thing at the moment."

If, in January 1971, a competitive league was the last thing on the minds of some NHL governors, a merger with the WHA was not considered possible by most observers in April 1973. Many NHL owners were embittered toward the upstart league because of player raids and the added dilution of talent. Merger talk was regarded as a good four or five years away.

But on April Fool's Day, 1973, Hatskin and William Jennings, president of the New York Rangers and one of the most powerful NHL owners, conferred in New York City about the possibilities of a merger between the two leagues. The news was as shocking as the formation of the WHA two years earlier.

On April 3rd, as reports of the preliminary merger talks spread across the continent, R. Alan Eagleson, executive director of the NHL Players' Association, denounced the plan and said that his group would fight it on both sides of the border. Conversely, Bobby Hull endorsed the idea as "the best thing for hockey."

Hull scoffed at suggestions that a merger would lower players' salaries. "The owners want to make a dollar and the players want to make a dollar. But our main objective is to put forth the best possible brand of hockey. A consistent 40-goal scorer is going to draw a good salary whether or not the two leagues join."

Prospects for a merger were dimmed by the endless hassling in basketball where the NBA and ABA had failed to unite. NHL owners were known to have misgivings and some WHA owners had second thoughts but the talks continued. "I think we're headed in the right direction," said Davidson. "Sure we had some shortcomings in our first year but we've come a lot farther than anyone ever expected us to."

The results on the ice were predictable. Winnipeg's Jets, powered by player-coach Bobby Hull, finished first in the West Division while the New England Whalers, fortified with numerous ex-NHL stars, captured the East Division crown. Both clubs swept past their opposition and into the finals for the Avco World Cup.

Considering the balance of the teams and the fact that Hull was the most potent scorer on either team, it was believed that Winnipeg would give New England a good run for the playoff money. But the Jets were wiped out in five games and the first WHA crown was bestowed upon Whaler captain Ted Green at Boston Garden.

Shortly after the playoffs were concluded more WHA action took place. The Philadelphia Blazers were purchased by a Vancouver group and moved to the British Columbia city. Ottawa's Nationals switched to Toronto and the New York Raiders were bought by syndicate which immediately changed its name to the Golden Blades.

In its first expansion move, the WHA also approved Cincinnati for a team during the 1974–75 season after the Ohio group revealed that it had given up hope of obtaining a team in the NHL.

When all was said and done it appeared that the WHA no longer was skating on thin ice. It was here to stay.

Russia–Canada

SPORTSWRITERS reached for superlatives as they strained to fence in the climax of the Russia-Canada series in September 1972, with exclamation marks.

There seemed to no adequate way for witnesses to tell it. The art of fiction, even on the sports pages, was dead. Reality had strangled invention. Only the utterly preposterous, the inexpressibly fantastic would ever seem plausible again.

The best way to tell it was with a half-boob air, aware as adults should be that, when all is said and done, hockey is a game that small boys play.

Thus, on the cool dark Moscow night of September 28, 1972, a Thursday:

Red Square became an embarrassed White Flag waving acceptance of defeat, pro tem.

The handle of the Hammer broke and the Sickle was an old rusty jacknife.

The Lenin Mausoleum trembled as though Richard Nixon was selling used cars in the Kremlin courtyard.

All the vodka turned sour in the Russian vats.

The Politburo disintegrated and 55 years of Communist rule became just another wretched Five-Year Plan.

The garlic went rancid in the Ukrainian sausage, and the cops in the KGB couldn't find the floor if they fell out of bed.

Pravda was nothing more than a soggy Soviet throwaway and Lennie Brezhnev's blood turned to cold beet borscht.

All because Team Canada—alias Team U.S. NHL or the Eagleson Athletic Club or Team Ugly—won a cozy little series at the summit in the last 34 seconds of the last game in the most discussed, most cussed tournament in hockey history.

The score was tied 5–5 and the eight-game series was snarled: three games for Canada, three for the Soviet Union, one tied. A tie in the last game would have been eminently satisfying, even to the most chauvinistic of Canadian fanatics.

Then, in the last minute, play boiled around the Russian goalkeeper, Vladislav Tretiak. Phil Esposito, refusing to leave the ice on a line change, controlled the puck out of a chaotic scramble.

"Somebody shot it into the Russian zone," Esposito explained later. "I whacked it toward the net. The goalie made the save, but here came Henny and he tucked the rebound in the net."

Henny—Paul Garnet Henderson—sprang approximately nine feet in the air, then landed in a heap of jubilant teammates. The twilight of civilization had been averted, momentarily. In Moscow's bright Luzhniki Arena, about 3,000 Canadians whooped and hollered as though they had won a world war.

Canada, in fact, never sent that many people overseas in one mob outside of a world war. The Canadian zealots were on an emotional treadmill for the duration of their 10-day mission to Moscow, gripped in a tourniquet of tension.

Few ever sang O Canada so loudly or so passionately off key. Staid Muscovite fans were startled by the noisily defiant chant, "Go, Canada, Go! Go, Canada, Go!"

They were insulted by another rude, inventive battle cry. "Da, Da, Can-a-da! Nyet, Nyet, Sov-i-et! Da, Da, Can-a-da! Nyet, Nyet, Sov-i-et!"

Henderson's goal gratified the chauvinists who traveled from Canada to Moscow in the biggest airlift since the relief of blockaded Berlin, in 1948. "By God, the Canada goose isn't a dead duck, not yet anyway. Let's get smashed!"

"When I scored that winning goal," Henderson said, "I finally knew what democracy was all about."

That seemed to be slicing the old salami a trifle thick, even Soviet salami. It is true that Henderson's winning score in the Super Bowlski conferred upon Canada a sense of exciting achievement in the one game that inflates the country's national ego.

Cooling out from a satiating orgasmic experience, an observer could reflect upon William Buckley's comment on the nature of games.

"If you win a basketball game by 50–30 or a hockey game 7–3," Buckley wrote, "you are the better team. If you win by a single point, what you have is two evenly matched teams, one of which is lucky."

Henderson, a fleet left wing who knocks down 75,000 soggy coconuts a year from the Toronto Maple Leafs, scored the winning goal for Canada in each of the last three games, and he could reasonably quote Budd Schulberg in rebuttal of Buckley.

"Luck," Schulberg once wrote, "is only a bulb that shines when the current is on."

Henderson was turned on as seldom before in his big-league career, allied with his Toronto associate, Ron Ellis, and Bobby Clarke of the Philadelphia Flyers on the most consistent Canadian forward line.

Other Canadian representatives have rarely played better, and may never reach such patriotic peaks again.

Few hockey experts believed big Bill White of the Chicago Black Hawks or solid Gary Bergman of the Detroit Red Wings could reach inside themselves and play as efficiently on defense.

Most of all, athletically, the summit series certified the rangy, moose-tall Phil Esposito as a superstar. He could always score—76 goals for Boston Bruins in 1970–71, 66 in 1971–72, 55 in 1972–73,—more than any other shooter in a three-year span—but in Boston he operated in the shadow of a prodigy, Bobby Orr. Earlier, in Chicago, he passed the pucks which Bobby Hull's celebrated slapshot converted into goals.

Orr was recovering from an operation to repair a damaged left knee and could not play against Russia. Hull abandoned the National Hockey League for the Winnipeg Jets of the rival World Hockey Association and was barred from playing by a spiteful NHL establishment.

Esposito strode into the vacuum created by the absence of Orr and Hull and, trying harder, No. 2 became No. 1. He played 30 or 35 minutes of every game—scoring goals (7), setting up goals (6), forechecking, killing penalties, on the power play, arguing.

He had been put down by a few directors of Hockey Canada as a "money grubber" and "unpatriotic" when he demanded certain guarantees in the event of injury. In Stockholm, en route to Russia, when the Canadians struggled in disarray in two Swedish exhibition, Esposito took charge in the dressing room.

"Anybody that doesn't want to stand up for Canada," he said, not quietly, "better take off their uniforms and go home. We don't want any god damn quitters on this club."

Four did quit after the Canadians arrived in Moscow. Vic Hadfield of New York Rangers, Jocelyn Guevremont of Vancouver Canucks, and Richard Martin and Gilbert Perreault of Buffalo Sabres defected after coach Harry Sinden did not pick them to play against Russia.

The defections, more than any other factor, seemed to cement the remaining players as a team.

Peter Mahovlich, the younger and bigger of two Mahovlich brothers on the team, muttered a statement to reporters after the last game.

"Don't forget to mention those fucking guys who deserted us," he said. "What the hell—we became a team after they left."

It was a pistol-paced sports story, with the bladed tension of Jean-Paul Parise's hockey stick poised menacingly above the haircut of a German referee, Joseph Kompalla.

Many in the Canadian contingent, Alan Eagleson prominent among them, regarded the confrontation as more than a hockey showdown.

Most of the players regarded it as Us versus Them, White Hats against Black Hats, Good Guys defying Bad Guys.

The older Mahovlich, Frank, devoutly insisted that the series was more than a contest between cultures. To the Big M, it became a paranoiac crusade of Right battling Might. His preoccupation with the Moscow menace was reflected in Mahovlich's play. He was benched for one of the eight games and, in total, contributed one goal and one assist.

Canada withdrew from world hockey tournaments on January 4, 1970, fed up with amateur bindlestiffs such as John (Bunny) Ahearne, a former London travel agent who is perennial president of the International Ice Hockey Federation.

"Amateurs?" the Canadian officials said in effect. "There ain't any. Let's open up the tournament to anyone good enough to play in it and the hell with hypocrisy."

The Europeans, adroitly manipulated or muscled by the Soviet Union, opted for a continuance of hypocrisy. Canada was restricted to a roster of nine minor-league professionals and 11 alleged amateurs. The Russians and every other country were allowed to employ their best, although you will find more amateurs in a crap game than you will on the Russian national team.

The prospect of a summit series seemed so much idle speculation, therefore, until a startling announcement out of Prague on April 18, 1972, pushed the Stanley Cup playoffs into overset newspaper type.

"PRAGUE—Officials of the Soviet Ice Hockey Federation and Hockey Canada and the Canadian Amateur Hockey Association have agreed to an eight-game series between Canadian professionals and a Russian all-star team. The likely date for such a series is September, before the start of the National Hockey League season."

Those bare details were negotiated by three men who met privately for several days in a room on the fifth floor of the International Hotel in Prague, site of the 1972 world championships.

Andre Starovoitov, a squat gray man with prominent blue eyes, haggled on behalf of the Russians. Gordon Juckes, executive director of the CAHA, and Joe Kryczka, president of the CAHA, dickered on behalf of Canada. Kryczka, a young articulate lawyer from Calgary, Alberta, is a second-generation Pole who has some linguistic rapport with the Russians.

"I speak some Polish," Kryczka explained, "and the Russians were impressed that at least some of the language barriers were down. Starovoitov and I could understand each other without always having to resort to an interpreter."

Other Canadian hockey executives approached Starovoitov from other angles. He is an operative in several dimensions.

He is the ranking Communist Party man in Soviet hockey, and he has been in Soviet hockey as a player, referee, and boss for more than 20 years. He played with Vsevold Bobrov, the current coach of the Russian Nationals, and their political-athletic alliance led to the expulsion of ebullient Anatoli Tarasov as czar of the Nationals.

"The Russians have only one system," Alan Eagleson testified, "and that's the muscle system. I'd rather be a bum in Toronto than a major-general in Russia."

Many Canadian fans and commentators were indignantly convinced that Eagleson behaved like a bum in Moscow.

"He is diplomatic disaster," John Robertson wrote in the *Montreal Star* after Eagleson hassled Russian policemen, and was hassled by them, during the last game.

Eagleson vocally protested that the Soviet goal judge did not turn on the red light for the fifth and tying Canadian goal. To lend force to his protest, he rushed from his seat toward the bench occupied by the official scorekeeper.

In its long quest for world peace, Russia has always stuck to its guns—even in hockey arenas. Thus, surrounded by Russian guards as he ranted, Eagleson almost had his right arm wrenched from its socket.

He was rescued by several Canadian players who piled over the boards in a mission led by Peter Mahovlich. Skidding across the ice toward the Canadian bench, surrounded by Canadian players, Eagleson seemed to lift the long finger on his right hand in the universal gesture which indicated that the jeering Russian fans should go commit an indecency against themselves.

"What I was really doing," Eagleson said, "was putting my thumb up in a thumbs-up gesture to the Canadian fans. Films of the game prove this to be so."

Eagleson, executive director of the NHL Players' Association, is a hard-nosed, mainchance Toronto lawyer whose ceaseless maneuvering on behalf of the union has earned him the respect of most NHL players. Since 1967 he has bargained for pension benefits and salary increases which the athletes have ample reason to appreciate.

Eagleson's unremitting scorn for the Russians probably welded Team Canada into a clubby attitude of mean-spirited myopia that shrunk their world in Moscow to the confines of the arena and welcomed few outsiders. His personal bonfire ignited just enough of the Canadian players to inspire them just to win.

In the series, the Russians proved that their best is about even with the NHL's best. They won the first game in Montreal, 7–3, causing a national shock summed up in black headlines on Canada's newspapers: DISASTER AT THE SUMMIT.

The Canadians tied the series in a swift, exciting game in Toronto, 4–1. They tied, 4–4, in Winnipeg, the Soviets bouncing back from a 2–4 deficit to gain a deadlock. The Russians won the fourth game, in Vancouver, chasing the outskated Canadians into a 5–3 defeat.

In the fifth game, in Moscow, the Canadians blew a 4–1 lead in the third period into a 5–4 defeat and were left reeling on the ropes. With three games remaining on enemy ice, they had one win, three losses, and a tie. Another tie or win would cinch the series for the Soviets.

Team Canada battled to a 3–2 win in the fifth game, goaltender Ken Dryden coming up big for the first time in the series. They won the seventh, 4–3, Henderson scoring the winning goal with fewer than three minutes to play.

There is no defense for Canadian sportsmanship that did not rise higher than snail spoor in the eighth and final game. Jean-Paul Parise threatened Kompalla, one of the neutral referees, with his stick and was expelled from the game.

Parise's expulsion prompted coach Harry Sinden and his riled assistant, John Ferguson, to heave towels and furniture on the ice.

It is difficult to endorse Eagleson telling a Russian interpreter, after the incident of the goal-light-that-didn't-flash, "You're a liar when you tell me the goal light was burned out! You Russians are all a bunch of god damned liars!"

That is how a vest-pocket war can affect normally rational Canadians. The malady lingers on, and the spectre looms of Russian hockey surpassing the Canadian kind, but nothing can obscure one vivid cameo after Paul Henderson scored the winning goal.

One good Russian player, the chippy Boris Mihailov, turned away from the joyful Canadians and skated toward the Soviet bench. The number on the back of his jersey looked huge; No. 13.

THE CANADIAN PERSONNEL

Goalkeepers

KEN DRYDEN—An All-American at Cornell University; top player in the NHL playoffs in the spring of 1971; NHL rookie-of-the year in 1972; 25; a law student at McGill University when his prolonged physique, four inches over six feet, isn't guarding the Montreal goal.

TONY ESPOSITO—The more serious of the two Esposito brothers; a year younger than Phil at 29; responsible for 15 shutouts in a NHL season, which is the modern record; winner of the Vezina Trophy in two of his first three professional seasons.

ED JOHNSTON—Oldest member of Team Canada at 36; a 10-year member of the Boston Briuns enjoying latter-day success.

Defensemen

GARY BERGMAN—Hub of the Detroit rearguard, reliable and steady.

BRAD PARK—Considered second best defenseman in the NHL, after Bobby Orr; good puck carrier and a first-team all-star last season.

BILL WHITE—Underrated Chicago veteran; picked for second all-star team last season.

PAT STAPLETON—Good playmaker for Chicago; responsible for 279 assists in eight seasons; a second team all-star in 1972.

ROD SEILING—A seven-year NHL veteran, at 27; member of Canada's Olympic team in 1964.

SERGE SAVARD—Top playoff performer in 1969, but susceptible to injuries; missed three of first six seasons with Montreal Canadiens because of broken bones.

GUY LAPOINTE—Has baleful slapshot; 24; one of several outstanding Canadien defensemen.

DON AWREY—An effective muscleman on the Boston blueline.

JOCELYN GUEVREMONT—One of the bright spots on bleak Vancouver Canucks; accumulated 51 points as a rookie last season.

BRIAN GLENNIE—Played against the Soviet Union in 1968 Olympics; rugged member of Toronto Maple Leafs.

DALE TALLON—Flashy Toronto junior who signed two years ago with Vancouver Canucks for big bonus.

Forwards

PHIL ESPOSITO—Rangy, 30-year-old center; scored 142 goals in last two seasons for Boston; first team all-star last four successive seasons.

JEAN RATELLE—Smooth New York pivot, broke ankle late in the 1971–72 season but still scored 46 goals in 63 games.

BOB CLARKE—Underrated Philadelphia center; drafted low by the pros because he is diabetic; scored 35 goals for the Flyers last winter.

STAN MIKITA—Born in Czechoslovakia; won NHL scoring title four times; bothered by bum back in recent seasons; skilled at winning face-offs.

GILBERT PERREAULT—First draft choice by Buffalo Sabres in 1970; set rookie record with 38 goals; 22.

MARCEL DIONNE—Good all-round Detroit center; scored 28 goals as a rookie last year; 22.

RON ELLIS—Strong checking right wing; has scored 199 goals in eight seasons for Toronto Maple Leafs.

PAUL HENDERSON—Fast skating, quick-shooting left wing for Toronto; walks beat with discipline; scored 38 goals last season.

JEAN-PAUL PARISE—Picked for thorough checking ability exhibited on behalf of Minnesota North Stars.

FRANK MAHOVLICH—A prodigy with the puck on big nights; scored 464 goals in 15 seasons; holds playoff record of 14 goals.

MICKEY REDMOND—Involved in trade from Montreal to Detroit for Mahovlich three years ago; scored 42 goals last season.

RICK MARTIN—Scored 44 goals as Buffalo rookie last year; 21.

RED BERENSON—Once scored six goals in one game for St. Louis Blues; played for Belleville McFarlands on world championship team in 1959; president of NHL Players' Association.

ROD GILBERT—Scored 43 goals for New York Rangers last season; stylish right winger who has developed pugnacious tendencies.

BILL GOLDSWORTHY—Consistent Minnesota shooter; averaging more than 30 goals a year over last three years.

DENNIS HULL—Possesses hard slapshot; younger and less flamboyant than brother Robert; scored 30 goals last season.

VIC HADFIELD—Robust left wing; scored 50 goals for New York last season; later signed a million-dollar contract.

WAYNE CASHMAN—Hard checker; diligent in the corners; truculent member of the truculent Bruins.

YVAN COURNOYER—Swift Montreal right wing, constantly moving; scored 47 goals last season.

PETER MAHOVLICH—Younger than Frank by nine years; less intense; ready to mix in rugged going; has scored 35 goals in each of the last two seasons for Montreal.

SOVIET PERSONNEL

Goalkeepers

VLADISLAV TRETIAK—Just 20; helped win Olympic title last year in Japan; a graduate of a crash course to improve Russian goaltending; Moscow Army.

VIKTOR ZINGER—International veteran; called to replace injured Vladimir Shepovalov.

ALEKSANDER SIDELNIKOV—22-year-old prospect from Wings of the Soviet.

Defensemen

ALEKSANDER RAGULIN—Has played 210 games for Soviet Nationals; bulky and hard to move; heavy shot from the point; Moscow Army.

VLADIMIR LUTCHENKO—At 23, has played on three world champions; member of Central Army.

VIKTOR KUZKIN—Central Army veteran; 32; member of nine world championship teams.

YEVGENI PALADIEV—From Moscow Spartak; 24; former Soviet all-star.

ALEKSANDER GUSEV—Central Army player; 25; new to international competition.

GENNADIY TSIGANOV—International veteran; from the Army squad.

VALERY VASILIEV—A three-year member of Soviet nationals; recruited from Moscow Dynamo.

VITALIY DAVYDOV—Well-known member of six world championship teams; 33.

YURI LIAPKIN—From Moscow Spartak; new to Russian nationals in 1971.

Forwards

VLADIMIR VIKULOV—Helped win six world titles and two Olympic tournaments; Moscow Army star; 26.

ALEKSANDER MALTSEV—Three-time all-star with Moscow Dynamo; scored 87 goals in 94 international matches; 23.

VALERY KHARLAMOV—Swift and wiry; Central Army winger; responsible for 77 goals in 89 international games; 24.

BORIS MIKHAILOV—Able and truculent; NHL-style rabble-rouser from Central Army; 27.

VLADIMIR PETROV—Joined Soviet nationals in 1969; 25.

VIACHESLAV STARSHINOV—Scored 135 goals in 165 international games; Moscow Spartak veteran; 32.

YURI BLINOV—National rookie from Moscow Army; 23.

YEVGENI ZIMIN—Defensive expert from Moscow Spartak; 25.

YURI LEBEDEV—A 21-year-old freshman from Wings of the Soviet.

YEVGENI MISHAKOV—Innovative veteran from Moscow Army; 31.

ALEKSANDER YAKUSHEV—One of the two or three best left wings on earth; from Moscow Spartak; 25.

VIACHESLAV SOLODUKHIN—Sophomore among Soviet nationals; rising Red star from Leningrad; 22.

VIACHESLAV ANISIN—Up from Wings of the Soviet; member of 1972 World Student champions; 22.

ALEKSANDER BODUNOV—Rookie from Wings of the Soviet; 21.

VLADIMIR SHADRIN—Substitute from Spartak; 24.

National Hockey League Trophies

THE STANLEY CUP is awarded annually to the team winning the NHL's best-of-seven final playoff round. The oldest trophy competed for by professional athletes in North America, and symbolic of the World's Hockey Championship, it was donated in 1893 by Frederick Arthur, Lord Stanley of Preston and son of the Earl of Derby.

The Prince of Wales Trophy is presented each year to the team finishing first in the East Division at the end of the regular schedule. It was donated by the Prince of Wales to the NHL in 1924. From 1927–28 to 1937–38 it went to the winner of the American Division. From 1938–39, when the NHL became one section, to 1966–67, it was awarded to the winner of the League's regular season championship. With expansion, it became a divisional trophy again.

The Clarence S. Campbell Bowl, presented in 1968 by the League in honor of the man who has presided over the NHL since 1946, is the West Division counterpart of the Prince of Wales Trophy.

The Hart Memorial Trophy is awarded to the player "adjudged to be most valuable to his team" as selected in a poll by the NHL Writers Association. (The Calder, Norris and Byng are decided in the same way.) The Hart Memorial Trophy was presented to the NHL in 1960 after the original Hart Trophy was retired to the Hockey Hall of Fame. The first Hart Trophy was donated in 1923 by Dr. David A. Hart, father of Cecil Hart, former manager-coach of the Montreal Canadiens.

The Calder Memorial Trophy goes to "the player selected as the most proficient in his first year of competition in the NHL." From 1936–37 until he died in 1943, Frank Calder, then president of the NHL, presented a yearly trophy to the outstanding rookie. After his death the League perpetuated the award as a memorial. To be eligible a player cannot have played more than 25 games in a single preceding season nor in six or more games in each of any two preceding seasons.

The James Norris Memorial Trophy is awarded to "the defense player who demonstrates throughout the season the greatest all-around ability in that position." The Norris Trophy was presented in 1953 in honor of the late owner-president of the Detroit Red Wings by his four children.

The Lady Byng Memorial Trophy is annually won by "the player adjudged to have exhibited the best type of sportsmanship and gentlemanly conduct combined with a high standard of playing ability." Lady Byng, at that time wife of Canada's Governor-General, presented the trophy in 1925. She donated another trophy in 1936 after Frank Boucher of the New York Rangers had retired the first one by winning it seven times in eight seasons. After Lady Byng died in 1949, the NHL presented a new trophy and made it a memorial.

The Art Ross Trophy was presented to the NHL in 1947 by Arthur Howey Ross, former manager-coach of the Boston Bruins. It goes to the player who leads the league in scoring points.

The Vezina Trophy is awarded to "the goalkeeper(s) having played a minimum 25 games for the team with the fewest goals scored against it." It was presented to the league in 1926–27 by Leo Dandurand, Louis Letourneau and Joe Cattaranich, former owners of the Montreal Canadiens, in memory of Georges Vezina, outstanding goalkeeper of the Canadiens.

The Conn Smythe Trophy is given to "the most valuable player for his team in the entire playoffs." The winner is selected by the League governors at the finish of the final game of the Stanley Cup. It was presented in 1964 by Maple Leaf Gardens Ltd. in honor of the former coach, manager, president and owner-governor of the Toronto Maple Leafs.

The Lester Patrick Trophy is awarded "for outstanding service to hockey in the United States." Eligible are players, coaches, officials, executives and referees, and the winner is selected by an award committee comprised of people from many branches of the sport. It was presented by the New York Rangers in 1966 to honor their late coach and general manager.

The Bill Masterton Memorial Trophy is awarded under the trusteeship of the NHL Writers Association to "the NHL player who best exemplifies the qualities of perseverance, sportsmanship and dedication to hockey." The selection is made by a poll among the Association's 16 chapters. The trophy was first presented in 1968 to honor the memory of the late Minnesota North Star player who died on January 15 of that year. A player must participate in at least 50 games to be eligible.

MONTREAL CANADIENS' YEAR-BY-YEAR RECORD

Season	GP	W	L	T	GF	GA	Pts	Finished	Playoff Result
1972–73	78	52	10	16	329	184	120	1st, East Div.	Won Stanley Cup
1971–72	78	46	16	16	307	205	108	3rd, East Div.	Lost Quarterfinal
1970–71	78	42	23	13	291	216	97	3rd, East Div.	Won Stanley Cup
1969–70	76	38	22	16	244	201	92	5th, East Div.	Out of Playoffs
1968-69	76	46	19	11	271	202	103	1st, East Div.	Won Stanley Cup
1967-68	74	42	22	10	236	167	94	1st, East Div.	Won Stanley Cup
1966-67	70	32	25	13	202	188	77	2nd, East Div.	Lost Final
1965-66	70	41	21	8	239	173	90	1st, East Div.	Won Stanley Cup
1964-65	70	36	23	11	211	185	83	2nd, East Div.	Won Stanley Cup
1963-64	70	36	21	13	209	167	85	1st, East Div.	Lost Semifinal
1962-63	70	28	19	23	225	183	79	3rd, East Div.	Lost Semifinal
1961-62	70	42	14	14	259	166	98	1st, East Div.	Lost Semifinal
1960-61	70	41	19	10	254	188	92	1st, East Div.	Lost Semifinal
1959-60	70	40	18	12	255	178	92	1st, East Div.	Won Stanley Cup
1958-59	70	39	18	13	258	158	91	1st, East Div.	Won Stanley Cup
1957-58	70	43	17	10	250	158	96	1st, East Div.	Won Stanley Cup
1956-57	70	35	23	12	210	155	82	2nd, East Div.	Won Stanley Cup
1955-56	70	45	15	10	222	131	100	1st, East Div.	Won Stanley Cup
1954-55	70	41	18	11	228	157	93	2nd, East Div.	Lost Final
1953-54	70	35	24	11	195	141	81	2nd, East Div.	Lost Final
1952-53	70	28	23	19	155	148	75	2nd, East Div.	Won Stanley Cup
1951-52	70	34	26	10	195	164	78	2nd, East Div.	Lost Final
1950-51	70	25	30	15	173	184	65	3rd East Div.	Lost Final
1949-50	70	29	22	19	172	150	77	2nd, East Div.	Lost Semifinal
1948-49	60	28	23	9	152	126	65	3rd, East Div.	Lost Semifinal
1947-48	60	20	29	11	147	169	51	5th, East Div.	Out of Playoffs
1946-47	60	34	16	10	189	138	78	1st, East Div.	Lost Final
1945-46	50	28	17	5	172	134	61	1st, East Div.	Won Stanley Cup
1944-45	50	38	8	4	228	121	80	1st, East Div.	Lost Semifinal
1943-44	50	38	5	7	234	109	83	1st, East Div.	Won Stanley Cup
1942-43	50	19	19	12	181	191	50	4th, East Div.	Lost Semifinal
1941-42	48	18	27	3	134	173	39	6th, East Div.	Lost Quarterfinal
1940-41	48	16	26	6	121	147	38	6th, East Div.	Lost Quarterfinal
1939-40	48	10	33	5	90	167	25	7th, East Div.	Out of Playoffs
1938-39	48	15	24	9	115	146	39	6th, East Div.	Lost Quarterfinal
1937-38	48	18	17	13	123	128	49	3rd, Cdn. Div.	Lost Quarterfinal
1936-37	48	24	18	6	115	111	54	1st, Cdn. Div.	Lost Semifinal
1935-36	48	11	26	11	82	123	33	4th, Cdn. Div.	Out of Playoffs
1934-35	48	19	23	6	110	145	44	3rd, Cdn. Div.	Lost Quarterfinal
1933-34	48	22	20	6	99	101	50	2nd, Cdn. Div.	Lost Quarterfinal
1932-33	48	18	25	5	92	115	41	3rd, Cdn. Div.	Lost Quarterfinal
1931-32	48	25	16	7	128	111	57	1st, Cdn. Div.	Lost Semifinal
1930-31	44	26	10	8	129	89	60	1st, Cdn. Div.	Won Stanley Cup
1929-30	44	21	14	9	142	114	51	2nd, Cdn. Div.	Won Stanley Cup
1928-29	44	22	7	15	71	43	59	1st, Cdn. Div.	Lost Semifinal
1927-28	44	26	11	7	116	48	59	1st, Cdn. Div.	Lost Semifinal
1926-27	44	28	14	2	99	67	58	2nd, Cdn. Div.	Lost Final
1925-26	36	11	24	1	79	108	23	7th	Out of Playoffs
1924-25	30	17	11	2	93	56	36	3rd	Lost Cup Playoff
1923-24	24	13	11	0	59	48	26	2nd	Won Stanley Cup
1922-23	24	13	9	2	73	61	28	2nd	Lost NHL Playoff
1921-22	24	12	11	1	88	94	25	3rd	Out of Playoffs
1920-21	24	13	11	0	112	99	26	3rd	Out of Playoffs
1919-20	24	13	11	0	129	113	26	2nd	Out of Playoffs
1918-19	18	10	8	0	88	78	20	2nd	Cup Final but No Decision
1917-18	22	13	9	0	115	84	26	1st and 3rd*	Lost NHL Final

* Season played in two halves with no combined standing at end.
From 1917-18 through 1925-26, NHL champions played against PCHL champions for Stanley Cup.

355

TORONTO'S YEAR-BY-YEAR RECORD

Season	GP	W	L	T	GF	GA	Pts	Finished	Playoff Result
1972–73	78	27	41	10	247	279	64	6th, East Div.	Out of Playoffs
1971–72	78	33	31	14	209	208	80	4th, East Div.	Lost Quarterfinal
1970–71	78	37	33	8	248	211	82	4th, East Div.	Lost Quarterfinal
1969–70	76	29	34	13	222	242	71	6th, East Div.	Out of Playoffs
1968-69	76	35	26	15	234	217	85	4th, East Div.	Lost Quarterfinal
1967-68	74	33	31	10	209	176	76	5th, East Div.	Out of Playoffs
1966-67	70	32	27	11	204	211	75	3rd, East Div.	Won Stanley Cup
1965-66	70	34	25	11	208	187	79	3rd, East Div.	Lost Semifinal
1964-65	70	30	26	14	204	173	74	4th, East Div.	Lost Semifinal
1963-64	70	33	25	12	192	172	78	3rd, East Div.	Won Stanley Cup
1962-63	70	35	23	12	221	180	82	1st, East Div.	Won Stanley Cup
1961-62	70	37	22	11	232	180	85	2nd, East Div.	Won Stanley Cup
1960-61	70	39	19	12	234	176	90	2nd, East Div.	Lost Semifinal
1959-60	70	35	26	9	199	195	79	2nd, East Div.	Lost Final
1958-59	70	27	32	11	189	201	65	4th, East Div.	Lost Final
1957-58	70	21	38	11	192	226	53	6th, East Div.	Out of Playoffs
1956-57	70	21	34	15	174	192	57	5th, East Div.	Out of Playoffs
1955-56	70	24	33	13	153	181	61	4th, East Div.	Lost Semifinal
1954-55	70	24	24	22	147	135	70	3rd, East Div.	Lost Semifinal
1953-54	70	32	24	14	152	131	78	3rd, East Div.	Lost Semifinal
1952-53	70	27	30	13	156	167	67	5th, East Div.	Out of Playoffs
1951-52	70	29	25	16	168	157	74	3rd, East Div.	Lost Semifinal
1950-51	70	41	16	13	212	138	95	2nd, East Div.	Won Stanley Cup
1949-50	70	31	27	12	176	173	74	3rd, East Div.	Lost Semifinal
1948-49	60	22	25	13	147	161	57	4th, East Div.	Won Stanley Cup
1947-48	60	32	15	13	182	143	77	1st, East Div.	Won Stanley Cup
1946-47	60	31	19	10	209	172	72	2nd, East Div.	Won Stanley Cup
1945-46	50	19	24	7	174	185	45	5th, East Div.	Out of Playoffs
1944-45	50	24	22	4	183	161	52	3rd, East Div.	Won Stanley Cup
1943-44	50	23	23	4	214	174	50	3rd, East Div.	Lost Semifinal
1942-43	50	22	19	9	198	159	53	3rd, East Div.	Lost Semifinal
1941-42	48	27	18	3	158	136	57	2nd, East Div.	Won Stanley Cup
1940-41	48	28	14	6	145	99	62	2nd, East Div.	Lost Semifinal
1939-40	48	25	17	6	134	110	56	3rd, East Div.	Lost Final
1938-39	48	19	20	9	114	107	47	3rd, East Div.	Lost Final
1937-38	48	24	15	9	151	127	57	1st, Cdn. Div.	Lost Final
1936-37	48	22	21	5	119	115	49	3rd, Cdn. Div.	Lost Quarterfinal
1935-36	48	23	19	6	126	106	52	2nd, Cdn. Div.	Lost Final
1934-35	48	30	14	4	157	111	64	1st, Cdn. Div.	Lost Final
1933-34	48	26	13	9	174	119	61	1st, Cdn. Div.	Lost Semifinal
1932-33	48	24	18	6	119	111	54	1st, Cdn. Div.	Lost Final
1931-32	48	23	18	7	155	127	53	2nd, Cdn. Div.	Won Stanley Cup
1930-31	44	22	13	9	118	99	53	2nd, Cdn. Div.	Lost Quarterfinal
1929-30	44	17	21	6	116	124	40	4th, Cdn. Div.	Out of Playoffs
1928-29	44	21	18	5	85	69	47	3rd, Cdn. Div.	Lost Semifinal
1927-28	44	18	18	8	89	88	44	4th, Cdn. Div.	Out of Playoffs
*1926-27	44	15	24	5	79	94	35	5th, Cdn. Div.	Out of Playoffs
1925-26	36	12	21	3	92	114	27	6th	Out of Playoffs
1924-25	30	19	11	0	90	84	38	2nd	Lost NHL Semifinal
1923-24	24	10	14	0	59	85	20	3rd	Out of Playoffs
1922-23	24	13	10	1	82	88	27	3rd	Out of Playoffs
1921-22	24	13	10	1	98	97	27	2nd	Won Stanley Cup
1920-21	24	15	9	0	105	100	30	1st	Lost NHL Playoffs
**1919-20	24	12	12	0	119	106	24	3rd	Out of Cup Playoffs
1918-19	18	5	13	0	65	92	10	3rd	Out of Playoffs
1917-18	22	13	9	0	108	109	26	2nd and 1st	Won Stanley Cup

* Name changed from St. Patricks to Maple Leafs.
** Name changed from Arenas to St. Patricks.

BOSTON BRUINS' YEAR-BY-YEAR RECORD

Season	GP	W	L	T	GF	GA	Pts	Finished	Playoff Result
1972–73	78	51	22	5	330	235	107	2nd, East Div.	Lost Quarterfinal
1971–72	78	54	13	11	330	204	119	1st, East Div.	Won Stanley Cup
1970–71	78	57	14	7	339	207	121	1st, East Div.	Lost Quarterfinal
1969–70	76	40	17	19	277	216	99	2nd, East Div.	Won Stanley Cup
1968-69	76	42	18	16	303	221	100	2nd, East Div.	Lost Semifinal
1967-68	74	37	27	10	259	216	84	3rd, East Div.	Lost Quarterfinal
1966-67	70	17	43	10	182	253	44	6th, East Div.	Out of Playoffs
1965-66	70	21	43	6	174	275	48	5th, East Div.	Out of Playoffs
1964-65	70	21	43	6	166	253	48	6th, East Div.	Out of Playoffs
1963-64	70	18	40	12	170	212	48	6th, East Div.	Out of Playoffs
1962-63	70	14	39	17	198	281	45	6th, East Div.	Out of Playoffs
1961-62	70	15	47	8	177	306	38	6th, East Div.	Out of Playoffs
1960-61	70	15	42	13	176	254	43	6th, East Div.	Out of Playoffs
1959-60	70	28	34	8	220	241	64	5th, East Div.	Out of Playoffs
1958-59	70	32	29	9	205	215	73	2nd, East Div.	Lost Semifinal
1957-58	70	27	28	15	199	194	69	4th, East Div.	Lost Final
1956-57	70	34	24	12	195	174	80	3rd, East Div.	Lost Final
1955-56	70	23	34	13	147	185	59	5th, East Div.	Out of Playoffs
1954-55	70	23	26	21	169	188	67	4th, East Div.	Lost Semifinal
1953-54	70	32	28	10	177	181	74	4th, East Div.	Lost Semifinal
1952-53	70	28	29	13	152	172	69	3rd, East Div.	Lost Final
1951-52	70	25	29	16	162	176	66	4th, East Div.	Lost Semifinal
1950-51	70	22	30	18	178	197	62	4th, East Div.	Lost Semifinal
1949-50	70	22	32	16	198	228	60	5th, East Div.	Out of Playoffs
1948-49	60	29	23	8	178	163	66	2nd, East Div.	Lost Semifinal
1947-48	60	23	24	13	167	168	59	3rd, East Div.	Lost Semifinal
1946-47	60	26	23	11	190	175	63	3rd, East Div.	Lost Semifinal
1945-46	50	24	18	8	167	156	56	2nd, East Div.	Lost Final
1944-45	50	16	30	4	179	219	36	4th, East Div.	Lost Semifinal
1943-44	50	19	26	5	223	268	43	5th, East Div.	Out of Playoffs
1942-43	50	24	17	9	195	176	57	2nd East Div.	Lost Final
1941-42	48	25	17	6	160	118	56	3rd, East Div.	Lost Semifinal
1940-41	48	27	8	13	168	102	67	1st, East Div.	Won Stanley Cup
1939-40	48	31	12	5	170	98	67	1st, East Div.	Lost Semifinal
1938-39	48	36	10	2	156	76	74	1st, East Div.	Won Stanley Cup
1937-38	48	30	11	7	142	89	67	1st, Am. Div.	Lost Semifinal
1936-37	48	23	18	7	120	110	53	2nd, Am. Div.	Lost Quarterfinal
1935-36	48	22	20	6	92	83	50	2nd, Am. Div.	Lost Quarterfinal
1934-35	48	26	16	6	129	112	58	1st, Am. Div.	Lost Semifinal
1933-34	48	18	25	5	111	130	41	4th, Am. Div.	Out of Playoffs
1932-33	48	25	15	8	124	88	58	1st, Am. Div.	Lost Semifinal
1931-32	48	15	21	12	122	117	42	4th, Am. Div.	Out of Playoffs
1930-31	44	28	10	6	143	90	62	1st, Am. Div.	Lost Semifinal
1929-30	44	38	5	1	179	98	77	1st, Am. Div.	Lost Final
1928-29	44	26	13	5	89	52	57	1st, Am. Div.	Won Stanley Cup
1927-28	44	20	13	11	77	70	51	1st, Am. Div.	Lost Semifinal
1926-27	44	21	20	3	97	89	45	2nd, Am. Div.	Lost Final
1925-26	36	17	15	4	92	85	38	4th	Out of Playoffs
1924-25	30	6	24	0	49	119	12	6th	Out of Playoffs

DETROIT'S YEAR-BY-YEAR RECORD

Season	GP	W	L	T	GF	GA	Pts	Finished	Playoff Result
1972–73	78	37	29	12	265	243	86	5th, East Div.	Out of Playoffs
1971–72	78	33	35	10	261	262	76	5th, East Div.	Out of Playoffs
1970–71	78	22	45	11	209	308	55	7th, East Div.	Out of Playoffs
1969–70	76	40	21	15	246	199	95	3rd, East Div.	Lost Quarterfinal
1968-69	76	33	31	12	239	221	78	5th, East Div.	Out of Playoffs
1967-68	74	27	35	12	245	257	66	6th, East Div.	Out of Playoffs
1966-67	70	27	39	4	212	241	58	5th, East Div.	Out of Playoffs
1965-66	70	31	27	12	221	194	74	4th, East Div.	Lost Final
1964-65	70	40	23	7	224	175	87	1st, East Div.	Lost Semifinal
1963-64	70	30	29	11	191	204	71	4th, East Div.	Lost Final
1962-63	70	32	25	13	200	194	77	4th, East Div.	Lost Final
1961-62	70	23	33	14	184	219	60	5th, East Div.	Out of Playoffs
1960-61	70	25	29	16	195	215	66	4th, East Div.	Lost Final
1959-60	70	26	29	15	186	197	67	4th, East Div.	Lost Semifinal
1958-59	70	25	37	8	167	218	58	6th, East Div.	Out of Playoffs
1957-58	70	29	29	12	176	207	70	3rd, East Div.	Lost Semifinal
1956-57	70	38	20	12	198	157	88	1st, East Div.	Lost Semifinal
1955-56	70	30	24	16	183	148	76	2nd, East Div.	Lost Final
1954-55	70	42	17	11	204	134	95	1st, East Div.	**Won Stanley Cup**
1953-54	70	37	19	14	191	132	88	1st, East Div.	**Won Stanley Cup**
1952-53	70	36	16	18	222	133	90	1st, East Div.	Lost Semifinal
1951-52	70	44	14	12	215	133	100	1st, East Div.	**Won Stanley Cup**
1950-51	70	44	13	13	236	139	101	1st, East Div.	Lost Semifinal
1949-50	70	37	19	14	229	164	88	1st, East Div.	**Won Stanley Cup**
1948-49	60	34	19	7	195	145	75	1st, East Div.	Lost Final
1947-48	60	30	18	12	187	148	72	2nd, East Div.	Lost Final
1946-47	60	22	27	11	190	193	55	4th, East Div.	Lost Semifinal
1945-46	50	20	20	10	146	159	50	4th, East Div.	Lost Semifinal
1944-45	50	31	14	5	218	161	67	2nd, East Div.	Lost Final
1943-44	50	26	18	6	214	177	58	2nd, East Div.	Lost Semifinal
1942-43	50	25	14	11	169	124	61	1st, East Div.	**Won Stanley Cup**
1941-42	48	19	25	4	140	147	42	5th, East Div.	Lost Final
1940-41	48	21	16	11	112	102	53	3rd, East Div.	Lost Final
1939-40	48	16	26	6	90	126	38	5th, East Div.	Lost Semifinal
1938-39	48	18	24	6	107	128	42	5th, East Div.	Lost Semifinal
1937-38	48	12	25	11	99	133	35	4th, Am. Div.	Out of Playoffs
1936-37	48	25	14	9	128	102	59	1st, Am. Div.	**Won Stanley Cup**
1935-36	48	24	16	8	124	103	56	1st, Am. Div.	**Won Stanley Cup**
1934-35	48	19	22	7	127	114	45	4th, Am. Div.	Out of Playoffs
*1933-34	48	24	14	10	113	98	58	1st, Am. Div.	Lost Final
1932-33	48	25	15	8	111	93	58	2nd, Am. Div.	Lost Semifinal
1931-32	48	18	20	10	95	108	46	3rd, Am. Div.	Lost Quarterfinal
**1930-31	44	16	21	7	102	105	39	4th, Am. Div.	Out of Playoffs
1929-30	44	14	24	6	117	133	34	4th, Am. Div.	Out of Playoffs
1928-29	44	19	16	9	72	63	47	3rd, Am. Div.	Lost Quarterfinal
1927-28	44	19	19	6	88	79	44	4th, Am. Div.	Out of Playoffs
***1926-27	44	12	28	4	76	105	28	5th, Am. Div.	Out of Playoffs

* Team name changed to Red Wings.
** Team name changed to Falcons.
*** Team named Cougars.

NEW YORK RANGERS' YEAR-BY-YEAR RECORD

Season	GP	W	L	T	GF	GA	Pts	Finished	Playoff Result
1972–73	78	47	23	8	297	208	102	3rd, East Div.	Lost Semifinal
1971–72	78	48	17	13	317	192	109	2nd, East Div.	Lost Final
1970–71	78	49	18	11	259	177	109	2nd, East Div.	Lost Semifinal
1969–70	76	38	22	16	246	189	92	4th, East Div.	Lost Quarterfinal
1968-69	76	41	26	9	234	217	91	3rd, East Div.	Lost Quarterfinal
1967-68	74	39	23	12	226	183	90	2nd, East Div.	Lost Quarterfinal
1966-67	70	30	28	12	188	189	72	4th, East Div.	Lost Semifinal
1965-66	70	18	41	11	195	261	47	6th, East Div.	Out of Playoffs
1964-65	70	20	38	12	179	246	52	5th, East Div.	Out of Playoffs
1963-64	70	22	38	10	186	242	54	5th, East Div.	Out of Playoffs
1962-63	70	22	36	12	211	233	56	5th, East Div.	Out of Playoffs
1961-62	70	26	32	12	195	207	64	4th, East Div.	Lost Semifinal
1960-61	70	22	38	10	204	248	54	5th, East Div.	Out of Playoffs
1959-60	70	17	38	15	187	247	49	6th, East Div.	Out of Playoffs
1958-59	70	26	32	12	201	217	64	5th, East Div.	Out of Playoffs
1957-58	70	32	25	13	195	188	77	2nd, East Div.	Lost Semifinal
1956-57	70	26	30	14	184	227	66	4th, East Div.	Lost Semifinal
1955-56	70	32	28	10	204	203	74	3rd, East Div.	Lost Semifinal
1954-55	70	17	35	18	150	210	52	5th, East Div.	Out of Playoffs
1953-54	70	29	31	10	161	182	68	5th, East Div.	Out of Playoffs
1952-53	70	17	37	16	152	211	50	6th, East Div.	Out of Playoffs
1951-52	70	23	34	13	192	219	59	5th, East Div.	Out of Playoffs
1950-51	70	20	29	21	169	201	61	5th, East Div.	Out of Playoffs
1949-50	70	28	31	11	170	189	67	4th, East Div.	Lost Final
1948-49	60	18	31	11	133	172	47	6th, East Div.	Out of Playoffs
1947-48	60	21	26	13	176	201	55	4th, East Div.	Lost Semifinal
1946-47	60	22	32	6	167	186	50	5th, East Div.	Out of Playoffs
1945-46	50	13	28	9	144	191	35	6th, East Div.	Out of Playoffs
1944-45	50	11	29	10	154	247	32	6th, East Div.	Out of Playoffs
1943-44	50	6	39	5	162	310	17	6th, East Div.	Out of Playoffs
1942-43	50	11	31	8	161	253	30	6th, East Div.	Out of Playoffs
1941-42	48	29	17	2	177	143	60	1st, East Div.	Lost Semifinal
1940-41	48	21	19	8	143	125	50	4th, East Div.	Lost Quarterfinal
1939-40	48	27	11	10	136	77	64	2nd, East Div.	**Won Stanley Cup**
1938-39	48	26	16	6	149	105	58	2nd, East Div.	Lost Semifinal
1937-38	48	27	15	6	149	96	60	2nd, Am. Div.	Lost Quarterfinal
1936-37	48	19	20	9	117	106	47	3rd, Am. Div.	Lost Final
1935-36	48	19	17	12	91	96	50	4th, Am. Div.	Out of Playoffs
1934-35	48	22	20	6	137	139	50	3rd, Am. Div.	Lost Semifinal
1933-34	48	21	19	8	120	113	50	3rd, Am. Div.	Lost Quarterfinal
1932-33	48	23	17	8	135	107	54	3rd, Am. Div.	**Won Stanley Cup**
1931-32	48	23	17	8	134	112	54	1st, Am. Div.	Lost Final
1930-31	44	19	16	9	106	87	47	3rd, Am. Div.	Lost Semifinal
1929-30	44	17	17	10	136	143	44	3rd, Am. Div.	Lost Semifinal
1928-29	44	21	13	10	72	65	52	2nd, Am. Div.	Lost Final
1927-28	44	19	16	9	94	79	47	2nd, Am. Div.	**Won Stanley Cup**
1926-27	44	25	13	6	95	72	56	1st, Am. Div.	Lost Quarterfinal

CHICAGO BLACK HAWKS' YEAR-BY-YEAR RECORD

Season	GP	W	L	T	GF	GA	Pts	Finished	Playoff Result
1972–73	78	42	27	9	284	225	93	1st, West Div.	Lost Final
1971–72	78	46	17	15	256	166	107	1st, West Div.	Lost Semifinal
1970–71	78	49	20	9	277	184	107	1st, West Div.	Lost Final
1969–70	76	45	22	9	250	170	99	1st, East Div.	Lost Semifinal
1968-69	76	34	33	9	280	246	77	6th, East Div.	Out of Playoffs
1967-68	74	32	26	16	212	222	80	4th, East Div.	Lost Semifinal
1966-67	70	41	17	12	264	170	94	1st, East Div.	Lost Semifinal
1965-66	70	37	25	8	240	187	82	2nd, East Div.	Lost Semifinal
1964-65	70	34	28	8	224	176	76	3rd, East Div.	Lost Final
1963-64	70	36	22	12	218	169	84	2nd, East Div.	Lost Semifinal
1962-63	70	32	21	17	194	178	81	2nd, East Div.	Lost Semifinal
1961-62	70	31	26	13	217	186	75	3rd, East Div.	Lost Final
1960-61	70	29	24	17	198	180	75	3rd, East Div.	**Won Stanley Cup**
1959-60	70	28	29	13	191	180	69	3rd, East Div.	Lost Semifinal
1958-59	70	28	29	13	197	208	69	3rd, East Div.	Lost Semifinal
1957-58	70	24	39	7	163	202	55	5th, East Div.	Out of Playoffs
1956-57	70	16	39	15	169	225	47	6th, East Div.	Out of Playoffs
1955-56	70	19	39	12	155	216	50	6th, East Div.	Out of Playoffs
1954-55	70	13	40	17	161	235	43	6th, East Div.	Out of Playoffs
1953-54	70	12	51	7	133	242	31	6th, East Div.	Out of Playoffs
1952-53	70	27	28	15	169	175	69	4th, East Div.	Lost Semifinal
1951-52	70	17	44	9	158	241	43	6th, East Div.	Out of Playoffs
1950-51	70	13	47	10	171	280	36	6th, East Div.	Out of Playoffs
1949-50	70	22	38	10	203	244	54	6th, East Div.	Out of Playoffs
1948-49	60	21	31	8	173	211	50	5th, East Div.	Out of Playoffs
1947-48	60	20	34	6	195	225	46	6th, East Div.	Out of Playoffs
1946-47	60	19	37	4	193	274	42	6th, East Div.	Out of Playoffs
1945-46	50	23	20	7	200	178	53	3rd, East Div.	Lost Semifinal
1944-45	50	13	30	7	141	194	33	5th, East Div.	Out of Playoffs
1943-44	50	22	23	5	178	187	49	4th, East Div.	Lost Final
1942-43	50	17	18	15	179	180	49	5th, East Div.	Out of Playoffs
1941-42	48	22	23	3	145	155	47	4th, East Div.	Lost Quarterfinal
1940-41	48	16	25	7	112	139	39	5th, East Div.	Lost Semifinal
1939-40	48	23	19	6	112	120	52	4th, East. Div.	Lost Quarterfinal
1938-39	48	12	28	8	91	132	32	7th, East Div.	Out of Playoffs
1937-38	48	14	25	9	97	139	37	3rd, Am. Div.	**Won Stanley Cup**
1936-37	48	14	27	7	99	131	35	4th, Am. Div.	Out of Playoffs
1935-36	48	21	19	8	93	92	50	3rd, Am. Div.	Lost Quarterfinal
1934-35	48	26	17	5	118	88	57	2nd, Am. Div.	Lost Quarterfinal
1933-34	48	20	17	11	88	83	51	2nd, Am. Div.	**Won Stanley Cup**
1932-33	48	16	20	12	88	101	44	4th, Am. Div.	Out of Playoffs
1931-32	48	18	19	11	86	101	47	2nd, Am. Div.	Lost Quarterfinal
1930-31	44	24	17	3	108	78	51	2nd, Am. Div.	Lost Final
1929-30	44	21	18	5	117	111	47	2nd, Am. Div.	Lost Quarterfinal
1928-29	44	7	29	8	33	85	22	5th, Am. Div.	Out of Playoffs
1927-28	44	7	34	3	68	134	17	5th, Am. Div.	Out of Playoffs
1926-27	44	19	22	3	115	116	41	3rd, Am. Div.	Lost Quarterfinal

PHILADELPHIA FLYERS' YEAR-BY-YEAR RECORD

Season	GP	W	L	T	GF	GA	Pts	Finished	Playoff Result
1972–73	78	37	30	11	296	256	85	2nd, West Div.	Lost Semifinal
1971–72	78	26	38	14	200	236	66	5th, West Div.	Out of Playoffs
1970–71	78	28	33	17	207	225	73	3rd, West Div.	Lost Quarterfinal
1969–70	76	17	35	24	197	225	58	5th, West Div.	Out of Playoffs
1968–69	76	20	35	21	174	225	61	3rd, West Div.	Lost Quarterfinal
1967–68	74	31	32	11	173	179	73	1st, West Div.	Lost Quarterfinal

LOS ANGELES KINGS' YEAR-BY-YEAR RECORD

1972–73	78	31	36	11	232	245	73	6th, West Div.	Out of Playoffs
1971–72	78	20	49	9	206	305	49	7th, West Div.	Out of Playoffs
1970–71	78	25	40	13	239	303	63	5th, West Div.	Out of Playoffs
1969–70	76	14	52	10	168	290	38	6th, West Div.	Out of Playoffs
1968–69	76	24	42	10	185	260	58	4th, West Div.	Lost Semifinal
1967–68	74	31	33	10	200	224	72	2nd, West Div.	Lost Quarterfinal

ST. LOUIS BLUES' YEAR-BY-YEAR RECORD

1972–73	78	32	34	12	233	251	76	4th, West Div.	Lost Quarterfinal
1971–72	78	28	39	11	208	247	67	3rd, West Div.	Lost Semifinal
1970–71	78	34	25	19	223	208	87	2nd, West Div.	Lost Quarterfinal
1969–70	76	37	27	12	224	179	86	1st, West Div.	Lost Final
1968–69	76	37	25	14	204	157	88	1st, West Div.	Lost Final
1967–68	74	27	31	16	177	191	70	3rd, West Div.	Lost Final

MINNESOTA NORTH STARS' YEAR-BY-YEAR RECORD

1972–73	78	37	30	11	254	256	85	3rd, West Div.	Lost Quarterfinal
1971–72	78	37	29	12	212	191	86	2nd, West Div.	Lost Quarterfinal
1970–71	78	28	34	16	191	223	72	4th, West Div.	Lost Semifinal
1969–70	76	19	35	22	224	257	60	3rd, West Div.	Lost Quarterfinal
1968–69	76	18	43	15	189	270	51	6th, West Div.	Out of Playoffs
1967–68	74	27	32	15	191	226	69	4th, West Div.	Lost Semifinal

PITTSBURGH PENGUINS' YEAR-BY-YEAR RECORD

1972–73	78	32	37	9	257	265	73	5th, West Div.	Out of Playoffs
1971–72	78	26	38	14	220	258	66	4th, West Div.	Lost Quarterfinal
1970–71	78	21	37	20	221	240	62	6th, West Div.	Out of Playoffs
1969–70	76	26	38	12	182	238	64	2nd, West Div.	Lost Semifinal
1968–69	76	20	45	11	189	252	51	5th, West Div.	Out of Playoffs
1967–68	74	27	34	13	195	216	67	5th, West Div.	Out of Playoffs

CALIFORNIA GOLDEN SEALS' YEAR-BY-YEAR RECORD

1972–73	78	16	46	16	213	323	48	8th, West Div.	Out of Playoffs
1971–72	78	21	39	18	216	288	60	6th, West Div.	Out of Playoffs
1970–71	78	20	53	5	199	320	45	7th, West Div.	Out of Playoffs
1969–70	76	22	40	14	169	243	58	4th, West Div.	Lost Quarterfinal
1968–69	76	29	36	11	219	251	69	2nd, West Div.	Lost Quarterfinal
1967–68	74	15	42	17	153	219	47	6th, West Div.	Out of Playoffs

BUFFALO SABRES' YEAR-BY-YEAR RECORD

1972–73	78	37	27	14	257	219	88	4th, East Div.	Lost Quarterfinal
1971–72	78	16	43	19	203	289	51	6th, East Div.	Out of Playoffs
1970–71	78	24	39	15	217	291	63	5th, East Div.	Out of Playoffs

VANCOUVER CANUCKS' YEAR-BY-YEAR RECORD

Season	GP	W	L	T	GF	GA	Pts	Finished	Playoff Result
1972–73	78	22	47	9	233	339	53	7th, East Div.	Out of Playoffs
1971–72	78	20	50	8	203	297	48	7th, East Div.	Out of Playoffs
1970–71	78	24	46	8	229	296	56	6th, East Div.	Out of Playoffs

ATLANTA FLAMES' YEAR-BY-YEAR RECORD

Season	GP	W	L	T	GF	GA	Pts	Finished	Playoff Result
1972–73	78	25	38	15	191	239	65	7th, West Div.	Out of Playoffs

NEW YORK ISLANDERS' YEAR-BY-YEAR RECORD

Season	GP	W	L	T	GF	GA	Pts	Finished	Playoff Result
1972–73	78	12	60	6	170	347	30	8th, East Div.	Out of Playoffs

STANLEY CUP WINNERS

Season	Champions	Manager	Coach
1972-73	Montreal Canadiens	Sam Pollock	Scotty Bowman
1971-72	Boston Bruins	Milt Schmidt	Tom Johnson
1970-71	Montreal Canadiens	Sam Pollock	Al MacNeil
1969-70	Boston Bruins	Milt Schmidt	Harry Sinden
1968-69	Montreal Canadiens	Sam Pollock	Claude Ruel
1967-68	Montreal Canadiens	Sam Pollock	Toe Blake
1966-67	Toronto Maple Leafs	Punch Imlach	Punch Imlach
1965-66	Montreal Canadiens	Sam Pollock	Toe Blake
1964-65	Montreal Canadiens	Sam Pollock	Toe Blake
1963-64	Toronto Maple Leafs	Punch Imlach	Punch Imlach
1962-63	Toronto Maple Leafs	Punch Imlach	Punch Imlach
1961-62	Toronto Maple Leafs	Punch Imlach	Punch Imlach
1960-61	Chicago Black Hawks	Tommy Ivan	Rudy Pilous
1959-60	Montreal Canadiens	Frank Selke	Toe Blake
1958-59	Montreal Canadiens	Frank Selke	Toe Blake
1957-58	Montreal Canadiens	Frank Selke	Toe Blake
1956-57	Montreal Canadiens	Frank Selke	Toe Blake
1955-56	Montreal Canadiens	Frank Selke	Toe Blake
1954-55	Detroit Red Wings	Jack Adams	Jimmy Skinner
1953-54	Detroit Red Wings	Jack Adams	Tommy Ivan
1952-53	Montreal Canadiens	Frank Selke	Dick Irvin
1951-52	Detroit Red Wings	Jack Adams	Tommy Ivan
1950-51	Toronto Maple Leafs	Conn Smythe	Joe Primeau
1949-50	Detroit Red Wings	Jack Adams	Tommy Ivan
1948-49	Toronto Maple Leafs	Conn Smythe	Hap Day
1947-48	Toronto Maple Leafs	Conn Smythe	Hap Day
1946-47	Toronto Maple Leafs	Conn Smythe	Hap Day
1945-46	Montreal Canadiens	Tommy Gorman	Dick Irvin
1944-45	Toronto Maple Leafs	Conn Smythe	Hap Day
1943-44	Montreal Canadiens	Tommy Gorman	Dick Irvin
1942-43	Detroit Red Wings	Jack Adams	Jack Adams
1941-42	Toronto Maple Leafs	Conn Smythe	Hap Day
1940-41	Boston Bruins	Art Ross	Cooney Weiland
1939-40	New York Rangers	Lester Patrick	Frank Boucher
1938-39	Boston Bruins	Art Ross	Art Ross

Season	Champions	Manager	Coach
1937-38—Chicago Black Hawks	Bill Stewart	Bill Stewart
1936-37—Detroit Red Wings	Jack Adams	Jack Adams
1935-36—Detroit Red Wings	Jack Adams	Jack Adams
1934-35—Montreal Maroons	Tommy Gorman	Tommy Gorman
1933-34—Chicago Black Hawks	Tommy Gorman	Tommy Gorman
1932-33—New York Rangers	Lester Patrick	Lester Patrick
1931-32—Toronto Maple Leafs	Conn Smythe	Dick Irvin
1930-31—Montreal Canadiens	Cecil Hart	Cecil Hart
1929-30—Montreal Canadiens	Cecil Hart	Cecil Hart
1928-29—Boston Bruins	Art Ross	Cy Denneny
1927-28—New York Rangers	Lester Patrick	Lester Patrick
1926-27—Ottawa Senators	Dave Gill	Dave Gill
1925-26—Montreal Maroons	Eddie Gerard	Eddie Gerard
1924-25—Victoria Cougars	Lester Patrick	Lester Patrick
1923-24—Montreal Canadiens	Leo Dandurand	Leo Dandurand
1922-23—Ottawa Senators	Tommy Gorman	Pete Green
1921-22—Toronto St. Pats	Charlie Querrie	Eddie Powers
1920-21—Ottawa Senators	Tommy Gorman	Pete Green
1919-20—Ottawa Senators	Tommy Gorman	Pete Green
1918-19—*a*—No decision		
1917-18—Toronto Arenas	Charlie Querrie	Dick Carroll

a In the spring of 1919 the Montreal Canadiens traveled to Seattle to meet Seattle, PCHL champions. After five games had been played—teams were tied at two wins each and one tie—the series was called off by the local Department of Health because of the influenza epidemic and the death from influenza of Joe Hall.

STANLEY CUP WINNERS PRIOR TO FORMATION OF NHL IN 1917

Season	Champions	Manager	Coach
1916-17—Seattle Metropolitans	Pete Muldoon	Pete Muldoon
1915-16—Montreal Canadiens	Geo. Kennedy	George Kennedy
1914-15—Vancouver Millionaires	Frank Patrick	Frank Patrick
1913-14—Toronto Ontarios	Jack Marshall	Scotty Davidson°
°°1912-13—Quebec Bulldogs	M. J. Quinn	Joe Malone°
1911-12—Quebec Bulldogs	M. J. Quinn	C. Nolan
1910-11—Ottawa Senators	————	Bruce Stuart°
1909-10—Montreal Wanderers	R. R. Boon	Pud Glass°
1908-09—Ottawa Senators	————	Bruce Stuart°
1907-08—Montreal Wanderers	R. R. Boon	Cecil Blachford
1906-07—Montreal Wanderers (March)	R. R. Boon	Cecil Blachford
1906-07—Kenora Thistles (January)	F. A. Hudson	Tommy Phillips°
1905-06—Montreal Wanderers	————	
1904-05—Ottawa Silver Seven	————	A. T. Smith
1903-04—Ottawa Silver Seven	————	A. T. Smith
1902-03—Ottawa Silver Seven	————	A. T. Smith
1901-02—Montreal A.A.A.	————	R. R. Boon°

* *In the early years the teams were frequently run by the Captain.* ° Indicates Captain.

°° Victoria defeated Quebec in challenge series. No official recognition.

Season	Champions	Manager	Coach
1900-01—Winnipeg Victorias			
1899-1900—Montreal Shamrocks			H. J. Trihey*
1898-99—Montreal Shamrocks			H. J. Trihey*
1897-98—Montreal Victorias			F. Richardson
1896-97—Montreal Victorias			Mike Grant*
1895-96—Winnipeg Victorias (Feb.) ..			
1894-95—Montreal Victorias			Mike Grant*
1893-94—Montreal A.A.A.			

PRINCE OF WALES TROPHY WINNERS

1972-73—Montreal Canadiens
1971-72—Boston Bruins
1970-71—Boston Bruins
1969-70—Chicago Black Hawks
1968-69—Montreal Canadiens
1967-68—Montreal Canadiens
1966-67—Chicago Black Hawks
1965-66—Montreal Canadiens
1964-65—Detroit Red Wings
1963-64—Montreal Canadiens
1962-63—Toronto Maple Leafs
1961-62—Montreal Canadiens
1960-61—Montreal Canadiens
1959-60—Montreal Canadiens
1958-59—Montreal Canadiens
1957-58—Montreal Canadiens
1956-57—Detroit Red Wings
1955-56—Montreal Canadiens
1954-55—Detroit Red Wings
1953-54—Detroit Red Wings
1952-53—Detroit Red Wings
1951-52—Detroit Red Wings
1950-51—Detroit Red Wings
1949-50—Detroit Red Wings
1948-49—Detroit Red Wings
1947-48—Toronto Maple Leafs
1946-47—Montreal Canadiens
1945-46—Montreal Canadiens

1944-45—Montreal Canadiens
1943-44—Montreal Canadiens
1942-43—Detroit Red Wings
1941-42—New York Rangers
1940-41—Boston Bruins
1939-40—Boston Bruins
1938-39—Boston Bruins
1937-38—Toronto Maple Leafs
1936-37—Detroit Red Wings
1935-36—Detroit Red Wings
1934-35—Toronto Maple Leafs
1933-34—Detroit Red Wings
1932-33—Toronto Maple Leafs
1931-32—New York Rangers
1930-31—Montreal Canadiens
1929-30—Boston Bruins
1928-29—Boston Bruins
*1927-28—New York Rangers
*1926-27—Ottawa Senators
1925-26—Montreal Maroons
1924-25—Montreal Canadiens
1923-24—Montreal Canadiens
1922-23—Ottawa Senators
1921-22—Toronto St. Pats
1920-21—Ottawa Senators
1919-20—Ottawa Senators
1918-19—Montreal Canadiens
1917-18—Toronto Arenas

* No intersectional playoffs took place during these years. Top three teams in each division played off independently. Rangers finished second in American Division in 1927-28, while Ottawa finished first in Canadian Division in 1926-27.

CLARENCE S. CAMPBELL BOWL WINNERS

1972-73—Chicago Black Hawks
1971-72—Chicago Black Hawks
1970-71—Chicago Black Hawks

1969-70—St. Louis Blues
1968-69—St. Louis Blues
1967-68—Philadelphia Flyers

NATIONAL HOCKEY LEAGUE INDIVIDUAL TROPHY WINNERS

Year	Art Ross Trophy		Hart Trophy		Lady Byng Trophy	
1973	Phil Esposito,	Bos.	Bobby Clarke,	Phil.	Gil Perreault,	Buff.
1972	Phil Esposito,	Bos.	Bobby Orr,	Bos.	Jean Ratelle,	N.Y. Rang.
1971	Phil Esposito,	Bos.	Bobby Orr,	Bos.	Johnny Bucyk,	Bos.
1970	Bobby Orr,	Bos.	Bobby Orr,	Bos.	Phil Goyette,	St. L.
1969	Phil Esposito,	Bos.	Phil Esposito,	Bos.	Alex Delvecchio,	Det.
1968	Stan Mikita,	Chi.	Stan Mikita,	Chi.	Stan Mikita,	Chi.
1967	Stan Mikita,	Chi.	Stan Mikita,	Chi.	Stan Mikita,	Chi.
1966	Bobby Hull,	Chi.	Bobby Hull,	Chi.	Alex Delvecchio,	Det.
1965	Stan Mikita,	Chi.	Bobby Hull,	Chi.	Bobby Hull,	Chi.
1964	Stan Mikita,	Chi.	Jean Beliveau,	Mtl. C.	Ken Wharram,	Chi.
1963	Gordie Howe,	Det.	Gordie Howe,	Det.	Dave Keon,	Tor.
1962	Bobby Hull,	Chi.	Jacques Plante,	Mtl. C.	Dave Keon,	Tor.
1961	Bernie Geoffrion,	Mtl. C.	Bernie Geoffrion,	Mtl. C.	Red Kelly,	Tor.
1960	Bobby Hull,	Chi.	Gordie Howe,	Det.	Don McKenney,	Bos.
1959	Dickie Moore,	Mtl. C.	A. Bathgate,	N.Y. Rang.	Alex Delvecchio,	Det.
1958	Dickie Moore,	Mtl. C.	Gordie Howe,	Det.	C. Henry,	N.Y. Rang.
1957	Gordie Howe,	Det.	Gordie Howe,	Det.	A. Hebenton,	N.Y. Rang.
1956	Jean Beliveau,	Mtl. C.	Jean Beliveau,	Mtl. C.	Earl Reibel,	Det.
1955	Bernie Geoffrion,	Mtl. C.	Ted Kennedy,	Tor.	Sid Smith.	Tor.
1954	Gordie Howe,	Det.	Al Rollins,	Chi.	Red Kelly,	Det.
1953	Gordie Howe,	Det.	Gordie Howe,	Det.	Red Kelly,	Det.
1952	Gordie Howe,	Det.	Gordie Howe,	Det.	Sid Smith,	Tor.
1951	Gordie Howe,	Det.	Milt Schmidt,	Bos.	Red Kelly,	Det.
1950	Ted Lindsay,	Det.	C. Rayner,	N.Y. Rang.	E. Laprade,	N.Y. Rang.
1949	Roy Conacher,	Chi.	Sid Abel,	Det.	Bill Quackenbush,	Det.
1948	Elmer Lach,	Mtl. C.	B. O'Connor,	N.Y. Rang.	B. O'Connor,	N.Y. Rang.
1947	*Max Bentley,	Chi.	Maurice Richard,	Mtl. C.	Bobby Bauer,	Bos.
1946	Max Bentley,	Chi.	Max Bentley,	Chi.	Toe Blake,	Mtl. C.
1945	Elmer Lach,	Mtl. C.	Elmer Lach,	Mtl. C.	Bill Mosienko,	Chi.
1944	Herbie Cain,	Bos.	Babe Pratt,	Tor.	Clint Smith,	Chi.
1943	Doug Bentley,	Chi.	Bill Cowley,	Bos.	Max Bentley,	Chi.
1942	Bryan Hextall,	N.Y. Rang.	Tom Anderson,	N.Y. Am.	Syl Apps,	Tor.
1941	Bill Cowley,	Bos.	Bill Cowley,	Bos.	Bobby Bauer,	Bos.
1940	Milt Schmidt,	Bos.	Ebbie Goodfellow,	Det.	Bobby Bauer,	Bos.
1939	Toe Blake,	Mtl. C.	Toe Blake,	Mtl. C.	Clint Smith,	N.Y. Rang.
1938	Gordie Drillon,	Tor.	Eddie Shore,	Bos.	Gordie Drillon,	Tor.
1937	Dave Schriner,	N.Y. Am.	Babe Siebert,	Mtl. C.	Marty Barry,	Det.
1936	Dave Schriner,	N.Y. Am.	Eddie Shore,	Bos.	Doc Romnes,	Chi.
1935	Charlie Conacher,	Tor.	Eddie Shore,	Bos.	F. Boucher,	N.Y. Rang.
1934	Charlie Conacher,	Tor.	Aurel Joliat,	Mtl. C.	F. Boucher,	N.Y. Rang.
1933	Bill Cook,	N.Y. Rang.	Eddie Shore,	Bos.	F. Boucher,	N.Y. Rang.
1932	Harvey Jackson,	Tor.	Howie Morenz,	Mtl. C.	Joe Primeau,	Tor.
1931	Howie Morenz,	Mtl. C.	Howie Morenz,	Mtl. C.	F. Boucher,	N.Y. Rang.
1930	Cooney Weiland,	Bos.	Nels Stewart,	Mtl. Mar.	F. Boucher,	N.Y. Rang.
1929	Ace Bailey,	Tor.	Roy Worters,	N.Y. Am.	F. Boucher,	N.Y. Rang.
1928	Howie Morenz,	Mtl. C.	Howie Morenz,	Mtl. C.	F. Boucher,	N.Y. Rang.
1927	Bill Cook,	N.Y. Rang.	Herb Gardiner,	Mtl. C.	Billy Burch,	N.Y. Am.
1926	Nels Stewart,	Mtl. Mar.	Nels Stewart,	Mtl. Mar.	Frank Nighbor,	Ott.
1925	Babe Dye,	Tor.	Billy Burch,	Ham.	Frank Nighbor,	Ott.
1924	Cy Denneny,	Ott.	Frank Nighbor,	Ott.	————	
1923	Babe Dye,	Tor.	————		————	
1922	Punch Broadbent,	Ott.	————		————	
1921	Newsy Lalonde,	Mtl. C.	————		————	
1920	Joe Malone,	Que.	————		————	
1919	Newsy Lalonde,	Mtl. C.	————		————	
1918	Joe Malone,	Mtl. C.	————		————	

NATIONAL HOCKEY LEAGUE INDIVIDUAL TROPHY WINNERS (cont.)

Year	Vezina Trophy		Calder Trophy		James Norris Trophy	
1973	Ken Dryden,	Mtl. C.	Steve Vickers,	N.Y. Rang.	Bobby Orr,	Bos.
1972	Tony Esposito, Gary Smith,	Chi.	Ken Dryden,	Mtl. C.	Bobby Orr,	Bos.
1971	Ed Giacomin, N.Y. Rang. Gilles Villemure, N.Y. Rang.		Gil Perreault,	Buff.	Bobby Orr,	Bos.
1970	Tony Esposito,	Chi.	Tony Esposito,	Chi.	Bobby Orr,	Bos.
1969	Glenn Hall, Jacques Plante,	St. L. St. L.	Danny Grant,	Minn.	Bobby Orr,	Bos.
1968	Lorne Worsley, Rogatien Vachon,	Mtl. C. Mtl. C.	Derek Sanderson,	Bos.	Bobby Orr,	Bos.
1967	Glenn Hall, Denis DeJordy,	Chi. Chi.	Bobby Orr,	Bos.	Harry Howell, N.Y. Rang.	
1966	Lorne Worsley, Charlie Hodge,	Mtl. C. Mtl. C.	Brit Selby,	Tor.	Jacq. Laperriere, Mtl. C.	
1965	Terry Sawchuk, Johnny Bower,	Tor. Tor.	Roger Crozier,	Det.	Pierre Pilote,	Chi.
1964	Charlie Hodge,	Mtl. C.	Jacq. Laperriere, Mtl. C.		Pierre Pilote,	Chi.
1963	Glenn Hall,	Chi.	Kent Douglas,	Tor.	Pierre Pilote,	Chi.
1962	Jacques Plante,	Mtl. C.	Bobby Rousseau,	Mtl. C.	Doug Harvey, N.Y. Rang.	
1961	Johnny Bower,	Tor.	Dave Keon,	Tor.	Doug Harvey,	Mtl. C.
1960	Jacques Plante,	Mtl. C.	Bill Hay	Chi.	Doug Harvey,	Mtl. C.
1959	Jacques Plante,	Mtl. C.	Ralph Backstrom, Mtl. C.		Tom Johnson,	Mtl. C.
1958	Jacques Plante,	Mtl. C.	Frank Mahovlich,	Tor.	Doug Harvey,	Mtl. C.
1957	Jacques Plante,	Mtl. C.	Larry Regan,	Bos.	Doug Harvey,	Mtl. C.
1956	Jacques Plante,	Mtl. C.	Glenn Hall,	Det.	Doug Harvey,	Mtl. C.
1955	Terry Sawchuk,	Det.	Ed Litzenberger,	Chi.	Doug Harvey,	Mtl. C.
1954	Harry Lumley,	Tor.	C. Henry, N.Y. Rang.		Red Kelly,	Det.
1953	Terry Sawchuk,	Det.	L. Worsley, N.Y. Rang.		————	
1952	Terry Sawchuk,	Det.	Bernie Geoffrion, Mtl. C.		————	
1951	Al Rollins,	Tor.	Terry Sawchuk,	Det.	————	
1950	Bill Durnan,	Mtl. C.	Jack Gelineau,	Bos.	————	
1949	Bill Durnan,	Mtl. C.	Penti Lund, N.Y. Rang.		————	
1948	Turk Broda,	Tor.	Jim McFadden,	Det.	————	
1947	Bill Durnan,	Mtl. C.	Howie Meeker,	Tor.	————	
1946	Bill Durnan,	Mtl. C.	E. Laprade, N.Y. Rang.		————	
1945	Bill Durnan,	Mtl. C.	Frank McCool,	Tor.	————	
1944	Bill Durnan,	Mtl. C.	Gus Bodnar,	Tor.	————	
1943	Johnny Mowers,	Det.	Gaye Stewart,	Tor.	————	
1942	Frank Brimsek,	Bos.	G. Warwick, N.Y. Rang.		————	
1941	Turk Broda,	Tor.	Johnny Quilty, Mtl. C.		————	
1940	Dave Kerr,	N.Y. Rang.	K. Macdonald, N.Y. Rang.		————	
1939	Frank Brimsek,	Bos.	Frank Brimsek,	Bos.	————	
1938	Tiny Thompson,	Bos.	Cully Dahlstrom,	Chi.	————	
1937	Normie Smith,	Det.	Syl Apps,	Tor.	————	
1936	Tiny Thompson,	Bos.	⁰⁰Mike Karakas,	Chi.	————	
1935	Lorne Chabot,	Chi.	Dave Schriner, N.Y. Am.		————	
1934	Charlie Gardiner,	Chi.	Russ Blinco, Mtl. Mar.		————	
1933	Tiny Thompson,	Bos.	Carl Voss,	Det.	————	
1932	Charlie Gardiner,	Chi.	————		————	
1931	Roy Worters, N.Y. Am.		————		————	
1930	Tiny Thompson,	Bos.	————		————	
1929	Geo. Hainsworth, Mtl. C.		————		————	
1928	Geo. Hainsworth, Mtl. C.		————		————	
1927	Geo. Hainsworth, Mtl. C.		————		————	

NATIONAL HOCKEY LEAGUE INDIVIDUAL TROPHY WINNERS (cont.)

Year	Bill Masterton Memorial Trophy	
1973	Lowell MacDonald	Pitt.
1972	Bobby Clarke,	Phil.
1971	Jean Ratelle,	N.Y. Rang.
1970	Pit Martin,	Chi.
1969	Ted Hampson,	Oak.
1968	Claude Provost,	Mtl. C.

Year	Conn Smythe Trophy	Year	Lester Patrick Trophy Winners
1973	Yvan Cournoyer, Montreal	1973	Walter L. Bush Jr.
1972	Bobby Orr, Boston	1972	Clarence S. Campbell
			John "Snooks" Kelley
			Ralph "Cooney" Weiland
1971	Ken Dryden, Montreal	1971	William M. Jennings
			Terry Sawchuk (Posthumously)
			John Sollenberger (Posthumously)
1970	Bobby Orr, Boston	1970	Eddie Shore
			Jim Hendy (Posthumously)
1969	Serge Savard, Montreal	1969	Bobby Hull
			Edward J. Jeremiah (Posthumously)
1968	Glenn Hall, St. Louis	1968	Thomas F. Lockhart
			Walter A. Brown (Posthumously)
			General John Reed Kilpatrick (Posthumously)
1967	Dave Keon, Toronto	1967	Gordon Howe
			Charles F. Adams (Posthumously)
			James Norris, Sr. (Posthumously)
1966	Roger Crozier, Detroit	1966	J. J. "Jack" Adams
1965	Jean Beliveau, Montreal		

CODE OF ABBREVIATIONS (FOR PAGES 365-367)

*	— Scoring leaders prior to inception of Art Ross Trophy in 1947-48
**	— Leading rookies to and including 1935-36
Bos.	— Boston
Buff.	— Buffalo Sabres
Chi.	— Chicago
Det.	— Detroit
Ham.	— Hamilton
Minn.	— Minnesota North Stars
Mtl. C.	— Montreal Canadiens
Mtl. Mar.	— Montreal Maroons
N.Y. Rang.	— New York Rangers
N.Y. Am.	— New York Americans
Oak.	— Oakland Seals
Ott.	— Ottawa
Phil.	— Philadelphia Flyers
Pitt.	— Pittsburgh Penguins
Que.	— Quebec
St. L.	— St. Louis
Tor.	— Toronto

INDIVIDUAL GOAL-SCORING LEADERS THROUGHOUT THE YEARS

Season	Player and Club	Games Played	Goals Scored
1972-73	Phil Esposito, Boston	78	55
1971-72	Phil Esposito, Boston	76	66
1970-71	Phil Esposito, Boston	78	76
1969-70	Phil Esposito, Boston	76	43
1968-69	Bobby Hull, Chicago	74	58
1967-68	Bobby Hull, Chicago	71	44
1966-67	Bobby Hull, Chicago	66	52
1965-66	Bobby Hull, Chicago	65	54
1964-65	Norm Ullman, Detroit	70	42
1963-64	Bobby Hull, Chicago	70	43
1962-63	Gordie Howe, Detroit	70	38
1961-62	Bobby Hull, Chicago	70	50
1960-61	Bernie Geoffrion, Montreal Canadiens	64	50
1959-60	Bobby Hull, Chicago	70	39
	Bronco Horvath, Boston	68	39
1958-59	Jean Beliveau, Montreal Canadiens	64	45
1957-58	Dickie Moore, Montreal Canadiens	70	36
1956-57	Gordie Howe, Detroit	70	44
1955-56	Jean Beliveau, Montreal Canadiens	70	47
1954-55	Bernie Geoffrion, Montreal Canadiens	70	38
	Maurice Richard, Montreal Canadiens	67	38
1953-54	Maurice Richard, Montreal Canadiens	70	37
1952-53	Gordie Howe, Detroit	70	49
1951-52	Gordie Howe, Detroit	70	47
1950-51	Gordie Howe, Detroit	70	43
1949-50	Maurice Richard, Montreal Canadiens	70	43
1948-49	Sid Abel, Detroit	69	28
1947-48	Ted Lindsay, Detroit	60	33
1946-47	Maurice Richard, Montreal Canadiens	60	45
1945-46	Gaye Stewart, Toronto	50	37
1944-45	Maurice Richard, Montreal Canadiens	50	50
1943-44	Doug Bentley, Chicago	50	38
1942-43	Doug Bentley, Chicago	50	33
1941-42	Lynn Patrick, New York Rangers	47	32
1940-41	Bryan Hextall, New York Rangers	48	26
1939-40	Bryan Hextall, New York Rangers	48	24
1938-39	Roy Conacher, Boston	47	26
1937-38	Gordon Drillon, Toronto	48	26
1936-37	Larry Aurie, Detroit	45	23
	Nels Stewart, Boston - New York Americans	43	23
1935-36	Bill Thoms, Toronto	48	23
	Charlie Conacher, Toronto	44	23
1934-35	Charlie Conacher, Toronto	48	36
1933-34	Charlie Conacher, Toronto	42	32
1932-33	Bill Cook, New York Rangers	48	28
1931-32	Charlie Conacher, Toronto	45	34

Season	Player and Club	Games Played	Goals Scored
1930-31	Charlie Conacher, Toronto	40	31
1929-30	Cooney Weiland, Boston	44	43
1928-29	Ace Bailey, Toronto	44	22
1927-28	Howie Morenz, Montreal Canadiens	43	33
1926-27	Bill Cook, New York Rangers	44	33

INDIVIDUAL PENALTY LEADERS THROUGHOUT THE YEARS

Season	Player and Club	Games Played	Penalties in Minutes
1972-73	Dave Schultz, Philadelphia	76	259
1971-72	Bryan Watson, Pittsburgh	75	212
1970-71	Keith Magnuson, Chicago	76	291
1969-70	Keith Magnuson, Chicago	76	213
1968-69	Forbes Kennedy, Philadelphia - Toronto	72	219
1967-68	Barclay Plager, St. Louis	49	153
1966-67	John Ferguson, Montreal Canadiens	67	177
1965-66	Reg Fleming, Boston - N.Y. Rangers	69	166
1964-65	Carl Brewer, Toronto	70	177
1963-64	Vic Hadfield, N.Y. Rangers	69	151
1962-63	Howie Young, Detroit	64	273
1961-62	Lou Fontinato, Montreal Canadiens	54	167
1960-61	Pierre Pilote, Chicago	70	165
1959-60	Carl Brewer, Toronto	67	150
1958-59	Ted Lindsay, Chicago	70	184
1957-58	Lou Fontinato, N.Y. Rangers	70	152
1956-57	Gus Mortson, Chicago	70	147
1955-56	Lou Fontinato, N.Y. Rangers	70	202
1954-55	Fern Flaman, Boston	70	150
1953-54	Gus Mortson, Chicago	68	132
1952-53	Maurice Richard, Montreal Canadiens	70	112
1951-52	Gus Kyle, Boston	69	127
1950-51	Gus Mortson, Toronto	60	142
1949-50	Bill Ezinicki, Toronto	67	144
1948-49	Bill Ezinicki, Toronto	52	145
1947-48	Bill Barilko, Toronto	57	147
1946-47	Gus Mortson, Toronto	60	133
1945-46	Jack Stewart, Detroit	47	73
1944-45	Pat Egan, Boston	48	86
1943-44	Mike McMahon, Montreal Canadiens	42	98
1942-43	Jimmy Orlando, Detroit	40	89*
1941-42	Jimmy Orlando, Detroit	48	81**

* Match Misconduct penalty not included in total penalty minutes.
** Three Match Misconduct penalties not included in total penalty minutes. 1946-47 was the first season that a Match penalty was automatically written into the player's total penalty minutes as 20 minutes. Now all penalties, Match, Game Misconduct and Misconduct are written in as 10 minutes.

INDIVIDUAL PENALTY LEADERS THROUGHOUT THE YEARS (cont.)

Season	Player and Club	Games Played	Penalties in Minutes
1940-41	Jimmy Orlando, Detroit	48	99
1939-40	Red Horner, Toronto	30	87
1938-39	Red Horner, Toronto	48	85
1937-38	Red Horner, Toronto	47	82°
1936-37	Red Horner, Toronto	48	124
1935-36	Red Horner, Toronto	43	167
1934-35	Red Horner, Toronto	46	125
1933-34	Red Horner, Toronto	42	126°
1932-33	Red Horner, Toronto	48	144
1931-32	Red Dutton, N.Y. Americans	47	107
1930-31	Harvey Rockburn, Detroit	42	118
1929-30	Joe Lamb, Ottawa	44	119
1928-29	Red Dutton, Montreal Maroons	44	139
1927-28	Eddie Shore, Boston	44	166
1926-27	Nels Stewart, Montreal Maroons	44	133

Each NHL team played 44 games per season from 1926-27 to 1930-31; 48 games per season from 1931-32 to 1941-42; 50 games per season from 1942-43 to 1945-46; 60 games per season from 1946-47 to 1948-49; 70 games per season from 1949-50 to 1966-67 season; 74 games in 1967-68; 76 games from 1968-69 to 1969-70; 78 games in 1970-71.

Index